BLACK WOMEN OF BRAZIL IN SLAVERY
AND POST-EMANCIPATION

Black Women of Brazil
in Slavery and Post-Emancipation

edited by

Giovana Xavier, Juliana Barreto Farias, and Flávio Gomes

DIASPORIC AFRICA PRESS
NEW YORK

This book is a publication of
Diasporic Africa Press
New York | www.dafricapress.com

All rights reserved. No part of this publication may be reproduced or distributed in any form or by any means, or stored in a database or retrieval system, without the prior written permission of the publisher.

Library of Congress Control Number: 2016952371

ISBN-13 978-1-937-30654-0 (pbk.: alk paper)

Mulheres Negras no Brasil Escravista e do Pós-Emancipação © Selo Negro Edições 2012

English translation © Diasporic Africa Press 2016

Obra publicada com o apoio do Ministério da Cultura do Brasil / Fundação Biblioteca Nacional

Work published with the support of the Brazilian Ministry of Culture / National Library Foundation

MINISTÉRIO DA CULTURA
Fundação BIBLIOTECA NACIONAL

Acknowledgments

We would like to thank Crystal Love and Laurelann Porter for their Portuguese language skill and assistance in this English translation. Portuguese language books and journals cited in notes and bibliographies are accompanied by English translations placed in brackets to help the reader.

Contents

Introduction i

1. *Women of Diverse "Types" and their Last Wills and Testaments in the Colonial, Slave, and Mestizo Captaincy of Minas Gerais* | Eduardo França Paiva 1

2. *Women of African Descent in Bahia: Gender, Color and Social Mobility, 1780-1830* | Adriana Dantas Reis 19

3. *Three Black Women Who Changed the Game in 18th Century Minas Gerais* | Luciano Figueiredo 35

4. *Queens and Judges: Black Women in the Black Sisterhoods of Central Brazil, 1722-1860* | Mary Karasch 59

5. *Among Characters, Typologies, and Labels of "Difference": The Slave Woman in the 19th Century Fiction of Rio de Janeiro* | Giovana Xavier 83

6. *Enslaved Women in 19th Century Paraíba: Work, Contradictions, and Fights for Freedom* | Solange P. Rocha 107

7. *Mônica da Costa and Teresa de Jesus: Free African Women, Status, and Social Networks in 19th Century Recife* | Valéria Gomes Costa 127

8. *Under the Rule of Women: Marriage and Divorce among the "Minas" African Ethnic Group in 19th Century Rio de Janeiro* | Juliana Barreto Farias 145

9. *A Certain Freedom* | Sandra Lauderdale Graham 175

10. *"With Her, He Lived Like a Dog Lives with a Cat": Emancipation, Maternity, and Gender on the Southern Border* | Paulo Roberto Staudt Moreira 195

11. *Gender Relations in the Daily Life of Black Women in 19th Century Bahia* | Isabel Cristina Ferreira dos Reis 227

12. *To Grandma Vitorina, With Love. Rio De Janeiro, Around 1870* | Sandra Sofia Machado Koutsoukos 245

13. *Between Two Benedicts: Stories of Wet Nurses in the Decline of Slavery* | Maria Helena P. T. Machado 263

14. *The "Livro de Ouro" (Golden Book), Emancipation Fund and Enslaved Women: Gender, Abolition, and the Meanings of Freedom in the Court, 1880s* | Camillia Cowling 283

15. *Teodora Dias da Cunha: Constructing a Place for Herself in the World of Writing and Slavery* | Maria Cristina Cortez Wissenbach 301

16. *Women of the House: Black Women and Domestic Work in the Imperial Court* | Flavia Fernandes de Souza 323

17. *Zizinha Guimarães: Between History and Memory* | Petrônio Domingues 343

18. *"Around the World" with Women of Capoeira: Gender and Black Culture in Brazil, 1850-1920* | Antônio Liberac Cardoso Simões Pires 371

19. *Histories of Differences and Inequalities Revisited: Notes on Gender, Slavery, Race, and Post-Emancipation* | Marcelo Paixão and Flavio Gomes 391

INTRODUCTION

In recent decades, studies of slavery have been consolidated in the vast historiography of colonial and post-colonial Brazil. Studies developed in graduate programs, the diversity in use of sources—especially approaches to quantitative data and of social history—and the abundance of approaches that refer to time and space are some of the principal characteristics of that historiographical turn. Up until the 1960s, enslavement was spoken of as something generic, later the systemic approaches of pro-slavery would lose ground to the analyses of the daily life and the culture of the slave, and of the enslaved person. New themes have gained prominence. We know more about slave society in different regions and their productive activities: plantation, mining, food production, livestock, and urban slavery.

Today, we analyze emancipations, *quilombos* (colonies of escaped slaves also called maroon colonies in some literature), brotherhoods, kinship, slave revolts, and families; we approach the slave quarters, the *zungu* (low-rent living quarters for freed slaves), the slums, and barracks; and closely examine the imagined discourse and material culture of the principal protagonists of slave society. Among the set of themes that were asserted, those that disappeared or reappeared, we evidence one theme even less explored: the experiences of black women. For this reason, we feature here the studies of pioneers Maria Odila Leite da Silva Dias, Sonia Giacomini, Mary Del Priori, Magali Engel, Martha Abreu, Luciano Figueiredo, Margareth Bakos, Liana Reis, Cecilia Moreira, Selma Pantoja, Rachel Soihet; and Maria Lúcia Mott; and the more recent analyses by Sandra Graham, Júnia Furtado, Sheila de Castro Faria, and Carlos Eugênio Líbano Soares.

The originality of this collection exists in the offering of a thorough and updated survey of the topic, by gathering the articles of 20 specialists, covering Brazil from North to South in theoretical terms and in the use of diverse sources. These are scholarly texts that not only tell the story of cities, mills, factories, and mansions, but which also fundamentally reconstruct scenes and design landscapes to reveal shadows, moments, and ways of life: the body, the mind and the soul of the women—*crioulas* (women of African descent born into captivity in Brazil), *escravas* (enslaved women), *mulatas* (bi-racial women), *africanas* (women born in Africa but brought to Brazil as slaves), *pardas* (women of mixed race, often a mix of white/European, indigenous, and African), *forras* (freed women), *pretas* (black women, typically used to refer to a woman with darker complexion), *negras* (also means black women but has less emphasis on the darkness of the shade), and *morenas* (women of African descent typically referring to a mixed race shade of brown)—during slavery and in the first decades post-emancipation. They were mixed universes, expanded approaches, and sources that gained attentions in other realms. Sounds and images multiplied in different concepts, theoretical perspectives, and methodologies. The principal idea was not only to trace the steps of these women, but also to walk with them and through them. These various texts hold at the center of the analysis pathways of mini-biographies as part of a larger search for model characters, among an array of inconclusive trajectories.

The arrangement of chapters is not as preoccupied with chronological order as with territorial diversity. We begin in a noble space for women in slavery. The chapter on 18th century Minas Gerais, by Eduardo França Paiva, offers the first examples. By examining testimonies and witness accounts—the principal source that will appear in other texts—envisioned are the cultural thoughts of *negras, pretas, crioulas, índias* (indigenous women), *mamelucas* (mixed race of indigenous and white/European), *mulatas, pardas,* and *cabras* (a woman of mixed race with a black parent and a "mulatto" parent) with different "attributes" and "conditions," who invented mixed spaces of experiences among villages and camps. We continue to Bahia in the transition to the post-colonial era. Adriana Dantas Reis brings to us the *experiences of liberty* under slavery. Strategies of freed slaves and their paths—sometimes shortcuts that were not always common—of mobility. Again, the testaments offer records of goods, attitudes, and expectations in narratives where men are revealed by voices no less strong than that of the *crioulas* and *africanas*. This throws us inside of a world woven together by pain and smiles. Before continuing, we return to Minas Gerais to change the image already drawn. Luciano Figueiredo, one of the pioneers in the research of gender and slavery, resumes analyses of the role of the women street vendors. In the narratives of the characters, including Luzias and Sebastianas, we are guided to the streets, to the scenarios of affirmation, to the markets, and to the life of the small, but strong network of the black women in Minas Gerais. Also, in the environment of mining, we reach Goiás and invade an important space addressed in slavery studies, but unknown from the perspective of black women: the sisterhoods and the role of queens and judges. Mary Karasch, responsible for distinguished research of slavery in central Brazil, presents us with a new approach. By way of her work, we get to know more closely the religious feminine life and association in the Catholic orders dedicated to Our Lady of the Rosary, São Benedito, and Santa Efigênia. Festivities and practices involving devotion to the saints and sisterhoods were also spaces of power and of status for black women.

The first trip the collection takes to Rio de Janeiro—the largest slave city and urban area of the Atlantic with the most Africans—we encounter more black women. Giovana Xavier guides this historical interpretation. Certainly, caricatured with views of social invisibility in the world of ideas we identify predetermined feminine roles of characters portrayed in romances, short stories, and poems. The repetition of stereotypes and labels suggests how black women were perceived, rejected, harassed, and battered. From Rio de Janeiro we make the first return to the Northeast. Initially, we land in 19th century Paraíba. Among baptisms and letters of emancipation, Solange Rocha addresses the hopes that mobilized black women. Limitations and setbacks marked the long and tortuous journey to liberty in a world surrounded by slavery. From there, we jump to Recife, one of the other large slave cities. Valéria Costa guide us to encounter the *africanas* and their networks—part of which are religious—also through witness accounts. In this manner, we follow two valiant West African women: Monicas and Therezas, residents of the parishes of São Frei Pedro Gonçalves of Recife and Boa Vista. With kinfolk and courage, they left goods and much solidarity to husbands, children, godchildren, and even slaves, in a city that became their space for projects, aspirations, and experiences.

Something complex and similar to the scenario reconstructed by Juliana Barreto Farias directs us back to the "black city" of Rio de Janeiro. *Africanas* and greengrocers/street vendors from West Africa are unveiled in divorce filings in the Arquivo da Cúria of Rio de Janeiro. Men and women tell us why they married, how they lived, and why they decided to break their unions. We enter the space of the home and from there we exit to the streets, seeing the couples between markets, shacks, and lifelong projects that transformed captives into freed women and converted them into a network of alliances and businesses that also involved frustrations of married life and dreams of family. We travel down the line to find the long-term stories of ex-slaves, narrated by Sandra Graham. As Balbina, a domestic captive, continues being sold from one property to another from the interior of Minas Gerais and the Vale do Paraíba in the middle on the 19th century into the streets and markets of Salvador and Rio de Janeiro, the *africanas* Rosa, Henriqueta, and Sabina experienced different, but also challenging situations. Enjoying the autonomy of a more urban environment, they could win their freedom, become recognized traders, and still form new families with aggregates and offspring of their slaves, to whom they left their belongings.

From there, we continue to Rio Grande do Sul. In Uruguaiana, very close to the border, Paulo Moreira stresses the routes of black women and the formation of families as one of the expectations that surrounded emancipations. Sounds of motivation, hope, and delusion are heard in the notary records and inventories. We see an exemplary portrait of a black family come to Salvador in the chapter by Isabel Reis. With the trajectories of Augusta, Ubaldina, and Domingas, again feminine histories drive us, in the daily functioning of life in which affection, marriage, neighborhood, and material resources were important items of many lives.

Lives with various images. The chapter by Sandra Koutsoukos shows images hardly revealed by historiography. Affection, ideologies, gifts, medical knowledge, and the labor market of wet nurses and maids are brought to life through the lenses of photographers. But still we must know more about the wet nurse, symbol of the slave society in the Americas. It is possible to take great strides by accompanying the analysis of Maria Helena Machado. The alleged burgeoning of the relationships between owners and slaves in the domestic world had thorns of suspicion, hatred, and murder. For many slaves, motherhood and familial protection were worth more than legal emancipation. If liberty had gender, on the eve of Abolition, the meaning was ambiguous. Many factors were at play including laws, hopes, perceptions, and expectations. Centered on the effervescent age of parliamentary abolitionism, the chapter by Camillia Cowling deals with the original form of the ceremonies in Rio de Janeiro in the second half of the 1880s, when Princess Isabel issued letters of freedom. In these occasions, the records were included in the book *Livro de Ouro* (The Golden Book) created by the Câmara Municipal (City Council) in 1884. Feminine images of freedom and its contemplations are the background to understanding the meanings of the ritual.

These thoughts held their own narratives, they were registered socially or written with pen and paper. With the original sources, Maria Cristina Wissenbach presents us with letters and the trajectory of the *africana* Teodora Dias da Cunha. It was in São Paulo in the 1860s that this domestic slave ordered these letters to be written. Beginning with registries and the other evidence, the author proposes to cross the blurred boundaries of the world of writing between literate and illiterate characters in a hierarchical society with defined social roles. If the historiography of slavery still was not able to enter the slave quarters—apart from the works of the occasional traveler and a few studies of archaeology—it has been possible to reach urban homes and find scenarios and practices through the actions of black women. In the chapter by Flávia Souza, they are hostesses; the hands of innumerous domestic workers open the windows and doors in the homes of the imperial elite. One example biography of someone reaching the last years of a slave society and the first decades of liberty is offered by Petrônio Domingues. In the interface of memory, we get to know the trajectory of the professor Eufrozina Guimarães, also known as Zizinha. In Sergipe, this woman reached a level of notoriety that still reverberates today with celebrations and tributes to her.

However, everything was not always a festival or carnival, nor were cultural practices devoid of female characters. As such, we see the game of *capoeira* (an Afro-Brazilian form of dance and martial art) from other angles in Antônio Liberac's chapter, which examines evidence of the presence of black women among *capoeira* practitioners in the 19th century and the first half of the 20th century. The collection closes by making a turn that jumps to the history of this time. Flávio Gomes and Marcelo Paixão combine narratives found in depositions of emancipated women in the 18th and 19th centuries with the population data and socioeconomics of the 21st century, exploring which aspects changed and which aspects remained from slavery, post-abolition, and the contemporary racial relations relative to the variation of the labor market and the resources left for black women.

Masters of pasts and presents, current and true, and solid as a rock, in the historiography of slavery and post-emancipation, black women are hardly approached as protagonists of more diverse stories. Although this is just the beginning, this collection takes important steps in this direction, revealing profiles previously concealed by hierarchies of gender and race.

I

WOMEN OF DIVERSE "TYPES" AND THEIR LAST WILLS AND TESTAMENTS IN THE COLONIAL, SLAVE, AND MESTIZO CAPTAINCY OF MINAS GERAIS

Eduardo França Paiva

Beyond Chica da Silva, the famed freed slave that won over the superintendent of Diamantes, the then captaincy of Minas Gerais, one of the richest regions of the 18th century world, brought forth many other characters that penned their stories, despite the conditions of their daily lives, often contrary to their claims. The majority of them remain in anonymity today, but their traces can be found in archives, museums, and libraries, as I will present in this essay. Almost always biographies are found, although short, but intense and fascinating, that bring with them important chunks of the history of Minas Gerais, closely connected with socioeconomic dynamics, political and cultural networks, and with the traffic of people that traveled throughout the Portuguese empire and even outside of it.

Connected Characters

Over the months that had elapsed, something peculiar had worried Joana da Silva Machada, the Christian name given to the slave coming from Costa da Mina to Brazil during the first half of the 18th

century. For some unknown reason, throughout the year 1745, the free woman sensed that her days would not be much longer, which led her to write her will, completed this same year, in Vila de Santo Antônio in Recife, the captaincy of Pernambuco. She had reason to worry, because she would pass away shortly after in 1747. However, between the creation of her will and her death, Joana had enough energy to travel from Recife to Minas Gerais, a very long route, and one so dangerous that it may explain the care that was taken to record her last will and testament. Before Recife, the African woman may have lived in Cidade da Bahia, where she requested that many chapel masses were held with the intention to ask for the repose of her soul after her death, which happened in the Arraial dos Carijós, near by the Vila de São João del Rei, in the capital of Minas Gerais. In this village, Joana lived at the inn of Manual Antunes.

Joana did not declare the reasons that made her leave Recife and migrate to Minas Gerais, from where she would no longer leave; but it does not seem to have been for the sake of getting to know another region of expansive Brazil, as a tourist of our time would. Travelers that sought to learn about the daily lives of others were rare in that age, and generally, they were linked with restricted groups of the rich, scientists, naturalists, or explorers, groups of which she certainly did not belong. The motivation seems to be linked to economic activities performed by the emancipated woman, which seem to be indicated in her will and involved the textile trade, clothing, and other objects. Joana probably earned a lot because the group of people who traveled between these regions was bringing in and taking goods to be traded. The largest part of these traders was composed of men, and many of them were called "road men." However, like Joana, there were some women who also performed the same job and could have been called "road women" (Ivo, 2009).

Our character must have been a determined woman, who traveled by markedly masculine routes, in which she obtained success, if we consider the fortune declared in her will and inventoried after her death. All that she owned seems to be a result of her business ventures that even included the market of Rio de Janeiro. Even the geographic range this black woman traveled is extraordinary. The ex-slave had ascended economically and had become, in her own time, owner of slaves, along with jewels, and other material goods. Her post-mortem inventory of 1748 listed, for example: fabrics of various types, readymade garments, sheets and towels, shoes and shoe buckles, two cups and a saucer from India, glass, silver spoons and forks, tin plates and bowls, copper cookware, scales, and tobacco. Among such items were her personal clothing, bedding and table linen, fabric and shoes, a velvet headdress trimmed with silver lace was found; skirts made of black silk adorned with flowers, black silk with velvet circles, blue cloth with gold lacing underneath, raw silk, raw wool, baize (coarse felt), gingham, "with normal wear" and one "of silk with much wear"; a goat-hair cloak lined with baize; one worn, marbled waistcoat; two cubits of "thread cloth" (possibly canvas or cheesecloth), eleven cubits of gingham, two cubits of used black wool cloth, and one cubit of pink-colored baize; two yards of Brittany cloth, and four with lace inset; a hat with embroidered edging; a nightgown of red baize; a box from Moscow; two linen bed sheets with embroidery and two flat sheets; eleven shirts of Brittany cloth, five of chambray and one "well-worn game hide"; four linen hand towels and one of Brittany cloth with lace; three little pillows; a white scarf; two napkins; a baize doublet and a worn Moroccan slipper. Forged from gold and silver, "some strings of beaded wire necklaces," three ropes of beaded coral, four fine strings, buttons with images of Our Lady of Conception and the baby Jesus, scapulars (clerical shoulder cloaks) of Mount Carmel, metal hook and eye fasteners with images of Saint Luzia, a filigreed cross; a "small icons on gold chain necklaces," padlocks with small pearls and diamonds and "short silver sash with gold chains and other silver items." She owned the slaves Antônio Angola and the "little black girl by the name of Maria, of the same ethnic nation," in addition to Francisca Mina, who had been unconditionally freed in 1745, and had continued following her ex-mistress. Joana did not claim to have family, home, or any fixed place of residence. Nor did she mention cargo animals, essential for the activities of this "road woman," which could indicate that she belonged to some network of traders who conveniently traveled together, sharing operational structures, support bases, and security strategies.

If an organization of drovers and traveling traders did not exist, how could Joana have used these routes infested with bandits and highwaymen, carrying so many goods and objects of value, accompanied, apparently, by a couple of adult slaves? How would she have moved through such expansive and widespread regions, and how would she have transported goods, in addition to personal items, some with high value, including gold dust (that served as currency), and sometimes money?

Such a nomadic life did not impede the African woman from establishing and maintaining emotional bonds with people from various places, and this helps to explain part of the complex organization of her ventures. Maybe the people she knew had given her operational support, welcoming her and her companions. Maybe they integrated networks of support for the activities of these adventurous traders. Joana met many people in various places and she demonstrated this in 1745, listing the beneficiaries of her will. The list was much bigger than the majority of those elaborated by rich, white testators. She, who had cultivated autonomy and lavished courage, requested:

> To Mr. Vitoriano Ribeiro and to Domingos Francisco Braga and to Francisco Álvares Ribeiro and to Bento de Bessa Barbosa and to Manuel Correa de Araújo, in Cidade da Bahia; to sergeant major Miguel Francisco de Araújo and to Sebastião Ribeiro da Silva, in Rio de Janeiro, and to Manuel Ribeiro Manso and to Antônio Álvares in Minas Gerais, and to Bartolomeu Álvares and to Antônio Rodrigues Coelho and Domingos da Costa Guimarães and, in Sabará, to Antônio Pereira Braga and to Joseph Vieira Antunes and to sergeant major João Vieira, in Serro do Frio, to João Ribeiro da Costa and to João Teixeira Leitão and to Francisco Martins and in Minas Novas, Antônio Gonçalves Chaves and to the captain-general Francisco Álvares, residents of Chapada, and to the reverend vicar of the parish where my death will be... my estate executors.[1]

Still in Recife, listing her beneficiaries, she indicated that the comings and goings were constant and that the trip in the direction of Minas, made right after, was not the first. During her travels, Joana had established contacts with important men in the locations where she traded. Women with a similar profile, so willing to adventure on journeys that lasted weeks, who were competent enough to leave captivity and create a personal and commercial network so widespread, were rare.

Minas Gerais in the 18th century constituted one of the most dynamic and rich regions of the world. Gold, diamonds, and precious stones; heavy commerce, connection with markets and ports of Brazil, of Spanish America and of other continents; important agriculture and livestock; delivery of services and complex administrative structure in towns and villages where the largest part of the greater population of free people, slaves, and freed slaves was found among the major captaincies of Brazil. This was the profile of the region that attracted people from all over. There were as many African slaves and Brazilian-born slaves arriving as there were free people and freed slaves coming from other captaincies of Europe (the majority, Portuguese). Early on, the population of those born in Minas had positive growth rates, fostering demographic growth. At the end of the 18th century, there were more than 360,000 inhabitants, of whom nearly half was composed of slaves and the other half of those born free and ex-slaves (Maxwell, 1978, p. 302). It was a melting pot of cultures and like other American areas, it was a society defined by the intensive transit of people and cultures and social mobility.

In a context like this, the countless emancipations and *coartações* (customary practice resulting in an agreement between owner and slave that allowed for parceled payment of emancipation in four or five years) were instrumental in the social dynamic, with strong demographic, economic, political, and cultural impact. In this society, ex-slaves and all "types" (a general term of identification) of non-whites who were born free, that is, Indians, whites, blacks, *crioulos* (Creoles, mixed race or blacks born into enslavement) *pardos* (mixed race, often a mix of white/European, indigenous, and African), *cabras* (a woman of mixed race with a black parent and a "mulatto" parent), *mamelucos* (mixed race, indigenous and white/European), mulattos, *mestizos*, etc., ascended economically and socially. They constituted families, acquired material goods, and became slave owners.

Fitting within this framework, and in search of the innumerable opportunities that it generated, a *mameluca* (daughter of a Portuguese and an Indian) decided to travel across forests, mountains, and rivers to settle down in Minas Gerais. Anastácia was her name, daughter of Pascoal Homem and Moxia Carijó. She was born in 1720, and lived in Vila de Itu, the then captaincy of São Paulo and Minas de Ouro, where she married and had a daughter with João Requeixo. According to her, the crude and violent man had abandoned her with the child to adventure through the territory of Minas, in search of quick riches. He had taken with him, without her permission, two *carijós* (natives of southern Brazil, the term also means a species of chicken) that Anastácia had been given by her uncle, Manuel Homem. The *mameluca* sought to fulfill her material and physical needs during her husband's absence, and ended up having two other children: João and Francisco, the fruit of a relationship she had with a student.[2]

Many months passed and Anastácia remained in Itu, where she had surely managed to build her life among family members, friends, and people she knew. However, all of a sudden, news arrived that would make her decide to immediately abandon her seemingly stable situation. Someone told her that her husband who abandoned her was returning from the "hinterlands," which further indicates her participation in networks of information that were organized among the population. Shortly after, she decided to avoid the encounter and to escape, precisely, to Minas Gerais. So she decided to take the path opposite of her husband and find a new life.

Her trip to Minas, from the beginning, was a risky adventure. After all, to cross such a large territory, probably by alternative routes, to avoid meeting Requeixo, "without any belongings other than what she herself could carry," according to what she wrote in her testament, facing days and days of difficulties of all kinds, must not have been an easy task. It is plausible that she had received, in some form, help from members of the same network that informed her of the return of her husband. Maybe, because of this, she was able to complete the long trip with success: having somewhere to stay overnight and eat and counting on companions who were able to protect her on trails that were quite rugged and considered to be decidedly masculine.

The strategy worked and Anastácia crossed the hinterlands of Minas without crossing paths with her husband. A short while later, she became pregnant again and gave birth to another son, child of Antônio Pereira, of Serro do Frio, a mining district which in that time stretched from the center to the north of the captaincy, all the way to the border of Bahia, and where the administrative headquarters of Vila do Princípe were. The relationship did not seem to last for a long time, because shortly afterward, Anastácia had another partner, the educated Domingos Maciel Aranha, from São Paulo, with whom she had a daughter and stayed with until she passed away in 1743. The couple spent some years on a farm they owned in Vila Nossa Senhora do Pilar do Pitangui, which was a part of the county Rio das Velhas, which extended from the center to the north and to the west of the captaincy, with administrative headquarters in Vila de Nossa Senhora da Conceição de Sabará. At this point, Anastácia had already changed her name, calling herself "Francisca," which she chose herself. The name change, as she declared in her testimony, she gave herself "when I entered this town [Pitangui]."[3]

Francisca had traveled quite a lot in her life before settling in Pitangui. Similarly, in addition to many travels, there were many romantic relationships in which she found herself involved. Furthermore, this woman who seemed to cultivate changes and adventures had opted for another alteration in her life: a new first and last name. In Minas Gerais, she called herself Francisca Poderosa (spelled like this in the testament) and Pedrosa (in documents related to her Episcopal visits in Pitangui). The *mameluca* from São Paulo had resorted to a custom of the time, maybe seeking to erase traces that could compromise her, thus constructing a new identity for herself.

The last years of Francisca's life were lived with more stability by the side of her educated partner, Aranha; but her personality must have gained her enemies and provoked the envy of others because the couple was denounced during an Episcopal visit, reprimanded by the inspector Francisco Pinheiro da Fonseca, for common-law marriage and were obliged to pay a fine of three thousand *réis* (currency of the time), "for a public and notorious relationship."[4] Even this did not separate them. With her last companion, Poderosa/Pedrosa experienced good conditions in life and acquired material possessions. She owned an Angolan slave, who was married to a slave belonging to her lover, Aranha. In addition to her, she claimed to have purchased the administration of a *carijó* (which meant having purchased an Indian slave, a prohibited practice, hence the "chicken" euphemism), Margarida de Brás de Sosa Arsão, for 160 eighths of gold (estimated around 240 thousand *réis*, a value close to that of a good slave), and her four children, with the oldest being free of bondage. The other three seem to have served Francisca as slaves: a girl, "Easter bastard girl," and two boys, "João and Inácio, a biracial boy and a *curiboca*" (*curiboca* is the mix of Indian and European). Among the material goods she accounted for garden tools, pots, tin dishes, two silver spoons, wooden bowls, chests, a basin, a saddled and bridled mule, towels, "clothing worn by me including four linen shirts from Brittany—one which will be given to my goddaughter," "a chain with three necklaces and a travel bed made of 'washed bread'... a rifle." Among the debts, she listed what she owed for having purchased seven yards of linen cloth for her daughter. Among the credits, one was regarding the assistance given on behalf of a biracial woman named Isabel (her ex-slave?) to Manual Barbosa, resident of "Abórboras da Contagem" (Contagem das Abórboras, today called Contagem), which indicates the sprawl of her business. This mixed race woman from São Paulo still owned two eighths of gold (gold-dust); "a brand new cloak of fine blue cloth with a lush lining of fine silver"; "some grass houses in Gouveia"; and "half of the farm behind the hill of this village... where I have a grass house."[5]

Escaped from São Paulo, without bringing anything with her, our mutating *mestiza* character ended her days enjoying economic and maybe social ascension since she had met Domingos Aranha in Pitangui. Before her death, she dictated her testament and fortunately she didn't avoid telling her extraordinary story. Although her trajectory was quite a rare one, it is important to highlight that she was also a sort of synopsis of many other similar and intertwined trajectories. Other women left detailed accounts in their wills about their lives, and in doing so, bequeathed us with information about life in Minas Gerais in the 18th and the beginning of the 19th century, which, in large measure, was similar to the life in other slaveholding urban areas in the Americas.

Realities like those that Minas produced promoted the emergence of characters whose stories strongly influenced the life of social groups and even entire societies. Many non-white women fall within these parameters, despite the collective imaginary of slavery that holds to this day, even with the advancement of historical studies, the images of victimhood imposed on slaves and their descendants born free. These images are customarily called *imaginário do tronco* (truncated imaginary) (Paiva 2001, p. 24). The rhythm of changes in this field seem to be much less frenetic than of historiography; in spite of each other, they always iterate dialogue. Nevertheless, the studies done in the recent decades reveal a colonial slave past much more complex, dynamic, and markedly feminine than was thought. We return, however, to our protagonists, leaving the extensive documentation existing in our archives, especially these rich testaments of the colonial period. These women still have much to tell us about that society and that time period.

Bárbara Gomes de Abreu e Lima was a *crioula*, that is, she was born in Brazil to an African mother and father. She probably had black skin, like her parents. She was born a slave in Sergipe del Rei, "lawful daughter of Antônio Benguela and his wife Maria Gomes of the gentile Mina" and had been emancipated, according to her testament, in Minas Gerais, where she headed accompanied by her owner, from whom she inherited the noble last name. Her life trajectory was fascinating, and once again, the dynamic of the mining society helped to mold this extraordinary character. Her economic and social ascension was rapid and notable. In 1735, when she dictated her last will and testament, she was already a rich woman, by the standards of that time. She lived in the "cosmopolitan" Sabará, one of the most populous towns of Minas, an obligatory stop for the "globalized" traders that negotiated products coming from the four parts of the world and traveled between Bahia and the central region of mining and gold. Bárbara owned a "villa" in "the plaza of the great church and in front of the parish church of the village." Her source of income was connected to the trade between Bahia and the county of Rio das Velhas, made along the "path of the corrals," where passed the cattle stock that supplied the region. She did not explicitly state which type of trade she was involved in, but the list of beneficiaries was extensive and included men who occupied important positions, responsible for caring for her interests in the mentioned county, in Vila de Sabará, in Minas, in Bahia, in the hinterlands, and in the path of corrals. Among the people she named was a Captain General, an archpriest, a man referred to as "Dom," a field master, two staff sergeants, and a lieutenant colonel.[6] Of course, the military positions stand out, which sheds light not only on this case, but the previous ones, especially when we question the apparent ease of movement of the women between extensive and dangerous colonial areas and the control that some of them exercised within business networks that operated in these same areas. Bárbara was, in this way, a precursor of Joana Machada, our first character. She also may have been one of the people whose lives and autonomy echoed the life and projects of various other people who lived around that time.

The emancipated *crioula* was one of those women who owned, and certainly wore, a rare object in Minas: a combination of jewelry, with distinctive adornment and set of charms that were later called "a bundle of *balangadãs*" (a word used for an adornment to clothing that was a collection of beads and amulets designed to "jangle" or make noise as they passed. Some say it was to ward off evil spirits). It was much more common in Bahia, where the custom seems to have been born among black women and *crioulas* who wore the bundle at the waist, attached to a strap or a chain, as seen in the images described below, other times held up by a large chain set perpendicular, from the shoulder to the bundle, laid over the breast and the back of the wearer. An object emblematic of the autonomy of some of these women, the bundle was made of a wide variety of styles and components. There were many symbols of bunches of grapes and pomegranates, which, since the middle ages at least, were associated with fertility and motherhood; even figs, which are ancient charms of Mediterranean origin; and axes of Xangô (a sacred Yoruba entity representing thunder, storms, and justice), tambourines, cocoa and cashew fruits, fish, dogs, keys, among many other symbolic objects.

Bárbara owned, however, much more than her various bangles or bundles of charms and amulets made of fine gold. Her clothes of expensive cloth must have called attention to the residents of 18th century Sabará. In her testament, she declared to have "four skirts, two of black silk, and one of [?], and one of fine white goat-hair,… three two-cubit cloths, one black, one blue, and one green."[7] Among the jewelry that she owned were cords and buttons of gold, ropes of coral trimmed in gold, amber, and pearl earrings. She owned tin plates; copper pots; and silver spoons, forks, and knives. She was the owner of three black women from Minas, two little *crioulas* (black girls born in Brazil) and two little *crioulos* (black boys born in Brazil), who were probably the children of Africans, which indicates the possible formation of matriarchal families (with the mother at the center) in her slave count. Moreover, the composition the groups of slaves dependent on her points to the internal reproduction, in place of the purchase of slaves imported from Africa. In her villa, in front of the parish church of Sabará, this ex-slave lived and, certainly, gave examples of living to many other women who sought to free themselves or to ascend economically and socially.

Another *crioula*, Bárbara de Oliveira, also lived in Vila de Sabará. In 1766 she resolved to record her last will and testament, and because of this, we still have to this day a registry of one of the largest fortunes accumulated during that time. Bárbara declared being the daughter of a "black woman known as Maria of the now defunct Mina nation," but she did not mention the name of her father. It is very much possible that she didn't know him, because matriarchal families were very common in the slave, emancipated, and non-white populations; in them fathers seemed to have played a secondary role and the children did not always know who they were. Bárbara dictated to the registrar that she had been a slave of Mariana dos Anjos and that, she presumed, the old mistress "dwelled in the Convent of Santa Clara," in Cidade da Bahia. After she became free (while still in Bahia) she moved to Minas Gerais, where she stayed until her death and remained single, still served by the 23 slaves that she owned, 70 percent of which were women. Among the women and girls there were: two black women of the "Courana" nation from Africa; six adult black men born in Brazil; two adult women without identification of "ethnic type"; three young girls born of mixed black/mulatto parents; three young *mulatta* girls, in addition to three children of the enslaved adult women, namely, one *cabrinho* (son of black/mulatto parents), one "little mulatto," and one without a defined "ethnic type." Among the male adults, all blacks born in Brazil, one had escaped to the region of Paracatu, according to Bárbara, and the other, she rented "a reasonable ¾ of the week" to father Antônio José de Araújo. The majority of the slaves were a part of the household; they lived together with, and apparently, shared the same house as Bárbara. If we count mothers and children, 77 percent of the slaves had close family ties nearby, which clearly indicates internal reproduction, from which came many of the black and mixed race children born into slavery, a pattern that was repeated amongst most slaveholding households in 19th century Minas Gerais.

The relationship Bárbara had with her slaves was very close, another characteristic of small and medium-sized slaveholdings. During the time she had her testament written, aware of *mors inevitabilis est et hora incerta* (Tuielman Kerver in Martins, 1969, p. 176), or that death is inevitable, she requested that a number of material inheritances should be left to her slaves, as well as emancipation for some and *coartações* (limited liberation—see above) for others. Her words, though written by others, reveal the closeness, and even complicity, existing in these relationships. At the same time, they inform us about the material world and the daily life she lived. As a show of appreciation for the services they provided, she emancipated and issued manumission arrangements to almost all of her slaves and their children, and in a manner of protecting one of her favorites, the little Josefa, aiming to prevent her from living a barbarous life in the future, she left "two boxes of clothes and also a basket with white linen... to become a wife when it is the right time, or being that you don't marry, but none the less live a life of honor, I will give to you said clothes," and also, "a skirt of flowered silk, one of black linsey-woolsey, and one of silk with gold tracing…, and a travel bed made of carved black jacaranda wood."[8]

To her other charge, Úrsula (the young mulatto girl), she left 32 eighths of gold (approximately 48,000 *réis*) so that she could marry (without making the same notes left to Josefa), additionally "a nearly new skirt of bright green silk and a little jacket of Berne cloth and three chambray shirts." How "the remainder of outstanding debts" (without identification of the sources), would be divided according to Bárbara, was "equally between Brás de Oliveira Perto, Ana de Oliveira, Bonifácia, Josefinha (mulatto), Maria de Olivera *crioula* and all of my servants of the house."[9]

The fortune accumulated by the emancipated *crioula* was even larger. Supporting this are numerous pieces of jewelry made of gold, silver, and precious stones; many pieces of clothing; and many loans. However, the economic and social ascension experienced by this ex-slave and her notable fortune did not settle the anguish that seemed to torment her. Facing her imminent death, she thought of the family that lived in the distant Cidade da Bahia. There was a mixed-race daughter, who had remained a slave of her own ex-owner Mariana dos Anjos when Bárbara moved to Minas. After that, this mixed race daughter had gotten her emancipation, married, and had a daughter, who also married and had "two strong boys." In spite of all the information she had of her already lengthy ancestry, Bárbara never returned to see her daughter and did not know her children or grandchildren. Nevertheless, she designated them as her universal heirs. This situation, along with the other information recorded about her, reinforces our initial suspicions: it is likely that one of the largest fortunes found among freed slaves who left wills in Minas Gerais was the result of prostitution, perhaps even of the testator herself and also of her slaves.[10]

Cases in which colonial women ascended economically and socially were common, especially in the most urban areas of the captaincy. When this happened, it was not rare for them to incorporate some Catholic and European values, pious attitudes and moralizing practices that, *a priori*, were more expected of white women. For example, although having remained single and having a daughter with whom she had lost contact, in addition to probably having exploited her slaves as prostitutes, Bárbara de Oliveira sought to persuade two of her young mulatto slave women to get married, leaving to them monetary goods, furniture, and clothes. Other testators around that time, some more than others, became Catholics by conviction, rather than for convenience, fervent devotees to the Virgin and various saints. In fact, this was very common among those who simultaneously proceeded with other religious rituals and believed in other divinities. However, this was not necessarily a situation that involved all slaves, emancipated slaves, and colonial non-white free people, including men and women from various parts of the African continent, who held various religious perspectives. Whether converted, Catholic-born, or practitioners of other distinct religions, before dying almost all of them resorted to the last will and testament as a form of constructing a profile left for future generations or what they tried to present in the Final Judgment. The invocation of saints to intercede with God on behalf of the soul of the testator, although being a characteristic formality in the beginning of this type of document, also informs us about the universal religiousness which was formed by non-white women (and men) of all "types" and "conditions" (free, emancipated, or enslaved) who lived in Minas Gerais.

One ex-slave brought from Africa to Brazil, Teodósia de Castro, declared her last will and testament in February of 1748 and left us with a good example of the incorporation of Catholic norms. On the day she decided to do it, the teachings she learned from listening to sermons, in the catechesis, in masses, and in sisterhood meetings weighed heavily and were imposed along with the official rules of the document preparation. The will of the emancipated slave began in a formal manner, but part of her beliefs and hopes were also registered.

> In the name of the Holy Trinity, Father, Son, and the Holy Spirit, three persons and only one true God. Let it be known that this legal instrument has been executed in the year of our Lord Jesus Christ seventeen-forty eight, on the third day of the month of February of said year, I, Teodósia de Castro, emancipated black woman, being in my right mind and understanding that Our Father gave me health, and fearful of death and wishing to put my soul on the path to salvation

and not knowing what Our Lord wants me to do and when it will
be fitting to take me to you..., I send my soul to the Holy Trinity
who created it and I beseech the eternal Father by the death and Passion of his Only Begotten Son who wishes to receive it... I ask and
beg of the glorious Virgin Mary, Our Lady Mother of God, and of
all the saints of the celestial court, particularly to my guardian angel
and to the glorious Saint Teodósia, saint of my name, and to the glorious Saint Gonçalo, and to the glorious Saint Benedito to whom I
have devotion, wish to intercede for me and beseech to my Lord Jesus Christ now and when my soul departs from my body, because as a
true Christian I profess to living and dying in the Holy Catholic Faith
and believing what it has and believing in the Holy Mother Church
of Rome and in this faith I hope to save my soul, not by my merits,
but by the Holy Passion of the Only Begotten Son of God... My body
will be buried in the chapel of Nossa Senhora da Lapa, affiliate of the
parish of Sabará in the custom of Saint Francisco and will be taken to
the grave with three priests and all will recite to me the funeral mass
for my soul and if on the day of my death, if unable to find anyone beyond the chaplain of said chapel, this let him take me to my grave.[11]

Six months after the will was made, she died. Teodósia de Catro, black woman from Angola, lived in Arraial de Nossa Senhora da Lapa, the end of Vila de Sabará, with her husband, Bonifácio de Castro, a black man and an emancipated slave. They did not have children. She did not list goods beyond eight slaves: Antônio, of the Mina nation, around 35 years old; Manuel, Angolan, around 28 years old; Bonifácio, little *crioulo*, around 8 years old; Teodósia, *crioula*, around 13 years old (she was given a *coartação*—a plan for manumission—in the will); Luísa, *crioula*, around 10 years old; Antônia, *crioula*, 4 years old, more or less; Ana, *crioula*, 2 years old, more or less; and Isabel, black woman from the Mina nation, around 40 years old (she was also given a *coartação* in the will). The sustenance of the family seemed to come from the garden that the slaves cultivated. Teodósia, like many characters of the colonial world, converted to Catholicism and, who knows, simultaneously kept up religious practices brought from Africa; she got married, became a slave owner, and, predicting the end of her days, made a will for man and for God. She made a very personal declaration that showed how she lived and understood the life in that society: "I declare that I was issued a deed of freedom from my already deceased owner Luís de

Castro, for 200 eighths of gold that I had given to him for my emancipation, as stated in said deed of freedom..."[12]

Some Conclusions

Pretas, crioulas, índias, mamelucas, mulatas, pardas, cabras (dark-skinned black women, black women born in captivity in Brazil, indigenous women, daughters of mixed white/indigenous parents, women daughters of mixed European/African/indigenous parentage, women of mixed black/mulatto parents), and non-white women of all types and conditions did not just populate mining towns and villages of the 18th century, but they were much more. They transformed themselves into active characters, in the dynamic, mobile, slave context that was mixed and connected with regions of the entire world, they transformed themselves into true historical agents, co-constructors of that world in all the dimensions of it. These women, for many years, remained hidden in the stories of Brazil that were told. Beginning in 1980, the historiography of Brazil came to see notable development and a renaissance occurred which was started by the history of slavery. From there, the roles of defenseless victims, poorly treated by cruel white owners were problematized and the research presented realities very different than what was known. These women, who remained anonymous, whose contribution to the formation of colonial society were not even a part of historiographical themes, came to the forefront of the colonial scene and many have rewritten it since then.

In this essay, I chose to write about some of these women who, like many others, helped to construct one of the principal societies of the world during that time. They took advantage of opportunities that arose and invented formulas that, in turn, were copied by others, which resulted in extraordinary individual and group situations. It is no exaggeration to speak of the essential role they performed in social networks. At the end of the 18th century, Minas Gerais had the largest population among the captaincies of Brazil, and it is very possible that women were the majority among the emancipated and the freeborn non-whites. Many emancipated slaves became slave owners, something very common in that time. Between one-third and two-thirds of slave owners in Minas must have been non-white and, among them, women also occupied a prominent position.

It is necessary to highlight that I didn't select exceptions, but rather cases that bring forth, in their complexity and detail, patterns, common practices, customs, strategies, and forms of coexistence that these women lived and left as a legacy for other women and men. The examples could have been different ones and could have spanned a larger space. These women, however, summarized many other cases and experiences, representing other women whose actions helped to construct a colonial mining society, an important piece of the experiences of displacement and of human and cultural blends in the modern world.

Notes

1. Instituto do Patrimônio Histórico e Artístico Nacional (IPHAN)/[Instituto Brasileiro de Museus (Ibram)]/Museu Regional de São João del Rei (MR)/Inventários (INV), box 145. Inventário *post-mortem* de Joana da Silva Machada – Recife de Pernambuco, 21 November 1745. Note that the first two names on the list were also universal heirs selected by Joana. The spelling has been updated to reflect current standards.

2. IPHAN/[Ibram]/Casa Borba Gato (CBG)/Cartório do Primeiro Ofício (CPO) – Testamentos (TEST) – códice (07) 13, f. 90v.-f. 95v. Testamento de Francisca Poderosa, Pitangui, 6 August 1742. The facsimile edition of the document and its complete transcription can be found in Paiva (2009, p. 264-81).

3. The spelling has been updated to reflect current standards.

4. Arquivo Eclesiástico da Arquidiocese de Mariana (Aeam), Devassas, June-Sep. 1737-1738, f. 22. *Proscrições do resultado final da visita. Domingos Maciel Aranha com a cúmplice Francisca Pedrosa fez a culpa em três mil réis*. I am indebted to Rangel Cerceau Neto, who I expressly thank, for access to this part of the documentation on Francisca Poderosa/Pedrosa.

5. The spelling has been updated to current standards.

6. IPHAN/[Ibram]/Museu do Ouro (MO)/CPO – TEST – códice 2, f. 86v.-91. Testament of Bárbara Gomes de Abreu e Lima – Sabará, 12 July 1735. The facsimile edition of the document and its complete transcription can be found in Paiva (2009, p. 217-34).

7. The spelling has been updated to current standards.

8. The spelling has been updated to current standards.
9. The spelling has been updated to current standards.
10. Arquivo Público Mineiro (APM)/Câmara Municipal de Sabará (CMS) – códice 53, 21v-f.16. Testament of Bárbara de Oliveira – Sabará, 12 August 1766.
11. APM/CMS – códice 20, f. 21v-f.3. Testament of Teodósia de Castro – Arraial de Nossa Senhora da Lapa, 3 February 1748. Note that the spelling has been updated to current standards.
12. The spelling has been updated to current standards.

Bibliography

Ivo, Isnara Pereira. *Homens de caminho: trânsitos, comércio e cores nos sertões da América portuguesa – século XVIII*. [Men on the Way: Transit, Commerce, and Colors in the Hinterlands of Portuguese America – 18th Century]. 2009. Diss. (Doctoral). – Programa de Pós-Graduação em História, Universidade Federal de Minas Gerais (UFMG), Belo Horizonte, MG.

Martins, Mário S. J. *Introdução histórica à vidência do tempo e da morte.* [Historical Introduction to Violence in the Time of Death]. Braga: Livraria Cruz, 1969, v. I.

Maxwell, Kenneth R. *A devassa da devassa; a Inconfidência Mineira: Brasil e Portugal – 1750-1808.* [The Inquiry of All Inquiries; Mistrust in Minas Gerais: Brazil and Portugal – 1750-1808]. Rio de Janeiro: Paz e Terra, 1978.

Paiva, Eduardo França. *Escravidão e universo cultural na Colônia: Minas Gerais, 1716-1789.* [Slavery and the Cultural Universe in the Colony: Minas Gerais, 1716-1789]. Belo Horizonte: Editora da UFMG, 2001.

____. *Escravos e libertos nas Minas Gerais do século XVIII; estratégias de resistência através dos testamentos.* [Slaves and Freedmen in Minas Gerais of the 18th Century: Strategies of Resistance through Testaments]. 3. ed. São Paulo/Belo Horizonte: Annablume/PPGH-UFMG, 2009.

2

WOMEN OF AFRICAN DESCENT IN BAHIA:
GENDER, COLOR AND SOCIAL MOBILITY,
1780-1830

Adriana Dantas Reis

As is already well established in Brazilian historiography, although being a slave society strongly marked by the hierarchy of gender, the result of power relations was not always negative for women. Various studies show that in relation to men in the same condition, female slaves stood out in the acquisition of emancipation, and free women, in the quantity of goods.[1] Bahia was no different. Between the end of the 18th century and the first decades of the 19th century, many free women of color and freed women owned slaves and managed businesses, becoming true bridges in the process of social mobility.

Emancipation or promises of emancipation—registered in notebooks and wills of owners—free or paid, conditional or unconditional were obviously the entryway to the world of the free and the trajectories of free women and their descendants reveal the specifics of slave relations in Brazil. Today we know that Chica da Silva was just one among many in the same condition who had extramarital affairs with white, well-to-do men (Furtado, 2003). They appear in the bibliography on family and sexuality, in ecclesiastical sources, wills, personal inventories, letters of emancipation, etc.

There are innumerous free men that, in their will, claimed or established as their heirs their children with slave women, freed women, or free women of color. On the other hand, various groups of freed women, legitimate or natural daughters, single, married and widowed, with or without children, were also fundamental in the processes of mobility for other slave women of diverse ethnicities: *crioulas* (black women born into captivity in Brazil), freed women, free women of color, *pardas* (women of mixed race involving black/white/indigenous parentage), mulatto women, etc. In an attempt to get closer to this universe, a study was done on 662 wills of deceased men and women, dated between 1811 and 1833 and distributed throughout 15 notary books that make up a collection in the Arquivo Público do Estado da Bahia (Apeb).[2]

Examining the information contained in these wills, among the 77 free men, married and single, 21 of them (27.2 percent—13 single and 8 married) claimed to have natural children with women of color. Among the single men, 7 had children with ex-slaves, 5 with *pardas* and 1 with a *crioula*. Among the married men with illegitimate children, 2 had children with slaves and the other 6 were children with *pardas*, *cabras* (women born of black and mulatto parents) or *crioulas*. The only illegitimate children identified as mulattos were children of slaves who had Portuguese fathers, while those identified as *pardos* were children of *crioulas*, *pardas*, or African-born women whose fathers were Portuguese men or men born in Brazil.

The majority of these men had been born in Portugal or in Portuguese territories, as was the case of Francisco de Paula, native of Ilha Terceira, Azores, legitimate son, who had a natural son, Francisco de Paul, with Paula de Tal, *parda*, single, deceased. In 1824, he named as his testators, Maria de Nazaré, "emancipated *crioula*," and his son Francisco.[3] In the same year, José Gomes da Costa, a Portuguese man from Braga, declared in his will that he had five children with three different women, three of the children from Florência Maria Pereira, *parda*, single. He owned a farm on the Cangurungu land, a house with 19 slaves, cattle, horses, and breeding animals. As for the remainder of his goods, he named as heirs the children of *parda*, Florência Geraldo Gomes da Costa, Josefa Gomes and Francisca Mariana,[4] which makes us believe that he, most likely, lived in the company of his children.

In 1811, Joaquim José Copque, native of Porto, owner of the Engenho do Jacaré, in the neighborhood of São Sebastião das Cabeceiras do Passé, acknowledged his natural children that he had after being widowed: Casemiro José Copque and Maria da Apresentação, who were children he had with Vitória Maria da Conceição, "slave" of his family.[5]

Some of these men, although not assuming their children, left strong indications of paternity. For example, the reverend canon José Telles de Meneses, native of Vila da Água Fria, ordered in 1814 that his farm, Jenipapo, should be sold and 15,000 *cruzados* (a currency of the time) be split among the daughters of the *parda* Quitéria: Vitória, Rosa and Eusébia, all married (the value was later increased to 20,000 *cruzados* in a codicil). In a private letter, he affirmed that these same beneficiaries had already received land for their dowries, leaving to Rosa the site of Brejões, and the other to Vitória, both daughters of the *parda* Quitéria. He also left the site Engenho Catêt Cacos and the small surrounding crop lands to Vitoriano Álvares da Fonseca, son of the *parda* Maria Angélica, and to Francisco, Maria dos Prazeres and Cipriano, children of the *cabra* (mixed race woman of black/mulatto parents) Maria Francisca.[6]

Independently of having natural children or not, single men were always surrounded by women, many of them being their principal beneficiaries. In 1827, Vicente Ferreira Milles, single, determined that his former slave Domiciana should choose and take ownership of two of his current slaves. He also left to her *coartadas* (an arrangement for manumission after a certain period of time) for the *negrinha* (young black girl) Felicidade, the *preta* (dark-skinned black girl) Possedônia and a slave by the name of Rita. Vicente also claimed to have in his camp more than 11 slaves that were not his; they all belonged to the *preta* Domiciana and were in the various cargoes from the Costa da Mina, and he named her as his universal heir.[7]

A minority of men that appear in the wills were men who owned land and slaves or they had businesses and dwelling houses, and in some cases the company of African women, freed and free, and women of color and their children were a choice rather than a shortcoming. However, the women, slave or free, were not just concubines; after all, many of them married with white men of great social and economic power.

One story that became famous in Bahia was that of the *parda* Rita Gomes da Silva, also known as Rita Cebola. Widow of the Portuguese captain Leandro de Souza Braga, she secretly married again in 1792 with another Portuguese man, Inocêncio José Costa, a wealthy trader.[8] The descriptions speak of the entourage of slaves and the luxuries of Rita Cebola (Bittencourt, 1992, p. 49-50). Her husband belonged to various third orders, such as that of Carmo, he was a brother of the Santa Casa de Misericórdia and knight of the Ordem de Cristo. In his testament, he asks the prior of the Ordem Terceira de Nossa Senhora do Monte Carmo that he had been a part of for years that he be buried, if possible, together with his third wife lady Rita Gomes da Silva, "to show how important she was to me."[9] A large part of the declarations of Inocêncio are requests made by Rita Cebola, who died without a will. A large part of his beneficiaries, in name of his wife, were also women. It should be noted that for some of them, he cites the origin as *pardas* and young *crioulas*; regarding, however, others such as Ms. Úrsula, he does not mention color—they were probably *pardas* like Rita Cebola, and maybe they were freed women. All of them made up a large circle of dependents raised by Rita. The will of her husband also shows that he aimed to establish a formal relationship with her, marrying her in secret, and being attentive to realizing the wishes of his wife; something that we did not see frequently in the wills we studied.

There were other cases of such marriages. Francisco de Mera, white man, native of the kingdom of Galícia, in his will created in 1814 declared to be married to Cecília Maria do Sacramento, a black woman from Angola, with no children. Furthermore, he states that with his wife, he had more than 16 years of "illicit communication and fulfillment of responsibility and co-living with her and [she had always helped me] to live." He named her as his universal heir.[10] There were also some marriages registered in the neighborhood of

Nossa Senhora do Ó of Paripe in the Recôncavo. In 1786, Inácia Maria, native of the Freguesia do Passé, *parda* woman, legitimate child, married Antônio José da Silva, white man, from Lisboa, legitimate son,[11] and in 1790 Bernardo Pereira, white man, married Joana, *parda* woman.[12]

In Bahia, many divorce requests in the 19th century were motivated by masters having affairs with their slaves or with women of color.[13] An interesting case is captured in a letter sent to the king of Portugal asking for a divorce. It states the following:

> ... the petitioner ended up living in contempt of the respondent, who, deaf to pleas, and insensitive to tears did not recognize the reason... on the same day in which the petitioner went to the house of the respondent, he slept in the same bedroom as two of the slave women... because of them she become so insolent that she made the petitioner the object of her contempt... admonishing the respondent with endless obscenities and harsh words; she to punish one of the fiercest with her own strength, but the strongest one tried to throw herself at the woman, grabbing her throat with her bare hands, to try to pin her down and end the life of the petitioner; and if voices calling for help hadn't alerted the respondent and the slave hadn't intervened in his behalf, grabbing one of the arms of the petitioner, and with a fierceness and force warned her that she was a free woman, showing her a letter that he had given her, making her read it as a proclamation of her blindness, with no mercy for the disgraced petitioner who fell on the ground as if dead, and she would have died right there if compassionate people hadn't shown up....[14]

This woman, neglected by her husband who preferred to share his bed with his slaves, was not a matronly woman with many children, but rather Maria Ana Rita de Meneses, a white woman, who married at 12 or 13 years old with her cousin/uncle, the colonel lieutenant of the militia of Cachoeira, Gonçalo Marinho Falcão. This happened in 1806. Right after the marriage, lady Maria got her divorce and after became the famous peasant of the Recôncavo Baiano, lover of the powerful Colonel Pereira Sodré, with whom she had an illegitimate child, Francisco Pereira Sodré, husband of Cora Coutinho (Dantas Reis, 2000, p. 147).

In another case, in 1830, Lady Luzia Maria de Jesus filed for divorce from her husband, captain José Bernardino de Melo. According to her, her husband had stopped giving her clothing and food and left her to live with a *parda* whore, with whom he already had some children in the same area they lived, Freguesia do Camisão na Vila de Cachoeira. Furthermore, he hit her every day and hurt her with foul words.[15]

In spite of many men choosing to remain in the company of women of color, socially it was a risky option. In 1784, for example, the governor of Bahia informed the king of Portugal that he had left the position he held as second lieutenant in the artillery of Salvador to Antônio Gomes Viana, "for having married with a black woman," which the governor characterized as a "perverse and scandalous practice."[16] However, the decision to formalize relations with freed women and women of color strongly indicates that there really was the option of staying with them and this not only happened because of lack of white women as it has been repeatedly claimed in Brazilian historiography.

The Case of Luzia Jeje

Among the wills of free men, we highlight that of captain Manuel de Oliveira Barroso, created in 1814. Resident of Engenho Aratu, in the neighborhood Nossa Senhora do Ó of Paripe, in the Recôncavo Baiano, the captain was a native of Freguesia da Sé and legitimate son of captain Manuel Barroso de Oliveira and Lady Antônia de Azevedo, both deceased. Despite never having married, Manuel de Oliveira Barroso acknowledged seven children: lady Teresa de Jesus Maria José, daughter of Rita Maria de Santo Antônio, white woman, single and without impairments; and six more children from Luzia Gomes de Azevedo, "black woman of Jeje origin" (descendent of the Ewe and Fon people of West Africa): Sutério, Domingos Antônio, Estevão, Gaspar, Ana Joaquina and Maria da Conceição. In his will, captain Barroso named his children as heirs of the two parts of his farm after paying his debts and also included that his six *pardo* children were already "exempted from all servitude seeing as they were already considered legitimate," as their mother Luzia was also emancipated and free.[17]

Contrary to the publicized insensitivity of masters for the natural children they had with slaves, the captain kept his family united. He purchased his son Domingos Antônio, separate from the others in the distribution of his parents' property, paying 40 thousand *réis* (currency of the time) to his brother, also a captain, José de Oliveira Barroso.[18] Manuel also named his children Sutério, Domingos Antônio and Estevão as his testators, giving them full decision rights, including the freeing of some of his slaves. In a society strongly marked by interpersonal power relations, the choice of the captain shows that he cultivated relationships of trust and loyalty with his offspring and he wanted, above all, to guarantee that his heirs were truly benefitted.

There are few details about Luzia. She is cited only in the will of her companion (1807) and that of her son Sutério de Oliveira Barroso (1822), appearing also in a marriage registry from 1790 in the neighborhood Nossa Senhora do Ó of Paripe. It is likely that she arrived in Bahia during the second half of the 18th century, a strong period of trade with the Costa da Mina, and she was a part of the Gbe-speakers, the cultural group that created the Candomblé ritual of the Jeje people (Parés, 2006, p. 46). It is almost certain that she had stayed some time on Ilha de Itaparica, where her son Sutério was born. However in 1783, after the death of Luzia's owners, captain Barroso decided to buy the Aratu mill located in the neighborhood of Nossa Senhora do Ó in Paripe, where he lived with his companion and her children until death in 1814.

Supposing that Luzia had lived on a sugarcane plantation in Itaparica or in some urban loft in Salvador, it is most likely that she was a domestic slave. The certainty captain Barroso had about the paternity of his children shows that there was very close control. During the time, many fathers recognized natural children, but not all of them showed certainty in their offspring. In 1824, for example, Sebastião Alves de Castilho, freed, native of Salvador, called attention in his will to the lack of "preservation of the womb" of the supposed mother of his daughter, the *crioula* Ana Maria, and highlighted that he left to his alleged daughter 50 thousand *réis* for the sake of his conscience and "for the reputation that follows my daughter."[19] There is also the hypotheses that Luzia had arrived in Bahia before becoming an adult, as happened with the freed woman Luísa Cardozo Maria de Jesus, native of the African coast, who declared in her testament to have been "baptized as a young girl in Conceição da Praia,"[20] or like the freed woman Joaquina de Santana e Melo, Jeje origin, who is said to have arrived in Brazil at 8 years old.[21] These slaves, coming from Africa very young, probably had an easier time adapting to the local culture and were closer to the masters than to the adult slaves.

Luzia shared the company of slaves of her origin in the Aratu mill, later coming to own a slave named Esperança, also of Jeje origin. Contrary to the contractor of Diamantes who did not mention the name of Chica da Silva in his will (Furtado, 2003, p. 244), captain Barroso not only freed and named Luzia as the mother of his *pardo* children, but he also left her 200 thousand *réis*.[22]

Luzia's children, identified as *pardos* in Barroso's will, appear in other documents without any reference to color. In the will of Sutério, for example, he does not define himself as *pardo*, and his mother is named only as Luzia Gomes de Azevedo. In the same way, Sutério's siblings lost their identification as *pardos* in the registries of baptisms and marriages in which they were godparents, or in the other documents researched, with the exception of a single document of a baptism registry in which Gaspar appears as "Mr. *pardo*" of baptized slaves.

The natural daughter of Sutério, lady Florinda Maria de Jesus and her husband Cristovão Pereira de Faria, appear without any reference to their color, both in the marriage registry and in the baptism of their daughter Clarinda in 1813.[23] Only during the judicial disputes of the inventory of Sutério do we discover the color of Cristovão Pereira in the transcription of his death record in 1852, in which he is identified as "widowed *pardo*," like his son José Alexandre Pinto, a "single *pardo*."[24] The color of a certain individual thus could appear or disappear depending on variables and circumstances that were not always clear.

Those facts highlighted the need for an aspect of research methodology that we developed. The pitfall of these sources should alert historians to the fact that the absence of any reference to color in the documents does not obviously signify that they were white.[25] A large part of the documentation on Luzia's children camouflages the history of a family of slaves that would have been lost if it weren't for the will of captain Manuel de Oliveira Barroso.

Fundamental in this story is its social result. The paternal benefits of the captain favored a group of slaves that became plantation and slave owners. Luzia's children represented some *pardos* that ascended socially at the end of the 18th century and the beginning of the 19th century, perhaps the same ones either classified as "mulattos" or *pardos* by Vilhena (1969, p. 136). According to the reports of this author, black women, especially *mulatas*, were women "for whom honor is a chimerical name," were "the first who began to corrupt the sons of the masters, giving them their first tests of lewdness." The result of these relations was a "troop of little mulattos and offspring, who later became extremely pernicious in families." According to the exposition by Vilhena, some owners never married, "only because they were not able to get rid of that harpy, to whom the boys were attached," just as there were "clergymen, and not just a few," who lived in "disorder with *mulatas* and black women, whose children they made heirs and to whom they left their property."

For Vilhena (1969, p. 136-7), those relationships between the owners and the *mulatas* and slave women caused "many of the most precious properties of Brasil" to end up "in the hands of arrogant, smug, lazy mulattos." The inherited plantations "would quickly be destroyed with grave damage to the state, something worthy of the royal attention of His Majesty; because if not, he will see the plantations and large farms fall into the hands of these uncultivated *pardo* men, who are generally rotten."

As the author indicates, in social and economic terms, it would be extremely disadvantageous for free men to share mobility and access to goods with freed slaves or free "bastards" of color. The subject of illegitimate *pardos*, for example, was argued "by the Conselho Ultramarino, in August of 1723, starting with a request from the governor of Minas that mulattos could not be heirs of their father, even if they didn't have white siblings" (Lara, 2007, p. 340). These critiques reinforce the idea of the choice that many men made: maintaining relationships with slave or ex-slave women and their children. Nevertheless, if these women and their children ascended socially, the action of the masters further confirmed their privileges in the slave and gender hierarchy, especially in confrontation and preservation of enslaved men. Meanwhile, slave women and free women of color paradoxically transformed the submission to their masters into elements of access to the world of the free for themselves and their children; again giving life to the questions about the efficiency of the patriarchal model to analyze slavery in Brazil.

Mobility among women

In 1814, Maria da Saúde, natural daughter of Maria Pereira and an unknown father, born in Nossa Senhora da Piedade do Cabrito, in the Recôncavo, declared in her will that her few possessions were acquired "by her own agency and work." She owned townhouses in Ladeira do Carmo on her own land, some small houses in Saúde on borrowed land, in addition to silver cutlery and an old black woman named Rosa. She freed her *crioula* Maria Francisca, mother of Maria José—who was already emancipated—and named her as an heir. She also freed the older slave Teresa, and presented a long list of freed slave women and beneficiaries. She left twenty thousand *réis* to the *crioula* Felipa, who had been her slave and was found in the convent of Soledade da Lapa as slave of Adriano Araújo Braga; five thousand *réis* and a bench to the *crioula* Francisca Romana, who had been a slave of Domingos da Rocha; thirty thousand *réis* to Joana, the little *mulatta* daughter of Sebastiana Rodrigues, a *cabra* woman, and resident of Pilar who had been the slave of João Rodrigues, deceased. She also left two chairs to Joaquim de Tal, brother of Francisca, as well as ten thousand *réis* to a *crioulo* by the name of José Maria, who had been her slave, son of the *preta* Rosa, and who was in Portugal.[26]

That is just one case among so many others of free single women who decided to name other women as beneficiaries in their wills, generally both slave and freed women. Unfortunately it is very difficult to define their color and origins, and of the 57 wills made by free, single women that we studied, only two relate their ascendance to slavery: one was a daughter of *pardos* and the other of *crioulos*. The number of slave or freed women named as beneficiaries by Maria da Saúde shows that her social circle and her dependents were predominantly feminine; even the men who were named were directly linked to women. That is to say, "her agency and work" was based on her slaves and by naming them as beneficiaries of her will was a form of recognizing the help they lent to her in growing her possessions.

Free women who were married or widowed also named other slaves, freed women, or free women of color as beneficiaries in their wills, making provisions that established emancipation or determined some benefit for ex-slaves and their children, which was usually some small value of *réis*, but sometimes included houses for them to live in. In 1817, for example, Teresa Maria de Jesus, a widow of "unknown parents," established in her will that the testator buy a small house of a value up to two hundred thousand *réis* for her freed slave Rosa and her three children: André Joaquim de Santana, Manuel, and Severiana. She also left to André and Manuel fifty-thousand *réis* and to Severiana twenty-thousand *réis*, in addition to her furniture. The possession of property would be lifelong and after their passing, it would go to the Igreja de Nossa Senhora de Guadalupe.[27]

In 1815, Ronalda Maria do Sacramento, also a widow and mother of four children, freed Quitéria, an albino shoemaker, Rafael a stonemason, Delfina, and Justa and asked her religious daughter for a villa of houses to go to this group of slaves.[28] Maria de Assunção Cintra, a widow with no children, named in 1829 her former slaves Teresa Angola, the mothers Escolástica and Silveira, and their children Marcelino, Alberto Alexandre, Jerônimo, José Mateus, and Rosa de Lima, as well as Maria Ludovica do Patrocínio as heirs, leaving to them residential properties with stores to rent.[29]

There were few slave women in Bahia, and they were the minority among the captive Africans that arrived in Salvador, proportionally they were more favored than men in the granting of emancipation, especially because there was typically no cost for them. According to Andrade (1988, p. 118-9), "the average percentage of female African slaves is 51.7 percent of the total of African and Brazilian women, while the percentage of female slaves with Brazilian origins is 48.2 percent of the same group." According to Oliveira (1988, p. 23), between 1779 and 1850, the number of "mulattos equaled 10 to 15 percent of the global population of slaves," and as such, the number of emancipated mulattos was equally high. Of the wills studied, the majority of the freed women were from the Costa da Mina or the coast of Africa; few were born in Bahia, just two. What happened with the *crioula* beneficiaries with letters of emancipation highlighted by Oliveira? It is possible that many of them are hidden in the wills of free women. Could this be the case with Maria da Saúde?

Some freed women owned residential properties; however, the principal investment was in slavery, although there were few slaves left. Many, like free women, left goods to the slaves who served them such as Maria Caetana Rodrigues, born on Ilha de Itaparica, a widow who divided twenty fathoms of land among her five emancipated slaves, four fathoms to each one, under the condition that they don't sell them.[30] In 1827, Ifigência da Silva, a widow and native of the Costa da Mina, in 1827, left her house to the slave Mereciana, also heir to the remainder of her possessions.[31]

The analysis of the wills made between 1811 and 1830 show the processes of social mobility in Bahia during the period. Single and married men, both free and freed, appear naming slave women, freed women, and free women of color as their beneficiaries by acknowledging paternity or as a result of a combination of relationships of dependence, affection, fidelity, and gratitude. Free women, married or single, also show much autonomy and interest in benefitting other women, especially freed women and women still enslaved, which not only represents solidarity in gender, but also indicates successful reproduction of ascending mobility among women. At the same time that they ascended the social hierarchy, they also shared ascension with other women in situations of dependence.

However, it is not possible to confirm that these processes of mobility were reaffirmed and deepened only among women of color. The lack of indicators of the color of free men and women in wills leaves the direct relationship between gender, color, and social mobility open-ended. In spite of this, it is possible to affirm that among men and women who named as heirs enslaved women, freed women, or free women of color, others of the same origin also existed. We could call them "afro-descendants," men and women with some African/slave heritage who, for the sake of social ascension, preferred to hide their color, such as the children of Luzia, who also wait for a reconnection to their slave past.

Notes

1. See Castro Faria, 2007 and Oliveira, 1988.
2. Study developed initially for the doctoral thesis of the author (UFF) and extended to a research project; *Libertos da Bahia: Gênero, cor e mobilidade social, 1700-1850* [Freedmen in Bahia: Gender, Color, and Social Mobility, 1700-1850]. (CNPq).
3. Arquivo Público do Estado da Bahia (Apeb) [Public Archive of the State of Bahia], Livro de Registro de Testamentos (LRT) [Registry of Witnesses] 10, 1824, p. 174.
4. Ibid, p. 96v.
5. Apeb, Judiciário. Tribunal de Justiça, Notificação. [Justice Court, Notice] Conta de Testamento [Witness Statement] 1822 – José Joaquim Copque, Santo Amaro, f. 5.
6. Ibid, LRT 07, 1814, p. 01v.
7. Ibid, LRT 15, 1827, p. 16v.
8. Apeb, Cartas para S. Majestade, 1799 in Vilhena, 1969, p. 365.
9. Apeb, Judiciário, 08/3465/02, 1805, p. 02.
10. Ibid, LRT 04, 1814, f. 29v-32v.
11. Laboratório Eugênio Veiga (LEV), Cúria Metropolitana [Metropolitan Papal Court], Livro de Assento de Casamentos [Book of Wedding Entries], Paripe, p. 61.
12. Ibid, p. 78.
13. Maria Odila Dias (1984, p. 142-3) also cites divorce cases in São Paulo in which women "accused their husbands who were ostentatiously living with their slaves discrediting them to the point of being diminished by their own slaves."

14. Apeb, Cartas do governo, v. 143, f. 265-265v. I thank professor João José Reis for recommending this document. See more about lady Maria Rita in Reis, 2008, p. 72-3.
15. LEV 483, caixa 02, doc. 10, p. 12v.
16. Apeb, Ordens régias, v. 77, doc. 17, 1720-1790.
17. Apeb, LRT, capital, n. 04, 1814. p. 80v.
18. Apeb, LRT, n. 4, 1814, p. 81.
19. Apeb, LRT 11, 1824, p. 05v.
20. Apeb, LRT 19, 19/8/1829, p. 276v.
21. Apeb, LRT 22, 1/8/1832, p. 04v.
22. Apeb, LRT 04, 1814, p. 83v.
23. ACMS (Arquivo da Cúria Metropolitana de Salvador) [Archive of the Metropolitan Papal Court of Salvador] – LEV, Livro de Registros de Batismos de Paripe [Book of Registry of Baptisms of Paripe], 1813, f. 12v.
24. Apeb, Judiciário, Inventário [Inventory], 04/1930/2402/05, capital, 1823, f. 462v.
25. Among other authors who called attention to the absence or move of free people, see Mattos, 1995, p.103-14; Faria, 1998, p. 135-9; Mattoso, 1992, p. 582; Guedes, 2006. p. 447-88.
26. Apeb, LRT 04, 1814, p. 87.
27. Apeb, LRT 09, 1817, p. 128v-30.
28. Apeb, LRT 05, 1815, p. 84v-89.
29. Apeb, LRT 19, 1829, p. 90v.
30. Apeb, LRT 15, 1827, p. 125v-129.
31. Apeb, LRT 15, 1827, p. 206-208v.

Bibliography

Andrade, Maria José. *A mão de obra escrava em Salvador (1811-1860)*. [Slave Labor in Salvador (1811-1860)]. São Paulo/Brasília: Corrupio/CNPq, 1988.

Bittencourt, Anna Ribeiro de Goes. *Longos serões do campo*. [Long Evenings in the Country]. Rio de Janeiro: Nova Fronteira, 1992, v. 1 e 2.

Dias, Maria Odila da Silva. *Cotidiano e poder em São Paulo no século XIX: Ana Gertrudes de Jesus*. [Daily Life and Power in São Paulo in the 19th Century: Ana Gertrudes de Jesus]. São Paulo: Brasiliense, 1984.

Faria, Sheila Siqueira de Castro. *A colônia em movimento. Fortuna e família no cotidiano colonial.* [The Colony in Movement. Fortune and Family in Colonial Daily Life]. Rio de Janeiro: Nova Fronteira, 1998.

____. "Damas mercadoras – As pretas minas no Rio de Janeiro (século XVIII a 1850)." [Merchant Ladies – Black Women in Rio de Janeiro (18th Century to 1850)]. In: Soares, Mariza de Carvalho (Org.). *Rotas atlânticas da Diáspora Africana: da Baía do Benim ao Rio de Janeiro.* [Atlantic Routes in the African Diáspora: From the Bay of Benin to Rio de Janeiro]. Niterói: Eduff, 2007.

Furtado, Júnia Ferreira. *Chica da Silva e o contratador de diamantes – O outro lado do mito.* [Chica da Silva and the Diamond Contractor – the Other Side of the Myth]. São Paulo: Companhia das Letras, 2003.

Guedes, Roberto. "Sociedade escravista e mudança de cor. Porto Feliz, São Paulo, século XIX." [Slave Society and Changes in Color]. In: Fragoso, João Luis Ribeiro et al. (Orgs.). *Nas rotas do Império: eixos mercantis, tráfico e relações sociais no mundo português.* [On the Routes of the Empire: Merchant Trade Routes, Traffic, and Social Relations in the Portuguese World]. Vitória/Lisboa: Edufes/IICT, 2006.

Lara, Silvia Hunold. *Fragmentos setecentistas: escravidão, cultura e poder na América portuguesa.* [Eighteenth Century Fragments: Slavery, Culture, and Power in Portuguese America]. São Paulo: Companhia das Letras, 2007.

Mattos, Hebe. *Das cores do silêncio. Os significados da liberdade no sudeste escravista – Brasil séc.* XIX. [Of the Colors of Silence. Meanings of Liberty in Southeastern Slavery – Brazil Cent. XIX]. Rio de Janeiro: Arquivo Nacional, 1995.

Mattoso, Kátia. *A Bahia no século* XIX. *Uma província no Império.* [Bahia in the 19th Century. A Province in the Empire]. Rio de Janeiro: Nova Fronteira, 1992.

Oliveira, Inês. *O liberto: seu mundo e os outros.* [Liberty: Its World and Others]. São Paulo: Corrupio, 1988.

Parés, Luis Nicolau. *Formação do candomblé: história e ritual da nação jeje na Bahia.* [The Formation of Candomblé: History and Ritual in the Jeje Nation in Bahia]. Campinas: Ed. da Unicamp, 2006.

Reis, Adriana Dantas. *Cora: lições de comportamento feminino na Bahia do século* XIX. [Shades: Lessons in Feminine Behavior in Bahia of the 19th Century]. Salvador: FCJA/Centro de Estudos Baianos da UFBA, 2000.

Reis, João José. *Domingos Sodré. Um sacerdote africano. Escravidão, liberdade e candomblé na Bahia do século* XIX. [Domingos Sodré. An African Prist. Slavery, Freedom, and Candomblé in Bahia of the 19th Century]. São Paulo: Companhia das Letras, 2008.

Vilhena, Luis dos Santos. *A Bahia no século* XVIII. [Bahia in the 18th Century]. Salvador: Itapuã, 1969, v. 2.

3

THREE BLACK WOMEN WHO CHANGED THE GAME IN 18TH CENTURY MINAS GERAIS

Luciano Figueiredo

The scenario is a vast territory, suspended by the mountainous upland irrigated by streams that plunge into the folds of dark stones. It earned the name "Minas" to identify the material that lay hidden in the earth waiting to sprout; accompanied by "Gerais" (literally, General Mines) to disguise the countless places that gold could be hidden. People of all origins climbed the mountains to get there, adding to those already inhabiting the area, inaugurating a time that seemed to flow forever. And then it ended. Or almost. Some papers and scribbles with the seal of officials remain, which historians observe curiously; and with their enchantments and a large dose of creative liberty, want to bring them to life.

There are three women who were freed from silence by the pen of scribes. There could have been more, because there were many of them. However, this selected trio insinuates the multitude of people who experienced the golden and crystalline 18th century. The fortune they had, in terms of weapons, law, or faith, hardly matters.

Ana

Exhausted from walking underneath the weight of the tray holding baked goods to sell, the black woman took a deep a breath when she saw before her a dozen slaves working in a nearby village grotto. It was near the end of the day and she was just about to finish her activities, but she relied on the hunger, thirst for alcohol, and fatigue of the diggers, waist-deep in the cold water striking the hard water of the river bed; surely, they needed to take a swig of a drink, have a bite of sponge cake, and smoke. Ana was right. As soon as she arrived in her colorful cloth dress, the slaves of the mine, belonging to a certain Domingos de Matos, eagerly crowded around the tray that promised some wealth in the poverty of the rest of the day. They had to be quick and discreet because it was with hidden gold that they paid for that fleeting comfort.

Suddenly, the climate changed and the black woman found herself surrounded by various armed men. She undoubtedly recognized the captains of the forest, who were following governmental orders to hunt down whoever got close to the mining zones with goods to sell. Ana tried to escape, looked around for an escape route, but keeled over before the evidence and fatigue. There was nowhere to run, her legs ached with no strength to climb the trails with the persistent officials on her heels. Caught "selling unmeasured spirits to blacks... from a tin bowl,"[1] as it was written later in the writ of her imprisonment by the bailiff of the chamber of Vila do Serro Frio, in the north of Minas Gerais.

To incriminate her was an empty liquor bottle, another that was half full, as well as tobacco, found on her tray. There were no doubts as to what she was doing there. Turned over to the hand of the court, the bailiff locked Ana into the village jail, "behind bars," as it was called. Being a slave, her release was resolved by her owner, which added to the loss of the confiscated goods and the days of lost work in the amount of 1,200 *réis* (currency of the time) paid to the court.[2]

There were many women like Ana, regularly challenging the authorities and putting themselves at risk in prohibited locations to sell goods to the population of Minas. In the mining zones, on roads and routes, and in the public squares, a vigorous trade stirred life—practiced by women who carried trays or leaned against sales stands to negotiate with their clientele. Almost always women, and usually women of color, they would eventually lend their color and gender to a designation that epitomized them: the *negras de tabuleiro*—"black women with a tray."

Freed or slaves, mulatto women, *pretas* (those who were born in Africa), or *crioulas* (those born in Brazil), they sold pastries, cakes, sweets, honey, milk, bread, fruits, tobacco, and drinks, especially spirits. They circulated through the villages with their goods without missing the busy roads and farms nearby. However, the preferred location was the rivers or grottos that were being mined and where gold rolled smoothly into their hands.

It was not like this only in the mountains of Minas Gerais. Practically in all of the centers of the Portuguese colony, such as São Paulo, Belém, Salvador, Rio de Janeiro, and Recife, there were women who cared for the staples through retailing. Brazil was the port of cultural traffic that molded the culture and social habits, adapted traditions that the Iberian Peninsula and the Atlantic coast of Africa already knew.

In the Portuguese seaside cities where the population paid dearly for the human costs of the naval expansion, widows and orphans earned special protection of the state, and reserved exclusively for them was minor urban trade. It was the state that assured "the honest practice and necessary sustenance of many poor women, natives of these regions, who… lived from these small trades," according to what was determined by the laws of the 18th century—for example, the Law of 19 November 1757—like an echo of an old custom. For those who doubted, the law stipulated: "without any man daring to disturb them."[3]

On the equator, these women would change color. The historian Sheila de Castro Faria (2001, p. 307) believes that the stigma created by the work done by African women in the tropics was responsible for the fact that white women had gradually ceased to practice this traditional craft; the reason being that once black women took these tasks, it became incompatible with social standards of the elite.

There was a union between two different cultural matrices. In the societies of the west African coast there were also women who took care of the food needs of the community. Alberto da Costa e Silva (2002, p. 237) tells us that "the business of retail… in almost all of Africa was dominated by women." They not only prepared the food, but they also planted, collected, and sold it, without any help from men. In Luanda, Angola, the same thing happened during the Portuguese domination of the 16th century, and the markets were controlled by women—*mubadi* (saleswoman) or *mukwa* (businesswoman)—who divided themselves by specializations according to the product of their stands (manioc/cassava, fruit, corn); they also offered services with their supernatural healing powers using amulets, clay, and herbs (Pantoja, 2001, p. 46). "The saleswomen," says the Africanist (Silva, 2002, p. 237),

> ...before sunrise, they left and headed for the road, from one village to another, with the *merces* [merchandise] on their head. Shrewd, experienced, and well-informed, they knew the best place to setup in each square.... Here, they sold pepper and bought the yams that they would offer later. There, they acquired white cloth, which they dyed to exchange later for fish in another market.... They bought in bulk and sold it little by little.

Street trader, Rio de Janeiro, Brazil, c. 1770

However, it was in Minas that they were immortalized by the beautiful colors and brushstrokes of Carlos Julião, in his record of customs made in the 18th century, illustrating the reality of submission and inferiority under colonial rule, according to the historian Silvia Lara (2007, p. 263). Even if he doesn't truthfully reflect the scenes as they were seen through their eyes, the women of his album "Fashions worn in Rio de Janeiro and Serro Frio," which was cultivated by a taste for the exotic, and beautifully records with extraordinary beauty details of the traits and colors, helped to show the colonizers the diversity of the population that lived in the colonies.

It was also in Minas that, without any romantic affairs, the *negras de tabuleiro* gained fame among colonial government authorities for threatening social and economic order. They were a danger. Their retail business activity seemed dreadfully linked to contraband gold, especially when they worked near the mining zones because the slaves stopped giving gold to their master (who, in turn, paid their right to a fifth) in exchange for liquor or food from their trays. In the captaincy, a large part of the slaves lived as "work for hire," that is, without an overseer on their heels, responsible for a certain amount that must be given to their master each day. The black women were accused of interfering with this "daily payment." Also, weighing on Ana's cohorts was the suspicion that they facilitated contact among the poor and oppressed, carrying information about slave escape plans, and even exchanging the basic goods to supply the *quilombos* (colonies of escaped slaves). Not enough being a "rosary of damage" (figuratively a string of successive damage), they were also considered immoral, because they prostituted themselves.

They faced heavy persecution and repression as clearly evidenced by the large number of laws dedicated to expunging them from mining zones and nearby areas. Even so, the authorities were in a delicate situation because they could not simply ban an activity of retail supply on which they all depended. For that reason, they tried to limit their movement, prohibiting them from the mineral mines and the highways. On the perimeters of the village, they tried to confine them to a specific area. Some laws, such as the Term of Agreement of 29 July 1720, ordered that the municipal council reserve "more comfortable stops... for the black women who go up the hill to disturb the blacks," whereas others they determined that they should make "divisions and stands for vendors to demonstrate what they wanted to sell."[4] If they infringed upon these orders, they would be imprisoned.

The day to day of Minas Gerais, above all, showed how it was all far from good intentions. The laws against the *negras de tabuleiro* revived relentless persecution each year, showing that the authorities faced many difficulties in controlling them. On a vertiginous scale, as more gold was extracted and more people depended on it to live, the subject was being taken more seriously each time and the punishment became more violent. The principal targets were black women, mulatto women, or *carijós* (indigenous women from a group near what is today the state of São Paulo), freed or captive; upon them fell all sorts of punishments when they transgressed prohibitive laws. In addition to the confiscation of the goods they were selling, the prison stay—which in the beginning of the century did not exceed eight days—was extended to 90 days, while the whipping in the public square that they were also given changed from 50 lashes to 200 lashes. The practice of whipping is an example of an act used to spread terror. Violence towards the body went beyond the pain inflicted on those women; after all, the body did not stop being, according to Arletter Farge (2008, p. 170), "the carnal cloth of history" and it was "on the body that politics was imprinted."

The intense effort to control street trading counteracted the earnings expected by the slaves' masters and of the freed women who dedicated themselves to selling via the trays. After all, the trade of supplies was extremely lucrative. Antonil the Jesuit wrote an important work about colonial riches in the first decade of the 18th century, in which he discussed the opportunities represented by buying and selling in mining lands; he called this phenomenon "from mine to flower of the land" (2007). He states: "...by selling edible items, spirits, and sugar cane juice, in little time many accumulated a considerable amount of gold. Since the blacks and the Indians customarily hid a significant amount of *oitavas* [currency of the time that equaled 1,200 *réis*] when they were gathering gold in the brooks… a large part of this gold is spent on eating and drinking…."

However, women themselves also accumulated resources. At great risk, there were many slave women who acquired emancipation due to the earnings from their business selling items from their trays. Others, already considered freed, could create a respectable inheritance by their small businesses. Minas Gerais was not just the land of opportunity for those coming from São Paulo or Bahia, or the Portuguese. Many of these emancipated black women accumulated a fortune of valuable goods such as slaves, jewelry, and homes; and they were surrounded by other women, among them slaves and ex-slaves.

With the African background and the opportunities in that region of mineral riches, it became easy, often combining trade and prostitution, to form legacies that were revealing of the vertiginous ascension of some black *sinhás* (mistresses) (Faria, 2001). Skilled and shrewd, they did not waiver; after emancipation, they invested in the purchase of slave women, the cheapest, who they could hire in commercial service. In São João del Rei, among the inventories of 18 emancipated women, 12 were owners of slaves. Sheila de Castro Faria (2001, p. 291) states that "the overwhelming majority of the emancipated testators that I studied had slaves that were mostly women."

The rest of their riches were jewelry, clothes, houses in the city, and gold powder. This group was active in trade and participated in the credit market: loaning money and powdered gold, with interest, as well as earning income from renting their houses. The jewelry derived its value from the decoration and dresses common among African women, especially from the Costa da Mina, where many of them originated. These African women in Minas "held cultural baggage that favored them, leading them to wealth and a certain level of autonomy" (Faria, 2001, p. 322). However, they didn't earn social prestige, because in addition to being women, they were black and they worked in manual labor, which degraded them, according to the cultural standards of that time.

Beyond this, they created a social group, which in Minas was one of the most expressive. The region held the largest population of emancipated slaves in the whole colony and within this group, according to historian Eduardo Paiva (1995, p. 109), the women were "more numerous than the emancipated men and constituted, as it were, the second most important category, only below free men." Paiva doesn't have any doubt as to the consequences of the phenomenon: "in the period of captivity they were closer to their owners and seem to have perfectly known how to take advantage of this opportunity." Adopting strategies to achieve emancipation, they prompted an inversion on the demographic balance, since women were already fewer in number than slaves of the masculine sex. They changed the game. "Women were the minority amongst slaves, but it was the women who freed themselves" (Faria, 2004, p. 115). According to Sheila de Castro Faria (2004, p. 126), they had better conditions than men to obtain freedom; "it was not only having the correct amount of money to pay for freedom that mattered, but the persuasion strategies women had more of than the men."

The celebrated life of Chica da Silva, former slave, daughter of a black woman from the Costa da Mina and a white man, illustrates the paths to freedom followed by thousands of other women. Chica lived by the side of the affluent contractor of Diamantes, João Fernandes, with "airs of a stable, but non-legal matrimony" for 17 years, as Júnia Furtado affirms (2003, p. 119 *passim*). As soon as they got together, he stopped being her owner thanks to the emancipation he gave her, in addition to the last name Oliveira that she went on to use, and a brood of 13 children.

Júnia Furtado (2003, p. 110) offers this synthesis: contrary to what men of color experienced, for whom it was always difficult to obtain extra earnings to purchase freedom, "black women for hire, given that they had access to savings, and slave women who lived as concubines with white men had greater chances of being emancipated." Like Chica, there were thousands of ex-slaves that established themselves. "The relations of gender and race were strongly linked in Minas Gerais. The life of Chica da Silva and other emancipated slave women from the village of Tejuco and adjacent villages prove this. Gender was key in the ease of access to emancipation" (Furtado, 2003, p. 109).

However, not all black women needed to move around. Many made sales that spread throughout Minas. There were fixed commercial establishments, of various sizes, a mix of bars, warehouses, and domiciles frequented by the population of slaves, freedmen, and craftsmen. It didn't matter if they were in the heart of the villages or far from everything; what mattered was being near the large brooks where the slave and free men mined. It was there where they purchased goods, but also danced, argued, and schemed. They were also meeting points for underhanded business deals, such as the sale of gunpowder, lead, or salt to *quilombos*. Nevertheless, sales were more difficult to prohibit, given that they represented a good volume of the tax revenues, and as such, the authorities preferred to control their operation more closely, regulating the hours of operation, who went there, or even who could be a seller. "No black man or woman could have a sales contract for edibles or drinks, nor could they open their houses to captive black men," proclaimed a law from 1719.[5] Other orders obliged sales to end early, "one-half hour after the *ave-maria*," or according to the ringing of the bell of the municipal chamber.

Transgressing the law was expensive for women. The authorities, as revealed by an edict from the Câmara Municipal de São João del Rei on January 13, 1720, could not leave out the economic danger that was caused to owners when in "many houses where food is sold… what followed was not only theft but also missing daily payments to their masters." There was still another cause of worry, that it put political stability at risk. The document refers to "other harm that idleness produced from such gathering brings, feeding slave rebellion that threatened the Republic with presumptions of bad consequences."

Rosa, an emancipated black woman who lived in Água Limpa, promoted in her shop, on holy days and Sundays, "*batuques* (drumming with African rhythms) and black dances, *capitães do mato* (literally, forest captains—a term used to refer to slave catchers), with scandals and disturbances." The presence of forest captains shouldn't be considered odd because despite their repressive occupation, they were almost always free or emancipated blacks and mulattos who would did not lose their original social stigma. Another was Ana Vieira, an emancipated black woman like Rosa who owned a lively shop in Passagem, Freguesia de Ouro Branco, where she "gathered blacks at night... to do business."[6]

With authorities fearing illegal trafficking of gold, women and their forms of trade became more limited as the years passed. Instead of shops located near the mines, the authorities were concerned with the violence and crime that the women promoted, fights, and drunkenness, or the misappropriation of the obligatory profit that the slaves had to pay to their masters (the day's wages earned off the backs of "for-hire" slaves), which would eventually affect collection of the 20 percent tax imposed by the Portuguese Crown. However, it was not easy to eliminate sales due to the risk of supply shortages. In one of the central mining regions in the beginning of the 18th century the custom was to permit street vendor activity under the condition that women were not in charge. In the gold extraction on the hill of Congonhas, near Sabará—as determined in the Proclamation of 11 September 1729—shops were permitted at "a two-hundred step circumference" around the hill, provided that they were in the hands of their owners and "in no way" could "black women, *mulatas*, slave women, or emancipated women be doing the selling."

However, the laws didn't stop the presence of women vendors in fixed establishments from slowly surpassing the number of men in this occupation that was traditionally masculine. In Vila Rica, the capital of Minas, at the start of the 18th century, there were just ten women against 180 shops in the hands of men. By the second half of the century, the situation had changed: of the 697 shops, 482 were owned by women. Certainly, contributing to this was the mining crisis, which put men on the road while the women became an element of stability.

The situation had already motivated a report completely dedicated to women, completed by the secretary of the captaincy government, Manuel Fonseca de Azevedo, who in 1732 was horrified with "the residents [who], in great number, have stores selling food and drink, where they put their black women to invite black men to buy." It was said that often owners of the shops left the establishment "to create a place for the black women to become more free to use their appetites" (in Barbosa, 1972, p. 120). It was not an exaggeration of a bureaucrat. The official data confirmed the complaint. In Serro Frio, in the region of diamond extraction, of the 52 men that owned shops in 1736, 32 of them allowed slave women to take over the business.[7]

It seems certain that many of these establishments became centers for amorous encounters, provoking moralizing condemnations from the authorities. However, they hid another danger because the shops under the control of slave women or free women became communication centers for escaped slaves and support for *quilombos*. These black women, said the attentive secretary Azevedo, are "advisors and participants," anyone can find "help and shelter in these black women who assist in the shops" (in Barbosa, 1972, p. 121). The action of these black women was fundamental in engaging solidarity among dispersed groups marked by innumerous ethnic, social, economic and functional differences.

Luzia

The house of Luzia Pinta rapidly gained fame in the humble village where it was located, deep in Vila de Sabará. It was there the neighbors ran when they faced a major affliction. High fevers, serious wounds, questions about love—all were tended to by the freed black woman Luzia. A known practitioner of *calundu* (religious practices with similar African roots as *Candomblé*), she led nighttime ceremonies in her house—called *calundus*—where she appeared dancing moved by the rumble of African drums and wearing a "Turkish style" headdress (Souza, 1986, p. 354), accompanied by snakes coiled on her arms and legs. Before the people who appeared there, Luzia, accompanied by black men and women, drank wine and her body was subjected to tremors, a kind of sacred trance. In this state, she served the afflicted: she cured with the use of herbs, gave advice, and scared away bad spirits.

Luzia, or Luísa as some called her, was Angolan and had arrived to Minas in the beginning of the 1720s in the 18th century. The ritual that she practiced, according to Laura de Mello e Souza, was manifestation of a syncretism (or, the expression that has been more recently used, a cultural miscegenation) that preserved elements of the African cultural universe, such as the snakes she used, combined with Catholic references, especially when she invoked collaboration from the Virgin Mary and from God in the cures that she provided (Souza, 1986, p. 354-5).

In the 1740s, she fell prey to the grasp of the Inquisition. She experienced hard times after having been captured by zealous visitors in Minas and shipped to Lisbon where the courts and inquisitors were waiting for colonists suspected of crimes against the Catholic faith. Nearly 50 years old, she was described as a "a dull-colored black woman, tall with a thick body, with a birth mark near the forehead and another on either side" (Souza, 1986, p. 352). In the metropolis, during two years, as Laura de Mello e Souza also tells us (1986, p. 352), she was interrogated, tortured, and as expected, condemned, parading publicly humiliated in the capital in 1744, when she received the sentence: four years of exile in Algarves.

There were many suspicions of her being a witch, and the more she affirmed her Catholic faith in the interrogations, that she was baptized and confirmed, there was a fear that she had made a pact with the devil to bring about her cures and divinations. To the inquisitors, the trance that she entered, the "winds of divination" that blew in her ears and the body tremors were proof of her pact with the devil. In the conclusive terms of Laura de Mello e Souza (1986, p. 353): "Faithful to the African rites, [Luzia] transforms them into a condemnable offense, unacceptable. This modest history thus bears the marks of Africa, Brazil, and Portugal, the triangle which supported the colonial system; and Luzia, a humble character, passed through this system with great suffering."

The massive presence of the African population in Minas Gerais filled the prisons of Santo Ofício with suspected women; and almost always, they were condemned like Luzia. The archives were also filled with papers from the Portuguese Inquisition and the colony missions in which the bishops covered the territory of Minas, complete with stories of *calundus*, shamanism, blessings, curses, divinations, and every type of magic. It is shocking the number of women in Minas who stood out, in relation to men, in this field as well, especially because magic was typically, in the African tradition, a masculine domain. "In the captaincy of Minas Gerais, in the 18th century," affirms Maria Beatriz Nizza da Silva (2002, p. 194-5)—in an article that adds the book of Laura de Mello e Souza as a source for identifying the complaints and trials against women in various regions of Brazil that reached the Inquisition—"it was the women who were most wanted as healers, while men continued to cure as it was tradition in the African culture."

There was no lack of women in action. Another woman accused of practicing *calundu* was Maria Canga, a black slave woman who amassed gold from the hands of her clients for whom she did divinations. Once again, traces of African beliefs appeared in the descriptions of the rituals that the woman adopted, starting with the "*batuque* dance, in the middle of which something entered and exited from a gourd, a thing she calls Wind." It was when she could "guess what she wanted."[8] More shocking still were the roads that *crioula* Rosa roamed, from Congonhas do Campo, where she would "at midnight dance with the devil at the foot of a cross," where they then communicated.[9]

Many times, slaves performed these magical practices, characterized as witchcraft by political and religious institutions, to ease the rigors of slavery. With the help of two friends under the same condition, the black woman Antônia Luzia promoted parties with dances by the "*negras* and *pardas*" to alleviate the cruelty with which they were treated by their masters, or as it was said then, "to tame the wills of the masters."[10] The black woman Josefa, with origins in the Costa da Mina, did not dance to calm her owner, but she recommended an infallible resource: "wash your lower parts and throw the same water you wash with in the food you make for your masters" (in Carrato, 1962, v. 3, p. 234-40).

It appears that sometimes such methods worked and often the dominion of this type of cultural artifact guaranteed the women conditions even to obtain emancipation or at least maintain a familial relationship without violence. It was suspected amongst the community that the slave Teresa had conquered the heart of her owner, "who cannot eat without her being at the table." The rumor spread in the nearby areas that he was just about to grant her emancipation, having even "bought slaves for the said black woman."[11]

The religious expression exercised by some African women or their descendants, marked by syncretism, cooled the conflict in the daily life of slavery; however, it also narrowed solidarity and pushed the captive slaves and emancipated slaves to a breaking point. If the ceremonies led by the women who ended up persecuted by the Inquisition served to cure and placate daily doubts; on the other hand, the parties, *batuques* and revelries that the black women participated in caused risk to the political and economic order. At least that was what was believed by some authorities who governed the captaincy in the 18th century, and they were not pleased with the waste of time that the black men and women dedicated to the parties which had an excess of music, dance, and drink. They feared, as happened in the mining town where the emancipated *crioula* Teresa lived, the "dances and drumming of the blacks and mulattos." As such, in accordance with one of the cases narrated by Luciano Figueiredo (1999, p. 175), the house of Inácia da Silva, emancipated woman of Vila Rica, where two mulatto women lived, was visited day and night by men, where they all came together "with dueling guitars." Another woman that tormented the local power was the emancipated black woman Margarida, this time for "scandalous drunkenness" during the *batuques* that happened "in her house many nights" and went through the middle of the night until morning.

The sociability of the slave population was wrapped up in practices of all kinds, sometimes contradictory, from *quilombos* and escapes to parties. Present in both the *batuques* and the parties, black women participated in this potential resistance. Perhaps because of this, a simple party in 1719, in the small district of Itaubira, gained the worry of the governor Dom Pedro de Almeida, the Count of

Assumar, who was informed that "there was in that district an emancipated black man who originated from the Costa da Mina called Manuel that was married to an emancipated black woman by the name of Mariana, in whose house they gathered others of the same origin, causing insolence and great disturbance to the residents with their revelries." There were more than innocent festivities there: it was certain "that said emancipated black man was elected among the others as head of an uprising of the blacks."[12]

Slave revolts were a huge risk there; some of which came to fruition both in 1719 and on other occasions. Such preoccupation was associated with the presence of Africans who had come from the Costa da Mina who dominated the composition of slaves in Minas Gerais in the first half of the 18th century, as Maria de Carvalho Soares (1999) observes. Ethnic groups originating from the area of the Costa da Mina, where they received the designation *minas*, as the so-called *Nagôs, Hausas* and *Jejes* (different ethnicities and languages from Africa), it seems they were preferred for their force and magical powers. The miners then said that they were "the strongest and sturdiest." In the judgment of a Portuguese authority, there was another reason: the reputation of the witchcraft of the Africans from the Costa da Mina. He stressed: "they introduced the devil (a curse) so that only they would discover gold." The result of this belief couldn't be any other: there was not a single "miner who could live without a black *mina* woman, saying that only they have good luck."[13]

Considered rebels of political order, sorcerers in relation to religious norms, and disseminating immorality in the Christian family order, the disputes between leaders of the ethnic groups always sabotaged slave revolts, whose differences were ancestral in Africa and remained so in the colonial world. Aware of the importance of these differences, the masters began to consider it quite advisable to bet on the distinction of the ethnic composition for the management of slaves. In that regard, there was no *calundu* that could be resolved.

Sebastiana

In Água Limpa, with much difficulty, Sebastiana bought her freedom and built a modest house; however, life seemed more difficult each day. With a little imagination, she was reminded that the privacy guaranteed by those walls could no doubt yield something: she resolved to loan her house to romantic encounters, or "shameful and dishonest purposes," as deemed by the authorities invested in moralistic fervor. It was there that the prostitutes from the nearby areas headed to be with the clients they picked up. "Black men and black women," summarized a neighbor who was vigilant of the practices. The man knew the reason behind Sebastiana's generosity, when he informed the authorities that she allowed "similar shames... she expected them to give her something for in return."[14]

Gold and prostitution were nearly synonymous. The black woman Sebastiana knew how to sniff out an opportunity that in Minas Gerais reached astonishing proportions in the mining zones, in which hundreds of lonely men were concentrated with heavy and itinerant work, ambition, and the hope of riches that the soil promised. The permanent mobility of the miners combined with the formation of urban centers resulted in a large concentration of people and services, an uncommon reality in colonial, rural, and agricultural Brazil up until then.

On the other hand, this population lived under consensual relations, avoiding official Christian marriage, which was expensive, prolonged, and very complicated. The number of women was always less in relation to the men—in 1776, an estimated 120,128 women to 199,641 men, of different colors and conditions. To further complicate the situation, they were almost always black and mulatto women, who were not encouraged to marry officially in view of racial prejudice. It was better to establish concubinage. The white women were the blatant minority there. According to a total population census of the captaincy of Minas Gerais presented in 1776 that reached the house of 319,769 residents, there were 120,128 women spread through the counties. Of these women, 28,987 were white women lost among 91,141 black and mulatto women. A few were also white men, totaling 41,677.

This is all without speaking of slavery. After all, many masters and mistresses put their slave women in the amorous market, earning even more. These factors seem to have facilitated a culture in which prostitution was a large business. An owner of captives didn't have the slightest shame in declaring "that he would really like the black men converted into black women because they yielded more in the daily earnings" (in Souza, 1982, p. 181).

In the general language of the 18th century, Sebastiana and many others set up "brothel houses," a term that designated the facilitation of prostitution by some means. Sometimes they were mixed in with the houses of the town; however, it seems more common that they had been functioning in the periphery, near the roads where men circulated. Even though there were not specific establishments for prostitution, it could occur in commercial establishments, such as shops or taverns, even being housed on the plantations themselves. Or, as in the case of Sebastiana, many domiciles of impoverished groups served as amorous refuges. An emancipated *parda* in Conceição do Mato Dentro named Adriana even gave up "her own bed for her shameless behavior."[15]

Other times, significant interest in the issue seemed inexistent. In this sense, the complaint that exposes the life of the *pardas* Rita Ribeira da Costa and her comrade Barbosa da Silva is revealing. The complaint tells that they received anyone in their home, "becoming outrageously drunk, making noise [drumming]… with great immorality," making the house "a public brothel."[16] Or the complaint that speaks of the emancipated black woman Eugênia, in the village of Paraúna, stating that under her roof she "gathers in her house black women street vendors" who, according to the moral language of the denouncer, "are making money off of their deceit." And the worst: "black men of the mines" were also there, right in the site where mining took place. Some would say "There are some [and] others who allow in their house at night for all types of deceit and lascivious acts."[17]

There were women who were persecuted for other stigmas beyond color and poverty. They received in their neighborhoods nicknames that assigned attributes recognized by the town, which became a part of history: *Sopinha* (little soup or "easy"), *Rabada* (literally, "tail" but also meaning something extraordinary—either very good or very bad), *Comprimento* (size or length), *Foguete* (firecracker), *Mãe do Mundo* (Mother of the World). It is suspected that the judgment had much more of the elite prejudices regarding the way of life of the popular groups. Women of color, almost always freed, appear frequently in the complaints, revealing an amorous sociability among peers.

Prostitution was the basis of survival for many poor families. Even with a masculine presence, in times of difficulty, the practice was permitted by parents, stepparents, and husbands. In contexts in which extreme poverty invaded the family structure, it was common that wives, daughters, stepdaughters, sisters, and sisters-in-law guaranteed the support of the house with prostitution. Widowhood was certainly one of the principal motives that pushed the *Enforcada* (literally, hanged or strangled, meaning pressed for cash), as the *mulata* Inácia was known in Mariana, to ignore her daughter, who had prostituted herself for eight years. Living in the same house, the mother saw "men enter to shamefully deal with her daughter." The reason was unarguably economic. It was said that she allowed these "insults [to] sustain and clothe themselves through the sin of her daughter."[18]

An example of this was the case of Josefa Maria de Sousa. Her house in Ouro Branco, in the middle of the road between Rio de Janeiro and Ouro Preto, functioned as an inn where she offered a special service: her young daughter to "dishonor herself with the guests." According to the complaints, Josefa, "doesn't have any other source of income to live from, and also survives by offering rooms for other women to prostitute."[19] Most precarious was the life of the emancipated Angolan *preta* Cristina, condemned by the bishopric visitor for the crime of "dishonoring" her daughter. After several days of languishing in prison, she appealed for the mercy of the "visiting doctor" that her condemnation be brief, because she had no way to pay for the costs of prison, seeing that she was "black, poor, and old."[20]

It was not just poverty that pushed women into prostitution. It can be assumed that a moral standard differentiated from the Catholic orthodoxy was established in this region, rapidly settled and constantly irrigated by different people—from Africans to people from São Paulo, from natives to the Portuguese—where the spiritual work of the church struggled to convince souls, making the Catholic constraints weigh less. Slavery corroded the guiding principles until even those for whom this type of conduct would never be expected, as was the case of the cleric Francisco Pereira de Assunção who lived in Itambira and was the owner of three black women—Antonia, Ana, and Juliana, "prostitutes exposed to all the men who seek them for illicit business."[21]

However, there would be just as many slave women to whom prostitution would show its crueler side. The exploitation of captive women involved regular work and extended to sexual exploitation, even to the slave's own body. A case that became famous, thanks to the important book of Luiz Mott (1993), was that of the African woman Rosa Egipcíaca of Vera Cruz, a slave who lived as a prostitute by obligation of her masters, but in virtue of the visions and prophecies that she announced, she became a notorious figure in Minas and in Rio de Janeiro, until the Inquisition put an end to her activity.

One of the actions that showed this dual exploitation of the slave woman was the small trade executed by the black women street vendors. Apparently, these women relied on great autonomy, since they could move about without the permanent supervision of their owner, as long as they brought the required income. Appearances fade as we approach the innumerable cases in which the masters, or mistresses, demanded very high daily payments that exceeded the value of the edible goods that were brought on the tray. If they didn't want to be punished for lacking what their condition imposed, these women could not avoid selling their bodies.

This was the cruel world that slavery created. Former slave women forgot the painful condition of captivity when it had to do with acquiring resources for bettering their life. If groups of women shared the home in which freed women laid out strategies for ascension, built savings as if they were mistresses, and often emancipated their slaves; a daily life of violence lurked around the work of the captives present there. The emancipated black woman Catarina de Sousa, resident of Rio de Santo Antônio in Conceição do Mato Dentro, "obliges her slaves, under threat of punishment, that they give her a daily payment for each day of service." If she were not satisfied, she was accustomed to demanding that on Sundays and holy days the daily payment was doubled, seeing that the clientele was more available. However, perhaps the greatest of all the problems resided in the fact that Catarina did not give her slaves "sales commission that was worth the daily payment asked of them," so there was no other solution left for them to obtain their daily payments other than "through offenses to God."[22] There was even a woman who didn't hide the dual function of her black female street vendors. Maria Franca, in addition to asking them "with whom did they sleep and who paid them best," she boasted, it was said "so shamelessly" that she had much work in bringing her slaves to Rio Abaixo "to satisfy the residents."[23]

Alongside the contingency that slavery determined for the occurrence of prostitution, the authorities committed themselves to controlling crime that, according to their considerations, not only wounded virtues, but also brought another risk along with it, namely multiplication of the population of color. The emancipated *parda* Eugênia Maria de Jesus, in Conceição do Mato Dentro, gave herself to white and black men in her own house, "disgracing herself first with some and then with others." From the complaint made regarding her, missing is a reference that seems to be key in understanding the other dimension of fear brought by prostitution in a society with a massive presence of women of color, whether mulatto women or black women: besides realizing that men were entering there, the denouncer also said that "she had given birth to mulattos and *crioulos.*"[24] (These choices of words hint at the fear of miscegenation apparent in the social order).

The excerpt is a beautiful synthesis of what the authorities feared and what, from the side of morality, weighed heavily in Minas Gerais where slave women were extremely active in the pursuit of their own emancipation and that their descendants. In a slave society, where the condition of "mulattos" and *crioulos*—the designation for the children of Africans born in Brazil—was joined with that of freed slaves, they (the authorities) could take all the care in the world and it would be too little.

Game Played

The modest cast of women who convened around Ana, Luzia, and Sebastiana, and circulated in these stories in territories marked by informality, indubitably does not exhaust the diversity of many other feminine lives. *Pretas, crioulas,* and mistresses were also present in the roles that tradition demanded, participating in the religious sisterhoods, bent over at the loom or sweating in domestic works.

The three black women that we gave preference to survived by employing the African culture that they still lived with. They relentlessly challenged inquisitorial visitors, bailiffs of the councils, bush captains, and masters. Their action imprinted political and social changes that marked the originality of Minas. The whip that burned the back of Ana, the prison in which Sebastiana was enclosed, the exile that took Luzia away from her African roots might appear to be failures. That isn't entirely true. If these women are present here in this book, it is because they won.

Notes

1. The spelling of the text has been adjusted to current standards.
2. Historical Archive of the Câmara Municipal do Serro, Registro do presos [prisoner list], 1762-1803, f.16. A large part of the story is fictional, and the document offers little more than that which is cited in the quotes.
3. *Coleção de leis, decretos e alvarás* [Collection of Laws, Decrees, and court orders],1761-62, Vol. 1, p. 257.
4. Atas da Câmara Municipal da Vila Rica [Acts of the Municipal Council of Vila Rica], in RAPM, XXV, p. 136-7.
5. Bando (official measure of the jurisdiction of the governor with legal power) of November 21, 1719. Arquivo Público Mineiro, Câmara Municipal de Ouro Preto, códice 6, f. 16-18.

6. Ecclesiastical archive of the Archdiocese of Mariana (Aeam), Devassa, July 1762 to December 1769, f. 70.

7. Register of petitions and orders, professions and stores in Serro Frio, 1736-1767, Arquivo Público Mineiro (APM), SC, códice 6.

8. Aeam, Devassas, May/Dec. 1753, f. 101v.

9. Aeam, Devassas, May/Dec. 1753, f. 58.

10. Aeam, Devassas, Jul. 1762/Dec. 1769, f. 114.

11. Aeam, Devassas, 1722-3, f. 38v.

12. APM, SC, códice 11, f. 124-124v.

13. Parecer do Conselho Ultramarino de 18 September 1728, Documentos Históricos, n. 94, 1951, p. 28-30, in Lara, 1999, v. 2, p. 681-8.

14. Aeam, Devassas, 1753, f. 132v.

15. Aeam, Devassas, 1756-7, f. 9.

16. Aeam, Devassas, 1759, f. 52.

17. Aeam, Devassas, Feb./May 1731, f. 102v.

18. Aeam, Devassas, May/Dec. 1753, f. 67.

19. Aeam, Devassas, Jul. 1762/Dec. 1769, f. 67.

20. Freguesia de Nossa Senhora do Pilar de Ouro Preto, 1731, in Francisco Vidal em Minas Gerais A vida cotidiana em julgamento.

21. Aeam, Devassas, 1765-7, f. 101.

22. Aeam, Devassas, 1765-7, f. 101.

23. Aeam, Devassas, Jul. 1733, f. 95v.

24. Aeam, Devassas, 1750-3, f. 76.

Bibliography

Antonil, André João. *Cultura e opulência do Brasil por suas drogas e minas*. [The Culture and Opulence of Brazil Because of its Drugs and Mines]. 3. ed. Belo Horizonte: Itatiaia; São Paulo: Edusp, 1982. (Coleção Reconquista do Brasil).

Barbosa, Waldemar de Almeida. *Negros e quilombos em Minas Gerais*. [Blacks and Escaped Slave Colonies in Minas Gerais]. Belo Horizonte: [s.e.], 1972.

Carrato, José Ferreira. "A crise dos costumes nas Minas Gerais do século XVII." [The Crisis of Customs in Minas Gerais in the 17th Century]. Revista de Letras, São Paulo, FFLA, 1962, v. 3, p. 234-40.

Costa e Silva, Alberto. *A manilha e o libambo. A África e a escravidão de 1500 a 1700.* [The manacle and the iron collar. Africa and Slavery from 1500 to 1700]. Rio de Janeiro: Nova Fronteira; Fundação Biblioteca Nacional, 2002.

Farge, Arlette. *Efusión y tormento. El relato de los cuerpos. Historia del pueblo en el siglo* XVIII. [Effusion and Torment. The tale of the Bodies. History of the People in the 18th Century]. Trad. Julia Bucci. Madrid: Katz, 2008.

Faria, Sheila Siqueira de Castro. "Sinhás pretas; acumulação de pecúlio e transmissão de bens de mulheres forras no sudeste escravista (séculos XVIII-XIX)." [Black Mistresses: Acumulation of Savings and Transmission of Goods of Freed Women in Southeastern Slavery (Centuries XVIII-XIX]. In: Fragoso, João (Org.). *Escritos sobre história e educação: uma homenagem a Maria Yedda Linhares.* [Writings on History and Education: Homage to Maria Yedda Linhares]. Rio de Janeiro: Mauad/Faperj, 2001.

____. *Sinhás pretas, damas mercadoras. As pretas minas nas cidades do Rio de Janeiro e de São João Del Rey (1700- 1850).* [Black Mistresses, Merchant Ladies. Black Women from Minas in the Cities of Rio de Janeiro and São João Del Rey (1700-1850]. Thesis for Professor Titular da Universidade Federal Fluminense (UFF), Niterói, 2004.

Figueiredo, Luciano. *Avesso da memória: cotidiano e trabalho da mulher em Minas Gerais no século* XVIII. [The Wrong Side of Memory: Daily Life and Women's Work in Minas Gerais in the 18th Century]. 2. ed. Rio de Janeiro: José Olympio, 1999.

Furtado, Júnia Ferreira. *Chica da Silva e o contratador de diamantes. O outro lado do mito.* [Chica da Silva and the Diamond Contractor. The Other Side of the Myth]. São Paulo: Companhia das Letras, 2003.

Lara, Silvia Hunold. "Os minas em Minas: linguagem, domínio senhorial e etnicidade." [The Mines in Minas: Language, Lordly Rule, and Ethnicity]. In: Nodari, Eunice et al. (Org.). História: fronteiras. São Paulo: Anpuh/Humanitas, 1999, v. 2, p. 681-8.

____. *Fragmentos setecentistas. Escravidão, cultura e poder na América portuguesa.* [Fragments of the 1700s. Slavery, Culture, and Power in Portuguese America]. São Paulo: Companhia das Letras, 2007.

Mott, Luiz. *Rosa Egipcíaca. Uma santa africana no Brasil.* [Egyptian Rose. An African Saint in Brazil]. Rio de Janeiro: Bertrand do Brasil, 1993.

Paiva, Eduardo França. *Escravos e libertos nas Minas Gerais do século* XVIII*: estratégias de resistência através dos testamentos.* [Slaves and Freedmen in Minas Gerais of the 18th Century: Strategies of Resistance Through Last Wills and Testaments]. São Paulo: Annablume, 1995.

Pantoja, Selma. "A dimensão atlântica das quitandeiras." [The Atlantic Dimension of the Female Street Vendors]. In: Furtado, Júnia Ferreira (Org.). *Diálogos oceânicos, Minas Gerais e as novas abordagens para uma história do império ultramarino português.* [Oceanic Dialogues, Minas Gerais, and new Embarkations for a History of the Portuguese Transoceanic Empire]. Belo Horizonte: Editora da UFMG, 2001, p. 45-67.

Silva, Maria Beatriz Nizza da. "Magia e heterodoxia femininas no Brasil colonial." [Magic and Heterodox Feminines in Colonial Brazil]. *Revista de Ciências Históricas*. [Journal of Historic Sciences]. Porto, Universidade Portucalense, 2002, p. 185-210.

Soares, Mariza de Carvalho. "Os mina em Minas: tráfico atlântico, redes de comércio e etnicidade." [The Mina People in Minas: Atlantic Traffic, Networks of Commerce and Ethnicity]. In: Nodari, Eunice et al. (Org.). *História: fronteiras*. [History: Frontiers]. São Paulo: Anpuh/Humanitas, 1999, v. 2, p. 689-95.

Souza, Laura de Mello e. *Desclassificados do ouro: a pobreza mineira no século* XVIII. [Outcasts of Gold: Poverty in the Mines/in Minas in the 18th Century]. Rio de Janeiro: Graal, 1982.

____. *O diabo e a terra de Santa Cruz. Feitiçaria e religiosidade popular no Brasil colonial.* [The Devil in the Land of the Holy Cross. Witchcraft and Popular Religiosity in Colonial Brazil]. São Paulo: Companhia das Letras, 1986.

4

QUEENS AND JUDGES: BLACK WOMEN IN THE BLACK SISTERHOODS OF CENTRAL BRAZIL, 1722-1860

Mary Karasch

In 1786, the black sisterhood of Our Lady of the Rosary was constructing a church in Natividade that would be the largest Catholic Church in central Brazil. According to a local belief, the slaves did not finish the church because of the abolition of slavery, but another bit of oral lore says that it was the decline of gold mining at the end of the colonial period that prohibited the slaves from being able to gather the resources to finish the work. Currently, only the walls remain as a silent testament of the enormous endeavor of this black sisterhood to construct their own church dedicated to Our Lady of the Rosary.[1] The ruins of a large church indicate the existence of a strong community of practicing Catholics, but we know little about them and their beliefs at the end of Colonial Brazil. We know even less about the role of the black women of this community, although among those who founded this building were free and freed black women. (The words "sisterhood" and "confraternity" will be used almost interchangeably in this essay as translations for the word *irmandades*. Whenever possible, sisterhood will be used to indicate the focus on women.)

This essay is an initial attempt to reconstruct a small part of the religious and social life of the black women in the captaincy of Goiás at the end of the colonial period. Considering the undertakings of the black sisterhoods from various parts of Brazil, I observed the role of black women in the sisterhoods that contrast strongly with the confraternities of Hispanic Latin America.[2] Why did black women play such an important role in the Brazilian sisterhoods? The answer to this question may be partly from the religious traditions coming from Africa, but there is little documentation in Goiás about the African-inspired religions relating to black women. Nevertheless, we managed to document the imprisonment of black women under the accusation of being witches and fortune-tellers. Among other sources, we find complaints from clerics about the nighttime dances in the churches of Goiás, while in the nineteenth century the women were often identified as healers. Other sources even refer to the use of talismans and amulets in the region such as the Mandinga bag.[3] (Mandinga is a word used to indicate sorcery but is also associated with the Mandingo people of West Africa). In the beginning of the nineteenth century black women even assisted in the control of smallpox in Goiás by way of arm-to-arm vaccination, a technique that some had learned in western Africa. A more detailed description of a black woman who conducted African religious rituals comes from Paracatu, which is located today in Minas Gerais, but was then a part of the captaincy of Goiás. In 1774, Caetana Mina, from Vila de Goiazes, led rituals that observers called the dance of thrashing.[4]

In contrast to the scarcity of documents concerning African religious traditions, there are many about the black confraternities of the region. The most useful in information surrounding the role of black women in the religious life are the minutes of the meetings of the Our Lady of the Rosary sisterhoods of Cidade de Goiás and of Natividade, today a restored colonial city in the state of Tocantins. Further serving as a source are the pledges from 1772 to 1788 from Our Lady of Mercy de Cocal, which was one of the richest mining cities at the end of the 18th century.[5] Also remaining are the lists of queens, judges, and sisters at the tables of some of the sisterhoods. To be an official in a sisterhood, it was necessary to donate gold, a motive for which the queens and judges must have been women with tenure and occupied social positions in the community. They also came to be a part of the historical registry when they donated houses and slaves to the black confraternities.[6] The older freed women were especially generous in donations to the Order of the Rosary and were accustomed to donating houses in exchange for care in their old age, for funerals, and for prayers for their soul after their death. Obviously membership in a sisterhood was mainly for the black women who didn't have an owner, a husband, or children to support them when they became sick, and to arrange their funeral, burial, and prayers for their soul after death.

Ruins of the Church of the Black Sisterhood of Our Lady of the Rosary

Most of the mining towns of Goiás in the 18th century had a significant number of enslaved Africans; there was, at least, one black sisterhood dedicated to Our Lady of the Rosary. Judging by the various remaining pledges, we are able to prove that this was the most common confraternity of blacks in the region. The second most popular were the sisterhoods dedicated to the black saints Benedito and Efigênia. For example, Natividade had another small church dedicated to São Benedito. Our Lady of Mercy wasn't as common in central Brazil, compared to her importance in Minas Gerais.[7]

Why did so many African women worship Our Lady of the Rosary? Obviously, those that had converted to Catholicism in Brazil could have come to believe in her as the Virgin Mary, but there is another explanation. In the city of Goiás, where many Angolans lived up until the end of the colonial period, those coming from this Portuguese colony could have already been accustomed to worshipping Our Lady of the Rosary in their native land. In other places of Brazil, many Africans had already adopted the use of the rosary: they wore it around their neck and prayed with it in their native tongue. As recounted by a British traveler, blacks in Brazil liked the stories of the rosary because they "seemed to arouse the sensation of being in their homeland." Many also considered the rosary a talisman against evil, like "artillery bullets."[8]

However, not all Africans and their descendants had roots in Angola; perhaps for this reason, they were able to devote themselves more to the black saints Benedito and Efigênia. São Benedito was one of the most popular black saints in Brazil. Since he was a cook in a monastery in Sicily, he became the protector of those who worked in the kitchen, as was the case of many black women.[9]

Although there were many other honored black saints in Brazil, only one was a woman, Santa Efigênia, often regarded as a Nubian princess.[10] She was the patroness of a confraternity of blacks in Rio de Janeiro, and other black men and women constructed a church in her name in São José do Tocantins. According to Paulo Bertran, this confraternity took care of her church for two centuries and held "festivities" in honor of Santa Efigênia and Our Lady of Carmo. In the mining city of Traíras, black men and women held a festival in her honor and placed "a flag with the image of their saint... on a tall mast at the door of the church."[11] Based on the colonial descriptions, there is no doubt as to her importance to those of African descent in the captaincy. But, why? Perhaps this first-century religious figure has attracted African women by having been born in Africa and led a religious community on that continent.

As the African-born blacks of the region had patron saints and their own confraternities, the same occurred with *pardos* (mixed race persons in Brazil, generally a mix of black, white, and indigenous heritage), who constructed churches in honor of Our Lady of the Good Death and Our Lady of Conception. These sisterhoods were supported by mulattos and *pardos,* both free and emancipated; but among them, there were also enslaved persons. Whites had other confraternities that were the richest of the captaincy.[12] Regardless of the color of the members, each confraternity erected their own churches or obtained permission to praise their saints in a side chapel of another church. In most cities, the black churches constructed by the Order of the Rosary and the Order of São Benedito were among the smallest and poorest of the captaincy. The ruins of the Church of the Rosary in Natividade were, without a doubt, an exception of the generalized poverty of the other black sisterhoods and their churches.

However, in spite of poverty, the black brothers and the women connected to them ran the confraternity and the church with a directorate, a type of advisory or ruling group of the confraternity. Due to the scarcity of clergymen at the end of the colonial period, many black churches had difficulty attracting a resident priest. They depended on visiting priests to occasionally celebrate mass and to administer the principal sacraments. As such, the sisterhoods were accustomed to having a lot of autonomy, allowing black women to fulfill roles of leadership and make significant financial contributions that were perhaps not allowed in the sisterhoods of whites or *pardas* (mixed race women).

For those who lived at the end of the colonial period, the most valuable services of the black sisterhoods were to praise Our Lady, to honor the black saints, and to comfort the brethren with fundamental religious rituals, especially prayers for the souls of the dead.[13] It can be proven that blacks valued these rituals by the significant quantity of gold they donated to the black sisterhoods to buy the candle wax, and for the payments of masses, funerals, and prayers for the dead. The most important festivals that the members sponsored were the processions and the solemn masses, with music on the Saint Days of Our Lady of the Rosary and São Benedito. A large part of the time was spent collecting resources to bring necessary articles to the rituals, such as wax, taffeta, and rosaries from distant places, such as Rio de Janeiro. The candle wax was essential to light the church or for evening processions; and robes were made with cloth, while rosaries were distributed in the celebrations in honor of Our Lady of the Rosary.[14]

Another important activity of the sisterhoods of central Brazil was distributing alms and performing other charitable acts, such as caring for the sick.[15] In other regions of Brazil, black sisterhoods were formed to free enslaved members from captivity, but there isn't enough concrete proof that in central Brazil sisterhoods were formed to obtain emancipation of its members. However, the members of the Order of the Rosary in the Cidade de Goiás were able to obtain their own freedom. In the beginning of the 19th century, the majority of the members of the board were enslaved, but by around 1860, almost all had been liberated from that condition.[16]

Finally, the black sisterhoods of central Brazil served as a hub for social and political organization of the communities. Every year, the confraternity elected a black king, a queen, a male judge, and a female judge, as well as other officials, that led the confraternity for a year. Apparently, one of the criteria for selection was the capacity to make donations in gold or in candle wax to help cover the high cost of the nine days of festivities, solemn masses, sermons, processions, and fireworks. The festival of Espírito Santo also required the donation of food. It seems that the costs were relatively high, because there were times in which the elected officials had to resign for not being able to donate the necessary gold.[17]

These generalizations about the functions of the black sisterhoods in the captaincy of Goiás constitute just one panel to begin to understand the significant role of black women within them. The following text is an initial attempt to glean from the fragmented documents related to the region what women were really doing in the black confraternities in central Brazil. We hope that this essay can then serve as a guide for future research on the role of black women in the religious life of colonial Brazil and of the 19th century.

The Position of Women

One of the first accounts of black women who participated in a Catholic religious ceremony was that in which four women carried a litter (sedan chair) with the Blessed Sacrament in a procession through the mining city of Pontal. The two Jesuit priests that allowed the black women to participate were forced to go in chains from the District of the North (Tocantins) to Rio de Janeiro. It was only two years later that it became known what the accusations against them were. Carrying the litter was a high honor normally granted to whites from the elite Order of the Blessed Sacrament. Another accusation against the two priests was that they had some relations with nearby *quilombolas* (fugitive slaves). The two Jesuits had clearly challenged the traditional hierarchal values of the captaincy that favored white men and excluded black women and *quilombolas*.[18]

This incident indicates that the two Jesuits supported the participation of black women in the Catholic rituals and probably helped to train the black Catholics in the north of the captaincy who, on the other hand, passed on their religious traditions to their children and grandchildren.

In the 1780s, free people and freed slaves participated in the construction of the church of Our Lady of the Rosary, of Natividade, a city not far from Pontal and the old Jesuit mission of Duro. The black Order of Our Lady of the Rosary, which constructed that church at the end of the 18th century, was considerably large, with an unusually large directorate of black men and women and many male and female officials, each one of which had to donate gold to become a part of the confraternity, and even more to become an official or advisor. The members had such a large quantity of gold to donate because of the rich mines of the region which had not yet been depleted in the 1780s, although the Portuguese collected less and less gold for the king (the fifth). Given the local lore about the gold buried in the Church of the Rosary, the question remains of how much gold the black miners, and the women who worked with them, siphoned to construct their church.[19]

The distinct role of free black women and emancipated black women in this sisterhood is especially notable, and the amount of gold that they donated attests to their ability to obtain it, either on their own, or by way of the men that were a part of their lives, including their masters. Unlike the Order of the Rosary of Cidade de Goiás, where the condition of the slave was carefully recorded, the scribes of Natividade did not attribute this social condition to any female member of the board from 1786 to 1801. In theory, all of them were free or emancipated slaves that had gained freedom because they had gold. Among the members of the board, there were up to 32 women from 1786 to 1794 (Table 1).

It is especially worth noting that the sisterhood had a "perpetual queen" from 1787 to 1800, named Joanna Maria de Assunção. Since there had been an enormous amount of enslaved Africans during that period, one could speculate that she had been a queen in Africa, but it is more likely that she had made a large donation of gold, as a part of a promise, to the point of the sisterhood honoring her with the title of perpetual queen. As her last name was that of a saint, and not Portuguese, she may have been a slave. Unfortunately, the wills and inventories from the colonial period in Natividade that allow us to assess the riches of Joanna Maria at the time of her death are missing.

Also impressive is the multiple times in which black women appear in high positions in the Order of the Rosary of Natividade, as queen or judge, or serving as sisters on the board, indicating that they enjoyed a social condition and wealth sufficient to be elected more than once. Just a partial list appears in Table 1. In addition to the queen elected for one year, this large confraternity also chose two judges, two judges for *ramalhetes* (flower arrangements, clusters, or collections), a judge for devotion in some years, and two trustees, all female. The Order of the Rosary of Natividade still had a number of sisters that was almost double that of the majority of the black confraternities between 1789 and 1793.

The lists compiled in the record books indicate the continuity of people in power, since the members of the board also served for years. Were these the leaders of the black community of Natividade? This is a sharp contrast to the more egalitarian—and less rich?—directorates of the city of Goiás, in which most officials served just once. The queens of both the confraternities also were elected just once, except Helena Barboza, from Natividade, who served as queen from 1791-1792 and for part of 1797. The sisterhood of Santa Efigênia, from Natividade, did not have a queen in 1795-1796.[20] Due to the large donation of gold required to be a queen, they could only do it once and in certain cases, only with the permission of their masters.

Table 1 Queens, Judges and Sisters in the Order of the Rosary, Natividade, 1786-1801

Year	Queens	Judges*	Sisters
1786-1787	Roza Fernandes da Silva	2	14
1787-1788	Marianna Correa de Mello Joanna Maria de Assunção†	3	16
1788-1789	Ritta da Cunha David	3	16
1789-1790	Herculia Teixeyra da Costa	4	20
1790-1791	Anna Luiza de Barros	5	32
1791-1792	Helena Barboza	5	25
1792-1793	Custodia Gonçalves Pereira	4	26
1793-1794	Quitéria da Costa Gomes	4	10
1794-1795	Thereza Dias dos Reyes Joanna Maria de Assunção	4	12
1795-1796	Anna Alves Varanda Joanna Maria de Assunção	4	18
1796-1797	Jozefa [illegible] Joanna Maria de Assunção	?	14
1797	Helena Barboza Joanna Maria de Assunção	4	25
1797-1798	Roza Gonçalves Lima Joanna Maria de Assunção	6‡	12
1798-1799	Getrudes Francisca da Silva Joanna Maria de Assunção	4	12
1799-1800	Sprianna Gomes Pereira Joanna Maria de Assunção	4	14
1800–1801	Maria Theresa Pinta de Carvalho	4	16

Source: *Cidade de Goiás*, BFEG, *Nossa Senhora do Rosário, livro de termo, Natividade, 1786-1801, f. 49-98.*

* In every year after 1789, there were two female presiding judges and two female judges for flower arrangements; A third or fifth was a judge for devotion.
† Perpetual queen, 1787-1788, 1794-1800.
‡ Included four presiding judges.

In Salvador and Rio de Janeiro, participation in the Order of the Rosary or in the Order of Santa Efigênia was almost always linked to ethnicity. However, the records of the officials of the confraternities of central Brazil did not restrict membership to one specific ethnic group or nationality. The confraternities had as many *crioulos* (blacks born in Brazil) as Africans, generally identified as originating from Angola or from Mina. In 1788, however, the pledge of Our Lady of Mercy of Captives from the mining city of Cocal required that the king and queen were black (Africans) one year, and *crioulos* in the following year. As in Bahia, this confraternity alternated the command between Africans and *crioulos*, thereby implying the existence of divisions based on birth origin within the sisterhood.[21]

Front Cover of the Pledge for the Order of the Rosary

In addition to ethnicity, we can also partly identify the legal standing of the members of the Order of the Rosary of Cidade de Goiás, whose records make a distinction between free people, emancipated slaves, and slaves. The highest position in this confraternity was the *juíza de vara* (presiding judge), situated before the queen. On the other hand, lists associated with other confraternities, the queen appeared before the judges. Women defined as free or emancipated occupied the positions of queen and judge in the Order of the Rosary in the city of Goiás. None of them were slaves, undoubtedly due to the financial resources necessary to be queen or judge. This confraternity also had another judge, called Judge of *ramalhetes*. No one knows for sure what her responsibilities were. Perhaps she took care of the valuable objects belonging to the confraternity? Or, was it merely a ritual role?

In the beginning of the 19th century the Judge of *ramalhete* participated in the festivities of the Order of São Benedito in Meia Ponte (today, Pirenópolis), where she and the male judge "symbolized the leaves of the trees" in the ribbon dance. What is interesting here is that few slaves were judges of *ramalhete*, probably because donations of gold were required, to which they didn't have access because of their slave status.[22] At the end of the colonial period, these judges were always listed after the presiding judges and the queens, which suggests less social importance. In the late 1830s, the Order of the Rosary of the city of Goiás added two new positions on the books, the "judges for devotion" and, in the 1840s, a "a queen of oaths."

Why were the female judges so important in the black confraternities? Roquinaldo Ferreira explains in his research on the role of the judges in Angola. As he documents, one of the most important institutions of Angola was the Court of the Mucanos, in which the African judges resolved cases involving Africans.[23] Perhaps the fact of the captaincy of Goiás having so many enslaved Angolans, they and their descendants valued black judges. Clearly Portuguese judges dominated the colonial judicial system of Goiás, in the same manner as colonial Brazil. Since women were prohibited from occupying the position of judge in Angola and in Brazil, it is notable that black women had held such a significant role as that of judge in the sisterhoods of central Brazil.[24] Was this region an exception? Or is it that the female judges had equally significant roles in the confraternities as in the rest of Brazil?

Because of the importance of the queens and the black female judges, today we know the name of those elected to occupy these positions, as well as the number of enslaved women who served on the board of the city of Goiás at the beginning of the 19th century. In Table 2, notice that the majority of sisters on the board were slaves in 1827, 1830-1832, and 1833-1834. Apparently, the queens came from those with either a free or emancipated status, because they all had surnames, except Custódia Thomazia. From 1830-1831, for example, Ignácia Luduvica de Almeida presided over a board that had nine slaves and only three non-slaves. The sisters on the board that were either emancipated or free women were indicated as such in the documents of the order.

Table 2: Queens and sisters of the Order of the Rosary in the city of Goiás, 1827-1835

		Slaves*	Freed / Emancipated
1828	Marta Antonia da Silva	8	4
1829	Custodia Thomazia	6	6
1829-1830	Barbara Maria da Silveira	5	7
1830-1831	Ignacia Luduvica de Almeida	9	3
1831-1832	Maria Rodrigues de Jezuz	9	3
1832-1833	Maria Joaquina Taveira	7	5
1833-1834	Maria Joaquina de Campos	8	4
1834-1835	Rosa Ferreira dos Santos	4	8

Source: Cidade de Goiás, BFEG, livros de termos de mesa, 1826-1835, f. 12-3.

*The total number of sisters at each board was 12.

However, we cannot show exactly what each official did in the Order of the Rosary in the city of Goiás. There is, however, an extraordinary pledge that was preserved in the Tribunal Archives of Goiânia for the beauty of the richly decorated, gilded manuscript. It is the pledge of the founding of the black order dedicated to Our Lady of Mercy in the mining city of Cocal, which had 4,002 inhabitants in 1789.[25] The pledge, from 1772, is not only significant for its beauty, but also for what it reveals about the functioning of the black sisterhood in the captaincy of Goiás, as well as the role of black women in their administrative structure.

The manuscript begins with a statement of respect in which the brethren identify themselves as "poor and humble natives from Ethiopia, slaves of your Majesty." They sought royal protection, particularly with a priest who required a high sum of gold for his services. After a formal appeal to the monarch, the brothers insisted that the reader knew that they were the only ones who had constructed a "spacious chapel" dedicated to Our Lady of Mercy in Cocal. This confraternity had a historical connection with the liberation of imprisoned Christians in northern Muslim Africa. The blacks probably chose this patroness precisely because she grants mercies, graces, and benefits. In Minas Gerais, the popular Order of Our Lady of Mercy had a special association with *crioulo* slaves.[26] In Cocal, however, the confraternity had African-born members not only because they identified as "natives of Ethiopia," which is African land, but also for the subsequent division of the leadership roles between blacks and *crioulos*, which comes into effect in the second pledge, revised in 1788.

To belong to this confraternity, each member—man or woman—had to pay an admission fee of two eighths of gold in 1772, which changed to one eighth of gold in 1788 (An *oitava* was the equivalent to an eighth of the former weight measurement, ounce, or 3.58 grams); afterward, the annual tax rose one eighth in 1772 and half of an eighth for those up to 25 years of age in 1788. The same amount appears in the pledge of the Order of the Rosary of Vila Boa de Goiás in 1796.

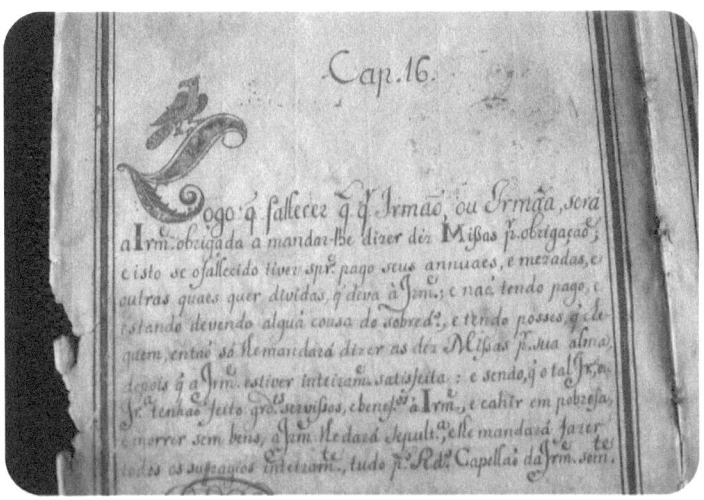

Front cover (left) and a chapter on the pledge of the Order of Our Lady of Mercy

The Order of Our Lady of Mercy must have been led by a board, which included an elected queen, a judge, and 12 sisters. In order to be queen, the woman had to donate 25 eighths of gold in 1772, a value that was lowered to 20 eighths in 1788, the same quantity as the dowry of the kind. In the year 1772, the female judge paid 16 eighths in donation and 12 eighths in 1788. In Vila Boa de Goiás, it cost 24 eighths of gold to be queen in 1796, and the judges paid the same.[27]

The pledge of the sisterhood also reveals how the queens were elected in Cocal. The ruling appointed four candidates, two of whom were emancipated and two were "captives." As such, slaves could be elected queen if they made the necessary donation of gold. The members of the board then chose who would be queen for the following year. Judges and sisters of the board also appointed successors.

One of the principal obligations of the confraternity was to celebrate the day of the festival of Our Lady of Mercy each year during the eight days of the Christmas holiday. The king and the queen presided over the festivities with the regalia of their majesty, probably short capes and crowns as in Minas Gerais, while the judge, dressed in the robe of the fraternity, carried his stick together with the female presiding judge. The obligation of each one of the 12 sisters of the board was to ask alms for the confraternity in the month designated to her. It seems that each sister walked through the city asking for contributions to sustain the sisterhood and its charities, the same way the sisters of the Order of Rio de Janeiro did, according to what artists have portrayed.[28] Obviously, the sisters had much greater importance in the activities of the sisterhood in gathering resources. All of the brothers (and also sisters?) were obligated to attend the board meetings and to help in the celebrations on the day of the festival wearing a white robe with a red cross.

The reason so many women would wish to pay such a high amount of gold to take on such major responsibilities in a confraternity can be justified partly by religious beliefs—difficult to determine based on 18th century documents, but the more practical explanations relate to death and concerns with having a good death, that is, receiving final sacraments and a dignified funeral inside of a church. Our Lady of the Good Death, whose order was supported by a congregation of *pardos*, and Our Lord of the Good Death, whose image was found in many private chapels, were very popular in the region.[29] Similar to the concerns of death and burial, concern about prayers for souls in purgatory showed up in the pledge of Cocal. The confraternity carefully listed the rights of each member and their relatives such as the funeral and the burial in the church. The fact is very interesting that those who had been queens were buried in the same place as the kings, near the main altar. Judges of both genders were buried from the archway to the railings, and the members of the board, from the railings to the front door. In other words, the same social status in life remained in death. On the other hand, the majority of slaves were buried outside next to the church or in poor conditions, without the Catholic rituals or their own African rituals.[30]

That same pledge also explains the duties of the black trustee—there was only one in Cocal. However, in Natividade, that confraternity had two men and two women who acted as trustees.

Maybe the responsibilities that culture defined as feminine, such as washing and ironing the altar panels, suited the female trustees of Natividade. In Cocal, on the other hand, the single trustee was responsible for sending them out to be washed and ironed. He also had to care for the ornaments and lamps of the church, make the communion wafers, ring the church bells, arrange the burials, and help any sick brethren whose lives were in danger. Did the trustees of Natividade cook and care for the sick, particularly the women? Or were they restricted to cleaning, washing, and decorating the statues of saints and the altar dedicated to Our Lady of the Rosary? The documents are not telling of the responsibilities of the female trustees. The fact is interesting that the confraternity in Natividade had black female trustees. In most pledges, the trustee was generally a white male.[31]

Because of the attention given to the aide of the sick and the dying, even *pardos* and whites were affiliated with black brotherhoods and occupied positions in them, especially the roles of trustee, treasurer, and scribe. Men of high social status belonged to as many confraternities as possible, and their status showed in the number of brethren that accompanied their funeral procession.[32] In Cocal, the pledge welcomed whites and *pardos*, but did not give them the right to vote, unless they were the scribe, treasurer, or trustee. The confraternity was also obliged to bury the whites that served them, unless they chose to be buried in another place. In this case, the black brethren were obliged to participate in their funeral procession. The language of the pledge suggests, however, that white males had a greater involvement in the black confraternities than white females. The Order of the Rosary of the City of Goiás had ties to free men with military titles, perhaps because the black women who lived with them participated actively in the directorates. The most famous man associated with that order was the artist José Joaquim da Veiga Valle, with an international reputation for the quality of his baroque sculptures.[33]

Through an examination of these incomplete documents of the sisterhoods, we are able to identify free black women, emancipated black women, and slaves. It is clear that they benefitted from a good social position and status in their community, exercising leadership roles as queens, judges, trustees, and sisters on the boards of the confraternities. They made donations in gold, equal to those of men, and were compensated for their services and contributions with burial in places similar to the men in the churches. Being a judge or a queen meant accumulating a certain degree of material wealth. The sisterhood's emphasis on treating the sick and dying, followed by burial in the church they had constructed, could have been a result of Catholic traditions as much as the African funeral organizations. African women and their descendants undoubtedly valued the Luso-Brazilian institution of the black confraternity, but why they did so is more difficult to determine. What we historians are able to document, however, are the annual donations of gold that sustained the confraternities dedicated to Our Lady of the Rosary and to Our Lady of Mercy. In conclusion, we can no longer exclude sisters in the attempt to understand how the black confraternities collected resources and constructed black churches in colonial Brazil in the 19th century.

Notes

1. Cidade de Goiás, Biblioteca da Fundação Educacional da Cidade de Goiás (henceforth BFEG) [City of Goiás, Library of the Educational Foundation of the City of Goiás], termo de assento [limit of entry], Nossa Senhora do Rosário, Natividade, 1786, f. 78. An image of the church with a roof can be seen in Ferrez, 1981, p. 144.

2. McCreery and Karasch, 2006. A preliminary version of the role of women in the black confraternities appeared in Karasch, 2004. Also see Karasch, 2010.

3. Goiânia, Arquivo da Cúria [Archive of the Papal Court], Edital que o Revmo. Visitor José Correa Leitão was served a decree... with respect to what was said about the sanctity of sacred places... Vila Boa, 28 Jul. 1784, cópia, f. 101A; and Karasch, 1999.

4. Karasch, 1999, p. 25-6, 46.

5. BFEG, Compromisso da Irmandade de Nossa Senhora do Rosário, 1796, and public records, 1826-1840; and fragments of public records of municipal seats of Nossa Senhora do Rosário de Natividade, 1786-1801. The two compromises of Cocal (1772-1788): Goiânia, Arquivo da Cúria [Archive of the Papal

Court], Agreements of the Sisterhood of Nossa Senhora das Mercês of the Slaves of São Joaquim do Cocal, 1772 e 1788.

6. BFEG, Cartório do Primeiro Ofício, Goiás, 1792-1799, Deed of donation made by Maria Francisca da Silva [freed woman of mixed race black and mulatto] of [a] villa/dwelling of houses in the Sisterhood of S. Benedito, 9 Nov. 1792, f. 41.

7. See the work of Borges and Palacin (1987), which has the image of the church Igreja do Rosário de Natividade on the cover. For the example of N. S. das Mercês, in Minas, see Scarano, 1975, p. 39.

8. In Africa: Thornton, 2002, p. 83-4; Kiddy, 2005, p. 15, 169; and Sweet, 2003, p. 206-8.

9. São Benedito: Karasch, 1987, p. 282-3; Kiddy, 2005, p. 220-1; Scarano, 1975, p. 38; and Borges, 2005, p. 155.

10. Santa Efigênia: Borges, 2005, p. 156.

11. Irmandade de Santa Efigênia: Karasch, 1987, p. 84; Soares, 2002, p. 64; and Bertran, 1985, p. 40-3, 72-6.

12. The best study on the sisterhoods in the captaincy of Goiás is that of Moraes, 2006.

13. BFEG, Rosário, Public Records, 14 May 1843, f. 58.

14. Cera e rosários [Wax and Rosaries]: BFEG, Rosário, Public Records, 4 June 1826, f. 10; tafetá: 16 Apr. 1837, f. 43-4; and 13 Jul. 1838, f. 47-8.

15. Goiânia, Arquivo da Cúria, Irmandade de N. S. das Mercês, Cocal, 1772, Chapt. 21. There is a photo of "caixinha para pedir esmolas" [offering box] from Minas Gerais in Borges, 2005, p. 249.

16. Mesa sem escravos: BFEG, Rosário, Public records, 29 May 1860, f. 126.

17. An elected king, the "negro Amador Pinto Caldeira not wanting to be the type that he is," he preferred not to be king "because I do not want to be a negro." BFEG, Rosário, 2 Junho 1827, f. 12-3; and 11 May 1828, f. 14.

18. Jesuítas: Lisboa, National Archive of Torre do Tombo, bundle 598, Ministério do Reino, Negócios do Ultramar, Letra B, 1753-1763, letter to the Vicar-General Pedro Barboza Cannaes de José dos Santos Pereira, São Félix, 5 Oct. 1761.

19. Registro de ouro: BFEG, Fragments from the treasury book of Nossa Senhora do Rosário de Natividade, 1810-1815.

20. Santa Efigênia: BFEG, Natividade, documents not catalogued, 1795-1796.

21. Africanos e crioulos: Goiânia, Arquivo da Cúria, Compromisso, N. S. das Mercês, 1792 [Africans and Creoles: Goiania, Tribunal Archives, Agreements, Our Lady of Mercy, 1792]; and Nishida, 1998, p. 331.

22. Pirenópolis: Brandão, 1978, p. 74. On "dança das fitas," see Moraes, 2006, cap. 8, p. 23-4.
23. Ferreira, 2012, chapter 3, p. 88-125.
24. Karasch, 2004, table 12.II, p. 260-1.
25. Cocal: Lisboa, Biblioteca da Ajuda, 54-V-12, n. 5, Notícia de todos os governadores e população das províncias do Brasil, 1782, [Notices of all governments and population of the provinces of Brazil], f. 33-4.
26. N. S. das Mercês, Minas Gerais: Scarano, 1975, p. 39.
27. See note 5.
28. To learn more about the use of poles in Rio de Janeiro, see Soares, 2000, p. 152-3, and Karasch 1987, p. 226.
29. Borges, 2005, p. 165-71; Karasch, 2004, p. 269, note 55; and Moraes, 2006, chapter 6.
30. Enterros nos sítios: BFEG, Natividade, Livro de Óbitos, 1801-1827.
31. Procuradores: Moraes, 2006, chapter 4; and in Rosário, Compromisso, 1796, cap. 10, f. 20.
32. Reis, 1993, p. 171-202; Moraes, 2006, chapter 9; and Borges, 2005, p. 165-71.
33. Veiga Valle: BFEG, Rosário, Livro de Termos, 26 de maio de 1849, f. 77; and 29 de maio de 1860, f. 127. The artist was the *capitão do mastro* in the Irmandade do Rosário in 1849.

Bibliography

Bertran, Paulo. *Memória de Niquelandia*. [Memory in Nickel-Land]. Brasília: Fundação Nacional Pró-Memória, 1985.

Borges, Anna Maria; Palacin, Luiz. *Patrimônio histórico de Goiás*. [Historical Patrimony of Goiás]. 2. ed. Brasília: Sphan/próMemória/8a Diretoria Regional, 1987.

Borges, Célia Maia. *Escravos e libertos nas Irmandades do Rosário: Devoção e solidariedade em Minas Gerais, Séculos XVIII e XIX*. [Slaves and Freedmen in the Brotherhoods of the Rosary: Devotion and Solidarity in Minas Gerais, 18th and 19th Centuries]. Juiz de Fora: Editora da UFJF, 2005.

Brandão, Carlos Rodrigues. *O divino, o santo e a senhora*. [The Divine, The Saint, and the Lady]. Rio de Janeiro: Campanha de Defesa do Folclore Brasileiro, 1978.

Ferreira, Roquinaldo. *Cross-cultural exchange in the Atlantic World—Angola and Brazil during the era of the slave trade*. Cambridge: Cambridge University Press, 2012.

Ferrez, Gilberto. *O Brasil do Primeiro Reinado visto pelo botânico William John Burchell, 1825-1829*. [Brazil of the First Kingdom as Seen by the Botanist William John Burchell, 1825-1829]. Rio de Janeiro: Fundação João Moreira Salles/Fundação Nacional Pró-Memória, 1981.

Karasch, Mary. *Slave life in Rio de Janeiro, 1808-1850*. Princeton: Princeton University Press, 1987.

_____. "História das doenças e dos cuidados médicos na capitania de Goiás." [History of Diseases and Medical Care in the Captaincy of Goiás]. In: Freitas, Lena Castello Branco F. de (Org.). *Saúde e doenças em Goiás*. [Health and Disease in Goiás]. Goiânia: UFGO, 1999, p. 46-9.

_____. "Free women of color in Central Brazil, 1779-1832." In: Gaspar, David Barry; Hine, Darlene Clark (Orgs.). *Beyond bondage—Free women of color in the Americas*. Urbana and Chicago: University of Illinois Press, 2004, p. 259-65.

_____. "Construindo comunidades: As irmandades dos pretos e pardos." [Constructing Communities: The Confraternities of Blacks and Mixed-Race People]. *História Revista* [UFGO], v. 15, n. 2, jul.-dez. 2010.

Kiddy, Elizabeth W. *Blacks of the Rosary: Memory and history in Minas Gerais, Brazil*. University Park: Penn State Press, 2005.

McCreery, David; Karasch, Mary. "Community building and identity formation—A comparative analysis of lay brotherhoods in Mesoamerica (Cofradías) and Brazil (Irmandades)," paper presented in Pretória, South Africa, 2006.

Moraes, Cristina de Cássia Pereira. *Do corpo místico de Cristo: Irmandades e confrarias na capitania de Goiás, 1736-1808*. [Of the Mystic Body of Christ: Brotherhoods and Confraternities in the Captaincy of Goiás, 1736-1808]. Diss. (Doctorate in History), Universidade Nova de Lisboa, Lisboa, 2006.

Nishida, Mieko. "From ethnicity to race and gender: Transformations of black lay sodalities in Salvador, Brazil." *Journal of Social History*, v. 32, n. 2 (inverno 1998), p. 331.

Reis, João José. *A morte é uma festa: Ritos fúnebres e revolta popular no Brasil do século XIX*. [Death is a Party: Funeral Rites and Popular Revolt in 19th Century Brazil]. São Paulo: Companhia das Letras, 1993.

Scarano, Julieta. *Devoção e escravidão: A Irmandade de Nossa Senhora do Rosário dos Pretos no Distrito Diamantino no século XVIII*. [Devotion and Slavery: The Brotherhood of Our Lady of the Rosary of the Blacks in the Diamantino District in the 18th Century]. São Paulo: Conselho Estadual de Cultura, 1975.

Soares, Mariza de Carvalho. *Devotos da cor: Identidade étnica, religiosidade e escravidão no Rio de Janeiro, século XVIII*. [Devotees of Color: Ethnic Identity, Religiosity, and Slavery in Rio de Janeiro, 18th Century]. Rio de Janeiro: Civilização Brasileira, 2000.

_____. "O império de santo Elesbão na cidade do Rio de Janeiro, século XVIII." [The Empire of Saint Elesbão in the City of Rio de Janeiro, 18th Century]. Topoi, Rio de Janeiro, Mar. 2002.

Sweet, James H. Recreating Africa—Culture, kinship, and religion in the African-Portuguese world, 1441-1770. Chapel Hill: The University of North Carolina Press, 2003.

Thornton, John. "Religious and ceremonial life in the Kongo and Mbundu areas, 1500-1700." In Heywood, Linda M. (Org.). *Central Africans and cultural transformations in the American diaspora.* Cambridge: Cambridge University Press, 2002.

5

AMONG CHARACTERS, TYPOLOGIES, AND LABELS OF "DIFFERENCE": THE SLAVE WOMAN IN THE 19TH CENTURY FICTION OF RIO DE JANEIRO

Giovana Xavier

> *A huge evil that disfigures, infects, demeans, misrepresents, and erodes our society is that to which our society still clings, like the disgraced woman.*
>
> —Joaquim Manuel de Macedo (n.d., p. 1)

The target of different intervention projects during African slavery in the Americas, the body of the black woman was seen as a mysterious piece of meat to be dissected. Although descriptions of the black woman are as present in the speech of curious masters and European travelers—as it is in the detailed narratives of doctors, jurists, police, and in ads for the purchase, sale, and escape of female slaves—it is the fiction of the 19th century (inclusive of novels, short stories, poetry, and plays) that is the privileged place to study a series of images produced during slavery.

Throughout the 1800s, different writers used images of black women as a metaphor of pathology, corruption, and primitivism, configuring the black female body as sickly and therefore harmful to the health of a nation under construction. Dozens of fictional narratives of the era converge in the same direction: the effort to demonstrate the connection between "abnormal" physical traits and "doubtful character" as the principle mark of the "colored" woman and her body. In this context emerged the literary stereotypes such as the *beautiful mulatto woman*, the *ugly crioula* (black woman born in Brazil), the *faithful slave*, the *resigned preta* (dark-skinned black woman), the *mischievous maid*, or even the *virtuous mestiça* (mixed-race woman).

Faced with such a vast gallery, it is time to give a voice to some of these characters, keeping in mind that they still belong to the same group (women of color—slaves, free, or emancipated), the construction of their stereotypes produced differentiated results according to the characteristics and personal style of each author.

Resigned Slaves

There is no one better than Mariana to begin our journey. Although not as famous as the controversial Capitu or the vivacious Helena, the little slave whose namesake story published in 1871 by Machado de Assis on the first page of the *Jornal das Famílias* mirrors the already known ability of the writer to dive into the complex relationships between masters and slaves in the domestic environment. In spite of having "intelligence of her situation" and of not sitting "at the table" or visiting the living room "when guests were present" (Machado de Assis, 2008, v. II, p. 1009), the "kind *mulatinha*" (diminutive term of endearment for a mulatto woman) is bold enough to fall in love with Coutinho, none other than her dear master. Aware of the impossibility to turn her dream into reality, the "girl" tries to hide her secret, guarded in her heavy heart in which she places "a certain brotherly affection." But her boldness does not go unreturned. The *morena* (a slightly politer term for *parda*, implying a mixed-race woman of medium or darker-than-white complexion) that "represented the type that was most perfect of her kind" is punished with a tragic end. "Born and raised as a daughter of the house," Mariana commits suicide by drinking poison in front of her great love.

The choice to portray a slave's love as a plot device is already, in itself, a distinctive feature in a literary world in which black women, especially mulatto woman, were consensually presented as prostitutes, lovers, wanton, and without any character. The story, however, goes further; after all, such impossible love is the background for larger discussions surrounding themes such as slavery, property, freedom, and paternalism, and that is seven months before the Lei do Ventre Livre of September 28 was decreed.

However, Mariana was not the only one to commit such an extreme act in the name of love. We searched our gallery for another kindhearted soul willing to do anything when it came to matters of the heart. Created in 1859 by José de Alencar, Joana is the protagonist of the play *Mãe* (Mother), "drama in four acts" dedicated to lady Ana de Alencar, mother of the author. "An old mulatto woman," a slave who knew how to "get to know people," was resigned with regard to her condition. Proof of this is that she shouted from the rooftops that she was happier serving Jorge than she would be "if she were freed" (Alencar, 1977, v. II, p. 259). Such happiness was not by chance and was due to a secret only known by her and Dr. Lima, a lawyer and friend of Jorge. Even though she acted as just a slave, Joana was also the biological mother of her dear *nhonhô* (a term slaved used to refer to their masters).

The farce of passing as a slave of her son was justified by love and by the fear of disgracing the life of the young man. Jorge, who had been raised without knowing the identity of his parents, found in Joana, a "second mother," the same way that Dr. Lima was a like a father. After becoming emotional over the absence of his mysterious mother, the theme that plagued his thoughts, the young man decides to grace the "old woman" with a letter of emancipation. Always submissive, the slave refuses the offer immediately, claiming that she wants to stay by his side. Dr. Lima, in turn, is alarmed with the attitude of the captive who shared such an intriguing secret.

In order to save Elisa, the love of Jorge's life, as well as the father of the bankrupt maiden, Joana herself suggests that Jorge use her as collateral for a loan. Initially, the "handsome young man" resists the idea of his "dear" friend, but later, facing a lack of options to obtain such a large sum of money, he ends up agreeing. During the negotiations for the terms of the loan, Joana, at the height of her "thirty-seven" years, insists upon proving herself far from the stereotypes that fall on slave women.

In accordance with what was already shown by historiography many times, male and female slaves created different bargaining strategies in search of reaching their objectives.[1] Joana was no different. In order to convince her future (and temporary) owner of the advantages of such a deal, she said: "I am not just any *mulatinha* (this use of the diminutive for mulatto woman implies disdain) like these other lazy ones who don't know how to do anything other than be in the window." The slave knew her value and also insisted upon differentiating herself from other women as the "fine, young, healthy slave," ready to fulfill "all the services needed within a family home," who an unhappy master tried to sell due to her only defect: "being very inclined to the male sex" (*Jornal do Comércio*, 24 Mar. 1828, p. 4),[2] or characters like the washwoman Eulália, a mulatto woman who, in spite of being very hardworking, had two serious problems: "passion for samba and an addiction to *cachaça*" (sugar cane liquor) (Almeida, 1888).

The wealth of skills and virtues of Joana echoed in the ears of the greedy Peixoto. After showing her feet and "beautiful teeth, pearls like no other" (Crespo, 1942a, p. 241), the slave was mortgaged by the trader for 600 thousand *réis* (currency of the day), a value higher that the debt contracted by the future father-in-law of Jorge, with the promise of being rescued by her idolized *nhonhô* the next day. The words spoken by the slave woman also help us to know a little more about the tasks that could be performed by maids in the 19th century. "Sewing, washing, and ironing" were some of them (Alencar, 1977, p. 290).[3] However, as we saw, the invaluable mulatto woman was the slave in which no one could find any defect. Her list of good qualities was extensive: "I sweep, clean, cook, set the table, and I still find time to do my sewing, mend the dishtowels, scour the pans..." So many skills certainly did not match the modest price of her mortgage value.

Already in the possession of Peixoto, Joana decides to visit her *nhonhô*, to make sure that everything was going well in her absence. Upon noticing the absence of his slave, however, the trader went after her to Jorge's house, who, at this point, received from his friend Dr. Lima, the value needed to get Joana back. When he discovered the transaction that was done the previous morning, Dr. Lima ended up revealing the tortuous secret: "You sold your mother!" Despite the terms of the mortgage (with the clause of the sale) being falsified by the sneaky trader, it was already too late. Aware that the boy had discovered his identity, Joana aiming to protect the honor and happiness of her son, swallows fatal poison and maintains her resignation until the end: "*Nhonhô*!... He lied to you!... I am not... I am not your mother, no... my son!" The identification of the audience with an ending so dramatic "since the curtain was raised"—here we take the words of Machado, in his critique of Alencar's play, published in the Revista Dramática of the Diário of Rio de Janeiro (Machado de Assis, 2008, v. III, p. 1038), in which he actually considered the drama a "perfect ending"—shows the verisimilitude between fiction and reality, after all, as Machado also left on the record, "the public began to see the dramatic spirit which, among us, could be a truth."

Next to Mariana and Joana, a third slave stands out for her intense resignation. A character in the novel *A Viúva Simões* (The Widow Simons), written by Júlia Lopes de Almeida, Josefa was "an *acaboclada* (term used to refer to someone with *caboclo* traits, indicating mixed racial heritage of white and indigenous blood lines), old woman, short and bony, with straight, broad shoulders, a square chin, and large hands." Loyal assistant of Ernestina (the widow Simões), to whom she had raised from "two years of age," the ex-slave "never left the house," not even after emancipation (Almeida, 1999, p. 122). Drawing upon animalistic characteristics to describe the slave population was a resource much used by writers of the time and was due to the active dialogue between science and literature, which culminated in the construction of typologies that made the blacks inferior and reinforced the genetic superiority of whites.

This crossing of ideas culminated in the rise of naturalist literature, in which the behavior of individuals would be determined through the manner in which they lived (called "social determinism"). In this literature, slave men and women had their physical and behavioral traits described as animalistic, whose origin was given due to the degenerating conditions imposed by slavery and inherited by African genetics. The disciple-like description of Ernestina fits like a glove in this context: "Stubborn, unstable mood, but unwavering and lovable like a dog." Devoid of charm and beauty, the character represents the exemplary slave: ugly, docile, and therefore, reliable.

Josefa's devotion to her mistress was such that she was able to apprehend letters, tear up photographs and make "many bouquets of flowers sent" by Luciano Dias—a character that the old slave "sensed" had bad intentions for the girl—disappear. In the face of the social conventions imposed on women of the bourgeoisie, the dedicated Josefa became the only confidant possible for the widow. Because of this, the slave listened to "secrets" from the protagonist, without consoling or advising her, and saying "amen" to everything. Actually, the blind loyalty is another recurring stereotype attributed to many domestic slaves in literary novels. Not considered friends, these women are treated as tireless watchdogs, devoid of critical sense and humanity.

The devotion of black women to their mistresses is also described by Gonçalves Crespo (1942b). Carioca, son of a Portuguese trader and a black woman, the poet announced in 1882, the sad end of the "old black women" in a poem of the same name "*As Velhas Negras*," dedicated to Madam Aline de Gusmão: "They knew many owners;/Lulled in much slumber/From so many kind masters!/They were loved maids./And now useless, bent over,/In stupid old age!" However, through Josefa it is possible to see the animalization of the slave woman in literary discourse; reading between the lines of her speech offers other interpretive possibilities in which dissimulation makes itself present. Her dialogue with the widow follows this form, as can be seen in the following example: "'Listen,' Josefa, interrupted Ernestina, 'today I am expecting a visitor here, in your house! I need the living room, hear? The house is all yours.'" Aware of the importance of silence to maintain harmony in the interdependency between her and her former master, the washwoman "was thinking that Ernestina was silly, a creature without any sense, and she concluded: "Why on earth will she not just get married?!" (Almeida, 1999, p. 153).

The stories of Mariana, Joana and Josefa, goodhearted house slaves with "feelings of a certain level, and a nobleness that contrasted with their social condition" (Machado de Assis, 2008, v. II, p. 1012), represent one of the few literary moments in which the virtues of the slave woman are highlighted. The narratives surrounding their "unequivocal affection" (idem, v. III, p. 1039) denounce the fragile borders between the world of the slaves and the world of their master, such as the stigmas of slavery and the barriers represented by social differences. However, it is not only these good creatures that compose the worlds of slavery.

Weeds: The Treacherous Slaves

The domestic slave (rural and urban), "a poisoned wave in that ocean of obliged vices" (Macedo, [s/d, b], p. 160), was a constant presence during the entire slavery period, according to the descriptions by European travelers such as Jean-Baptiste Debret, Johann Moritz Rugendas, and so many others who recorded their impressions of Brazil. Fixtures in the midst of the lordly family, they fulfilled "the duties of the house and for the family": cooking, washing, ironing, cleaning, knitting, nursing, shopping, etc. This daily life shared among slaves and masters will not escape the pages of novels and serials. Such publications portrayed the fear that such undesirable and necessary creatures awakened in the slaveholding families:

> The old ones believed that every house was inhabited by a familiar demon that depended on the calm and tranquility of the people in which it lived. We, Brazilians, realize this belief; we have, in our homes, this familiar demon. How often does it not share with us the caresses of our mothers, the frolics of our siblings and our family's kindness! But a day will come, like today, in which he [sic], in his ignorance or malice, disturbs domestic peace; and makes love, friendship, reputation, all of these sacred things, a child's game. This familiar demon of our homes, that which we all recognize (Alencar, 1903, p. 193).

The play *O demônio familiar* (The Familiar Demon) has a slave as a protagonist, the *moleque* (young boy, bratty child) Pedro. However, this masculine example is a good point for us to dive into the imagination of the elites on what they believed to be one of the greatest dangers of slavery: its moral corruption. In the middle of the debates on the continuity or extinction of that system in Brazil, the noble master Eduardo, taken back by the antics of the "boy" who dreamed of being a "coachman," advised family and friends on the necessity of cleansing their homes of the slave element. To make his argument more convincing, he highlighted the moral devastation that such an institution imposed on homes.

Blaming "all" the members of the seigniorial class for the persistence of slavery, Pedro's owner decided to punish him by granting his freedom. The reasoning was simple. The "little naughty child" had not been deserving of living in the middle of a white family. For this, the solution to correct him was making him a "self-sustaining man," giving him back "to society" and expulsing him from "within" the family. To Eduardo, once freed, the results of the blackmail, threats, and attacks of the slave would fall only on himself. Simply, a "letter of freedom" would be the best "punishment" that Pedro could receive, as well as the best remedy to preserve the integrity of the white family who closed the doors of their house to him "forever."

José de Alencar was not the only fiction writer to defend the end of captivity for fear of the nefarious influence this "pest called slavery" (Macedo, s/d, a, p. 162) represented for the white family. In the note "To our readers," Joaquim Manuel de Macedo explains to his audience one of the intentions of the novel *As vítimas algozes* (The Cruel Victims), painting "the picture of the evil that the slave brings to his master either purposefully or sometimes thoughtlessly." It is in this context that we return to our character and we meet Lucinda, "a very perverted girl and very desirous to become even more perverted."

The terrible, 12-year old maid, who "knew everything she needed to ignore so that she wouldn't harm her mistress," had been a present for the eleventh Christmas birthday of Cândida. The close relationship between the two, the "swamp and clear fountain" that made the little mistress a "girl" in the form of a "delicate and beautiful creature," "who loved with the purity of the love of the heavens," became the "slave of her slave." After learning from her slave all the secrets to being a "woman," the maiden was deflowered by Souvanel, a seductive Frenchman of whom Lucinda becomes a lover. However, the "corruption" of the girl by the slave, "with the most scandalous and repulsive behavior," would go further. Later, Cândida gives herself to Dermany, a "lackey" and "criminal" sought by the police. In the story, we follow the transformation of a childlike girl into a lying, promiscuous, curious, and vain young lady. Cândida's chance for regeneration arrives at the end of the story, however. In it, the young girl, who at this point had stopped "being an angel," goes to the altar with the virtuous Frederico, her stepbrother, thus saving the name of her family. By this time, the "immoral maid," Lucinda, had already escaped and is impeded, by government order, from returning to her old mistress.

Another slave that disrupted seigniorial peace was Simplícia. Character of the same novel *A viúva Simões* inhabited by Josefa, the little mulatto girl was "skinny, short, with a snout like a weasel, and small eyes, piercing and terrible." Upon discovering Ernestina's passion for Luciano Dias, a *bon vivant* newcomer from Europe, the slave began to demand from her owner clothes, fabrics, drinks, and money as payment for keeping such a secret considered vexing for a widow and mother. In unison with Simplícia, we learn of a "little coquettish girl" (Guimarães, 1992, p. 36). She had a "flexible body" and "charming black eyes." Rosa had "wavy black hair that could very well be on the head of the whitest aristocrat." However, over the course of the story, we find that behind the "kind" slave was a "malevolent" woman who fed "deadly hatred" towards the poor, sweet slave Isaura. Considered her "sworn enemy," Isaura will go through a real ordeal at the hands of her "petulant" rival.

The slave woman—an ever-present figure in the nineteenth century Rio landscape—was seen as the center of physical and moral corruption within the seigniorial family. For this reason, Lucinda's creator warned: "Oh! Parents, think, meditate for just one hour of the dangers that threaten your poor daughters, condemned, subject to the influence of slave maids!!!" Pedro, Lucinda, Simplícia, Rosa. Weeds planted in the seigniorial environment. Each one, in her own way, represented the dilemmas and contradictions stemming from the intimate ties constructed between masters and slaves in the domestic environment.

"I am Black, but I Have Feelings": Resignation or Resistance?

Among the hundreds of literary characters that populated the pages of novels and serials in the 19th century, Bertoleza is certainly one of the most recognized. *Quitandeira* (a woman street vendor who sells fruits and vegetables), the *preta* had as an owner "an old blind man in Juiz da Fora" and she was "friendly with a Portuguese man who had a hand cart and made deliveries in the city" (Azevedo, 1998). A Slave "working for herself," a form of slavery that intensified in the 19th century (Santos, 2010), Bertoleza is a good example of the autonomy that some slaves were able to acquire from their masters by way of work.

After the passing of her lover, who from "pulling a load larger than his strength, fell dead in the street, next to the cart, exhausted like a beast," the "thirty-something" *crioula* sought help in João Romão, a Portuguese man "crazy to become rich." Seeing in the cook an excellent opportunity to fulfill his ambitions, the businessman became her "bookkeeper, lawyer and counselor," being responsible for the administration of her estate as well as the slave payment of 20 thousand *réis* monthly to her master.

Contrary to the declared racial segregation, historiography already demonstrated that interethnic cohabitation was very common within the working class in various work, living, and recreation spaces, which is not to say that there were no conflicts among these groups. In this context, it is not surprising that the captive had affairs with two Portuguese men throughout her life.[4] Introduced by Aluísio de Azevedo as foolish and submissive, the character described as a "smelly black woman" represents the ultimate animalization of the slave woman in Brazilian literature. Her ingenuity is such that João Romão is able to coax her with a false letter of emancipation, becoming her second lover. The false freedwoman is portrayed by the writer as a natural manual laborer due to her resigned behavior and subservience in addition to her ugliness and bad smell: "Nevertheless, next to him the *crioula* snored with her mouth in the air, fat, exhausted from work, reeking of a mixture of sweat with raw onion and stinking fat" (p. 91).

After being able to considerably expand his business at the cost of the *crioula* ("João Romão rose and she remained here at the bottom, abandoned like a beast we no longer need to continue the journey"), the trader decided to marry the young Zulmira, daughter of a Portuguese couple living in a tenement near his market in the Botafogo neighborhood, but for this reason, it would be necessary to free himself of the encumbrance that was his "friend." Facing such a goal, the trader setup a preposterous trap so that the police would catch his concubine as a runaway slave.

When Bertoleza realizes this macabre plan, she takes the extreme action of suicide. It is not by accident that the place where the slave chooses to stab herself is her abdomen, the part of the black female body that was the topic of heated debates in the last two decades of slavery; debates that culminated in, among others, the Lei do Ventre Livre de 1871 (The Law of the Free Womb). Although her story is distinctive, uncontrolled rage was not exclusive to this character. In a classic study on the blacks in literature, Raymond Sayers tells the story of Mão Rosa. Introduced in 1843 in the weekly magazine *Museu Universal* (*Jornal das Famílias Brasileiras*), from the same owners of the *Jornal do Comércio*, Rosa was a jealous black woman, taken by her "wild and African" anger, who decided to castrate her partner with the same knife that was "often used to slice bread between the two," motivated by excessive jealousy coming from "black love" that ran through her veins (Sayers, 1956, p. 155).

Returning to Bertoleza, key moments of the character of the plot offer other interpretive possibilities than that which reduce her behavior to "*bertoldo* [foolishness]"[5] (conforming to what her name itself suggests). One of them is that when she realizes the real intentions of the Portuguese man and reclaims her free working condition: "He who ate my meat has to bite my bones! So shall a creature, year in and year out, being pulled by its body every holy day God gives, from early in the morning until late at night, be thrown in the middle of the street like a stinking chicken?! No! It shall not be this way, Mr. João." After all, she had not played to lose. She wanted the portion that she was rightly due.

In her logic, her life with the businessman had shared benefits: "I want to enjoy what we earned together! I want my part in what we made with our work! I want my prize, like you want yours!" Here, it is interesting to note the expressions "my part" and "our work" as representative of the codes of subordinate classes, in which the feminine social roles were not restricted to just marriage and motherhood, but also to work and the income of the household (Soihet, 1985). Another interesting phrase professed by the victim, puts humanity at the center of the debate: "I am black, yes, but I have feelings!" It is important to note the opposition between blackness and feelings in her discourse, because this was the form that the character ("dirty *preta*") chose to highlight her human level in the middle of animalizing stereotypes that erased the humanity of the black population.

Another time in which Bertoleza emerges as an agent can be seen in this line: "I will not be a *quitandeira* until I die! I need to rest! For this, I toiled next to you while God, Our Father gave me strength and health!... Hear this! I want to stay by your side! (p. 166). These speeches of the character create gaps for interpretations that extrapolate from the black woman as "dirty," "stinking," and "stupid." We have here a final speech with this idea:

> Now, I am worth nothing! However, when you needed me it was not bad to serve you with my body and sustain your house with my work! Then, the black woman was useful for everything; now she is worth nothing, and you throw her to the heap of dust! No! God does not command this! If old dogs are not shooed away, why shall I be put out of this house that put so much sweat on my face?... If you want to marry, wait until I close my eyes first, don't be ungrateful (p. 167).

In all of the lines in which her voice is heard, the slave reinforces her human condition and reclaims the rights that she thinks to be legitimate. Contrary to the narrow view of classic, naturalist literary production—in which poor populations (white and black) are animalized, each in their own way—Bertoleza forces us to hear her wishes through a narrative sustained by the rationalization of the dual role of companion and worker that she represented.

"Favorite Muses": The Sensual and Voluptuous Mulatas[6]

The little elegant *mulata* (mulatto woman) "*de cor morena sempre amena*" (a rhyme implying that her light brown shade of skin was always amenable)—as said in the popular *lundu* song *Mulatinha do caroço* (little mulatto woman of the seed), recalled by Moraes Filho (1981, p. 108)—was undoubtedly one of the most fascinating characters used among nineteenth century writers. Faced with such irresistible charm, fiction and reality revealed their porous borders and, on various occasions, the enchanting physical gifts of the *cabrochas* (little mulatto girls) would end up in the ads for missing, sale, and purchase of slave women who populated the country. This was the case of Joana, a "little *mulata* almost passing for *sarará*" (mixed race person with white skin but features such as curly hair or thicker lips) with her "whitish skin" and her "very fine legs and hands she could be a true flower of sin" (The phrase *flor do pecado* refers to the young woman being sexually attractive) (*Diário de Pernambuco*, 4 Jan. 1865).[7]

Among many "bewitching graces" (Moraes Filho, 1981, p. 108), one of them reigns supreme; as such, it is not surprising that Rita Baiana, from *O cortiço* (The slum house) is selected to begin the journey through this gallery. Neighbor of Bertoleza, the washwoman appears described as *mestiça* or as *mulata*. The use of the two categories on the same page drives us to the associations among gender, color, sexuality, and behavior in the definition of racial classifications. A lady of a sway "full of an irresistible grace, simple, primitive, made up entirely of sin and heaven and serpent and woman alike," the *baiana* (woman from Bahia) was deceptive like a "cursed snake" and used her beauty to get what she wanted. She was aware of her physical attributes like the "vain *mulata*" of the *lundu* song written by the folklorist Mello Moraes Filho. Contemporary of Rita, the beauty took pride in never having been beaten in samba and for having beauty to rival that of white women:

> I am the vain *mulata*
> Beautiful, graceful, delicate
> Which many white women are not!
> I have the most beautiful sway,
> If the night is my hair,
> My heart is the day....

(Moraes Filho, 1981, p. 82)

Oozing sensuality, vitality and happiness, the physical description of Rita is made up of synesthesia, figurative language that mixes tastes and feelings, which we see in the expressions such as "breast the color of cinnamon" and smell "of marjoram," attributed to them by their creator. The ultimate representation of the sensual *mulata* in Brazilian literature, Rita, "burning light of midday," "green snake and treacherous," was naturally an "aphrodisiac." If the animalization of Bertoleza justified her submission and "idiocy," in Rita's case, the same resource was used to explain her cunningness. The power of her charm was such that not even Jerônimo, an obstinate Portuguese worker could remain unscathed: "And the primal smell of the first class woman, *mestiça*, that stirred the blood [of Jerônimo] with the shake of her skirt and hair." In short, because of Rita, the young man became an "idiot." She made him "silly" and he lost "his complete mind" (Calado Júnior, 1981).

Not only theatre and literature turn their attention to black women. Since the colonial times, from Gregório de Mattos to Castro Alves and his contemporaries, different poets dedicated their efforts to portraying the feminine representatives "of the color of sin" (the same title of the song recorded by the composer Bororó in 1939: "That brown body you have, fragrant and tasty/is a slender body/the color of sin/that does so well...."). In the 1830s, the man from Minas Gerais João Salomé Queiroga described traits that he believed composed the "Portrait of the *Mulata*," among them, "curly tresses," "rosy cheeks," "eyebrows the color of charcoal," and an "elegant, beautiful waist." Given to such a magical creature, a "Venus born here in Brazil," the poet recited that she was able to capture the "five senses": "In your face/shines serene/your brown color/from the *buriti* (a type of plant that produces a reddish brown fruit)/your lips pour/pink freshness/smell of the honey/of the *jataí* (type of bee that produces clear, sweet honey) (Queiroga, 1870).

Machado de Assis, in "Sabina" (2008, v. III, p. 550), also recorded his impressions of a certain domestic slave who, due to her beauty, took the breath away from the overseer and all the guests who passed by the farm: "Sabina was a maid of the farm/20 years old/and in the whole province/ there was no *mestiça* more in fashion/With her clothes of chambray and lace." Best we leave that story for later. Another who was not immune to such charm was Aubrey Bell (1956, p. 234), who in his poem *Canção* (Song) he describes another beautiful *mulata* loved by an overseer. In addition to his commiseration with the old black women, the already mentioned Gonçalves Crespo was a poet who, attentive to the beauty of the *mestiça* woman, as in the poem *A sesta* (The Siesta) (Crespo, 1942c, p. 77), turned his gaze to a "beautiful *crioula*" who rested with arms "delicate and bare" in the "snowy web." While such physical qualities attracted men, they could also intimidate them. In this case, instead of *morena*, *mulata* or *mestiça*, the preferred classification was the *negra* (black woman), as we can see clearly in *A negra* (Crespo, 1942a): "Your eyes, Oh robust creature./Oh tropical daughter!/Recall the terrors of darkness/ Tropical forest/For it is black."[8]

The literary typologies of *morenas*, *crioulas* and *mestiças* solidify the contradictions of an intellectualism that defended a project of a *mestiça* nation, but at the same time appeared to be fearful of that which it believed to be nefarious influences: slavery and African heritage.

Out of Place? The Virtuous Mestiças and Their Skin

Not only faithful slaves, perverse maids and *morenas*, who were "fickle like all *mestiças*," existed in nineteenth century fiction:

> She found herself alone, seated at the piano, a beautiful and noble figure of a girl. The lines of the profile take shape distinctly between the ebony piano box, and the even darker bushy tresses. They are so pure and smooth these lines, that they fascinate the eyes, enlighten the mind, and paralyze all analysis. Complexion like the ivory of the keys, dawn that doesn't dazzle, dimmed by a delicate nuance, not know-

ing whether to call it a light pale or a faint pink (Guimarães, 1992, p. 12-3).

That could be just one among hundreds of bourgeois maidens with pure hearts that populated the fictional narratives of the time. However, the beautiful "girl" and the owner of the "noble figure" is none other than the famous slave Isaura. Among stereotypes of women of color, perhaps the most clearly constructed is this: the virtuous *mestiça*, because, at first sight, her character and her beauty represent the success of the mix between the white and black races: "She is beautiful and has a beautiful color, that no one will say has a single drop of African blood in her veins" (idem, p. 14)." In summary, the body of the slave created debates about a Brazil under construction. It was not by chance the young Henrique, amazed with such a beautiful creature, highlights that she "is a perfect Brazilian... superior to all" (p. 21).

Isaura was the daughter of Miguel, a "good and honorable" Portuguese man and "old overseer of the plantation," and the slave Juliana "a pretty *mulata*, who for a time had been the favorite maid" and died due to "cruel treatment" from her master, unhappy with the resistance of the slave to his "brutal solicitations" (idem, p. 17). The character from 1875 was the embodiment of a certain "Brazilian-ness" so desired by the elite: *mestiça*, maiden-like, educated and, last but not least, lady of a noble soul.

As we have seen, in cases like that of Rita Baiana, the terms *mestiça* and *mulata* were often used synonymously. In Isaura's case, the situation is more complex. She is before anything, *mestiça*, illustrating the role of literature in the construction of a national *mestiça* identity with sights set on whiteness (Schwarcz, 1993). However, erasing the African heritage was not one of the simplest tasks. Reading between the lines of the romance shows that in spite of embodying the success of whitening, the character also carried in her body, traits of the dangerous African heritage.

These marks of blackness were represented by her unnerving beauty. Possessing an irresistible physical appearance, Isaura (like Rita) drew a legion of fans that ranged from Leônico, her obsessed owner, and Henrique, brother of her mistress, even the gardener André and the slave Belchior. One of the only moments of the plot in which the slave is described as a "little *mulata*" opens pathways for us to observe a racialized concept of beauty constructed by associations between physical appearance, stereotype and social condition:

> Little *mulata*, he said—you have no idea *Mulatinha*, how enchanting you are. My sister is right; it is a shame that such a beautiful girl is nothing more than a slave. If you had been born free you would be, incontestably, the belle of the ball. (Ibid, p. 22)

Isaura exuded a certain "mulatto-ness," simultaneously written and invisible. Like an "enchantress" of whom no one could place any kind of defect, the "nearly white" heroine left nothing to be desired of the other ebony muses. Her charms, in addition to taking the prudence from the young men who lived with her, also awakened the rage and mistrust from women, from the envious slave Rosa to the ladies of high society. Like her mother a "beautiful *mulata* with a sway," Isaura's complexion would be motivation for "cases of exclusion or fixation" (Freyre, 2003, p. 368), representing (although in another way) the sick nature of the black woman and her body.

The different adjectives attributed to the character's color reveal the shadows of her skin, skin "like the ivory of the keys" (a tone we would call "dingy" white), "dawn that doesn't dazzle," and, finally, "dimmed by a delicate nuance." All of these terms, clearly constructed by the writer, bring the reader to think about the injustice of her captivity. The adoption of this complex game of words is also one of the reasons that explain the roaring success of this abolitionist serial that spans centuries. *Mulata* and white at the same time—and it is this aspect that is the source of her charms—the power of Isaura to transcend from her skin because it is exactly from her complexion "not knowing whether to call it light pale or faint pink" that creates this feeling of outrage towards the "painful situation" that she experienced. On the question of slavery, it is through a nearly white skin that we are invited to discuss the miserable place of the girl: "This education, that they gave me, and this beauty, that they boast about, what good do they do me? … They are luxury fodder placed on a plantation of Africans. The plantation does not stop being what it is: a plantation." Like a good *mestiça*, at the end of the plot, Isaura overcomes all the hardships and goes to the altar with the "handsome young gentleman," Álvaro (Guimarães, 1992, p. 13-4).

However, let us not fool ourselves into believing that *mestiçagem* (mixing races) represented a guarantee that all would end well in the lives of young people of color created by the quills of nineteenth century fiction. Among many with the same physical appearance, Isaura was one of few, if not the only *mestiça*, to achieve a happy ending for her character. In this context, another novel in which skin comes to life, overlapping the character, is, once again, in *A viúva Simões*. The protagonist, Ernestina, widow of the commander Simões, was presented in 1897 to readers in *Gazeta de Notícias*, where the text was originally published as a serial in 1895. Despite being considered by critics of the time and also in some recent works, a white woman of the bourgeoisie, a closer examination of the work produces a contrasting interpretation (Côrtes, 2005). In the first lines, her skin appears to define her character: in which "her temperament, apparently cold, some times gave her, momentarily, an air of strong authority, very contradictory to her Brazilian *Moreno* type" (Almeida, 1999, p. 180).

Contrary to her daughter Sara, the prototype of a sanitized woman, with her "fair, white and rosy flesh," the widow represented the "fire," and her "ardor" and "dominion came from her skin, her gaze, her presence, and her smile." It is Luciano Dias himself (a love of the past that she had never forgotten) who best synthesizes that counterpoint: "Ernestina was a fiery woman that burned you to the flesh, her daughter was a benevolent woman of light that lit the future, and he loved the two, one with the senses, and the other with the heart"(idem, p. 122).

Facing the tormenting effect of her complexion, Ernestina is idealized by her great love as a *bacante* (follower of Bacchus). The *morena* was not desirous as a wife—"it was not exactly as a husband that he wanted to kiss the small, red mouth of the widow of Simões" (p. 118); and the physical description of her body attests, once again, to the space reserved for women of color in literature: "The slender, billowy body of the girl, the blue black of her thick hair, the sweetness of her wide, dewy eyes, the warm brown of her rosy skin lit up his heart, not with the pure and chaste love that a man should dedicate to his eternal companion, but the sultry heat of a violent and transient passion" (p. 118).

Among the African descendants, the price to be paid for beauty could be very high. If determining a standard to define the destiny of these beautiful women were the case, we could say that sadness, barbarous punishments, and madness were a part of it, as we see in the saga of Domingas. Enchanted by her beauty, José Pedro da Silva falls in love with the *mulata* and has a child with her, the "mulatto" Raimundo, who is freed by his father at baptism, along with his slave mother. Discontent with her husband's cheating, the old mistress of the now freed slave inflicts the most heinous punishments, bringing the beautiful *mulata* to the deepest point of dementia (Azevedo, 1996).

The virtuous *mestiças*, as much as the sensual *mulatas*, enchanted the men around them. However, what differentiated them was the fact that the *mestiças*, being innocent creatures, did so unintentionally. This is the case, for example, of the "naïve virgin" Sabina (Machado de Assis, p. 552). A character already known to us, she was another *morena* that had her heart broken. To summarize the story, the "little *trigueira*" (girl having the color of ripe wheat) fell in love and gave herself to Otávio in the most "sincere and ardent" form (p. 554). The innocence of the maid with "soft eyes" and "black hair" kept her from seeing that the "soul" of "her young master" was never with her. Thus, what a surprise it must have been to her to witness the student "who was attending school" taking to the altar another young girl that wasn't her? With the child of her beloved in her arms, the only thing left for Sabina was to wait, "barren and silent," for death (p. 550).

The stories of Isaura, Juliana, Ernestina, Domingas, and Sabina show that the African heritage also confined these characters full of virtue and goodness in their souls to sexualized stereotypes commonly attributed to women of color during and after slavery, despite their proximity to whiteness.

As we saw, the black woman and her body occupied a special place in nineteenth century literature. Considering the dialogues between history and literature, it is important to historicize this group of typologies in which the female of color was framed. In this proposal, rather than seeing the stereotype as a static category, it is essential to pull out its dynamic character, because as we can see, the meanings are altered by variables such as class and color. In this way, the articulation among race, gender, and sexuality must be understood as a privileged stage for the perception of the social conflicts within the movement of the history.

It deals not only with denouncing or deconstructing the discourse of different authors, but rather confirming the space and voice of conflicting visions surrounding the honor and sexuality of characters such as Isaura, Sabina, Rita, Bertoleza, and many others imprisoned by a range of stereotypes in intellectual discourse.

Notes

1. See Reis, 1989 and Slenes 1999.
2. The spelling in Portuguese has been updated to current standards.
3. See Graham, 1992.
4. See Chaloub, 2001 and Ribeiro, 1990.
5. "Bertoldo: *s.m.* Fool, brute"; "Bertoldice: *s.f.* Silly speech or behavior. (Bras.) Nonsense, idiocy, foolishness." See Caldas Aulete, 1958, v. I, p. 669.
6. The expression appears in Moraes Filho, 1900, p. 144: "The sultans of Bahia/ These favorite muses/Of popular poetry…."
7. The spelling in Portuguese has been updated to current standards.
8. The spelling in Portuguese has been updated to current standards.

Bibliography

Alencar, José Martiniano de. *O demônio familiar: comédia em quatro atos*. [The Familiar Demon: a Comedy in Four Acts]. (Presented at Ginásio on 5 December 1857). Rio de Janeiro: H. Garnier, 1903.

____. "Mãe: drama em quatro actos." [Mother: Drama in Four Acts]. In *Teatro completo 2*. Rio de Janeiro: Serviço Nacional de Teatro, 1977, v. II, p. 253-310.

Almeida, Júlia Lopes de. *Memórias de Martha. A Tribuna Liberal*, [Memories of Martha. The Liberal Tribunal]. 14 December 1888, Year 1, n. 14.

____. A *viúva Simões* [The Widow Simons]. [1. ed. 1897]. Florianópolis: Edunisc, 1999.

Azevedo, Aluísio de. *O mulato*. [The Mulatto] [1. ed. 1890]. Rio de Janeiro: Ediouro, 1996.

____. *O cortiço*. [The Seed] [1. ed. 1890]. Rio de Janeiro: Click, 1998.

Bell, Aubrey. "*A literatura portuguesa*" [Portuguese Literature]. Coimbra: Imprensa da Universidade, 1931, p. 447. In: SAYERS, Raymond. *O negro na literatura brasileira*. [Blacks in Brazilian Literature]. Rio de Janeiro: Edições O Cruzeiro, 1956.

Calado Júnior. "As clarinhas e as moreninhas." {The light-skinned and the Brown-Skinned]. In: Moraes Filho, Mello. *Cantares brasileiros: cancioneiro fluminense*. [Brazilian Folk Songs: A Collection of Songs from Rio]. [1. ed. 1900]. Rio de Janeiro: Seec-RJ/Departamento de Cultura/Inelivro, 1981, p. 94.

Caldas Aulete. *Dicionário contemporâneo da língua portuguesa*. [Contemporary Dictionary of the Portuguese Language]. Rio de Janeiro: Delta, 1958, v. I.

Caulfield, Sueann. *Em defesa da honra: moralidade, modernidade e nação no Rio de Janeiro (1918-1940)*. [In Defense of Honor: Morality, Modernity, and Nation in Rio de Janeiro (1918-1940)]. São Paulo: Editora da Unicamp/Centro de Pesquisa em História Social da Cultura, 2000.

Chalhoub, Sidney. *Trabalho, lar e botequim: o cotidiano dos trabalhadores no Rio de Janeiro da Belle Époque*. [Work, Home, and Tavern: The Daily Life of Workers in Rio de Janeiro in the Belle Epoque]. São Paulo: Editora da Unicamp, 2001.

Côrtes, Giovana Xavier da C. *Coisa de pele: relações de gênero, literatura e mestiçagem feminina (Rio de Janeiro, 1880-1910)*. [A Skin Thing: Gender Relations, Literature, and Femininse Mixed Race Figures]. 2005. Master's Thesis (História). Niterói, Universidade Federal Fluminense, Rio de Janeiro.

Crespo, Gonçalves. "A negra." [The Black Woman]. In: *Obras completas de Gonçalves Crespo*. [The Complete Works of Gonçalves Crespo]. Pref. Afrânio Peixoto. [1. ed. 1887]. Rio de Janeiro: Livros de Portugal, 1942a.

____. "As velhas negras. A Mme. Aline de Gusmão." [The Old Black Women. To Madame Aline de Gusmão]. In: *Obras completas de Gonçalves Crespo*. [The Complete Works of Gonçalves Crespo]. Pref. Afrâ- nio Peixoto. [1. ed. 1887] Lisboa: Edições Livros de Portugal, 1942b, [s. p.].

____. "A sesta." [The Siesta]. In *Obras completas de Gonçalves Crespo*. [The Complete Works of Gonçalves Crespo]. Pref. Afrânio Peixoto. [1. ed. 1887]. Rio de Janeiro: Livros de Portugal, 1942c.

Diário De Pernambuco, Recife, 4 January 1865.

Freyre, Gilberto. *Casa-grande e senzala: formação da família brasileira sobre o regime da economia patriarcal*. [The Masters and the Slaves]. São Paulo: Global, 2003.

Graham, Sandra L. *Proteção e obediência: criadas e seus patrões no Rio de Janeiro (1860-1910)*. [Protection and Obedience: Maids and Their Masters] in Rio de Janeiro (1860-1910)]. São Paulo: Companhia das Letras, 1992.

Guimarães, Bernardo de. *A escrava Isaura*. [The Slave Isaura]. [1. ed. 1875]. Rio de Janeiro: Ediouro, 1992.

Jornal Do Comércio, Rio de Janeiro, 24 March 1828, p. 4.

Macedo, Joaquim Manuel de. "Aos nossos leitores." [To Our Readers]. In: *As vítimas algozes: quadros da escravidão*. [The Cruel Victims: Portraits of Slavery]. Rio de Janeiro: Scipione; Fundação Casa de Rui Barbosa, [1991 s/d, a], (3a Edição Comemorativa do Centenário da Abolição).

_____. "Lucinda, a mucama." [Lucinda, the Slave]. In: *As vítimas algozes: quadros da escravidão*. [The Cruel Victims: Portraits of Slavery]. Rio de Janeiro: Scipione; Fundação Casa de Rui Barbosa, [1991 s/d, b], (3a Edição Comemorativa do Centenário da Abolição).

Machado De Assis, Joaquim Maria. "Mariana," *Jornal das Famílias*, Jan.1871. In: *Machado de Assis: obra completa em quatro volumes*. [Machado de Assis: Complete Works in Four Volumes]. (Organização de NETO, Aluizio Leite; CECILIO, Ana Lima; JAHN, Heloisa). Rio de Janeiro: Nova Aguilar, 2008a, v. II, p. 1007-19.

_____. "Revista Dramática" [Dramatic Journal] (*José de Alencar: Mãe*), *Diário do Rio de Janeiro*, Rio de Janeiro, 29 Mar. 1860. In: *Ma- chado de Assis: obra completa em quatro volumes*. [Machado de Assis: Complete Works in Four Volumes]. (Organização de NETO, Aluizio Leite; CECILIO, Ana Lima; JAHN, Heloisa). Rio de Janeiro: Nova Aguilar, 2008b, v. III, p. 1037-9.

_____. "Sabina." In: *Machado de Assis: obra completa em quatro volumes*. [Machado de Assis: Complete Works in Four Volumes]. (Organização de NETO, Aluizio Leite; CECILIO, Ana Lima; JAHN, Heloisa). Rio de Janeiro: Nova Aguilar, 2008c, v. III, p. 550-6.

Moraes Filho, Mello. *Cantos do Equador*. [Songs from the Equator]. Rio de Janeiro: H. Garnier, 1900.

_____. *Cantares brasileiros: cancioneiro fluminense*. [Brazilian Folk Songs: A Collection of Songs from Rio]. [1. ed. 1900]. Rio de Janeiro: Seec-RJ/Departamento de Cultura/Inelivro, 1981.

Queiroga, João Salomé. "Retrato da mulata." [Portrait of a Mulatto Woman]. In: *Canhenho de poesias brasileiras*. [Remembrance of Brazilian Poetry]. Rio de Janeiro: Laemmert, 1870, [np].

Reis, João José; SILVA, Eduardo. *Negociação e conflito: a resistência negra no Brasil escravista*. [Negotiation and Conflict: Black Resistance in Pro-Slavery Brazil]. São Paulo: Companhia das Letras, 1989.

Ribeiro, Gladys S. *Mata galegos. Os portugueses e os conflitos de trabalho na República Velha*. [Foreign Jungle: The Portuguese and Labor Conflicts in the Old Republic]. São Paulo: Brasiliense, 1990.

Santos, Ynaê L. dos. *Além da senzala. Arranjos escravos de moradia no Rio de Janeiro (1808-1850)*. [Neyond Slave Quarters. Living Arrangements of Slaves in Rio de Janeiro (1808-1850)]. São Paulo: Hucitec, 2010.

Sayers, Raymond. *O negro na literatura brasileira*. [Blacks in Brazilian Literature]. Rio de Janeiro: Edições O Cruzeiro, 1956.

Schwarcz, Lilia Moritz. *O espetáculo das raças: cientistas, instituições e questão racial no Brasil (1870-1930)*. [The Spectacle of Races: Scientists, Institutions, and the Racial Question in Brazil (1870-1930)]. São Paulo: Companhia das Letras, 1993.

Slenes, Robert W. *Na senzala uma flor: esperanças e recordações na formação da família escrava*. [A Flower in the Slave Quarters: Hopes and Memories in the Formation of the Slave Family]. Rio de Janeiro: Nova Fronteira, 1999.

Soihet, Rachel. *Condição feminina e formas de violência: mulheres pobres e ordem urbana, 1890-1920*. [The Feminine condition and Forms of Violence: Poor Women and Urban Order]. Rio de Janeiro: Forense Universitária, 1985.

6

ENSLAVED WOMEN IN 19TH CENTURY PARAÍBA: WORK, CONTRADICTIONS AND FIGHTS FOR FREEDOM[1]

Solange P. Rocha

> *It is useless for me to become familiar with something that I cannot change.*
>
> —Paul Valéry, 1871-1945

Three women and their fights for freedom in nineteenth century Paraíba

On November 8th, 1830, in the city of Paraíba do Norte, the black woman I recognized as Gertrudes came into my office and she told me that, in order to continue with the terms of *a civil action* [against Carlos José da Costa], that for this reason she asks this judge to make a motion to add the reverend Frei João da Encarnação and José Francisco das Neves to the suit, *she names lawyers Francisco de Assis Pereira Rocha and Feliciano José Henriques Júnior to be her custodians* to whom she gives all necessary power to seek and request her rights and justice.[2]

The document tells us of a civil suit involving a conditionally emancipated woman, Gertrudes Maria, that began in 1828 when a "petition of embargo with forced seizure" arrived to the capital to apprehend the "slave of the justified," Carlos José da Costa who owed "over 17 thousand *réis*" (currency of the day) to José Francisco das Neves, from a total of "more than 33 thousand [*réis*]" José loaned to Carlos. It was José who stated that Gertrudes Maria was the only possession that the debtor owned. According to Carlos, in the attempt to pay the debt, he had made a "lien on a straw house" that had been auctioned, but the value was insufficient to cover the debt. Therefore, from the perspective of the creditors, it was necessary to sell the other goods belonging to Carlos José da Costa.

Gertrudes Maria was a *crioula/preta* (dark-skinned black woman born in Brazil) around 30 years old, who lived in the capital of the province of Paraíba where she worked as a *quitandeira* (street vendor selling food). In 1826 she bought her letter of emancipation for 100 thousand *réis* with the condition that she accompany her "patrons" until death. In spite of the conditional freedom, three of the witnesses from the trial confirmed that in the years prior, she "enjoy[ed] her freedom, negotiating with the types of people that correspond to/with... her own power of herself, without reporting to her owners," Carlos José da Costa and Maria Antônia de Mello, but lived in "[their] company as stated in her letter of freedom."[3] However, she ran the risk of losing her conditional freedom and being traded to pay the debts of her owners. However, she did not apathetically wait for the unraveling of the legal action and sought support from lawyers to keep her freedom.

We will later see more details on this woman's fight for her "rights and justice," between 1828 and 1842, a period in which few people condemned the institution of slavery and in which Brazilian society considered this practice natural. This perspective, that judicially and morally legitimized the slave system, was gradually interrupted beginning in 1850 with the end of the transatlantic trade of Africans.[4]

Three decades after Gertrude's suit, on July 20 1858 in the capital of the province, in a new economic climate—marked by the intensification of inter-state trafficking and the valorization of the slave—Juliana requested her letter of emancipation from the Livro de Notas.[5] She was a *parda* (a woman of mixed-race, generally a combination of white, black and/or indigenous), 23 years old, daughter of the slave Luísa, a *mulata* (biracial black/white woman), and belonged to the orphan Ana Tertula Pinho who inherited her from her father. Her letter of freedom was obtained after the hearing, which included the widow Cândida Irineia d'Asenção, mother and guardian of Ana T. Pinho, along with the judge presiding over orphans who authorized that the slave remain:

> ...completely *free*, as if she had been born from a free womb, very freely, without any constraint, *I grant full liberty with no condition for the price of 1:000$000 réis, because she has been legally evaluated and yesterday gathered the public deposit* by the order of the same court, so that from today forward she can fully enjoy her freedom, without I or any other person ever [again bringing her] to slavery.[6]

In this historical experience, attention is called to the fact that the young Juliana purchased the letter of emancipation during a time of high prices for captives, with the end of the international traffic of slaves after the proclamation of the Eusébio de Queirós law in 1850, which prohibited this activity. It can be concluded that she had been preparing in advance, because she purchased her freedom for the market value (a thousand *réis*), a relatively high amount in the 1850s, and difficult to be collected by poor slaves.[7] As we will see, in addition to Juliana, other members of her family were freed through the purchase of emancipation.

Lastly, we have the story of Salústia who, at the end of the slave regime in 1885, also petitioned the courts in defense of her freedom. She was 30 years old, *preta* (dark-skinned black woman) and lived in Engenho Curral Grande in Mamanguape (north coast of Paraíba), and her "custodian" was the lawyer José Luís Peixoto de Vasconcelos. March 18, 1885 was the beginning of Salústia's defense. She was alleged to have lived "for more than thirteen years in the barbarous state of slavery, unjustly and illegally because she was not registered—not in the registry book of this municipality, nor anywhere outside of it."[8] Salústia showed, with this information, that she had some knowledge regarding the legislation of the time and sought to take advantage of these breaches to plea her freedom.

Slavery, population and economy

The trajectories of these three black women from nineteenth century Paraíba provide fragmented evidence of the fights for freedom in different decades and have in common the fact of having been born in a province of the "North," with a low enslaved population, in comparison to provinces in imperial Brazil. To illustrate, I highlight some data from the captive population of Paraíba. In 1874, Pernambuco's population was 12.4 percent captive, while a smaller province like Alagoas had 10.3 percent of its population as captives and Paraíba only held 7 percent of its inhabitants in this condition.[9]

However, this is not to say that there were few black people in this province: from the end of the 18th century, the majority of the population were of African descent. In 1798, the total population of Paraíba was 39,894 inhabitants, with 62 percent being descendants of blacks.[10] In 1811, this population grew significantly (totaling 122,407 people), predominantly black (60.2 percent), and 14.4 percent slaves.[11] According to the first national census (1872), the population of the province tripled to 376,226 households, with the majority of the people being black: 58.9 percent—of which 50 percent were classified as *pardo* (mixed race) and 8.9 percent as *preto* (dark-skinned black); only 5.7 percent of the population were enslaved.[12]

Despite slavery being considered "the base of Paraíba's economy," it cannot be denied that the indigenous groups and free people—poor and black—were important for the economic life of the province, especially in the development of export agriculture (sugar and cotton) and animal breeding. Between 1835 and 1836, the province produced 116,655 *arrobas* (measure of weight equivalent to about 15kg) of sugar and 99,804 *arrobas* of cotton. In 1848 and 1849, production significantly grew: sugar rose to 369,087 *arrobas* and cotton reached 187,914 *arrobas*. In the second half of the 19th century, sugar cane farming largely fluctuated: a production high of 574,274 *arrobas* in 1863, and a low of 300,937 in 1868.[13] The production of cotton expanded beginning in the 1860s, from 446,937 *arrobas* (1865) to 533,609 (1869), contributing to the economic and political growth of the coast and rural municipalities (between the coastal region and the interior back lands) such as Mamanguape, Areia, and Campina Grande.

Thinking in terms of the capital, which then was the City of Paraíba, it had rural characteristics although administrative organizations, commercial buildings, and religious temples were concentrated there. Surrounded by plantations and small rural properties, the landscape was vast forest area. According to Henry Koster, in 1810, the capital had a "peculiar view," with "vast, green forests, embroidered with a row of hills, irrigated by various canals that divide the river" and shaped "by lofty trees."[14] Even at the end of the nineteenth century, memoirists pointed out that, beyond the geographical limits of the most populated neighborhood of the capital, Tambiá, one could see "woodlands, true forests" that became the "hideout of runaway slaves and evildoers" (Medeiros, 1994, p. 26). The neighborhood was in Cidade Alta, where there were residences, churches, and administrative buildings. Conversely, Cidade Baixa (or Varadouro) was dominated by the port area and commercial stores, near the river Sanhauá, tributary of the main river of the province, the Paraíba river.

Fights for "rights" and "justice" to "live as if born from a free womb"

It was in this scenario, in the capital of the province—with strong ties to the rural world—where people such as Gertrudes Maria and Juliana lived. They represented a population composed mainly of blacks of different social conditions (free, freed, slave), of various colors and origins (*pretos, pardos,* whites, indigenous, *cabras* [mixed race black and mulatto], *mamelucos* [mixed race white and indigenous], "semi-whites," *caboclos* [indigenous word for copper, indicating an indigenous or mixed race white/indigenous person with copper colored complexion], and Africans). Among these groups, the majority were rural workers and city dwellers of Paraíba such as the *quitandeiras*, who moved throughout the streets of the city trading foodstuffs and small products.

The work of the *quitandeira* demanded Gertrudes Maria move frequently throughout numerous urban arteries, creating opportunities to form social networks with people—free and enslaved, poor and rich—who could help her in a crucial moment such as the judicial action against her "patron" who put her partial liberty at risk.

Throughout the lawsuit, she depended on four lawyers. The first two took care of the case for a short time and in 1830, Feliciano José Henriques Júnior and Francisco de Assis Pereira Rocha took over her defense, the latter acting in the case of Gertrudes Maria for more than ten years. Pereira Rocha was a representative of the Paraiban elite, having held many administrative positions. When he took on the case, he had not yet entered law school; however, before obtaining his bachelor's degree, he was twice the "head of government," was a part of the General Advisory Council of the Province of Paraíba (1826-1833), participated in the first legislature of the Provincial Legislative Assembly (1835-1836), and was one of the founders of the Conservative Party of Paraíba.[15] In the judicial area, he must have been a *rábula* (a provisioned lawyer, legally authorized to practice law but had not attended law school): self-taught, who worked in the position without graduating in law, as was common in imperial Brazil.

In court, the main argument of the lawyer of Friar João and José das Neves was that the "freedom papers the plaintiff put together [were] false and fraudulently made much later than the embargo ruling for forced confiscation on the defendant." Ultimately, the goal was to prove that Gertrudes was a "legitimate slave" to be apprehended and sold for the purpose of paying a debt. He further alleged that Carlos José da Costa had, in 1827, made a mortgage deed, giving the creditors the right to go to court for the debt.

Gertrudes' lawyers got seven testimonies that were favorable to her defense. One of the witnesses confirmed that she got her emancipation for 100 thousand *réis*, the amount required by her owners. Another witness highlighted that Carlos José da Costa was disreputable in the area for being a spendthrift who, marrying with Maria Antônia, received "thirteen slaves, in addition to gold, silver, and many gifts." However, all of it "he lost, wasted and destroyed with his vagrancy"; in 1827, he escaped to Alagoas, abandoning his wife who became a beggar in the streets of the capital—a statement that seems exaggerated, as Gertrudes was responsible for their livelihood, according to the other testimonies.

In Gertrudes' defense, there was also information about her efforts to pay for her freedom: results of the "costs of sweat, sacrifice, and much hardship [she was able to amass savings] to obtain her manumission and see herself free from the abomination of captivity." With respect to the testimonies favorable to the creditors, it can be verified that they were firmly resolved to receive the value of the debt and had already made contact with a possible buyer for Gertrudes. One deponent confirmed:

> The aforementioned slave [is the] last property [of Maria Antônia], seeing as her husband… found himself indebted and his creditors all had their sight on the slave, and if the creditors won, her husband still had to make the sale, for [that is] what [they] told Francisco de Amorim.[16]

As we can see, there were various interests involved in this lawsuit. On one side, the owner of a conditionally emancipated slave, with financial difficulties, trying to maintain some type of "possession" that still belonged to him; and, in that moment, it seemed to be the only way to guarantee her livelihood. On the other side, the creditors hardly worried that they would have to dispute with an enslaved woman claimed to be, and lived as, an emancipated woman. Finally, Gertrudes Maria herself who, after convincing her masters to free her, still had to litigate in the court for this freedom, given that the title had not been officially registered.

When the issue was finally decided, on April 20, 1831, the judge ruled in favor of the creditors, considering the letter of freedom "null, useless and void." Therefore, an "arrest" could be put in effect against Gertrudes, who also had to pay for the cost of the trial.

The official sentence was published almost three months after it started and four days after the ruling, and was totally in favor of the creditors of Carlos José da Costa. Getrudes' custodians entered into an appeal, which sent the trial to the superior court, the General Auditor of the District, in the province of Paraíba. There were two public hearings (July 1, 1831 and July 5, 1831), but the creditors of Carlos José da Costa surprisingly did not appear. In the following days, measures were taken aiming for the suit to be sent to the "Superior Judge," passing by the "Dr. General Auditor and Magistrate of the District, Raimundo Felipe Lobato" (August 6, 1831) and finally "the case [was] settled" on August 31, 1831. Therefore, it would fall upon the Appeals Court of Pernambuco to rule on the case, something that did not happen until 1842, the year in which one of Carlos José da Costa's creditors reopened the trial. José Francisco das Neves contracted a new lawyer, who demanded the apprehension of Gertrudes Maria and her two children because, according to the complainant, Gertrudes' custodian,[17] José Bernardino de França, allowed her "to live on a loose rein and she was living with an Indian who lived... in-house, and with whom she has two children."

This action must have surprised Gertrudes, seeing that for more than ten years she lived without being challenged by the court. But, again, she did not get discouraged, she asked for a new custodian, and was released from prison. She immediately contracted the lawyer Francisco de Assis Pereira Rocha, who resumed the lawsuit. The first hearing (April 20, 1842) only included lawyer Francisco Inácio Peixoto Flores, new representative of José Francisco das Neves, who entered into a "lawsuit" to sell Gertrudes Maria and her two children in the public square to cover the debt. However, Pereira Rocha requested that the case be continued in the superior court, that is, in the "District Court of Appeals," in Recife. However, this is the last information that we have about this civil suit. That is, on May 30, 1842, the "case [was sent] to the District Court of Appeals." Although we do not know the result of the appeal, history allows us to visualize fragments of a relationship between a freed woman and her master in Paraíba City in the 19th century, as well as aspects of slave relations, and the ways an enslaved woman in search of a new place in society perceived her freedom and acted upon it.

Juliana also had a significant experience in slavery in Paraíba during those times. Her story bears similar resemblance to the diverse trajectories of so many enslaved women in imperial Brazil, creating strategies to free themselves from captivity. However, to reach freedom, it was first necessary to face the challenges of daily life for emancipated people since society had laws and social practices that limited social participation and, in extreme cases, could lead to the re-enslavement of freed people.

To recuperate the fragments of Juliana's story, I used the "nominative connection" of sources. In this methodology, the name of the individual serves as the conducting wire in the historic investigation, in a series of distinct types of documents, allowing part of her life to be reconstructed. In this manner, Juliana's name, and that of her owners, found in the baptism registry were cross-referenced with those found in a series of letters of emancipation, which made it possible to track some of her and her relatives' strategies for winning their freedom.

Her mother was named Luísa (a *mulata*) and she baptized Juliana in the church Igreja Nossa Senhora das Neves on July 19, 1835. Her godfather was a free man, but no one was named as her godmother. Three years later, in 1838, her sister Margarida was also baptized. During this time, the three women belonged to Antônio Soares de Pinho. Fifteen years later, Margarida baptized her daughter in the same church. On an unknown date, she married Manoel Francisco Ramos and when she baptized her daughter Joana, she did it as a "legitimate" and freed woman, forming a nuclear family. With the death of Antônio Soares de Pinho, the couple then belonged to his heirs.

At 20 years old Juliana had a daughter, however, contrary to her sister, she did not marry in the church. Maria, her daughter, was baptized as "natural daughter" on February 19, 1855 under the status of "slave," having as a godfather João do Rego Moura and as a godmother Ana Sidoneia Pinho. During this time, the mother and daughter appear as the property of Ms. Cândida Irineia d'Assunção, indicating that the old owner was deceased. In some documents, Juliana and her daughter appear with their owner being the widow Cândida Irineia d'Assunção; other times being the heiress, Ana Sidoneia Pinho.

Juliana's godfather, the clergyman João do Rego Moura, was one of the founders of the "abolitionist society" of the capital, *Emancipadora Paraibana*, which had the presence of the well-known abolitionist José do Patrocínio in its creation on February 25, 1883 when ten letters of emancipation were "donated" to enslaved men and women of the province.[18]

There is no evidence that proves if Juliana lived with the father of her daughter, nor is there any evidence if he was captive, emancipated, or free. However, they must have maintained a sexual-emotional relationship because on May 10, 1857, she baptized her son, Cassiano, as emancipated. The godfather was José Gonçalves dos Reis and there was no godmother named. Our character, at 22 years old, was close to winning her freedom and was the mother of two children. Regarding her relatives, Juliana knew her mother and she had a sister who gave her a brother-in-law (slave) and a niece (emancipated). In two decades, the "slave family," formed by women, grew to seven people, with two of them being emancipated children. It is likely that there was a great effort on behalf of the parents and the grandmother Luísa to free the third generation of the family from slavery.

Additionally, the evidence relating to Juliana and her family shows the growth of the familial links in two decades: biological (children, grandchildren, and nieces and nephews), affinities (brother-in-law), and spiritual (godfathers and godmothers). It can be deduced that such relationships increased the possibility of providing material support to enslaved women and men to help them win their freedom. Through Juliana's actions, she was working towards or creating alternative pathways to gaining her own emancipation. One year after she baptized her son, her title to freedom was written up and four days later, the notary made the registry in the Livro de Notas.

In 1863, the emancipated Juliana purchased the freedom of her daughter for the amount of 800 thousand *réis*: "Ana Tertula de Pinho gave a letter of freedom in favor of her little slave Maria, 9 years old, daughter of *parda* Juliana, for the amount of 800$000."[19] Two years before, in 1861, Luísa, Juliana's mother, around 50 years old, also was able to obtain her own letter of freedom. She belonged to Joaquim Soares de Pinho, heir of Antônio Soares de Pinho. Her value was estimated to be around 700 thousand *réis*, but after negotiation, Joaquim "forgave" half the value, for the "good service" she provided, and freed her for 350 thousand *réis*, received in "legal and current tender," granting the letter of "unconditional" freedom that was quickly registered.[20] As we can see, Juliana, her mother and her daughter were able to free themselves from captivity. They could have amassed savings doing extra services or, perhaps, relied on some support, for example, from her godfather João Moura.

It is worth highlighting that Juliana lived during a time in which inter-state trade intensified and in which slaves reached their highest value. Even so, she and her family overcame the difficulties and freed themselves with the purchase of "unconditional" emancipation becoming a part of the emancipated population of Paraíba.

Salústia's story is that of an astute slave woman who was alerted that her name was not in the *Livro de Matrícula de 1873* and who, if she was able to prove that fact in court, would be able to get her letter of freedom. Thus, she filed a lawsuit under the allegation of not having been registered as a "slave." Salústia lived in Mamanguape, on the northern coast of Paraíba—promoted to a city in 1855, and eight years later, a district receiving judicial structure and attending other areas of the region as well. In the 1850s, Mamanguape's economy went through a good phase, with the development of activities such as trade, agriculture (sugar, cotton and basic goods), and coastal navigation. In this city, there were about 20 sugar plantations and mills that produced *rapadura* (raw, bulk, brown sugar) and spirits. In 1854, its population was composed of 8,213 free people and 2,150 captives, totaling 10,363 residents. Many of these residents surely toiled in the arduous routine of agricultural work and, among them, there could have been indigenous people since Mamanguape had Potiguara villages.[21] However, with the inauguration of the railroad Conde D'Eu (in 1884), linking Paraíba City to Independência (currently Guarabira), the economic activity of Mamanguape declined.

On March 18, 1885 the suit for Salústia's freedom began. Her custodian was José Peixoto de Vasconcelos, and Captain Vicente F. de Carvalho was named as her trustee. During the rapid case proceedings, the court of orphans requested certification of the index of income from Mamanguape to check her registration and twice summoned the man who claimed to be her owner (Captain João Maria

Pereira de Souza) to prove with "legal title" ownership of the slave. However, de Souza never appeared nor did he send a representative, which made the judge conclude the trial, issuing a certification that Salústia's registration was negative. However, he did not issue her letter of freedom, preferring to send the case to the district court judge, Antônio da Cunha Xavier de Andrade.

Upon concluding the trial on May 22, 1885, that judge denied Salústia's freedom, considering her registration legitimate and advised her to enter into a "suit for indemnity" with her owner. Her custodian still preferred to bring the case to the higher courts and on June 8, 1885, her case was examined by the judges of the Appeals Court in Recife, with Luís Correia de Queirós Barros as the "reporting commissioner" and Carlos Eugênio as general trustee. The latter stressed that the judge of Mamanguape did not prove that the alleged master had ownership of Salústia and, as a result, considered her free because the owner did not comply with the legal rules regarding the obligation of registration defined by the Rio Blanco law (1871). He also pointed out that the lack of any documentation proving Captain João Maria's ownership of Salústia and noted that he could be punished for committing the "crime of reducing a free person to slavery."

On October 30, 1885, Salústia's custodian requested that her letter of freedom, dated October 26, 1885, and signed by João Maria Pereira Souza, be annexed to the court proceedings of her case. In the letter of emancipation, Salústia was freed "freely with no conditions for her to enjoy as if she had been born from a free womb."

In addition to Salústia's astuteness and courage in going to court against her owner, I highlight an issue regarding the writing of her name, which could have made the beginning of her law suit possible and may have been fundamental for the favorable ending for her. That is because, at the time of her owner's death in 1878, her ownership was legalized and with the transfer of ownership, she came to belong to "Francisca Glicéria Rodrigues de Mello," and, according to law, included in the inventory was the "certificate of the registration of all the slaves... including the slave Salústia, 30 years old, under number 28 of the registration and number 6 in the list." The judge of the district of Mamanguape, Antonio da Cunha Xavier de Andrade, pointed out that there was a slave named Salústio, but in his opinion, it was a spelling error, the change of the letter "a" for "o," and this was an issue of "little importance in the case." In the closing of the suit, he recorded that he believed that the person registered was the captive Salústia, not Salústio," and this misunderstanding did not guarantee the freedom of the litigant. However, as we saw, she exploited this discrepancy to seek her freedom, according to what was stated in Article 8 of the law of Rio Branco (1871), in which the second paragraph determined that "slaves who, by fault or *omission of the interested*, were not registered within one year after the closing of the matriculation, will be considered *freed*." Then, for her name being written incorrectly, she claimed to have not been registered and sought her "rights" in the court, having complete success in her quest for freedom, since, after various judicial debates, on October 26, 1885, her supposed owner, João Maria Pereira de Souza, signed an emancipation letter, closing the case.

What the three stories have in common is the search for strategies in the quest for freedom within the slave regime, that is, seeking to take advantage of breaches in the system in different periods and junctions of slavery. It should be noted that Gertrudes' story is extraordinary for her having faced slave society in the beginning of the 19th century, when it was not common for slaves (male or female) to use the courts to defend their "rights"; contrary to the era of Salústia, who sought the courts during a more favorable time, as much in the legal aspect as in the fact of taking place during the time of the abolitionist movement. And Juliana, in the 1850s, a time of various legal changes and the hyper valorization of slave labor, she was able to buy her own freedom and the freedom of some of her relatives. Without a doubt, they are emblematic figures in the 19th century who show enslaved women played an important role in a society whose relations were guided by the oppression and domination of a significant number of people throughout nearly four centuries.

I highlight that they had some autonomy and could form savings to pay for their freedom, even if partial, to compensate their owners. Gertrudes Maria's freedom was conditional, even though we have discovered that she lived free, although precariously, between 1828 and 1842; and she created family ties. Juliana, after purchasing her emancipation, was able to "support herself" and afterward worked to free her relatives.

This type of fight for freedom was a path that—although risky and tortuous—permeated the period of slavery in Brazil, demanding great persistence, patience, exemplary work, and furthermore, intense and constant negotiation. All this for an uncertain result, seeing as it depended on various political, economical arrangements, etc. In Gertrudes Maria's case, a rupture of agreement occurred, resulting in difficult times for her because, after all, her freedom was at stake. This type of fight often required pretense in the relations with owners such as making oneself seem submissive to the dictates of the enslavers in order to convince them that he or she deserved to be "rewarded" for their "good services" and "obedience." That is, the slaves had to wear false masks to convince their owners that they deserved a letter of emancipation. In this sense, the thoughts of Joaquim Manuel Macedo in his 1869 novel *As vítimas-algozes* (The Cruel Victims) are provocative and important for understanding the actions of slaves who were inside the system. Despite the book having been written with the objective of showing the atrocities and perversions of the slave system, especially of the seigniorial family, perhaps the strategies adopted by the slave characters Simeão and Esméria are plausible; they constructed images of good servants—passive and loyal—and they deserved to receive, in the future, their freedom.

Finally, it is worth noting that even though documents showing the fight of captive women trying to obtain their own letters of freedom, or one for a family member, are predominant in Paraíba, I found a single case of a slave that refused a letter of freedom. Her name is Hilária, 41 years old, mother of Félix, 14 years old and property of Ms. Delfina Maria de Jesus. In 1883, she was considered eligible for a letter of emancipation from the emancipation fund, by the Classification Board of Cajazeiras, in the backcountry of Paraíba. This had been happening since the proclamation of the Rio Branco (1871) law, but she stated that she "did not want to be emancipated and that her mistress was more like a mother." The members of the board did not know whether to heed the request or not and for this reason, they consulted the vice-president of the province, Antônio Alfredo de Gama e Melo, who confirmed that Hilária could not "renounce the right to freedom," since renouncement would affect the "right of [her] minor child." Her request was not heeded; on February 21, 1884, she was a part of a new group of "qualifying slaves" and in less than three months was liberated by the fund.

However, it is difficult not to question Hilária's motive for refusing freedom through the emancipation fund. Perhaps it will never be possible to have an exact response; however, it is supposed that, at 41 years old, she could have felt too old to begin a new life as a freed woman without savings, living in the backcountry, which had gone through "major droughts" between 1877 and 1879. Due to the difficulty of survival, it would have been adequate for her and her child to remain with their owner, making the claim of the affective connection with the mistress a strategy for survival.[22]

Final Considerations

Through the trajectories of the enslaved women of imperial Paraíba, as in other parts of Brazil, we can identify various political actions within the system which redefined the social conditions of these women who positioned themselves before the slave regime, facing it and fighting for freedom. In many cases, fighting for the freedom of their children, conquering new spaces in slave society, becoming free or living, even though dangerously, in freedom. Such actions qualify them as historical agents and their trajectories are more relevant than what traditional historiography proposes. Moreover, the unveiling of their stories proves not only the social dynamics of slave society, but also the diversity of experiences for women in the 19th century, and the complexity of the lives of enslaved people characterized for having their own logic for action, resulting in multiple behaviors and social interactions.

Recovering such experiences contributes not only to a better understanding slave society, but also, as Del Priore (2001) confirms, to make such women from the past exist as well as making it possible to acknowledge their pains, joys, failures, and victories.[23] I further add that, presently, the actions of these historical characters have inspired political action in defense of the full citizenship of black women and men; among them, many who are not satisfied with just knowing the history, and they search, in their daily life, to transform society by fighting against existing social inequalities in Brazil.

Notes

1. This text is based on my other academic works such as Rocha, 2001 and 2009. I offer thanks for the comments and suggestions made by Cristina Lima, Vitória Barbosa Lima, and Surya A. P. Barros.
2. The facts about Gertrudes Maria are found in *Ação Civel de* GM, of which a copy is available in Arquivo do Tribunal da Justiça da Paraíba (ATJPB) [author's emphasis]. There is also a published version, published in Mello, Albuquerque, and Silva, 2005, in which the trial was transcribed by myself and Vitória Barbosa Lima. The spelling in the text was updated to current patterns.
3. ATJP, Ação Cível de Gertrudes Maria, 1828-1842, f. 136.
4. According to Reis e Silva, 1989; Rodrigues, 2000.
5. Like many historians, I used the term "enslaved" to refer to the people who experienced captivity to understand that language expresses views of the world constructed by different social subjects and, where the use of the vocabulary "slave" refers to the view of the seignorial class and as such, denies the action of the other, of the "active agent of the process of enslavement," that is, the enslaver, the owner of slaves. For a more substantial discussion, see Carboni and Maestri, 2003.
6. Manuscript document in the Livro de Notas do Tabelião José Jerônimo Rodrigues Chaves, 1856-61, f. 93, deposited in the archive Instituto Histórico e Geográfico Paraibano, doravante IHGP (author's emphasis).
7. The amount of 1 million *réis* was sufficient to buy a small rural property in the province such as a cattle farm, according to what is included in the document Inventário de Josefa Antônia de Albuquerque Maranhão (1855), ATJPB.
8. The information on the Ação Cível de Salústia (1885) is in Lima, 2010, p. 186-92.
9. See Conrad, 1978, p. 345.
10. "Habitantes que existiam na capitania da Paraíba do Norte, 1798" [Inhabitants who lived in the Captaincy of Paraíba do Norte], Arquivo Histórico Ultramarino de Lisboa, in Oliveira, 2007, p. 162.

11. The data from 1798 and 1811 are in Medeiros and Sá, 1999, p. 55. The figures from 1851 are in *Mapa Estatístico da População Livre e Escrava da Província da Paraíba* (1852). Also in Conrad, 1978, p. 353 and 359.

12. See Alencastro, 1997, p. 474 and 481.

13. According to Galliza, 1979, p. 23-4 and 43-4.

14. See Koster, 1942, p. 70.

15. Information on the life of Francisco de Assis Pereira Rocha is included in Leitão, no date, p. 18-9.

16. The spelling has been updated to current standards.

17. When a lawsuit involved a captive, he or she left the guardianship of his or her owners, being sent to a third party after the creation of a "deposit agreement" in which the custodian was responsible for keeping the "good" and returning it when required. See Grinberg, 1994, p. 22.

18. According to Medeiros, 1988, p. 39-55.

19. ATJPB, Livro de Distribuição, 1861-1865, f. 22.

20. Livro de Notas do Tableião José Jerônimo Rodrigues Chaves, 1856-61, f. 164. The letter of freedom was given on March 2, 1861 and registered on April 8th of the same year.

21. In Mariz, 1939, p .39-40.

22. The information about Hilária is in *Lista nominativa de escravos para serem liberto* [List of names of slaves to be freed], Cajazeiras, stored in Arquivo Histórico da Paraíba, Caixa 65-A (1883-1884).

23. According to the content in the Apresentação de Del Priore, 2001.

Bibliography

Alencastro, Luiz Felipe (Org.). *História da vida privada no Brasil: Império*. [History of Private Life in Brazil: Empire]. São Paulo: Companhia das Letras, 1997.

Carboni, Florence; Maestri, Mário. *Linguagem escravizada: língua, história e luta de classes*. [Enslaved Language: Language, History, and Class Struggle]. São Paulo: Expressão Popular, 2003.

Conrad, Robert. *Os últimos anos da escravatura no Brasil (1850-1888)*. [The Last Years of Slavery in Brazil (1850-1888)]. 2. ed. Trad. Fernando de Castro Ferro. Rio de Janeiro: Civilização Brasileira, 1978.

Del Priore, Mary (Org.). *História das mulheres no Brasil*. [History of Women in Brazil]. São Paulo: Contexto, 2001.

Galliza, Diana S. *O declínio da escravidão na Paraíba, 1850-88*. [The Decline of Slavery in Paraíba, 1850-88]. João Pessoa: Universitária/UFPB, 1979.

Grinberg, Keila. *Liberata, a lei da ambiguidade. As ações de liberdade da Corte de Apelação do Rio de Janeiro no século XIX*. [Freed, the Law of Ambiguity. Cases for Freedom in the Court of Appeals in Rio de Janeiro in the 19th Century]. Rio de Janeiro: Relume Dumará, 1994.

Koster, Henry. *Viagens ao Nordeste do Brasil*. [Travels in the Northeast of Brazil]. Trad. Luís da Câmara Cascudo. 2. ed. São Paulo: Nacional, 1942.

Leitão, Deusdedit. *Bacharéis paraibanos pela Faculdade de Olinda, 1832-1853*. [Paraiban Bachelor's Degrees Awarded by the College of Olinda, 1832-1853]. João Pessoa: A União, s/d.

Lima, Maria da Vitória Barbosa. *Liberdade interditada, liberdade reavida: escravos e libertos na Paraíba escravista (século XIX)*. [Forbidden Freedom, Freedom Regained: Slaves and Freedmen in Paraiban slave society (19th Century)]. Diss. (Doctoral) Recife, Programa de Pós-Graduação em História (PPGH) da Universidade Federal de Pernambuco (UFPE), 2010.

Mapa Estatístico da População Livre e Escrava da Província da Paraíba (1852) [Statistical Map of the Free and Slave Population in the Province of Paraíba (1852)]. Available at: <http://www.brazil.crl.edu/>. Accessed: 12 June 2006.

Macedo, Joaquim Manuel de. (1869). *As vítimas-algozes: quadros da escravidão*. [Cruel Victims: Portraits of Slavery]. 4 ed. Porto Alegre: Zouk, 2006.

Mariz, Celso. *Evolução econômica da Paraíba*. [Economic Evolution of Paraíba]. João Pessoa: A União, 1939, p. 39-40.

Medeiros, Coriolano de. *Tambiá da minha infância*. [Tambiá of my Childhood]. João Pessoa: Conselho Estadual de Cultura/SEC, 1994.

_____. "O movimento da abolição do Nordeste." [The Abolitionist Movement of the Northeast]. In: Silva, Leonardo D. *A abolição em Pernambuco*. [Abolition in Pernambuco]. Recife: Fundaj, 1988, p. 39-55.

Medeiros, Maria do Céu; Sá, Ariane. *O trabalho na Paraíba. Das origens à transição para o trabalho livre*. [Labor in Paraíba. From the Origins to the Transition into Free Labor]. João Pessoa: Universitária/UFPB, 1999.

Mello, Virgínia; Albuquerque, Marcos; Silva, Rita de C. *História da ordem terceira do Carmo da Paraíba*. [History of the Third Order of Carmo da Paraíba]. João Pessoa: A União, 2005.

Oliveira, Elza Régis de. *A Paraíba na crise do século XVIII: subordinação e autonomia (1755-1799)*. [Paraíba in the Crisis of the 18th Century]. João Pessoa: Universitária/UFPB, 2007.

Reis, João José; Silva, Eduardo. *Negociação e conflito: a resistência negra no Brasil escravista*. [Negotiation and Conflict: Black Resistance in Brazil's Slavery Society]. São Paulo: Companhia das Letras, 1989.

Rocha, Solange P. *Na trilha do feminino: condições de vida das mulheres escravizadas na província da Paraíba (1828-1888)*. [On the Trail of the Feminine: Life Conditions of Enslaved Women in the Province of Paraíba (1828-1888)]. Master's Thesis. Recife, PPGH/UFPE, 2001.

____. *Gente negra na Paraíba oitocentista: população, família e parentesco espiritual*. [Black Folk in Paraíba of the 1800s: Population, Family, and Spiritual Kinship]. São Paulo: Unesp, 2009.

Rodrigues, Jaime. *O infame comércio: propostas e experiências no final do tráfico de africanos para o Brasil (1800-1850)*. [The Infamous Commerce: Proposals and Experiments at the end of the Trafficking of Africans to Brazil (1800-1850)]. Campinas: Unicamp/Cecult, 2000.

7

MÔNICA DA COSTA AND TERESA DE JESUS: FREE
AFRICAN WOMEN, STATUS, AND SOCIAL
NETWORKS IN 19TH CENTURY RECIFE

Valéria Gomes Costa

Mônica Da Costa Ferreira lived on Guia street, in the neighborhood Freguesia de São Frei Pedro Gonçalves, in Recife. She was a widow and mother of two illegitimate daughters. She died at 62 years old in April of 1864. In the neighborhood Freguesia da Boa Vista, on Conquista Street, n.17, Teresa de Jesus e Sousa made her home. She was married, but she did not have children. Owner of an inheritance valued at more than 30 million *réis* (currency of the time), she also died at 60 years old—almost nine years after Mônica—in February of 1873. These two women experienced slavery and freedom: they achieved emancipation, built families, wove networks of solidarity, both inside and outside of captivity; and in business, they made a fortune. The trajectory of each one of them crisscrossed in the urban mesh of the city, and their lives are a part of a collective trajectory revealing of the formation of social networks woven by free African and Brazilian-born black men and women in nineteenth-century Recife.

We encounter Mônica and Teresa for the first time in last will and testament registries and post-mortem inventories. Such documentation enables the verification of the material life of the testators, raising questions about the complexity of the choices and negotiations made by captive men and women, ex-slaves, and free people of color in the slave society and post-abolition. The testaments, when compared with other documents (crime trials, ecclesiastical settlements, letters of emancipation, etc.), make it possible for us to follow these people by name and reassemble their individual and collective paths, reducing our scale of observation and allowing us to closely follow the unfolding of historical processes—in this way we allow subjects and groups who have been silenced by history, those known as "anonymous," to take on the role of the protagonist.

However, what importance did the 19th century society attribute to the will? Who were the people that created wills and for what reasons did they proceed in this manner? Most often, it was those who had some property or goods to leave as an inheritance, particularly the more fortunate, but also people who were concerned about their funerals. There was, above all, concern with choosing who would receive the inheritance built over the course of the life of the subject.

From this discussion, we observe, by way of reading of the wills of these two women, Mônica and Teresa, that the naming of their heirs and executors raises questions in reference to the family structure of freed slaves and the mechanisms that the ex-captives, especially the women, used to secure their social spaces in the city. Ultimately, the connections between these two women suggest the possible formation of a community of freed slaves with possessions in the second half of the 19th century.

The Recife of Mônica and Teresa

The city of Recife, much like every other urban center in the mid-19th century, was marked by slave relations, which not only defined the socio-economic boundaries but cultural boundaries as well. The capital city of Pernambuco was formed by four neighborhoods. The neighborhood of Freguesia São Frei Pedro Gonçalves do Recife was the port area, the center of merchant activities of the city. Concentrated in this place were large scale national and foreign trading houses, sugar and cotton warehouses, and the majority of "houses of ill repute." A large part of the foreign consulates were also in this part of the city, in addition to many establishments focused on the slave trade. A large concentration of male slaves settled in the neighborhood. Many manual labor jobs were performed here such as stowage; loading and unloading of barges, rafts, and cattle carts that brought cotton and sugar from the interior of the province to be traded in the capital; carpentry services, metalsmithing, and maritime repair in general. But it was not only slaves for hire who were employed in the services of the port that lived there; since the second half of the 19th century many freedmen had also settled in this locale. For example, streets such as Senzala Velha, São Jorge, Guia, and Apolo became the addresses of freed men that were employed in trade or in port activities. There was also room for domestic work, including inside the houses of the richest of the rich, where cooks, laundresses, and nurses were employed.[1] The house where the freed black woman Mônica lived was located on Guia, one of the longest streets in the neighborhood.

Mônica also owned another property in the city, in the neighborhood of Freguesia de Santo Antônio, where the church of São Francisco was located and that housed the confraternity, Irmandade de São Benedito, to which she belonged and where she asked for her body to be placed when she passed. In this area, the trade of dry and wet goods, most retail and wholesale stores, and the most numerous population of slaves—mostly black women for hire such as vendors, grocers, and *quituteiras* (women who make and sell sweets and candies)—were concentrated. The movement of women was so heavy that it became a problem routinely debated in the town council. Various municipal ordinances were applied to prohibit the movement of captive and freed women and men after 8:00 p.m. in this neighborhood because of disorder in the streets. Still, it was in this area where the finest shops in the city predominated. For this reason, it had the largest number of luxury houses, inhabited by the merchants of nearby areas. To the south, in São José, was the center of housing for freed men and women and those born free and who had modest possessions. On Santa Rita Street, where Mônica's house in Santo Antônio was located, is where the fish trade of the city was concentrated. It was also where the first artisans guilds and the popular carnival clubs of Recife emerged.[2]

The Freguesia Boa Vista neighborhood is where the black woman Teresa de Jesus e Sousa resided. It was a typical residential place, with large river-facing houses, with expansive backyards, farms, and wide streets. It was the location preferred by the "sugar elite," but also inhabited by freed Africans such as Teresa, who in addition to her single-story residence with a large backyard had other properties dispersed throughout the four central neighborhoods. Teresa was a typical example of a person with assets. Open markets and black men and women for hire completed the landscape of Boa Vista.

The census of 1872 estimates a population of more than 1,686 female slaves to 1,231 male captives in Boa Vista. That is, the neighborhood was becoming, in the final decades of slavery, a place not only of domestic slaves, but also of women. On the other hand, not only women but also enslaved men divided themselves in the daily activities of "indoor and outdoor tasks." They were governesses, wet-nurses, laundresses, cooks, farmers, coachmen, messengers, farm and garden keepers, and *quituteiras*. These jobs were also filled by the freed migrant population, from the rural areas in which the sugar industry had declined, who came to the urban center in search of better living conditions and competed with the ex-slaves for work.[3]

Statistical data is always subject to doubt. However, the census of Recife in 1872, in addition to signaling the decline of the slave population and the growth in the number of free and emancipated people as a part of the political and economic changes of the age—especially the rural exodus caused by the sugar and cotton crisis in the province—brings us to reflect on the agency of the captives in the quest for emancipation and of world of urban work, to which they were linked. For a neighborhood typical of people of the socio-economic elite, there was, however, a significant quantity of free people of color in Boa Vista including females. In this neighborhood the sum of free and emancipated black women was second only to that of the neighborhood Freguesia de São Frei Pedro Gonçalves do Recife.[4]

Family Ties and Relations to Gender

The black woman, Mônica, was the mother of Romana Maria dos Prazeres and of Antônia, both conceived before her marriage to João Antônio Marques. About the ethnic origin of her husband or his experience with slavery, we could not obtain much information; we only know that he had been Mônica's husband and was Antônia's father. Romana married Joaquim Batista da Silva and Antônia was the wife of Antônio Gomes de Moura, with whom she had two children: Francisco and Feliciana.[5]

When Mônica decided to will her assets, her husband and daughter, Antônia, had already died. Her son-in-law, Antônio Gomes de Moura, was in charge of her business affairs. It was he who guided her in financial investments. Sometimes, it was Gomes de Moura himself who took responsibility for the money that she saved. Mônica even invested 400,000 *réis* in a deal whose nature was not revealed, through this son-in-law. Unfortunately, the African woman lost this money because she declared at the time that she was broke and still involved in court, with Gomes de Moura as the cause of her financial failure.

At first sight, Mônica appears to us as just another woman among many that lived in the city of Recife in the mid-19th century. When she married, she was under the guardianship of her husband. As a widow, she was dependent upon her son-in-law, who took care of her business affairs, while her daughters cared for her in her sickness. According to the laws and customs of a patriarchal society, economic, bureaucratic, and legal matters were considered masculine, while domestic jobs were the responsibility of the women. For Mônica, being a freed African woman, this arrangement would be no more than an example of ex-slaves grouping themselves within the social context of the era; however, the patriarchal model was not always the rule.

After realizing her financial damage due to the mistakes of Gomes de Moura, Mônica took some measures to reverse the situation. To begin, she sought legal methods to recuperate her lost money. Next, she reassigned the tasks of each person in her family; she separated her son-in-law from the administration of her assets and named as her executors, first, her other son-in-law Joaquim Batista da Silva and, second, her daughter Romana Maria dos Prazeres. Mônica also made that daughter heiress to one-third of her assets. According to her, she did this because she considered Romana to have been her friend and because Romana provided good service to her throughout her entire life. Nevertheless, as prescribed by the law, spouses and blood children were already direct heirs of a third of the assets of the testator. Because Romana was Mônica's only living daughter, her part was, of course, guaranteed. Emphasizing that she would receive one third of her inheritance may have been Mônica's strategy to prevent her son-in-law Gomes de Moura from putting the family's legacy at risk once again. In turn, it was Romana who was caring for her already old and sick mother. She and her husband also began to take care of their niece and nephew (Francisco and Feliciana), whose guardianship was already the responsibility of Joaquim. He remained the executor of his mother-in-law's estate and became the head of the family after her death.[6]

It was still Mônica who dictated the rules of the house and the finances, and who even decided the future of the family members until the last day of her life. Like many other women of various social groups of the age, this African woman upheld the prevailing patriarchal model and at the same time deviated from it. There were men who could not provide for or direct their families, having to count on the help of their female companions in sustaining the house and raising the children. There were also women who managed their lives and families, conceived children before marrying, like Mônica, or that continued as single mothers. They lost their husbands and assumed leadership of the home, they traded partners, and they worked outside the home. They probably learned to better manage their relationships with their men, increasing their areas of expertise, and minimizing the boundaries of patriarchal standards of conduct.

On the other hand, the African woman Teresa was married to a black man named Alexandre Rodrigues de Almeida, but never conceived children in marriage or outside of it. She was a part of a large family, however, from her role as a godparent, collecting various godchildren, with as many Africans as Brazilian-born blacks. The couple christened nine people, children and adults, among which six were wedded parents who brought more than one child for them to baptize: Carolina[7] and Úrsula, children of João Diogo da Costa and Margarida do Rosário; Joana and Felipe, children of Joaquim Cardoso and Ifigênia de Tal; Bernardina, daughter of Francisco Lourenço and Joaquina de Tal; Ana, daughter of José Coutinho and Raimunda de Tal. Among their godchildren, there are also slaves: Maria, *creole*, and ex-slave of Joaquina de Tal; Lourença, *creole*, slave of unknown masters; Joanna, *creole*, child of a certain Maria do Pilar. The slave goddaughters probably found in their godparent's possibilities of obtaining help, mainly financial, for securing their emancipation, while the freed godchildren found, in the couple, names that would help them enter not only religious areas, but especially social areas.

When Teresa made her will, it didn't inform the strategies that she or her husband had designed to guarantee social positions in the city for their godchildren. However, it did declare that 1,200,000 *réis* would be left to them. Carolina, Joana (daughter of Joaquim Cardoso and Ifigênia de Tal) and Bernardina received 200,000 *réis* each, while the others each inherited 100,000 *réis*, when their godmother passed.[8] We don't know how Teresa's godchildren used their inheritances. With the majority of them being females, they could have saved the money to secure their future dowry, or invested in jewelry, or even slaves. With 200,000 *réis*, one could buy a domestic service slave between the ages of 50 and 60 years of age. With 100,000 *réis*, jewelry or even a sewing machine, for example, could be bought. We assume that for the *creole*s—Joana (child of Maria do Pilar), Lourença, and Maria—buying objects such as a sewing machine meant having ways of providing for themselves, having a specialized craft, an important step in the agency of "being self-sufficient." As such, the gestures that Teresa made towards her godchildren, particularly those who were captives, included, above all, mechanisms elaborated by slaves and freedmen in their collective projects of autonomy.

It is worth highlighting that the godparent relationship was a method that families found to establish alliances, protection, and mutual respect among people of the same group or of different *status*.

In other words, true relations of clientelism, in which not only were they privileged to favors, but also owing reciprocal promises of service, obedience, respect, and loyalty.⁹ It must have been this way for Joaquim Cardoso and his wife Ifigênia de Tal, as well as for João Diogo da Costa and his wife Margarida do Rosário. It seems that João Diogo and family were even neighbors in Teresa and Alexandre's neighborhood.¹⁰ Francisco Lourenço and his wife Joaquina de Tal, who in addition to being the parents of Bernardina, were the ex-owners of the *creole* girl, Maria; and José Coutinho and his wife Raimunda de Tal were also neighbors. These families strengthened their kinship ties, which perhaps already existed before they were free. They certainly solidified their friendship with Teresa and her husband, strengthening their social web.

Next, these expanded familiar ties were, in particular, characteristic of the restructuring of families of Africans who had been freed. Many times they reflected the continuity of the experiences of captivity or were produced with new networks created since their freedom. In one way or another, it was such bonds—formed by those considered relatives or by fellow shipmates (*malungos*) and colleagues—which transformed into maids of honor, best men, godmothers, godfathers, "children," friends, children of friends, "students," "comrades," "partners," and neighbors. These were always mentioned in the wills as heirs, or at least as recipients of legacy donations, especially when there were no birth parents. One example of this is what happened with the family structure by this African couple from Boa Vista, especially by way of Teresa's actions with her godchildren, godfathers, godmothers and friends.¹¹

The experiences of the family life of Mônica and Teresa reveal, however, measures of protection for their children, grandchildren, in-laws, companions, godchildren, godmothers, godfathers, and households. Also revealing are strategies of maintaining marriage as well as the autonomy of the family and kinfolk. The agency of the black woman manifested itself greatly in daily life, in which African-born and Brazilian-born black women developed and redeveloped mechanisms on many fronts, in order to change not only their lives, but also those of their family members, relatives and friends, contradicting many popularly held ideas: from the assumptions about passivity in captivity to the overlapping relations of patriarchy in freedom.[12]

Material Possessions and Social Status

As stated in the beginning of this essay, the experiences of Mônica and Teresa were peculiar, making them part of a small, almost unknown group of well-to-do Africans in 19th century Recife. They were from "Costa da Mina," the region known as the Gulf of Benin. These two *minas* (Africans from the Costa da Mina) in Brazil stood out in their commercial activities, especially the female street vendors, both captive and free, who dominated the trade in the streets and public squares of Rio de Janeiro and Salvador, with their trays of delicacies, dressed with turbans and their famous cloth from the coast (a type of shawl), that they used as a part of their outfits. The women in Rio de Janeiro, in addition to their occupations as peddlers or street vendors, were also involved in the hard work of carrying barrels of water into the city. That is, the world of urban work for *mina* African women was not limited to the trade of food or small objects. Another trait attributed to these women was that the free ones, when they made a fortune, bought slaves, especially females ones; and they also hired them as sellers (Gomes, 2007, p. 204; Faria, 2000, p. 65-92).

In Recife, the presence of *minas* slaves was small; more predominant were those from the central-west region of Africa—Angolans, Benguelas, Cabindas, Congolese, and Mozambicans. Mário Sette (1981, p. 80-1) describes the "black women from the coast," mainly those of Cabinda origin, both captive and free, as dressing in round skirts, wearing colored turbans on their heads, adorned with gold rings and bracelets, and wearing a dressy shawl. These women sold delicacies, *dendê* (palm) oil, and china in the streets of the city. "'They spoke gently in a mix of Portuguese and African' and called their customers 'Iaiá,' 'Ioiô' [shortened names slaves used for their master and mistress], '*sinhazinhas*' [little mistress]." In the second half of the 19th century, they inhabited Coelhos, the poorest region of the neighborhood Freguesia da Boa Vista.

The description given by Sette leads us to the image of a black *mina* woman in Rio de Janeiro. It is possible that in the city of Recife, as was common in Rio, the various groups of origin and ethnicities of Africans were grouped under one "umbrella": African Coast, or Mina Coast. Moreover, in slaveholding Brazil, the identifications with African nations were strategically configured. In the mid-19th century, the more specific identities were losing ground, giving way to the generic "African" and "African coast," terms that covered the more specific identifications of Africans in the same way that "Mina Coast" did.[13]

The *mina* Mônica didn't make it clear what type of work she did to sustain herself and her family, however, she created business networks with traders. Of the witnesses that she chose to record her last wishes, four were businessmen and one was the public official, Francisco João Honorato Serra Grande, who lived in Olinda, was married and a bailiff. Among the businessmen were: João Francisco de Souza, married, who lived on the same street as her; Manoel José Pereira, single, resident of Senzala Velha street, neighbor in Mônica's neighborhood; José Pinto Ferreira, single, resident of Apolo street, located behind Guia street; and Flôrencio Pereira Braga, married, living on São João street, in the neighborhood Freguesia de São José.[14] Although Mônica lived in the neighborhood with the highest concentration of business activities in the city, it was not very common in the mid-19th century for a widowed woman, apparently without any profession, to establish private relationships with businessmen to the point of appearing as witnesses in her will.

We believe that this *mina* in fact was a part of the urban trade, though we still don't have clues as to what type of trade. Listed among her declared assets was the 30 years old *creole* slave, Luzia. In addition to her residence, she also owned the house on Santa Rita Street, which she undoubtedly rented, and some objects of gold.[15]

Paying a little more attention to the witnesses of Mônica's will, we can see that she chose people who had some type of influence in the city. Businessmen, in addition to having wide range of movement in the urban area, were people of social prestige. In general, they were wedding witnesses, baptism sponsors, and executors of wills. The bailiff was already a public official who executed the mandates of judges and magistrates. In the society of the age, in addition to complying with judicial determinations, informing people of summons, subpoenas, imprisonment, bails, and licenses, the officials were also inspectors. As such, there was no one more appropriate than Francisco João Honorato Serra Grande to inform and guide Mônica in her court trials, which resulted from the failed business dealings advised by her son-in-law. Serra Grande, however, lived in another city, which makes us believe that the business networks Mônica coordinated had a reach outside of the geographical area of Recife.

Teresa was also a businesswoman. It seems that her principal economic activity was renting houses, because she owned property in every urban city center. In the Boa Vista neighborhood she owned three houses on the street she lived; two "gates" (a type of housing complex) that consisted of four one-bedroom units and six additional small rooms with only a door and no window; and five other residences in the surrounding area. In the twin neighborhoods,[16] she bought seven buildings, including houses 14 and 16 on Santa Rita Street, the same street where Mônica also had a small rental residence. On São Jorge Street, in the neighborhood where Mônica situated her own home, Teresa owned two more houses.[17]

Teresa's enslaved work force—valued at 2,200,000 *réis*—consisted of four domestic slaves: Antônia (50 years old), Joana (44 years old), and Maria (44 years old), described as "black origin," and the 30 years old *creole*, Adriana. Antônia, Joana, and Adriana also possibly prepared snacks and delicacies that were sold by the black woman, Maria, the only one of Teresa's slaves whose occupation was listed as grocer. There were still the "young of the house," who had already reached adult age such as Martinho (22 years old), Brasilina and Marcolino (17 years old), Elias (15 years old), the little boys Malaquias (almost 8 years old), and Contança and Evaristo (almost 7 years old). For half the price of their value, Teresa freed these young children and determined that they would continue to serve her husband until his death.

Rental properties and slaves allowed Teresa and her husband to build an estate valued at 30,487,000 *réis*. In contradistinction to many freed African women in good financial condition, she did not declare ownership of jewelry, another indicator of wealth and social status for freed Africans who had become rich. Different from Mônica, she didn't have objects of silver and gold, or cash in her house when she made her will. In the descriptions of travelers and historians of the age, generally African women of the coast—ex-slaves—in Recife were black women who sought luxury by way of their dress and wealth in adornments: rings, bracelets, and beads. Even though Teresa did not acquire jewelry, she must have at least been somewhat concerned with dressing well, that is, with luxurious dresses made of English cloth, which were well accepted among women with fine taste, both black and white. After all, Teresa had 10 pieces of furniture dedicated to storing clothing in her house: one dresser for clothes, a standing coat rack, two wall hangers, four tin chests, and two trunks, which were maybe used to transport the belongings of her and her husband in their travels.[18] Perhaps she was even a trader of small objects and clothes in the city? Apart from the dresser, there were more than enough trunks for a couple without children. Maybe her wealth came from the profits of possibly an occupation in retail. The buildings spread throughout the center suggest that she and her husband circulated widely in the city. The fact is that Teresa and her husband realized that the safest investments were slaves and real estate, mainly renting houses. It is likely that the income from the rental properties brought them more than just money: it must have also brought influence and *status* in the city.

Generally, in the houses of freed Africans—even those with wealth—old and used objects predominated, but as signs of the refined taste of the rich. Gilberto Freyre (2004, p. 339-42) even mentions that among the desires of the ex-captives with modest finances in Recife, above and beyond the single-story brick and mortar house, Africans decorated their homes in a way that approximated the style of the two-story homes of the rich. Mônica didn't list her furniture, however the widower of Teresa, Alexandre, didn't fail to mention each object in the residence. The couple had many pieces of furniture: in chairs alone, there were 32, of various styles, in addition to three small benches; there were pine tables, china cabinets, chandeliers, *marquesa* style sofas. There were many utensils and furniture typical of the urban elite. We assume that a residence like hers, with many chairs distributed throughout the living room and the dining room and kitchen, indicated that people sat around the table in chairs, straying from the use of grass mats placed on the floor for people to sit and have their meals, as was done in the homes of the poor. Moreover, the quantity of chairs indicated that Teresa was accustomed to having many visitors, throwing parties, holding meetings, etc. The terrace next to her house was suitable and inviting. Old and used, Teresa's furniture symbolized that this African woman had acquired a certain social position.[19]

Another way of thinking about the social place of the subjects is by way of their funeral celebrations. Until the abolition of slavery in 1888, there were distinctions between the graves of the free people and those of enslaved persons. Even though in the second half of the 19th century the grandiose burial requests among free people (and freed slaves) had lost some meaning (for economic reasons, but mainly because of the secularization that accompanied the burial reforms), they continued to symbolize a person's *status*. In Recife, with the inauguration of the public cemetery in 1851, death became a lucrative business. The funeral procession stopped being done on foot and became driven by passenger vehicles—carriages, desired by the rich and poor, with no distinction of color or social class. But it was in the quality of cloth, chains, and the ornaments of the carriages and in the quantity of these cars, as well as the total cost of the funeral, that the hierarchies were evident. For instance, a luxury carriage that cost 40,000 *réis* during the time of Mônica's death, cost between 180,000 and 200,000 *réis* when Teresa passed. The funeral expenses in general cost up to 1,794,000 in the 1870s.[20]

For not having access to Mônica's testamentary accounts, we don't know the value of her burial. But, we know that her body was deposited in a catacomb in the confraternity of São Benedito, which cost around 50,000 *réis*. If her family had buried her in a simple grave, they would have spent just 3,000 *réis*.[21] Suppose we imagine the expenses of Teresa's funeral. Her husband financed not only a first-rate funeral car with four horses, covered with blankets and rich cloth worth 180,000 *réis*, but also spent more than 176,000 *réis* on the rental of 15 cars for the burial escorts of his wife. In addition to the expenses of the music orchestra, the funeral mass in the church of Carmo, where her funeral was held, cost more than 20,000 *réis*.[22]

Intertwined Lives in the Urban Area

Until now, we have followed the individual, although very similar, trajectories of Mônica and Teresa. What now remains is to show how they were connected to the same social network. Incidentally, there were several ties that united freed people, such as family ties, from mothers and fathers that freed their children, from lovers and spouses that freed each other, in addition to the ties that originated from the extensive spiritual kinship, driven by the relationships of sponsorship and patronage. In the case of Africans, there was even a solidarity based on ethnicity, the grouping by "nation" in the neighborhood and religious spaces such as the confraternities that also acted in the promotion of the manumission of its members when they were captives; and the *candomblés* and *xangôs*,[23] in which the "nations" and the family ties frayed by the slave trade were recreated. We tracked some of these meshes through fragments of the lives of our characters. Evidently, solidarity doesn't signify the absence of conflict within the community. There were tensions among very close comrades and neighbors, cases of theft, various disputes, scenes of jealousy between lovers. Complaints to the authorities and slave owners, for example, pervade everything from the police documentation to civil sources of the time. Mônica's own experience revealed the disagreement between her and her son-in-law Antônio Gomes de Moura.

In the specific case of our two characters, the fact is that Mônica and Teresa didn't leave many indicators of friendship between them in their wills. However, they were contemporaries, they had similar life experiences, they were even business neighbors as they both had rental properties on Santa Rita street. We even believe that they attended masses together in the Igreja do Carmo church that was located in their neighborhood. Both of them were buried with the Carmelite habit shroud made in the convent of that church.[24]

These two *mina* African women, however, were closer friends than we believed. One of the links between them was Alexandre Rodrigues de Almeida. The same black man from the coast that married Teresa was named as Monica's third will executor. Generally, people select those that are closest to them to be executors because they know the secrets that will be revealed after the person's death; they are also those who are knowledgeable about business, property, heirs, debtors, and creditors. They also have in their hands the entire life story of the testator. At the very least, the selected executors were in charge of arranging the funeral with proper prayers for the soul of the deceased and a burial ceremony according to the will. In this case, the husband of one woman was the close friend of the other. Alexandre also had the same ethnic origin of the two women.

Maria Inês de Oliveira (1996, p. 177) found that Africans in Bahia, in the 19th century, even when grouped in more general descriptive categories, held onto names, personal characteristics, and life stories that referenced their past in Africa. In Recife, they must have been organized in a similar form. Alexandre, who worked in real estate, seemed to have acquired a certain prestige in the African community. In addition to many relationships of patronage and sponsorship, he was called upon by other freed Africans—such as the butcher Lívio Taques—to serve as a will executor. Who knows, maybe Alexandre had been a "partner" of Monica's deceased husband? Maybe Mônica, Teresa, and Alexandre had been owned by the same master, or their solidarity was built upon the business affairs they had in the urban center, or even the fact that they were all *minas*.

The simple fact of being free Africans with some wealth made them the minority in the city. On the other hand, freed Africans were seen as foreigners without the same rights as Brazilian citizens or those extended to the emancipated natives. They were subjected to more embarrassment and discrimination. The Constitution of 1824 did not allow them to participate in politics of the country;

they were prohibited from voting or being elected for public positions; they could not, in any manner, act in the government. In 1830, a decree prohibited free Africans, like slaves in general, from moving around freely outside of their homes unless they presented a passport—for a limited period of time—that was only issued by after an examination of their conduct.[25] On the other hand, a large part of the population of ex-slaves was poor and without any possessions: modest workers who earned the bare necessities for survival in urban areas or in the countryside of Brazilian cities during the time. In Recife, free colored people and freed slaves continued to suffer the stigmas of captivity, falling even more so on freed women, seen by society as prostitutes and disorderly people. In the fight for daily survival, they fought for work not only with poor white women, but also with captives, free men, and freed men.

However, the *minas* Mônica and Teresa, were an exception to the rule. One bias is seen through their trajectories as former African captives who attained a certain social status; another is through the economic situation of the general population who faced urban poverty and misery that covered the region, especially after the uprisings of 1824 and the drought of the 1830s. But, they were not alone. Among them, there were other freed women who did business with men and women of their time. Their experiences reflect how the African women built their autonomy facing the patriarchy and slave order in Recife.

Notes

1. See Carvalho, 1998, p. 51-3.

2. See Carvalho, 1998, p. 63-6 e p. 86.

3. See Carvalho, 2003, p. 65-8; Instituto Arqueológico, Histórico e Geográfico Pernambucano (IAHGPE), Censo de 1872, p. 10.

4. According to the data from IAHGPE, Census of 1872 (p. 1, 4 and 7), the total of free women of color in Santo Antônio was 2,956 and in São José was 3,623, totaling 6,579 in the whole physical area that encompasses both neighborhoods; the men in Santo Antônio totaled 2,854 (*pardos* and *pretos*) and in São José they totaled 6.221. The neighborhood of Recife remained in third place with just 1,053 free women of color and 1,219 men.

5. Memorial de Justiça de Pernambuco (MJPE) [Written Record of the Justice Courts of Pernambuco], Registry of the Statement of Mônica da Costa Ferreira, Mapoteca 13, Gaveta F, Livro 1862-65, f. 44-5.
6. Arquivo da Cúria Metropolitana do Recife (ACMR) [Archive of the Metropolitan Papal court], Livro de Óbito (LO) [Registry of Deaths] 34, 1862-74, Registry of the Death of Mônica da Costa Ferreira, 24/4/1864, f. 20v.
7. Arquivos da Matriz da Boa Vista (AMBV) [Archives of the Main Office of Boa Vista], Livro de Batismo (LB) [Registry of Baptisms] 11, Registry of the Baptism of the Black Girl, Carolina, *crioula*, 4/8/1864, f. 17v.
8. IAHGPE, Inventário de Teresa de Jesus de Sousa [Death Inventory of Teresa de Jesus de Sousa, Mapoteca], 1873, box 229, f. 70 (witness accounts).
9. MJPE, Testamento de Teresa de Jesus de Sousa [Last Will and Testament of Teresa de Jesus de Sousa], Mapoteca 13, Drawer F, 1873-1875, f. 3-3v. Cf. Rocha, 2009, p. 221-5.
10. AMBV, LB 11, Registro de Batismo da preta Carolina, crioula, 4/8/1864, f. 17v.
11. See Graham, 2005, p. 75.
12. See Gomes, 2007, p. 191-224.
13. The idea of an ethnic "umbrella" to consider the re-creations of African identities in Brazil was started by João José Reis.
14. Testamento de Mônica da Costa Ferreira, f. 44v.
15. On 19th century residential furniture, see Freyre, 2004, p. 339-42.
16. Santo Antônio and São José.
17. Inventário de Teresa de Jesus e Sousa, f. 21-6.
18. Inventário de Teresa, f. 15-6.
19. Inventário de Teresa, f. 15-6.
20. See Castro, 2007, p. 190-211.
21. See Castro, 2007, p. 165.
22. See Inventário de Teresa de Jesus e Sousa, witness accounts.
23. The religious practices associated with the *orixás* named in Bahia—from *candomblés*—are called *xangôs* in Pernambuco.
24. ACMR, Registro de Óbito de Mônica da Costa Ferreira, 24/4/1864, f. 20v; AMBV, LO 13, Registro de Óbito de Teresa de Jesus de Sousa, f. 44v.
25. See Reis, 2008, p. 87-8.

Bibliography

Carvalho, Marcus J. M. de. *Liberdade: rotinas e rupturas do escravismo no Recife, 1822-1850*. [Liberty: Routines and Ruptures of Slavery in Recife, 1822-1850]. Recife: EdUFPE, 1998.

____. "De portas adentro e de portas afora: trabalho doméstico e escravidão no Recife, 1822-1850." [Of the Door to the Inside and the Door to the Outside: Domestic Work and Slavery in Recife, 1822-1850]. Revista Afro-Ásia, Salvador: Editora da UFBA, n. 29/30, p. 65-8, 2003.

Castro, Vanessa Sial de. *Das igrejas aos cemitérios: políticas públicas sobre a morte no Recife no século XIX*. [Of Churches and Cemeteries: Public Policies about Death in Recife in the 19th Century]. Recife: Fundação de Cultura Cidade do Recife, 2007.

Faria, Sheila de Castro. "Mulheres forras – Riqueza e estigma social." [Freed woman – Wealth and Social Stigma]. *Revista Tempo*, Rio de Janeiro, n. 9, p. 65-92, 2000.

Freyre, Gilberto. *Sobrados & Mocambos: decadência do patriarcado rural e desenvolvimento do urbano*. [The Mansions and the Shanties: The Making of Modern Brazil] 15. ed. rev. São Paulo: Global, 2004.

Gomes, Flávio dos Santos; Soares, Carlos E. L. "Negras minas no Rio de Janeiro: gênero, nação e trabalho urbano no século XIX." [Black Woman from the Mina Coast in Rio de Janeiro: Gender, Nation, and Urban Work in the 19th Century]. In: Soares, Mariza de C. *Rotas atlânticas da diáspora africana: da baía do Benin ao Rio de Janeiro*. [Atlantic Routes of the African Diaspora: From the Bay of Benin to Rio de Janeiro]. Niterói: EdUFF, 2007.

Graham, Sandra L. *Caetana diz não: história de mulheres da sociedade escravista brasileira*. [Caetana said no: History of Women in Brazilian Slavery Society]. São Paulo: Companhia das Letras, 2005.

Oliveira, Maria Inês de. "Viver e morrer no meio dos seus." [To Live and Die in the Middle of Yours]. *Revista da USP*, São Paulo, n. 28, p. 174-93, Dec./Feb. 1996.

Reis, João José. *Domingos Sodré, um sacerdote africano: escravidão, liberdade e candomblé na Bahia do século XIX*. [Domingos Sodré, an African Priest: Slavery, Liberty, and Candomblé in 19th Century Bahia]. São Paulo: Companhia das Letras, 2008.

Rocha, Solange Pereira. *Gente negra na Paraíba oitocentista: população, família e parentesco espiritual*. [Black Folks in Paraíba in the 1800s: Population, Family, and Spiritual Kinship]. São Paulo: Unesp, 2009.

Sette, Mário. *Maxambombas e maracatus*. [Urban Trains and Carnival Dancing]. 4. ed. Recife: Fundação de Cultura Cidade do Recife, 1981.

8

UNDER THE RULE OF WOMEN: MARRIAGE AND DIVORCE AMONG THE "MINAS" AFRICAN ETHNIC GROUP IN 19TH CENTURY RIO DE JANEIRO

Juliana Barreto Farias

> *That the plaintiff not only fulfilled all the duties of a married woman; but also for her continued work and business as a fruit seller, which was already busy before her marriage, she was earning money to sustain herself and the defendant, her husband, not giving him any reason to mistreat her.*
>
> —Fortunata Maria da Conceção, Rio de Janeiro, 1848

> *The defendant, far from meeting the love that the plaintiff has dedicated to him, and in the services that she has rendered to build his fortune, and the belongings of the couple, he has neglected her, where she is lacking food and clothing, to be with his black mistress Fausta, whose house he visits every day and where he spends the afternoons and evenings.*
>
> —Maria Joaquina, Rio de Janeiro, 1854

> *The defendant atrociously beat the plaintiff, sometimes with wood, and most of the time with punches and kicks, becoming so ferocious to the point of closing himself in a room with her, as he had done on three occasions, to hit her ruthlessly, throwing her to the ground, trampling her body with his feet and hitting her many times with all his strength, for a long time, for many hours, almost killing her.*
>
> —Henriqueta Maria da Conceição, Rio de Janeiro, 1856

These short stories were extracted from the divorce proceedings that Fortunata, Maria Joaquina, and Henriqueta, three freed African women from Costa da Mina, filed against their husbands. Like many women of the time, they didn't hesitate to resort to the Ecclesiastical Court of Rio de Janeiro to free themselves of "barbaric," "vagrant," and "cruel" men. Although marriage was considered to be an institution "completely insoluble," the Catholic Church recognized that for "many reasons the partners can be made to separate, regarding the bed or the housing, for a specified or unspecified time."

In the *Constituições Primeiras do Arcebispado da Bahia* (First Constitutions of the Archbishop of Bahia) (Vide, 2010), canonical legislation dealt with the subject at least until the final decades of the 19th century. These cases were carefully clarified. In situations of "serious abuse or guilty parties," for example, the split was guaranteed when one of the spouses, "with such hatred to treat the other so badly, that living together, runs the risk of his/her life or suffers from serious illness."[1]

But, during this time, divorce meant just the separation of bodies and the division of assets in the civil court. Even though legally separated, the couple could not remarry. Since the first union had not been annulled—and annulment was only granted in extremely specific cases—a new marriage would be considered bigamy, which was also condemned.[2] Moreover, it was recommended that the divorced spouses continued living "chastely as married."[3]

Even so, women did not give up withdrawing from their marriages. In various Brazilian cities, they seemed to be the main plaintiffs in divorce requests. However, in much of the studies on the subject, slaves and emancipated slaves were practically absent. In Rio de Janeiro, the sample (20 cases) analyzed by Sílvia Brügger (1995) didn't include black men or women. Only more recently Sandra Graham (2011) published an article, in *Slavery & Abolition*, exhaustively examining the trial of a separation involving a freed Minas couple that lived in 19th century Rio de Janeiro.[4]

Despite this presumed invisibility, *africanas* (African born blacks) and *crioulas* (Brazilian born blacks) were at the forefront of lawsuits. In the Curial Metropolitan Archive of Rio de Janeiro (ACMRJ), I found 19 indictments opened by emancipated black women between 1830 and 1860. Checking this documentation from the organized content of the archive itself—which, sporadically, indicates if the plaintiff and the defendant are emancipated blacks, Minas blacks, or Brazilian-born blacks—also requires cross-referencing the data contained in different sources. For example, this can be seen in the case of Fortunata Maria da Conceição and João José Barbosa. In the nominal list of cases of the Curia, there isn't any information on the legal status, the origin, or the "color" of the couple. Yet, consulting the petitions sent to the city council of Rio, I found that Fortunata and João were freed slaves, of Mina origin and were "dealing with their divorce" in 1848.[5]

In any case, in this group of lawsuits, nearly all of those involved—husbands, wives, and many witnesses—were from Costa da Mina. It was only in two cases that it wasn't possible to determine the origin of the "emancipated blacks" in the dispute. Among the others, there were two cases of Mina men married to *crioulas* and a couple made up of a *crioulo* (Brazilian-born black man) and an African woman from Cabinda. The 14 remaining indictments were from husbands and wives of Mina origin. Despite most them having been generically identified as "blacks of Mina origin," I found in seven cases more details about their origins. In addition to two wives identified as "Mina Jeje" and "Mina Ussá" (Hausa ethnic group), there was a man "Mina Nagô" (Yoruba ethnic group). There were still three other Mina women and two Mina men that had moved from Salvador to Rio de Janeiro and were identified sometimes as Nagô.[6]

However, we can question what brought these African women to file for divorce from their husbands? To what extent did their complaints approach—or depart from—those made by other women of different origins and social status? How did they *react* to the gender standards imposed by the ecclesiastical laws and by society itself? And what did these disputes reveal about the new and old forms of identification of these ex-slaves? We examine some of these issues closely, seeking not only to understand the meanings that the Catholic marriage could have had for these men and women originating from Africa as well as evaluating what motivated the black Mina women to often quickly abdicate their legal unions.

In the "Law of the White Man"

Almost every time the black Mina woman, Henriqueta Maria da Conceição, warned her husband Rufino Maria Balita, also Mina, he asked her "if she didn't know the white law." And, immediately, he answered himself:

> [The law] mandates that everything the woman has, half belongs to her husband—telling her, for example: if you have four *vinténs* (currency of the day), two belong to your husband; if you have a handkerchief, it will be torn in half, giving half to your husband.[7]

Sticking to the "lesson," the African man used to take half of the money that Henriqueta earned with her street vendor fruit selling business, taking her jewelry, and the money that was safeguarded in a drawer in their home. For the black Mina woman, the bigger problem was that he only understood, intended, and exercised this communion of assets "to his individual advantage." Even so, she didn't give up: she continued reiterating that her husband should work as well. Only in this way the "white law" could "be seen exactly as it then should be." Finding the woman insolent for wanting to "govern her husband" and even daring to call his attention to it, Rufino would become infuriated and abuse her with many blows and insults.

The marriage of the two went bad. And in June of 1865, they were in the middle of a divorce trial. However, Rufino, although somewhat lewd, was not completely mistaken in his claims. According to the Brazilian civil legislation of that time, such "white law," matrimonies were made under the communion of assets, also known as the "license to half." As in all countries ruled by Roman law, this type of union was considered a universal association, in which the properties and the debts of each spouse, present and future, belonged equally to the two parts. Those that didn't want to follow this model had to establish rules through prenuptial agreements, which determined an exact separation of assets between the couple, but, in that era, they were not common.[8]

It is no wonder that so many were concerned with these issues. From at least the 18th century, marriage was a family affair in Brazil that, almost always, involved social and economic interests. In these arrangements, property seemed to be fundamental elements, including choice of spouse. In the richer groups, the female's family sought sustenance, security, and protection for their daughters by way of a marriage that brought a good financial situation. Men, on the other hand, sought unions that would increase their wealth, or that made them rich easily.

Among the poorer social groups, especially among slaves and emancipated slaves, there was more freedom at the time of choosing partners. But they also considered socioeconomic interests. Some personal "dowries"—such as "work potential' of a Mina female food seller, for example—seemed to be powerful attractions. Not to mention that African parents and other "relatives" would equally pressure children and friends to arrange fiancés within their own community.

In Western Africa, marriages among the Yoruba were also comprised of strategic alliances between families, and were agreed upon during childhood. Certainly, a good part of the enslaved Africans that arrived in Bahia or in Rio de Janeiro left a suitor or a spouse on the other side of the Atlantic. At any rate, when a Yoruba woman reached marrying age, a kind of engagement confirmed the arrangement, via a ritual with a cola nut, payment of the dowry by the groom's family, and feasts and offerings (*ebó iaô*) to the *orisa* (Yoruba spiritual forces). On the day of the wedding, there were also many festivities split between the house of the bride's family and the house of the groom's family, where she would go to live (Reis, 2003, p. 408).

According to Sandra Graham (2011), these new alliances brought many advantages to the husband as well as the wife. For example, an entrepreneurial merchant joining a new family could even increase her commercial networks. Men, on the other hand, could count on the economic help or advice of his father-in-law. However, unlike the situation in Brazil, in the lands of the Yoruba, the spouses were the sole proprietors of their own assets, during the marriage and after divorce. As Graham also tells us, the missionary Thomas Bowen observed upon visiting this African region in 1849, that women were free traders, who worked to support themselves, without claiming their husbands' assets, and their husbands' not claiming theirs.

In Brazil, Yoruba men and women scarcely managed to follow all the protocols of an African marriage, or even a genuine Brazilian matrimony, since they almost never had families that "negotiated" their marriages. Nevertheless, they could revive, adapt, or combine some of these practices. Separated from their blood relatives, they outlined—according to ethnic identification—the profile of a large symbolic family that often was the main channel of solidarity and organization of their lives and the lives of their offspring.[9] Living "among his own," to use the expression of Cortês de Oliveira (1995/1996), these "nation relatives" met up in specific houses, markets, religious orders, and in "spell houses." In these spaces, they were accepted, though symbolically, as children, brothers, partners, or parents of other members.

In the divorce indictments, we are able to see, occasionally, a glimpse of that ancestry of the "national family" in the marital arrangements of the Mina Africans. This doesn't deal with arranged marriages in the Yoruba manner, or in that of the families of the Brazilian elite—although it is very likely that emancipated Minas *promised* their young daughters suitors from their "people" or even from other groups. One way or another, friends, godparents, and other Mina partners did not fail to indicate and, within limits, pressure the choice of the future spouses.

To seal the union, the emancipated Minas couple formed by the street vendor Joaquina Justiniana Vitória and the cook José Guilherme were under certain *pressure* from their "nation" people. And, following a recurring theme, the couple did not have a very happy outcome. The story of the two began complicated. A slave in Salvador, Joaquina had arrived in Rio de Janeiro with her master in a brief stopover before continuing a trip to the south of the country. Since she did not want to accompany him there, she requested to be sold in Corte.

The first buyer that had appeared was the Mina, José Guilherme. Providing just half of the money, he then borrowed the rest from the black Mina João Barbosa. Entangled in debts and new loans, José ended up losing the captive to a black man, Justiniano Vitória. It did not take long, however, for Joaquina to acquire her freedom. Later, she confessed that:

> ...thus now being free, she was seduced by the defendant and by his friends who all wanted her to marry him, under the pretext that it was the best way to free herself from the market; and it was this that obliged her to take this step; however it was not of her free will, nor did it appear that she had the slightest fondness towards the defendant or the marriage.[10]

The Mina African reported all of this throughout the divorce process, which began in 1851. Surely the feelings and opinions of this age were different from those in the early days. Since they had to convince the Ecclesiastical Court of the pertinence of their complaints and accusations, many times, women (and not just African women) adopted a more convincing rhetoric or even exaggerated some points via their lawyers and custodians. Even so, these indictments and all the connected documentation are precious resources, perhaps the best, to examine, in detail, the experiences and the marital conflicts of these emancipated Africans. Joaquina's claims, for example, allow for an understanding of the influence of her Mina husband's friends and the likely motives (dismissal from the Army) that brought them to legalize their union.

Although "reciprocated love," friendship, and "deep understanding" were identified as the motivations for a Catholic marriage, other issues almost always seemed to have more influence on the emancipated Minas couples. To the Catholic Church, marriage was mainly the answer to the necessity of procreation of the human species. It was not for love that the bride and groom united, but to fulfill responsibilities: paying the marital debt, procreating, and finally, fighting against the temptation of adultery (Brügger, 1995). Among the couples studied here, a good part had illegitimate children; and none of them mentioned that more children were among the priorities of the couple. If it was neither for having new legitimate heirs, nor for escaping extramarital relations, what exactly drove the Minas "to face the church"?[11]

Like Joaquina Justiniana, the freed Jeje Mina Maria Joaquina also alleged that she consecrated her relationship with the black Mina João José Rodrigues "solely because she took pity on him, because he was threatened with being drafted into the army, and with this favor she freed him."[12] According to the Orders of 1822 (that were in effect until 1875), marriage was among the cases that exempted men from recruitment into the army or the navy.[13] We don't know, however, if this would have freed João José. Moreover, according to the claims of the black Mina woman, she had other reasons that brought her to the consortium: "Of course it wasn't for love, nor friendship she had with him, but for her own advantage, or to walk away with the small fortune he earns with the sweat of his brow."[14]

In the marital agreements and disagreements of these African couples, the women also spoke of "interest" and for their assets and "fortunes." In the mid-1830s, the emancipated Cabinda woman (of the Bantu ethnic group) Rita Maria da Conceição reported that she had married the *crioulo* Antônio José de Santa Rosa for "reciprocated love" and that they were "mutually devoted." Yet, before long, the husband began to give "evidence that couldn't be ignored that he had married the plaintiff, not for the friendship he had with her, but solely for the interest of what the consortium resulted in for him, for everything the couple has, mostly belongs to the plaintiff."[15]

In the 1850s, the emancipated Yoruba slave, Lívia Maria da Purificação, went even further. When she met the Mina man, Amaro José de Mesquita, he was still a slave belonging to Barão de Bonfim, "serving as purchaser and butler." However, according to Livia's testimony, he wanted "to live a leisurely life, handsome and equally skilled in the art of seduction, as it was his usual occupation." As soon as he met her, he was "fascinated" with her assets: 12 slaves, jewelry, and money in the Souto banking house.[16] He did whatever he could to enter the "good graces" of the African woman. They soon began a relationship and he asked her to "supply" 300 thousand *réis* (currency of the day), the amount he needed to supplement the money necessary for his emancipation. She gave him the money, but under the "condition of marriage." Amaro resisted, because he knew that if she were "well-advised," the woman would make a prenuptial agreement. In the end, he ended up "deciding to marry her" on November 23, 1857. However, three months later, Lívia asked for separation in the Ecclesiastical Court.[17]

As we will further observe, the African women had plenty of motives to be protective of their estate, and civil legislation protected them in this sense. Not all however took action like Lívia.[18] In November of 1857, a few days before marrying, she and Amaro signed a contract that established a union "according to the laws of the country, but without reciprocal transmission of assets, except those accrued after marriage and the income they have." Emancipated just three days before signing this document the black Mina man did not indicate any estate. The African woman, on the other hand, included her 12 slaves (that totaled in value 16 million *réis*), not including the other property listed in the divorce proceedings. Amaro could not, in any manner, sell, rent, or loan any of the captives. And, since she already had four illegitimate children (one of them just three weeks old and still needing to be baptized and, apparently, an illegitimate son of the Mina black man), they—and the others that she had—would be heirs of all of her goods and half of what she acquired in the "constancy of the marriage."[19]

In the cases cited here, we observe the Africans speaking directly of the reasons that brought them to Catholic marriage. However, in most cases, resentment and mutual accusations permeate their claims. Even so, reading between the lines of their testimonies and the witness in the proceedings (mainly neighbors and Mina friends of the couple), it is possible to understand what matrimony represented in peaceful times of marriage. In addition to providing a certain *status* and respect in an often hostile "world of whites," it could reinforce solidarity and mutual help between these freed people. Even caught in moments of great conflict, certain scenes described in the separation proceedings reveal a daily life of concerns with the health of the other spouse, worries of "building a nest egg for old age," and especially, a joint effort aimed at the "growth of the fortune of the couple." Among the Mina people that I have been analyzing, there was a type of implicit agreement that did not take long to be formalized: defining that the money and the assets acquired by each one, with his own work, would belong to the two, in the same way that the expenses would be equally shared. Additionally, they no longer left out issues of a more strategic nature: issues linked to the rights of inheritance, as noted by João Reis (2003, p. 410-1), the "legalization of marriages among Africans guaranteed the spouse was included as legitimate heir of the property of the couple." It was the "white law" in action. All of this seemed so important that, when these pacts were broken, or simply torn up, many times it resulted in very troubled divorces.

In Dispute

Abuse and accusations of adultery were the principle motives that brought women to plead for separation in the Ecclesiastical Court. However, almost always "ancillary reasons" explained in their petitions held more weight than the easily recognized allegation of abuse. In the case of the Mina black women, this was very evident. Not that they did not complain of their husbands' violence, or of their many lovers. On the contrary. Blows, verbal offenses, and extramarital relationships were cited profusely. Despite this, other issues seemed equally as important—if not more so—in the disputes between the couples.

In 1848, the emancipated Mina woman, Fortunata Maria da Conceição, initiated a divorce trial against the Mina man, João José Barbosa. Like many women who could not respond for themselves in lawsuits, she had to contract a custodian to represent her. In the indictment presented to the general vicar of the Diocese of Rio, it informed:

> That the plaintiff married to the defendant in the face of the church in the manner of the Sacred Council of Trent, and the Constitution of the Diocese.
>
> That the plaintiff not only fulfilled all the duties of a married woman, but also for her continued work and business as a fruit seller, which was already busy before her marriage; she was earning money to sustain herself and the defendant, her husband, which nonetheless.

> That the defendant mistreated the plaintiff, his wife, giving her cruel beatings, many blows, leaving wounds on her head and bruises on her body, to the point of bleeding.
>
> That the defendant did not have any honest occupation; he did not work nor did her care for making a living, and he only tried to destroy and squander what the plaintiff acquired with her efforts, going as far as selling the slaves that she bought as the product of her continued works, to spend wildly....[20]

Comparing the plea of Fortunata with those of the other Mina African women, there is a clear feeling that all of them followed the same script at the time of accusing their husbands. Despite the "lack of occupation" of the spouses and the dilapidation of the estate of the couple not being among the legal reasons for ecclesiastical divorce, the majority mentioned in situations such as this, also adding, that this "licentious" behavior was the cause or the consequence of a lot of adultery and excessive violence.

In 1857, the emancipated Mina woman, Isabel Maria da Conceição, alleged that the freed Mina man, Fortunato Ribeiro, was far from fulfilling his "marital duties." In addition to supporting him, she had to pay all his debts, even selling one of her slaves to pay them off. Accusing him of being a "complete vagrant," who spent night and day in game houses ("his only occupation"), she also became obliged, every morning, to give him part of the money that she earned from her business selling food on the street. When this didn't happen, he beat her so much that once, he almost killed her with a knife.[21]

Certainly, women of other social groups—including "ladies" of the elite—also complained of lack of sustenance; of the misappropriation of property, and the expenses incurred by husbands spending money on their lovers. So the civil legislation sought to protect them from the harmful actions of their spouses. The Philippine Ordinances determined that:

> ...the husband can neither sell nor transfer any property without power of attorney, or express consent of his wife, nor assets, wherein each of them has only one use and result, either by marriage; or by 'license of half,' according to the custom of the Kingdom; or by dowry. Consent of which cannot be proved, except by publicly registered deed;

and being made otherwise, the sale or transfer is null and void (Almeida, 1870).

To the Catholic Church, however, these situations were not sufficient reasons for couples to separate. Even so, in some cases, they could be considered after a trial. In 1847, the black Mina woman, Esméria Alves Correia, sought separation from the Mina man, João Pereira, because he had "become involved in a liaison with the couple's very own slave" and was dilapidating the goods of the two, spending money on this captive, going as far as emancipating her for free.

João tried to defend himself saying that the expenditures were made to settle the debts of the woman, acquired to increase her food selling business in the Praça do Mercado. He even added a receipt for the mortgage of a Yoruba slave and her son, in case she didn't pay the loan made by the Portuguese José da Costa e Sousa, market trader. At the end of the dispute, Esméria received indefinite separation, with the right to the division of goods in the civil court. In conclusion, the canon justified his decision, noting that:

> The defendant did not prove what he explained in his opposition, nor did he produce a witness, and only settled with the combination of the paper of f.18 [the receipt from the mortgage], which affirms nothing he intends to do with it, rather it gives strength to that allegation made by the plaintiff in the 4th article of the indictment: how being the head of the family, all of the good and bad of the administration of the business falls on him.[22]

The husbands didn't always let go of their defense quite so easily. In some cases, we find replies and rebuttals to the indictments of the African women. In those instances, they were accustomed to vehemently denying their accusations and even initiating ferocious counter-attacks. On the other hand, when witness testimony left no room for doubt about the "culpability" of the accused, they did not even trouble themselves with appearing in court, allowing the litigation to run its course without them. At times, they appeared, but they abandoned all opposition "with the declaration of not paying any costs" (Silva, M. B. N., 1984, p. 216).

These games of accusation and defense among the Mina Africans of Rio were, at many points, similar to those of other ethnic and social groups in various Brazilian cities.[23] However, their marital disputes bore some unique characteristics. The first was with respect to the "social roles" given to men and women. In their divorce indictments, the Mina women also made use of an entire rhetoric to convince the Ecclesiastical Court. White Brazilian women of varying status, *crioulas*, and even other African women sought to show evidence of their good behavior, because, in this manner, they highlighted the unjust mistreatment that they received from their spouses.

"Fulfilling all of the duties of a married woman," they were expected to "always keep the marital faith," living with "the greatest honesty and modesty, serving the husband without giving reason for the least displeasure." The Mina woman, Henriqueta Maria da Conceição, remembered how she always vigorously followed her duties, "never forgetting to behave with all honesty." Maria Joaquina Borges, African woman of the same "nation," also esteemed, obeyed, and loved her husband, as did "good and virtuous women," without giving him cause to engage in "the least infidelity, always behaving in an irreproachable manner."[24]

But what exactly were these "marital duties"? According to the Catholic Church—and also to the state—women, in their "ideal" state, should carry themselves as faithful and honored wives, always focused on the inside of the home, caring for the domestic space, and raising the children. Her honesty was linked to privacy, anonymity, and living indoors. While the house represented the place of reserving feminine dignity and, consequently, her family, the street was the space of the dishonest, the prostitute. The husband, on the other hand, had the role of family protector, responsible for the physical security and for financial sustenance, and watching over his wife's actions; and he may even punish her (Zanatta, 2005, p. 57).

As we see, the emancipated Mina women—by way of their custodians and lawyers—tried, at all costs, to fit into these standards expected by the church, and with that, obtaining the desired divorce. They acted with caution inside of their tenuous limits between accusing and being accused, as the canonical law itself reiterated their inferior position in marital relations and granted certain privileges to men, as Aline Zanatta (2005, p. 57) also observes. The husbands knew very well how to manipulate these standards of conduct in their favor, seeking to escape the accusations or even avoiding separation. This is what is seen in this story told by the Mina man Rufino Maria Balita. On June 17, 1856, he asked the Ecclesiastical Court for removal of the black Mina woman, Henriqueta Maria da Conceição, from the house in which she was *confined*. Throughout the course of the divorce proceedings, the woman remained in a "serious and honest home," and could only leave it with the permission of the Church or of its new "leaders." But these decisions were not always strictly followed: some did not wait for the authorization of the vicar to abandon the conjugal home. Others, even *deposited women*, continued working or leaving the house alone.

According to Rufino, Henriqueta was being "seduced" by the caretakers of her depository, the black Mina man, Venâncio Francisco dos Santos, and his wife, the Mina woman, Joaquina Matildes. Taking advantage of her "beauty and the nice features which nature has bestowed upon her," they led her to prostitute herself and live as a whore, "because even Joaquina and other people indulge themselves in this art, and become rich at the expense of the honor of the plaintiff and his wife, who has been, up until now, honest." With that, he asked the judge that she be removed and sent to another location, preferably subjected "to the power of white people."[25] Henriqueta, defended herself, alleging that:

> The people in whose house she was confined were groomsmen of the wedding: poor, yet honorable, living decently from the fruits of their labor; and thus the aforementioned Venâncio earns 2:500 daily at the Army Arsenal, and his wife with an income from her food vending and slaves earn enough to subsist decently without making use of the dishonest means that the defendant recalls....

In the end, the African woman ended up staying in their house. Yet, later, countering the indictment she opened, Rufino returned to the position against the other black Mina. He said that until then, his woman lived peacefully, "fulfilling the duties of a good wife."

However, recently Joaquina Matildes had been luring her to nighttime "dances and entertainment," without respecting him or asking his permission. Although he had claimed not to have mistreated the woman (which Henriqueta denied), he often scolded her, "giving her good advice and showing her that such behavior was ugly, and not appropriate for a woman as honest as she."[26]

It is not necessary to produce more examples that reveal how the Mina African men and women, each in their own way, used and abused these patterns of behavior to reach their objectives. Rufino could very well have been uncomfortable with the work and the constant outings of his wife, but if we examine more closely his testimonies and other details present in the divorce, we will see that it was not always like this. Practically all the Mina women involved in these processes were accustomed to peddling through the streets and markets of Rio de Janeiro ever since they were slaves. Very far from what Catholic moral teaching disseminated, they did not live as recluses in their homes; and often, they alone supported—or still were supporting—their children or other relatives. Their own husbands agreed with these arrangements.

José Guilherme was said to have "consented that [his wife] be employed in the grocery business," while he, "to increase his fortune," worked as a cook. The Mina woman, Henriqueta Maria da Conceição, labored from the time when she was a captive, as a street vendor in Largo do Capim. The Mina couple, Fortunata Maria da Conceição and João José Barbosa, before even marrying in the church, already lived together and had their "food vendor trading" in the Praça do Mercado, where they "did business together."[27]

The men and women were judged before the church according to the ideal forms of living together. Not by chance did they tend to emphasize images of themselves that, sometimes, did not correspond to their daily experiences. However, the difference of the disputes involving elite couples or even those of other social status, we can capture in their marital conflicts, experiences of shared work and a very much autonomous female life. Mina women certainly felt displeased with partners who weren't giving them food or clothing, and not even paying their rent. After all, that was expected, in that society, of a "good husband." Not even this stopped them from going out to guarantee sustenance for the family at their "own expense," or from fighting in the Ecclesiastical Court for their rights. Moreover, many took advantage of these disputes to *get even* with the slave past, when, for instance, they had helped their companions pay the *daily salaries* to the masters or even bought their freedom. Furthermore, this was another peculiarity of the Mina people that emerges from these divorce processes.

Marriage and Freedom

In the 19th century, marrying in the Catholic Church seemed to be a very complicated task. To begin with, it was necessary to file a case—known as washing or dispensing of impediments—proving certain basic conditions that would enable the bride and groom to marry. Among the requirements were, for example, the presentation of baptismal certificate and proof that the person was free;[28] hence the efforts that many couples made to free one of the spouses before formalizing their relations. After emancipation, the next step of a freed slave, according to Mary Karasch (2000, p. 474-5), was the ratification of a consensual union with a religious wedding, perhaps a symbol that their families could no longer be divided and sold separately, which was frequent in the times of slavery.

The canonical and financial barriers did not seem to discourage the freed Mina people. In Freguesia do Sacramento, the city in which most Catholic marriages were performed, 344 unions involving at least one emancipated slave as spouse occurred between the decades of 1830 and 1860.[29] Considering that, in accordance with the facts collected by Eulália Lobo (1978, p. 437-8), Sacramento counted 2,871 marriages between 1835 and 1869; unions legalized by ex-slaves (304) during this period of time corresponded to 10.5 percent of the registries made in this parish. Throughout the 1840s, there were 1,184 entries, of which 166 (or 14 percent) included emancipated slaves. From 1850 to 1859 there were 103 (or 9.24 percent) in 1,114 entries.[30]

In this set of 344 registries, I found information about the origins or the "color" of 652 emancipated slaves.[31] Among the men (328), there were 290 Africans, 36 *crioulos*, one *pardo* (mixed race with varied ancestry including white, indigenous, and/or black), and one "Brazilian." Separating the Africans according to their regions of origin, we have 114 from western Africa; 92 from central-western Africa, and 22 from eastern Africa. If we isolate the "nations"—or groups of origin—highlighted are Minas (100), Cabindas (26), Angolans (17), Congolese (14), and Mozambicans (12). For the 324 women, I found 258 Africans, 64 *crioulas*, and two *pardas* (female *pardo*). Among those with origins in Africa, 90 came from the western region; 87 from the central-west, and 13 from the eastern area. In these groups, there were 75 Minas, 23 Cabindas, 18 Benguelas, and nine Rebolos.

As you can see, the majority of the engaged had origins in the western coast of Africa. Generically known as "Minas" in Rio de Janeiro, they also were identified by their subgroups in these entries Yoruba (7), Mina Yoruba (10), Hausa (1), Mina Hausa (2), Calabar (8), and Mina Calabar (1). It is certain that the fact that many of them dwelling in Freguesia do Sacramento explains the predominance of their unions in the region. According to the Census of 1849, Santana and Sacramento were locations that united most of the African residents in the city. It was in these areas where the Minas were very concentrated,[32] which ended up making it even easier to choose a partner among their "nation" comrades.

From 1830 to 1859, 75 western African couples contracted in marriage in Sacramento. The Mina women, in the majority, chose husbands of the same "nation." Of the 90 that married during this period, 83.3 percent (75) did so with partners from western Africa (Mina, Mina-Yoruba, and Yoruba). Just five united with central-eastern Africans (two Cabindas, two Congolese, and one Benguela), three to eastern Africans, two to Africans with no identified "nation," two to *crioulos*, one to a *pardo*, and one to a man without any type of identification. Among the Mina men, also noted is this trend of endogamy, 65 percent arranged wives of the same origin. For others, we have the following division: 11 married with women from central-western Africa, two with women of eastern Africa, 11 with African women without any identification of their area of origin, and 14 with *crioulas*.

Despite studies on the marriages of emancipated slaves being scarce, particularly in Rio de Janeiro, in almost all of the analyses available, this practice of marrying within one's ethnic origin is found.[33] Usually, African marries African, and *crioulo* marries *crioula*. Even though they remained inferior in numerical terms in the capital of Rio, Minas and Yorubas became accustomed to marrying amongst themselves rather than to central-western Africans or eastern Africans. Between the decades of 1830 and 1860, 49 (or 53.2 percent of 92) men from central-western Africa married African women of the same origin in the principal church of Sacramento. But, just 16 of these couples had the same "nation" (for example, Cabinda with Cabinda; Angolan with Angolan, etc.). Unlike western Africans, the men and women from central-western Africa—slaves as well as emancipated slaves—were presented in distinct groups (Congolese, Cabindas, Angolans, Benguelans, and Cassanges were the most recognized). As such, many of them ended up choosing partners of the same African macro region, but of "nations" different than their own.[34]

In any case, these facts allow us to infer that in the *labyrinth of nations* of the Imperial Court, the freed African had differentiated behaviors in the reduced marital market in the city. Even if the majority sought partners with African origins, not all of them did so with men and women of the same region of origin. Such a choice was not always necessarily linked to the demographics of the village or of the city. The Cabindas, for example, appear in almost every major compilation of the main "nations" in Rio as one of the most numerous groups, next to the Angolans and Congolese. A good part of them lived in Santana and in Sacramento. Even so, of the 52 Cabindas that married in the latter village between 1830 and 1859, just six chose partners of their own "nation." Very different from the Minas, that, as we saw, almost always arranged spouses among their own "nation relatives." However, they were not "closed" to other groups; they tended to organize themselves ethnically in this and other markets of the city, and in social, religious, and leisurely spaces.

In the market of freedom in nineteenth-century Rio de Janeiro, men and women from Costa da Mina paid the most for their letters of emancipation. As recent analyses have shown, the prominent role of these Africans—often translated into hegemony—in paid services and in small business, contributed to their great ability to organize resources, and consequently, to the disposition they had to free themselves. In the same way, the efficiency of their "ethnic institutions," such as Catholic confraternities, mutual support groups, and family groups also facilitated the collection of these savings.[35] Moreover, many relied on loans (even the full values) offered by parents, uncles, godparents, husbands, friends, and other "relatives."

In the documents of emancipation, there are few cases in which we find more detailed information about the ways of obtaining such sums or about the people that helped them to save. Yet, comparing and analyzing diverse sources, it is possible to clarify these and other questions. Cross-referencing the marital registries of freed slaves in Sacramento with their letters of emancipation, I obtained information about at least one of the spouses among the 70 Minas couples. Even though it is not possible to estimate an average time between freedom and marriage, I found that these emancipated Africans did not wait long to marry in the church. In many of the cases, the interval was just a few months or even days.

The Mina man, Paulo Joaquim Botelho, earned his emancipation for free on July 13, 1833, and just 14 days later, he married the ex-slave, Maria Rosa de Oliveira, of the Benguela "nation." The Yoruba-Mina woman, Felicidade, and the Mina man, Joaquim, sealed their union in the principal church of Sacramento on April 10, 1854. Two months before, each one of them had paid one million *réis* to free themselves from captivity. The men, as soon as they were freed, seemed to be in more of a hurry to marry an African woman. Some black Mina women could take more than ten years to carry out a marriage. This was the case with Teresa Maria, who received her freedom for free on July 16, 1833, and only went to legalize her relationship with the emancipated Cabinda man, João Francisco, on November 23, 1844.

In the divorce proceedings, I could follow all of that more closely. For the Ecclesiastical Court, the artifices—or the sparked conflicts—to attain emancipation did not have any importance in the granting of a temporary or indefinite separation. However, in some cases, the discussion became known with force, sometimes becoming the center of the dispute. In five cases, it was the man who brought up the subject first, to contradict the appeal of the wife. As they had to defend themselves from the accusations of the women, they tried to invert the trial and tried to present them as unjust and ungrateful women. However, in the end, the attacks ended up hurting them.

In the indictment sent in 1856, the black Mina woman, Henriqueta Maria da Conceição, reported that, "following the impulses of her heart," she didn't doubt her decision to "make the sacrifice of giving the amount necessary" so that the Mina man, Rufino Maria Balita, could be emancipated, and "*so he could join in legitimate nuptials*" with her. As one might expect, the husband disagreed. Before marrying, they were "lovers and had illicit relations." Being captive, Rufino recalled being afraid to have money in his possession. As such, "all that he earned, he was putting in the hands of the plaintiff, who was already emancipated, to obtain his freedom; for this reason it seems that for those who don't know these particulars, it was the plaintiff who freed the defendant with her money."

According to the woman, that was "completely false." When he was a slave, Rufino had to give 800 *réis* to the master, José Maria Balita. However, he did not always punctually comply with this obligation, "because many days he didn't earn enough to make the *daily salary*," and then fled to escape punishment. Compassionate, "and so as not to see him distressed, persecuted, outlawed, and punished," Henriqueta gave him the amount necessary to make up for what he was missing (sometimes, for entire weeks). In this way, the African woman recapitulated; the time from the beginning of the couple's relationship to the date of emancipation of the black Mina man was about ten months. She further questioned: if he could not acquire enough money to pay his *daily salaries*, how would he be able, in this short period, to have "amounts left over to have put (as he states) in the hands of the plaintiff, and gather the large sum of 1:400$000 *reis* for his freedom?!"

Once again, Rufino contested her assertions, and even added that they were together "from the time in which they were both captives, close to eight or nine years." Wanting to see her free before himself, he gave to her what he was saving, "and did not stop buying her jewelry, clothing, and everything within his power." Since the dispute also had not ended, the custodian of Henriqueta ended the complicated dispute, again arguing:

> She freed him, even at her own sacrifice, paying the cost of his freedom; and owing to the fact that the defendant was so grateful for such a great benefit that he agreed to marry her; on the contrary, he has mistreated her continuously with blows....[36]

As noted, the subject seemed to matter a lot to the couple, but very little to the church. For this reason, the debate did not go beyond the allegations by either party or the ratification of the arguments by their witnesses. How to determine who was, in fact, "right"? Consulting the letters of emancipation issued in the 1850s, for example, I verified that Rufino received his emancipation for free on April 1, 1854.[37] If the African man didn't have to pay anything to his master, then why all the disputes two years later? Which side was the "truth"? Perhaps revealing it is not fundamental here. The point is that the divorce trials and the other documents examined allow us a glimpse at just how important the pursuit of freedom and the legalization of marriage were in the lives of these ex-slaves. Many began to live together even during their captivity. Doing *service-for-hire* work in the streets of Salvador and Rio de Janeiro, they lived "on their own" and were pocketing money for their emancipation. Like the women, especially Mina women, they were liberated easier; it is likely that they were emancipated first and later helped their partners. However, a good part of the companions also preferred to see them freed as soon as possible, because this guaranteed that their children would be born free. When they were finally no longer slaves, they ran—almost literally—to the church to legalize their relationship. With that, they earned a new social *status* and ensured the stability of their family. However, when these ties, bound with such patience, began to come apart, the wives didn't spare any efforts to break them at once. During these times, hurt and blame flourished. For these African women, to be "treated like a slave" was much more than a metaphor for the female condition.

Under the Rule of Women

Indeed, the references to slavery were not random. In her divorce indictment, the black emancipated slave, Amélia Maria da Glória, said that "she worked more than a slave, because she washed clothes, ironed, and cooked, giving all the products of her labor to her husband." In the process opened by the Mina woman, Faustina Dourado, one of her witnesses, the "white" proprietor, Anselmo Luís Ribeiro, affirmed that the Mina man, Tibério Tomás de Aquino, charged Faustina "a sum every day, a type of salary, and if the plaintiff didn't give it to him, he would hit her." Without being as explicit, the black Mina woman, Isabel Maria da Conceição, also declared that Fortunato Ribeiro, her husband, an African of the same "nation," fed his addiction to gambling, demanding from her every morning part of the money that she earned with her food vending. When she did not give him everything, he would beat her "savagely."[38]

After many years living as captives, they were not hoping to find replicas of their masters in their partners. Surely this type of complaint was not exclusive to emancipated slaves. Women of other "colors" and status alluded to this in their divorce filings. In a case from 1805, for example, Sebastiana Rosa de Oliveira complained that her husband, "in addition to treating her like his slave, doing all the work of the house as well as that of a tavern," he demanded that she go to the beach and to the grocery store to buy coal, fish or meat, although "they had slaves that [could] serve in this capacity" (Brügger, 1995). Sebastiana seemed to be fighting against the attitude of her partner more so than the work itself. For Sílvia Brügger (1995), what felt most like slavery was the fact of not having freedom of action and still receiving punishment when she didn't fulfill responsibilities that were for slaves, or those of her own husband. Although they performed different functions, *parda* (mixed race) and white women like her considered themselves equal to their husbands because they contributed equally, or even more, to establish domestic unity, since generally, they brought dowries to the marriage.

Among the black Mina women, the discontentment was similar. However, to them, slavery was an old reality, of which, only after much labor and energy, they could pull themselves away. In many cases, they had pulled away from their own husbands. Maybe some also no longer wanted to peddle in the streets or go out and do the daily shopping, and for this they got captives to do these tasks. A good part, even though free, continued in small business, alongside slaves, husbands, other "nation" comrades, or even alone. As such how could they accept returning to being treated as captives, being forced to pay *daily salaries* and still receive severe punishment when they didn't fulfill their wishes? How could they lose their freedom that was such an arduous quest?

In 19th century Rio de Janeiro, these African women were recognized for their pride and independence. As "excellent street vendors," they scoured the streets of the city, maintaining their clientele in the busy Candelária Market; they even went as far as building "small fortunes." Perhaps, as some authors suggest, they recreated here experiences they lived, or observed, in Yoruba land. There, women were accustomed to traveling through networks of markets that ranged from small villages to large cities. Mastering this trade, they acquired independence, authority, and wealth.[39]

In one way or another, in addition to inheritance or recreation of African commercial traditions and practices, the Mina women—and their husbands—knew, and knew well, how to manipulate the "white law" on this side of the Atlantic. Marrying—and if necessary, divorcing—seemed fundamental to them to maintain a life of respect and freedom. In recently analyzing the wills and inventories of emancipated Minas in Rio and in São João del Rei during the 19th century, Sheila de Castro Faria (2004) observed that a large part of them preferred not to marry and still chose to live with another *family* formed by their female slaves and their offspring. In addition to emancipating them, these women tried to teach them a more appropriate way of life and keep their estate in female hands. As we have seen, however, not all of them opted to follow this familiar pattern. For many Mina women, especially for those that kept themselves busy in stands and greengrocers in the Praça do Mercado of Rio, marriage meant, among other things, security and strengthening of joint efforts between partners of the same "nation."

Howsoever, in the group of African women analyzed here, almost all of them could distance themselves from reckless and tyrannous husbands, at least temporarily, if not forever. Faustina Dourado ended up dropping her case, and in July of 1860, returned to live with Tibério Tomás de Aquino. Lívia Maria da Purificação didn't have such luck. Her case was dismissed and she appealed to the Court of Appeals of Bahia, where she was also defeated. The rest of the black Mina women remained divorced women, since they couldn't remarry in the Catholic Church. But this certainly didn't stop them from taking care of their homes and children, peddling in the streets, preserving their estates, and even finding new love.

Notes

1. Além de Vide, see also Silva, M B. N., 1984, p. 213-4.
2. About the accusations of bigamy and other sexual sins in colonial Brazil, see Vainfas, 2010.
3. See Brügger, 1995, specifically chapter 5, and Silva, M. B. N., 1984, p. 211.
4. See Graham, 2005, the first part in particular. Other works that deal specifically with divorce in the 19th century in different Brazilian cities, but also highlight women of the elite, are Silva M. .S., 1998; Zanatta, 2005. For Rio Grande do Sul, consult Soares, U. R., 2006.
5. In the petition, Fortunata complained that her husband tried to transfer the lease of the stand where they worked in the Praça do Mercado of Rio. See the General Archive of the City of Rio de Janeiro (hereafter AGCRJ), codex 61-2-2: Candelária Market (1844-49), p.102-4. In other petitions, preserved in the National Archive, Fortunata and João Barbosa disputed, after the divorce, ownership of the slaves that belonged to the couple. National Archive (hereafter AN), Appeal Court of Rio de Janeiro, n. 7658 volume 10, 1859-60.

6. In 19th century Rio de Janeiro, the Africans originating from the western coast—especially the Yoruba men and women—were identified, generically, as Minas. Inclusive of captives shipped from the Gold Coast, as well as those that came from the Ivory Coast, and the Slave Coast (Togoland, Benin, and Western Nigeria), the expression referred to the Castle of Saint Jorge of Mina (or Saint Jorge d'Elmina), constructed by the Portuguese on the Gold Coast, currently, Ghana—encompassed almost all the people from the Gulf of Benin, from the Ashanti to the Yoruba. In Salvador, they were generally known as Yorubas. On the term "Mina" and the trade with the western coast, see, among others, Soares, M. C., 2000, principally the second chapter, p. 63-92; Parés, 2006, p. 27-9; Law, 2006. Also, Farias, Gomes, and Soares, 2005.

7. ACMRJ-LD 1174, p. 15-20. Sandra Graham (2011) also analyzes this indictment.

8. See Silva, M. B. Nizza da, 1984, p. 223; Zanatta, 2005, p. 183-6.

9. On these topics and the concept of "nation relative," see Reis, 1991, p.55. See Soares, M. C., 2000, p. 145 and 264 (notation 44), in addition to chapter 6, "Conflict and Ethnic Identity," p. 197-230; Farias *et al.*, 2005.

10. ACMRJ-LD-1907, p. 25-30.

11. Expression used during the time to refer to marriages in the church. It also appeared in divorce cases and marriage registries.

12. ACMRJ-LD-1136, p. 155.

13. On the military recruitment in Brazil, see the works of Kraay, such as the article "Rethinking the Military Recruitment in Imperial Brazil," 1999.

14. In the final considerations of the case, the lawyer of José Rodrigues further added: "…the plaintiff continues to swear that she was friends with the defendant when they married; the adversaries know very well that the word friendship is not synonymous with the verb to love nor its participle loved, or from the verb that grammar books call substantive; and consequently, few questions arise, because we are abound with expressions to singly reject them." ACMRJ-LD-1136, p. 155.

15. ACMRJ-LD-766, p. 8.

16. One of Lívia's witnesses stated: "Knowing by witnessing, that Lívia's husband threatened her multiple times, occasionally saying that he only considered himself her husband as long as she had money to sustain them, because once it was gone, he would return to the house of his ex-master where he lacked nothing." ACMRJ-LD-1235, p. 34-9.

17. ACMRJ-LD-1235 p.54.

18. Sheila de Castro Faria (2004) says that prenuptial agreements were not rare in Brazil, although they were not the rule. Even so, she claims how surprising it is

how often freed slaves appeared in this type of document. Even with these claims, the author does not present numbers or cases that show this frequency.

19. ACMRJ-LD-1235, p. 9v-10.

20. ACMRJ-LD-1026, p. 20.

21. ACMRJ-LD-1204, p. 3.

22. ACMRJ-LD-1030, p. 36.

23. See, for example, the analyses of Nizza da Silva, Brügger, Zanatta, and Marilda Silva, previously cited in the beginning of this article.

24. See ACMRJ-LD-1174; LD-1136. Even though her husband was a slave (the *crioulo* Adão), the emancipated *crioula* Maria Correa Ramos also resorted to this "model" of the ideal wife to obtain her divorce from the Ecclesiastical Court. In 1796, an indictment was sent that stated: "she was married and was received in the face of the church with the defendant, *crioulo*, Adão Xavier sixteen years ago, and for all of this time, she always served and behaved with the obedience of a wife to her husband, cherishing him in all things, carrying herself with honor to the union, and fidelity to the marriage without remarks or contrary directions. ACMRJ-LDL37, p. 6.

25. ACMRJ-LD-1174, p. 2 (justification for the removal of the deposit).

26. ACMRJ-LD-1174, p. 9-12.

27. ACMRJ-LD-1907; LD-1174; LD-1026. The Minas Tibério Tomás de Aquino e Faustina Dourado had a similar agreement: since he had arrived from Bahia, he had become a fish merchant in the Praça do Mercado of Rio, even before marrying. Faustina, on the other hand, also sold groceries in the same square.

28. The person also needed to prove their unmarried and unattached state with any institution (for example, had not taken a vow of chastity or of another religion). If the person was a widow, they also had to include the death record of the other spouse, according to Faria, 1998, p. 58-9. See also Brügger, 1995.

29. The research was done from the books of marriage of free people from Freguesia do Sacramento, kept in ACMRJ. I thank Sirlene Rocha for the help in collecting this data.

30. Also see Brügger, 1995.

31. Excluded from the example were six men and ten women who were simply identified as emancipated or did not have any identification about their *status*. The slaves and the "free" were also kept out of the analysis.

32. See Hollaway, 2008; Farias *et al.*, 2005; Soares C. E. L., 2001.

33. Faria, Sheila, *op. cit.*; Brügger, *op cit.*; Lima, 2000.

34. Among the 26 emancipated Cabindas that wedded in this period, for example, four were with Cabinda women and five with central-western African women (two Angolans, one Benguela, one Banguela, and a Cassange).

35. See Florentino, 2002, p. 9-40; Farias and Gomes, 2005, p. 117-21.

36. ACMRJ-LD-1174 and 1856, p. 3, 9-10, 21 and 51. During the interrogations, the subject was only mentioned by one of the witnesses of Henriqueta, the Brazilian Cândido Meneses, son of Mina Africans. He said that "Due to having heard from his parents who are Minas, as well as other individuals of this nation, who frequented her house, he knows that the plaintiff had been the one to give the money for the freedom of the defendant, in order to marry him."

37. AN, 2nd Ofício de Notas, Book 87, f. 79. I thank Flavio Gomes for sharing his records of Western slave emancipations, with more than two thousand entries.

38. ACMRJ-LD-1316; LD-1227; LD-1204.

39. See Graham, 2005; Soares, C. E. L., 2005, p. 193 -247; Gomes and Soares, 2002, p. 3-16; Gomes and Soares, 2007; Faria, S., 2004.

Bibliography

Almeida, Cândido M. de (Org.). *Código Filipino ou ordenações do reino de Portugal, recompilados por mandado de el rei d. Filipe I (1603)*. [Philippine Code or ordinances of the kingdom of Portugal, recompiled by order of the king, Dom Filipe I (1603)]. Rio de Janeiro: Instituto Filomático, 1870.

Brugger, Sílvia. *Valores e vivências conjugais: o triunfo do discurso amoroso (bispado do Rio de Janeiro, 1750-1888)*. [Values and Conjugal Lives: The triumph of Loving Discourse (Bishop of rio de Janeiro, 1750-1888)]. 1995. Masters Thesis in History, Universidade Federal Fluminense (UFF), RJ.

Faria, Sheila de Castro. *A colônia em movimento: fortuna e família no cotidiano colonial*. [The Colony in Movement: Fortune and Family in Colonial Daily Life]. Rio de Janeiro: Nova Fronteira, 1998.

____. *Sinhás pretas, damas mercadoras: as pretas minas nas cidades do Rio de Janeiro e de São João del Rei (1700-1850)* [Black Mistresses, Merchant Ladies: Black "Mina" Women in the Cities of Rio de Janeiro and São Jão del Rei (1700-1850)]. 2004. Thesis publication for full professorship in História do Brasil, Universidade Federal Fluminense (UFF), Niterói, Rio de Janeiro.

Farias, Juliana B.; Gomes, Flávio S. "Descobrindo mapas dos minas: trabalho urbano, alforrias e identidades, 1800-1915." [Discovering Maps of the Mina People: Urban Labor, Freedom, and Identities, 1800-1915]. In: Farias, Juliana Barreto Farias; Gomes, Flávio S.; Soares, Carlos E. L. *No labirinto das nações: africanos e identidades no Rio de Janeiro, século* XIX. [In the Labyrinth of Nations: Africans and Identities in Rio de Janeiro, 19th Century]. Rio de Janeiro: Arquivo Nacional, 2005, p. 117-21.

Farias, Juliana B.; Gomes, Flávio S.; Soares, Carlos E. L. *No labirinto das nações: africanos e identidades no Rio de Janeiro, século* XIX. [In the Labyrinth of Nations: Africans and Identities in Rio de Janeiro, 19th Century]. Rio de Janeiro: Arquivo Nacional, 2005.

Florentino, Manolo. "Alforrias e etnicidade no Rio de Janeiro oitocentista." [Freedom and Ethnicity in 19th Century Rio de Janeiro]. *Topoi*, Rio de Janeiro, p. 9-40, Sep. 2002.

Gomes, Flávio; Soares, Carlos E. L. "Dizem as quitandeiras...: ocupações e identidades étnicas numa cidade escravista: Rio de Janeiro, século XIX." [So say the Street Vendors ...: Occupations and Ethnic Identities in a Slaveholding City: Rio de Janeiro, 19th Century]. *Acervo*, Rio de Janeiro, v. 15, n. 2, p. 3-16, Jul.-Dec. 2002.

_____. "Negras e minas no Rio de Janeiro: gênero, nação e trabalho urbano no século XIX." [Black Women and "Mina" Women in Rio de Janeiro: Gender, Nation, and Urban Labor in the 19th Century]. In: Soares, Mariza C. (Org.) *Rotas Atlânticas da diáspora africana: da Baía do Benim ao Rio de Janeiro*. [Atlantic Routes of the African Diaspora: From the Bay of Benin to Rio de Janeiro]. Niteroi: Eduff, 2007. p. 191-224.

Graham, Sandra. *Caetana diz não: histórias de mulheres da sociedade escravista brasileira*. [Caetana Says No: Histories of Women in Brazilian Slavery Society]. São Paulo: Companhia das Letras, 2005.

_____. "Being Yoruba in Nineteenth-century Rio de Janeiro." *Slavery & Abolition*, v. 32, n. 1, p. 1-26, 2011.

Hollaway, Thomas H. Preface: Haddock Lobo e o recenseamento do Rio de Janeiro em 1849. [Haddock Lobo and the Census of Rio de Janeiro in 1849]. Preface written by Roberto Haddock Lobo, titled "Texto introdutório do recenseamento do Rio de Janeiro de 1849," [Introductory Text of the Census of Rio de Janeiro in 1849], reproduced together with statistical data in *Boletim de História Demográfica*, year XV, n. 50, Jul. 2008.

Karasch, Mary. *A vida dos escravos no Rio de Janeiro (1808-1850)*. [The Life of Slaves in Rio de Janeiro (1808-1850)]. São Paulo: Companhia das Letras, 2000.

Kraay, Hendrik. "Repensando o recrutamento militar no Brasil imperial." [Rethinking Military Recruitment in Imperial Brazil]. *Diálogos*, v. 3, n. 3, 1999.

Law, Robin. "Etnias de africanos na diáspora: novas considerações sobre os significados do termo 'mina.'" [Ethnicities of Africans in the Diaspora: New Considerations about the Meanings of the Term "Mina."] *Tempo*, UFF, Niterói, v. 10, n. 20, Jan.-Jun.2006.

Lima, Carlos A. "Além da hierarquia: famílias negras e casamento em duas freguesias do Rio de Janeiro (1765-1844)." [Beyond Hierarchy: Black Families and Marriages in Two Parishes of Rio de Janeiro (1765-1844)]. *Afro-Ásia*, n. 24, 2000.

Lobo, Eulália M. L. *História do Rio de Janeiro: do capital comercial ao capital industrial e financeiro*. [History of Rio de Janeiro: From the Commercial Capital to the Industrial and financial Capital]. Rio de Janeiro: Ibmec, 1978, v. 1.

Oliveira, Maria Inês Cortês de. "Viver e morrer no meio dos seus. Nações e comunidades africanas na Bahia do século XIX." [To Live and Die in the Middle of Theirs: Nations and African Communities in 19th Century Bahia]. *Revista* USP, São Paulo, n. 28, p. 176-9, Dec. 1995/Feb. 1996.

Parés, Luis N. *A formação do candomblé: história e ritual da nação jeje na Bahia*. [The Formation of Candomblé: History and Ritual in the Jeje Nation in Bahia]. Campinas: Editora da Unicamp, 2006.

Reis, João J. *A morte é uma festa: ritos fúnebres e revolta popular no Brasil do século XIX*. [Death is a Party: Funeral Rites and Popular Revolt in 19th Century Brazil]. São Paulo: Companhia das Letras, 1991.

____. *Rebelião escrava no Brasil: a história do levante dos malês*. [Slave Rebellion in Brazil: The History of the Muslim Uprising]. 2 ed. São Paulo: Companhia das Letras, 2003.

Silva, Maria B. N. da. *Sistema de casamento no Brasil colonial*. [Marriage Systems in Colonial Brazil]. São Paulo: Edusp, 1984.

Silva, Marilda S. da. *As mulheres no Tribunal Eclesiástico do Bispado de Mariana (1748-1830)*. [Women in the Ecclesiastic Tribunal of the Bishop of Mariana (1748-1830). 1998. Masters Thesis (História). Universidade Estadual de Campinas (Unicamp), SP.

Soares, Carlos E. L. *A capoeira escrava e outras tradições rebeldes*. [Capoeira of Slaves and Other Rebellious Traditions]. Campinas: Editora da Unicamp, 2001.

____. "A 'nação' da mercancia: condição feminina e as africanas da Costa da Mina, 1835-1900." [The "Nation" of Commerce: Feminine Condition and the Africans of the Costa da Mina, 1835-1900]. In: Farias, J. B.; Gomes, Flávio S.; Soares, Carlos E. L. *No labirinto das nações: africanos e identidades no Rio de Janeiro, século XIX*. [In the Labyrinth of Nations: Africans and Identities in Rio de Janeiro, 19th Century]. Rio de Janeiro: Arquivo Nacional, 2005, p. 193-247.

____. "Negras minas no Rio de Janeiro: gênero, nação e trabalho urbano no século XIX." [Black "Mina" Women in Rio de Janeiro: Gender, Nation, and Urban Labor in the 19th Century]. In: Soares, Mariza C. (Org.). *Rotas atlânticas da diáspora Africana*. [Atlantic Routes of the African Diaspora]. Eduff, 2007, p. 191-224.

Soares, Mariza C. *Devotos da cor: identidade étnica, religiosidade e escravidão no Rio de Janeiro*. [Devotees of Color: Ethnic Identity, Religiosity, and Slavery in Rio de Janeiro]. Rio de Janeiro: Civilização Brasileira, 2000.

Soares, Ubirathan R. *Os processos de divórcio perpétuo nos séculos XVIII e XIX: entre o sistema de aliança e o regime da sexualidade*. [Divorce Cases made in the 18th and 19th Centuries: Between the System of Alliance and the Regime of Sexuality]. Diss. (Doctoral). Porto Alegre, Programa de Pós-Graduação em História, Universidade Federal do Rio Grande do Sul (UFRGS), 2006.

Vainfas, Ronaldo. *Trópico dos pecados: moral, sexualidade e Inquisição no Brasil colonial*. [Tropic of Sins: Morality, Sexuality, and the Brazilian Colonial Inquisition]. 2. ed. Rio de Janeiro: Nova Fronteira, 2010.

Vide, Sebastião Monteiro de. *Constituições primeiras do Arcebispado da Bahia*. [First Constitutions of the Archbishop of Bahia]. Eds. Bruno Feltier and Evergton Sales Sousa. São Paulo: Edusp, 2010.

Zanatta, Aline A. *Justiça e representações femininas: o divórcio entre a elite paulista (1765-1822)*. [Justice and Feminine Representations: Divorce Among the São Paulo Elite (1765-1822)]. 2005. Master's Thesis (História). Universidade Estadual de Campinas (Unicamp). Campinas, SP.

9

A CERTAIN FREEDOM

Sandra Lauderdale Graham

Only a wide and intricate mosaic would be able to portray the history of black women in Brazil; so richly complex and diverse are their origins in Africa and in Brazil, their many languages and dialects, religious practices, ways of work, marrying, having and taking care of children, the ways in which they were enslaved, and how some of them returned to being free. There is not a single story that tells it all. Instead, here is the history of some women—a slave born in Brazil, the others born free in Africa and brought by force across the Atlantic as slaves. I cannot say that the stories are typical, but they do allow us to catch a glimpse of specific black women in distinct situations. The particularities of their experiences reveal options that they identified for themselves or forged while they were trying to obtain what they wanted, the earnings they made, the prices they paid, and the difficulties they faced. I found these women in archives in Bahia and Rio de Janeiro and in the coffee producing regions of the valley of Paraíba—fragments of lives captured in small packets of old papers, although they lived in a much larger world.

Comparing these women reveals that they were different in many aspects—the families they lived in, the work they did, their age, their cultural and ethnic origin, the economy they worked in, and the social ties they formed. But, what stands out and unifies the various aspects of their lives is the fact that each one had lived in the country or in the city. Slaves and freed women traveled through the city, getting to know its streets and squares. They came across many different kinds of people and were able to make a place for themselves in the midst of a variety of people. They could better control their own lives—make choices. A certain degree of independence was possible and necessary in the city. The rural zone, on the other hand, reduced to farmhouses far from one another, seemed more confining, more limiting. The slaves were not used to leaving the farm alone unless work required them to do so; and even so, only the most trustworthy—a mule team driver, for example, could transport coffee to the nearest port. The plantations and workshops were generally visible from the big house, and the captains patrolled the fields. Vigilance was constant. Differences mattered.

Florença da Silva, knowing that her daughter Balbina had been sold by her master, decided to sue for her daughter's freedom in April of 1862.[1] Writing to Balbina and the man who she thought to be the current owner of her daughter, Manoel Esteves Otoni, she initiated a series of inquiries and initiatives. First, she warned Balbina: "Treat your masters very well so they have pity on you, in order to help me in my [intent]."[2] Later, she appealed to Otoni requesting that he might do the favor of freeing Balbina for a certain price. The distance that separated the actors of this short drama was discouraging. Florença believed that her letter, sent from her city, Grão Mogol, in the far northeast of Minas Gerais, would reach Otoni in the remote south of the city of Filadélfia (current Teófilo Otoni), a region that was just beginning to develop; it was still not a place with good communication. However, the letter arrived, even though we do not know how long it took to be carried from one little city to the other. By the time Otoni read it however, Balbina had already been sold to his wife's uncle, João Vieira Machado da Cunha, rich farmer in the city of Valença in the valley of Paraíba, very far from Filadélfia and even further from Grão Mogol. The social ties and the commercial calculations added to the geographic distance made Balbina's freedom more tangled and less certain. From Otoni's point of view, the sale of a valuable domestic slave made sense. He had moved to Filadélfia some years before to work on a large colonization program directed by his cousin Teófilo Otoni, who had opened an access point to the ocean for the lands of Minas Gerais, which ran through Santa Clara, along the Mucuri river, allowing goods to be shipped both upstream and downstream to the coast. Teófilo also tried to tear down the forest and open the lands to cultivate coffee and sugar on a commercial level, driving away the Indians and substituting them, not with slaves—he was against slavery and wanted to free himself from the dependence upon slave labor—but with European immigrants hired as settlers to work on lots of land that would eventually be theirs.[3]

Manoel Esteves Otoni supervised the construction of warehouses, docks, a brickyard, and a dredging from the falls of Santa Clara to the mouth of the river, while another brother and a cousin accompanied the construction and plantation in Filadélfia and created methods of communication by way of land, constructing the road that would link Santa Clara to Fildélfia.[4] During these years, Manoel also had time to clear a large area of the forest to raise his crops in Fildélfia, which he called Fazenda de Itamonhec, with sugar cane and corn plantations, extensive pastures, and sturdy buildings. On his farm, his wife had his six children, having the first in 1851 or 1852. When Manoel planted roots in the colony, he apparently did not have any misgivings about using slaves on his property. Balbina became one of these slaves, surely as a domestic slave working in the house. Could it be that she was one of the "seven very decorated slaves," servants that showed the "wealth" of their master?[5]

Despite these first years of enthusiasm and expectation, in 1858 things were already going poorly for almost all involved in the project. A report that was requested by the Brazilian government and written by a German doctor was gloomy. About 500 settlers worked without a place to live or adequate food, while the healthiest ones did what they could to perform the intensive work of clearing the forest and planting. All of the families had members that were sick, dying, or dead. Some seemed to be exhausted and defeated; others moved about with wounds and painful cuts on their legs and feet;

one woman gave birth with no assistance; others were fallen by fever; others died of typhus. Those that complained were punished; their letters, censored. And those that escaped in search of a coastal city were returned by company workers and obligated to fulfill the contract.[6] Paradoxically, a slave like Balbina, a member of the family of her owners, received care much better than the settlers.

In 1862, when Florença sent that letter, Manoel's investment had weakened and he spoke of "our displacement, abandoning our property that has cost us so much. I am so overwhelmed with tasks," as he wrote to his uncle.[7] Manoel certainly had sufficient motive to sell a slave. If the slaves were accustomed to being terrified of being sold to an unknown master in a strange place, Balbina, who in the end changed hands within a large family, must have—in such circumstances—felt alleviated to leave this den of disease and unfruitful hopes.

In the same letter, Manoel wrote about "a great obligation he had for the freedom of a slave named Balbina." The mother wants to know "if he agrees to giving her freedom, and for how much." He attached Florença's letter, adding: "You will find [the letter] to do as you see fit"—recognizing his role as a mere intermediary, indicating his position on the issue, but leaving the decision to his uncle. The words of Manoel Esteves Otoni sound serious and pressing, strong for a man who owned slaves. His uncle must have listened when he spoke of this person.

Could it be that the uncle would be willing to free the slave that he had just purchased and for which he probably paid a tidy sum? Exactly during this period, between 1860 and 1864, the price of slaves born in Brazil, such as Balbina, between 15 and 40 years old, reached its peak in Minas. Although the residents of the place did not have tables and graphs available for the time, they certainly knew that they paid more for the slaves in recent years, perhaps attributing this increase to the end of the traffic of African slaves in 1850.[8] João Vieira Machado da Cunha was a rich farmer and an experienced owner of slaves. He must have known Balbina's value. If he agreed, João Vieira must have acted quickly because, although no one knew this in January of 1863, by the end of November, he would be dead and Balbina would belong to his estate, to be given to an heir along with his other possessions, or sold to pay for debts.[9] Even though João Vieira had agreed with the sale in time, the issue of money remained. It seems unlikely that Balbina, a domestic slave, taken three times from a remote, rural residence to another, had any way to earn the money necessary to purchase her freedom. Would her mother pay? Was she able to pay? We do not know.

In contrast, how is it that an urban slave would be able to succeed in an independent life? We think of three women whose life experiences differed in every way from Balbina, but whose lives reveal great similarities. All three were urban slaves and each one worked "for hire," renting out their services, perhaps living on their own and pocketing any money they earned beyond the amount paid to their owner for their daily or weekly payment. With this extra money, each woman saved sufficiently to buy her freedom. And much more. How did they do this?

Different from the slave Balbina, who inherited her slave status from her mother, Sabina da Cruz, Rosa do O'Freire and Henriqueta Maria da Conceição began life as free people in Africa.[10] Each one was sold through the slave trade to Bahia. Sabina and Rosa remained in Salvador, and Henriqueta was sold to a new owner in Rio de Janeiro.[11]

Rosa do O'Freire is said to have come from the "African Coast" to Salvador "at a young age" without her parents, who remained in Africa. Sabina da Cruz said "I came from my land of Africa, where I was born, arriving in this capital many years ago," without the date or her age at that time.[12] Inevitably, the memories of Africa that these women had varied. Rosa did not have any memories to construct anything that resembled an African identity in Brazil. What she learned of her African roots had been heard not from her parents (it was in Brazil that she received notice of their death), but from others, who were older than her, that came to the country and told her stories about Africa. At most, Sabina had the sparse memories that every child has, perhaps embellished by the later tales of others.

Only Henriqueta Maria da Conceição, taken as a young girl from Costa da Mina, could remember an authentic African past.[13] To a certain degree, all three took from their African heritage, whether invented or remembered, material to construct their lives in Brazil. Selling in the market was what most African women did; whether in their villas, traveling to other villas, sometimes alone, sometimes in caravans, collecting as much prestige as wealth.[14] Henriqueta and Sabina—and probably Rosa too—became traveling saleswomen or merchants, first as slaves, later as freed women, fulfilling in Brazil the occupations they could have had in Africa.

Henriqueta

As a slave, Henriqueta sold *quitanda* (fruits, vegetables, and other small grocery items) in the streets with a big basket balanced on her head, in her neighborhood of Santa Rita, near the pier of Rio de Janeiro. It was a hard job, competitive. She shared the space not only with men and black Brazilian-born women, but also with many African women.[15] In July of 1853, she had saved enough money, 1:300$000 (one *conto* and 300 thousand *réis*—currencies of the day) in cash, to buy her freedom from Roza Maria de Jesus, who, judging by the name, was probably a freed black woman herself. Without a doubt, Roza Maria understood the importance of the piece of paper that she, being illiterate, dictated to the scribe. "And to be clear and for [her] to present where she sees fit, I give this letter of freedom."[16] Henriqueta was an ambitious and successful saleswoman. Less than one year later, in April of 1854, she also purchased the freedom of the African man she wanted to marry. However, this exhausted her resources and she borrowed about one-third of the money, which she quickly repaid.[17]

The marriage that she had planned for such a long time, insisting that they married as free people, quickly unraveled in violence and bitterness. The marriage was realized in January of 1855 and it ended a year and a half later in June 1856 when Henriqueta asked the church for an ecclesiastical separation, with the argument that her husband continuously caused her serious bodily injury. Witnesses described her body as full of "wounds" and "her face was bloody."[18] What was also as important to Henriqueta, however, were her husband's debts, which she paid. Since she bought fruits and vegetables on credit to sell, it was essential that she maintained her reputation as a trustworthy woman who paid her bills. Henriqueta wanted a separation to protect her good name as well as her physical well-being. With the separation being granted by the church, she went to a civil court to permanently split their property, which was nothing, because everything had been consumed by her husband's debts. At least she would no longer be responsible for them.[19] She continued to sell *quitanda* as a freed woman and, in 1861, proving her success, she was able to acquire two stalls in the square of Rosário, with a charter from the city.[20] The interval between the events was painful, but Henriqueta resurged recuperated and perhaps was even able to by a slave of her own, an ambition that she had previously abandoned for lack of money.[21]

Sabina

Marriage was not in the plans for Sabina da Cruz. For her, freedom was something else. Her owner, Manoel Gonçalves da Cruz, drove a ferry for transporting food and groceries across the bay, Baia de Todos os Santos, so that his slaves could sell them in Salvador.[22] Sabina probably started as one the "sellers" who sold goods in the street with a basket or a tray. She learned well, and later, as a free woman, worked as a wholesaler of commodities from Western Africa, buying in large quantities—barrels of cowry shells, cola nuts, soap, gourds, peppers, and meters and meters of striped fabric called *pano da costa* (cloth from the coast), a favorite of Yorubas in Brazil—commodities that she resold to dealers to be sold to the public.

Although she bought on credit from dealers in Salvador, Sabina paid her accounts on time. One declaration from a creditor, João do Prado Carvalho, showed that in the months of April, June, July, November, and December of 1871, and March of 1872, she owed him a heavy sum of 532$120, but by the time of her death, in July of that year, she had paid everything less 63$920. Similarly, she still owed, to two other dealers of the city, only what she had purchased recently in the months before her death. Her most notable debt was that to the "freed African man" Pompeu Justino Fernandes. Sabina knew that these debts would be paid by her estate before it was divided among her heirs. She also "sold items on good faith," but her executor could not say who had bought on credit because she, illiterate, did not keep notes.[23]

A former slave herself, Sabina came to be an owner of slaves. She did not say when she freed herself, but with respect to her master Manoel Gonçalves da Cruz, "I freed myself from his power many years ago, giving him two slaves for my freedom."[24] Free, like other freed people, she bought slaves; a reflection of the penetration that the ownership of human beings had in all layers and facets of Brazilian society. During the time of her testimony in 1868, Sabina owned five slaves "free and free from embargo," which means that she owed nothing for them and they could be sold. Three were African—Lino, a *jeje*; Maria Luíza, *nagô*; Antonio, also *nagô* (Jeje and Nagô are two Yoruba ethnicities)—and two *crioulas* (Brazilian-born black women), Maurícia and Francisca. When Sabina died four years later, only two slaves remained. Maria Luíza, a *nagô*, then a 50 year-old traveling saleswoman, had deposited her assessed value of 500$000 in the "public safe" in exchange for her freedom, money that served to cover the debts of the estate. When the executor refused to free José immediately—an African, 90 years old, not listed in 1868; too old and broken down to work and valued at only 40$000—he paid the estate so that he could finally be free.[25]

Sabina used her wealth to have a group of dependents surrounding her, a type of invented family. Among them were Maria Cezária da Cruz (later called Maria Cezária do Nascimento, widow of her executor, the shoemaker Plácido Félix do Nascimento) and the minors Seraphina Maria do Nascimento (Maria Cezária's daughter), Idalina da Cruz, Simplícia da Cruz, and Félix Sabino da Cruz. Sabina's relationship with them was not always clear. Could it be that Maria Cezária da Cruz had been a slave belonging to Manoel Gonçalves da Cruz? Had she later married Sabina's executor and become his widow? There is no doubt that Seraphina was the daughter of Maria Cezária, and Idalina da Cruz and Simplícia da Cruz are clearly identified as daughters of a slave belonging to Sabina named Jesuína, who was deceased at the time. It is clear that Sabina especially protected the two young slave girls—house children.[26] The ties between Félix Sabino da Cruz and Sabina remain unknown. Could Jesuína have been his mother also, making him one of Sabina's young, as his last name indicates?

Sabina wanted them to stay together. In 1860, she bought a house for common use. Although Sabina paid the sellers the total value in addition to 6 percent tax, she is cited on the deed as the "benefactor," putting the house in their name and further designating them as heirs. Along with her generosity, however, Sabina imposed restrictions. They could exercise their right to the property only after her death, and only after the death of the rest of the heirs could the last surviving heir sell the house and use it as he wished.

The price and the description suggested an impressive house. Located on the street Direita da Saúde and costing 5:500$000, it had a covered entrance, varnished wooden floors and ceilings in the front rooms, the other rooms "tiled with brick," two bedrooms in front and the other five in the back, "dining room, kitchen and pantry." On the top floor, in addition to two sitting rooms, "three rooms with windows placed on the roof and her backyard." With the same money, Sabina could have bought—according to the prices of 1860—five female or male slaves, healthy and able, and sent them to work as sellers and collected a weekly payment from each one.[27] In addition to the price of the purchase, she let go of a considerable income in order to create an enjoyable house for those she considered family.

Rosa

The sources do not tell where Rosa do O'Freire worked, nor how she got her savings, although, most likely, she also sold sweets or sundries or *quitanda* in the streets or a booth in Salvador. In time—like Sabina—Rosa not only bought her freedom, but she also bought slaves that she put to work; and she received daily payments from each one.

From her last will in 1863, when she was 50 years old—sick but still standing and "of sound mind"—we know that she wanted to distribute her wealth.[28] During that time, Rosa owned nine slaves.

She granted freedom to two African female slaves under the condition that they paid to the executor: in the case of Umbilina, 400$000 for the expenses of Rosa's burial; and in the case of Rita an amount of 600$000, to be paid in two years to Rosa's estate. Without payment, they would not be freed. If either one of the women did not pay, she would be sold and the money would be returned to the estate. Rosa reserved the best for her six "young"—five children from her African slave Leocádia, and one named Guilhermina, whose mother is not identified; all *crioulinhos* (little Brazilian-born black children) and children of the house. Each one would receive a letter of freedom as proof that they were freed. In an uncommon gesture, she gave a letter of freedom to Leocádia so that she could continue to care for her minor children. Upon freeing both the mother and children, Rosa guaranteed that they no longer ran the risk of being separated by sale to different owners.

There was more. In 1861, two years before her death, Rosa did what Sabina had done some years later. She bought a house and land in the name of her favorite children, Guilhermina and Leonico. The property was in Freguesia de Santa Anna, on the street behind Quartéis da Palma; she paid to the owner, Felisberto Gomes de Argollo Ferrão, the amount of 2:000$000. Rosa explained her action: "...with me being an African woman, due to the laws of the country, I cannot own property, I had to buy it in the name" of others. She chose her "two children." And she did so, she said, with the authorization of the Judge of Orphans, the court that managed the properties inherited by minors.[29]

However, her will is a mystery because I was not able to discover any law that prevented freed Africans from owning homes. It is true that anything a slave acquired belonged to its owner, as the slave himself did—both were property—which was equally applied to African slaves or those of Brazilian birth. There was, however, an exception: according to Roman law, this law could not impede a slave from trying to gain freedom and, for that purpose, saving money to purchase freedom—called a *pecúlio* (a reserve of money)—that belonged to the slave. In practice, it is clear that owners often did not honor these savings.[30] Maybe Rosa equated being African to being a slave. Sabina did not give any explanation. It is possible that her intention was to guarantee that the house would not be included in her inventory of possessions and eventually sold to pay her debts, and for this reason she took it from her estate, buying it in the name of her children.

In any case, Rosa mentioned that she was living in the house, and that with her death, it would be passed to her godchildren—all six named as heirs—who would continue to live in the house and receive the title of the house when they reached adulthood.[31]

What do these short stories tell us? We undoubtedly see the operation of the clientele, accomplished in different situations. They are ties that grew personal influence and imposed obligations. On the coffee farms of the rural zones, the mother of a female slave fought, from a far, for the freedom of her daughter with letters that she most likely paid someone to write and send to recipients that she did not know personally. Florença da Silva, perhaps a freed woman—note the last name, inherited from her old owner—knew how to appeal by linking her clientele to the "Doctor Mister" Manoel Esteves Otoni to assure Balbina's freedom. Otoni supported the request, but now it was he who requested sponsorship and the favor of someone more powerful, richer, with more familial authority than him, in the name of a family slave and her mother. Otoni also knew to ask favors in this society of vertical ties. This network of favors and obligations was widespread, socially and geographically, well in addition to the immediate work locations; it took months to become effective and depended on a certain exchange of letters, the last of which perhaps never arrived to the destination.

For Henriqueta, Rosa, and Sabina, the omnipresent exchange of favors operated in another manner. For them being urban slaves working in a cash economy, responsible for their own work, they were able to save enough of what they earned to buy freedom. Henriqueta paid in cash while Sabina paid with two slaves she had bought—solutions they arrived at only in direct negotiations with their owners. As free women, they were part of networks of patronage that were formed amongst themselves or connected them with people that they dealt with face to face, generally equal or nearly so. Upon giving freedom and property to their young—children of their slaves—they weaved ties of dependence and loyalty. Because they bought and sold on credit—business that linked them to rich dealers and small sellers, relationships on which they depended and which protected them—they also received favors as much as they granted them. Henriqueta and Sabina, although they did business on immensely different scales, valued their reputation as being trustworthy women who paid their debts. Reliability was the currency in the exchange for favors. Henriqueta and her husband borrowed money from friends, a couple—also African, a little older and much more established—to get through a difficult phase. Henriqueta was referred to the woman as her friend and "godmother"; but friendship did not erase the debt and Henriqueta insisted on paying it. This was how the urban networks of patronage functioned: woven from daily and occasional encounters, in conversations with people of similar social condition who knew each other and needed to find ways to get along with each other well.

As Rosa and Sabina explained, by the fact of neither of them having married nor having children or parents, they counted on the freedom of choosing their heirs and distributing their possessions as they saw fit. Nevertheless, surprisingly they bought property in the name of third parties. After bequeathing freedom as well as property to their young, Rosa and Sabina are examples of a recurring pattern among slaves coming from the African coast who, in Brazil, never married, much less had children. Generally, they designated as heirs not their slaves, but the children of their slaves—and often, if not always, as Rosa shows, the daughters were freed and given resources in money or property to begin life. As Sheila Siqueira de Castro Faria (2004) noted, these women established invented lineages to endow property to female heirs.[32]

Among our three African saleswomen, none of them had a protective mother in Brazil that advocated for them as Florença did for Balbina and as Sabina and Rosa tried to act with respect to their invented families. In the 1860s, the attorney Perdignao Malheiro wrote, lamenting, "among us, unfortunately, slaves live in illicit unions." He blamed not the church that approved marriages, but the institution of slavery, which had for centuries impeded the marriage of slaves. Then Malheiro presents this exception: "In some parts, I must confess it is true, mainly among the farmers, it is not rare to see them become families of slaves, husband, wife, children."[33]

The historians of today firmly reject this judgment that consensual unions were "illicit"; however, they recognize the difficulty of finding familial ties among urban slaves. Luckily we have available to us the lists of residences of rural municipalities at the end of the 18th century, especially in the province of São Paulo, which sometimes present slaves in familial groups or at least refer to the slaves as married, single, or widowed. In the rural regions already studied by historians, no less than 25 percent to 30 percent of the adult slaves were married and sometimes, many more. In Paraibuna, in 1830, on the farm of the widow Ms. Maria Custódia de Alvarenga, 90 percent of the adult slaves were married. Little more than half of the 60 adult slaves of Inácio Ferreira Braga were married. At one point or another, the slaves appear grouped and listed as families. The 53 slaves belonging to a farmer in 1835 consisted of 11 families; the majority had children.[34] Balbina's mother does not seem to be an uncommon case.

Balbina also lived with another family. Her owners sold her internally to other members of their extensive and powerful clan. Balbina da Silva apparently got her two names from members of the Otoni family.[35] And, due to a marriage between the Otoni family of Minas Gerais and the Vieira Machado da Cunha family from Valença in Rio de Janeiro, Balbina ended up in Saudade, the prominent coffee farm in the valley of Paraíba.[36]

For the three African women, the city—Salvador and Rio de Janeiro—became a place of possibility. There, they started as slaves; each working for herself as a street vendor or merchant, and each one then buying her own freedom. Two of them used it to become the owners of properties and slaves, and both freed their slaves. These two even forged family lineages. The three paid their creditors, one got divorced, and they all created personal networks of favors and obligations. It was not their "African-ness" that made a difference, because as entrepreneurial as the African woman was, since she was on a large agricultural property, her mobility was more likely from the field to the kitchen.

However, independence in the city had a price. The competition to sell on the streets was fierce. The sellers fought for space, sometimes reaching physical aggression. One morning in July of 1854, Amélia, a *mina* slave (descendent of the Mina coast in Western Africa), gave Josefa, an emancipated *preta* (black woman), "a strong blow to the face" and then dragged her to the well of Paço square. Both sold *quitanda* and Amélia evidently wanted Josefa to leave her territory.[37] Henriqueta once fought with a client, "in view of everyone in the middle of the day," according to her husband's accusation. The client ended up with a ripped shirt and she ended up in jail until her husband convinced the police that his wife was a free woman, honest and hardworking.[38] The freed women were sometimes confused with slaves; and honest women with prostitutes, with whom they shared the streets and squares, especially in the evening when the "public women"—the cheapest prostitutes—took to the streets.[39]

It is unlikely that Balbina had an independent life. It is difficult to imagine her walking about the streets alone, buying a house, or negotiating credit. She was spared from the fights of the street, failed business deals, cheap housing; but, wrapped in the protective orbit of a prominent family, she was also deprived of opportunities to test her abilities, make decisions, and become herself. If we remember her mother's warning to treat her owners well, we see that protection also had a price.

Of course these sources do not tell us if the family of the farmer granted Balbina's freedom or, if they did, how she used it. Balbina was young, with her entire life ahead of her. We know that Sabina and Rosa at the end of their lives, when they were nearing death, were choosing burial clothes, arranging masses, distributing alms, and influencing other lives with their legacy. Henriqueta disappears from our view after the divorce, determined to rebuild her life for the third time at middle age.

A Brief Epilogue

It was the late afternoon, and the work of the day had ended when the young black women went up the steps of a covered veranda of a large house. They went to the front door, knocked and waited. They explained to the maid that came to greet them and that they wanted to see Ms. Cecília, the lady of the house. The women were sweaty and rough-looking, not only because of the long day cutting sugar cane, but from the weeks and months of work in the field. Their clothes did not match, they were mended, torn; they wore sandals on their feet and scarves wrapped on their head. After 20 minutes or so, Ms. Cecília appeared. She stopped at the door, not inviting the women to enter nor meeting them on the veranda. They spoke quietly in a respectful manner. They probably rehearsed what they were going to say. They asked for a transfer from the field to domestic work. "For what reason?" asked Ms. Cecília. "Because," they responded, the field work destroyed their clothes. Ms. Cecília would think about it and advise them later of her decision. The women received permission to leave. Thanking her, they descended the stairs. It was a safe request, one that would not be dismissed because, after all, they did not complain of the exhausting work of cutting sugar cane with a short knife. The concern about their own clothes showed that they wanted to take care of their things. They would be good maids in the laundry or in the kitchen. Could it be that it was common on this farm to recruit domestic servants from the experienced agricultural workers, or were these women trying to make an exception for themselves? It is not clear.

Even in 1973, upon witnessing this eternal scene when I was the guest of said farm, black women from the countryside still had, at most, the hope of moving from the field to the kitchen.

Notes

1. Florença da Silva to Balbina da Silva, city of Grão Mogol, Minas Gerais, April 14, 1862, Arquivo Nacional, Rio de Janeiro, Secção de Arquivos Particulares (doravante AN-RJ, SAP), família Werneck (henceforth FW), códice 112, v. 8, Cartas Avulsas, f. 13-q.

2. Here and in several places where historical documents were reproduced, the original spelling was maintained.

3. On the Mucuri Project, see Chagas, 1956 and Otoni, 1983. On the Ottoni family, see Ferreira, 1998. Téofilo inherited the dream of his uncle, José Eloi Ottoni, a poet who, writing from Lisboa in 1798, insisted that Minas Gerais should develop agriculture for exporting and business to avoid the damaging control of Portugal, and in achieving this goal, it was essential to open roads and river navigation. "Memória sobre o estado atual da capitania de Minas Gerais (1798)" [Memoir about the current state of the captaincy of Minas Gerais], 1908, p. 301-18, especially p. 307-8.

4. Chagas, 1956, p. 291, 296-297. On the contract, see Ottoni, 1979, p. 56.

5. Avé-Lallemant, 1980, p. 193; quote: p. 195.

6. Scully, 1868, p. 124. Avé-Lallemant, 1980, especially p. 159-75, 194, 202-3, 218-9, 257, 259. Chagas, 1956, p. 359-95.

7. Manoel Esteves Ottoni to João Vieira Machado da Cunha, Filadélfia, Minas Gerais, 9 Jan. 1863, AN-RJ, SAP, FW, códice. 112, v. 8, doc. 47.

8. Bergad, 1999, p. 189.

9. Barata e Bueno, 1999, v. 2, p. 2274

10. "Inventário, Sabina da Cruz, africana liberta, Bahia, 1872" [Inventory of Sabina da Cruz, Freed African woman], Arquivo Público do Estado da Bahia, Salvador (henceforth Apeb), Judiciário, 3/1100/1569/07, f. 1 (henceforth "Inventário, Sabina da Cruz, 1872"). Note that this is not the same Sabina da Cruz who played a crucial role in the Levante dos Malês, in 1835. "Testamento, Roza do O'Freire, africana liberta, Bahia, 1863" [Last will and testament of Roza do O'Freire, Free African Woman, Bahia, 1863], Apeb, Judiciário, Registro de Testamentos, 1863-64, Salvador, book 43, f. 50-2 (henceforth "Testamento, Roza do O'Freire, 1863"). "Henriqueta Maria da Conceição, *preta mina* (black mina woman), against Rufino Maria Baleta, *preto mina* (black Mina man), *libelo de divórcio* (divorce indictments), Rio de Janeiro, 1856" (henceforth "Divórcio, 1856"), Arquivo da Cúria Metropolitana, Rio de Janeiro (henceforth ACM-RJ), *libelos de divórcio*, 1174, case 68; Juízo da 2.a Vara Cível, "Divórcio, Rufino José Maria Baleta, *réu* (respondent), Rio de Janeiro, 1857" (henceforth "Divórcio, 1857"), Arquivo Nacional, Rio de Janeiro (henceforth AN-RJ), Seção do Poder Judiciário (henceforth SPJ), Stack 877, n. 686 [transcribed]; Juízo Municipal da 3.ª Vara Cível, "Inventário, Rofino Joze Maria Baleta e Henriqueta Maria da Conceição, Rio de Janeiro, 1858" (henceforth "Inventário, 1858"), AN-RJ, SPJ, Case 300, n. 828, Gal. A.

11. "Divórcio, 1857"; Rufino (Maria Baleta) e Henriqueta (Maria da Conceição), Rio de Janeiro, 16 Jan. 1855, *casamentos* (weddings), Freguesia de Santa Rita, Book 5 (1852-60), ACM-RJ, AP552, f. 40v-41.

12. "Testamento, Roza do O'Freire, 1863," f. 50; "Inventário, Sabina da Cruz, 1872," f. 1.

13. See a longer version of Henriqueta's story in Graham, 2012, p. 25-65.

14. Johnson, 1996, p. 245; Lander and Lander, 1837, p. 121-2; Clarke, 1972, p. 13, 33-4, 45, 54, 184.

15. "Rellação nominal das cazas de negocios da Freguesia de Santa Rita pertencente ao anno de 1841" [Report of names of businesses in the parish of Santa Rita in the year 1841], "Estatística da Freguesia de Santa Rita"[Statistics of the Parish of Santa Rita], Arquivo Geral da Cidade do Rio de Janeiro (henceforth AGC-RJ), códice 43-1-42.

16. "Carta de liberdade que dá Roza Maria de Jesus à Henriqueta" [Letter of Freedom that gives Roza Maria de Jesus to Henriqueta], 21 Jul. 1853, AN-RJ, 2.º Ofício de Notas do Rio de Janeiro, Registro Geral, Book 86, 3/5/1853-14/1/1854, f. 92v.

17. "Divórcio, 1856," f.3,38v; "Carta de liberdade, conferida por José Maria Warleta a Rufino" [Letter of Freedom issued by José Maria Warleta to RUfino], 2 Apr. 1854, AN-RJ, 2.º Ofício de Notas, Rio de Janeiro, Registro Geral, Book 87, 16/1/1854-7/8/1854, f. 79.

18. "Divórcio, 1856," f. 2-52.

19. Inventário, Rufino José Maria Baleta e Henriqueta Maria da Conceição, 1858.

20. "Barracas, […] 1846, 1847, 1850, 1853, 1857, 1861 e 1863-1865," AGC-RJ, códice 53-3-36, f. 14-5.

21. "Divórcio, 1856," f. 35v-36.

22. "Licenças, Manoel Gonçalves da Cruz,"16 Jan. 1819, Arquivo Municipal de Salvador, Salvador, Bahia, 88.5, f.169.

23. "Inventário, Sabina da Cruz, 1872," f. 22, 25, 33, 39, 39v, 57, 58, 61-1v.

24. Ibid, f. 1.

25. Ibid, f. 1v, 15, 17, 19, 39-40v.

26. Ibid, f. 1v, 1-2.

27. Ibid, f. 1v, 5, 5v, 6. In respect to the prices of slaves, see Andrade, 1988, p. 207-208.

28. "Testamento, Roza do O'Freire, 1863" [Last will and testament of Roza do O'Freire], f. 50, 50v.

29. Ibid, f. 50v.

30. Malheiro, 1967, Chapter 3, Section 1.ª, art. IV, §31-35; laws, statutes, etc., *Coleção das leis do Brasil*, [Collection of the Laws of Brazil], Lei 2.040, 28 Sep. 1871, art. 4.º

31. "Testamento, Roza do O'Freire, 1863," f. 50v.

32. Lauderdale Graham, 2012, p. 60-4; Faria, 2004, p. 180-91, 191-208.

33. Malheiro, 1967, Chapter III, Section 1.a, art. III, § 30.

34. "Mappa Geral [illegible] da Villa de Jacarehy do anno de 1828" [General Map of the Villa of Jacarehy of the year 1828], Arquivo do Estado de São Paulo, seção de Manuscritos (henceforth Aesp-SM), maços de população, Jacarehy, Santa Branca, Parahybuna, 1830-50, Stack 2, Case 86, Order 86; "Mappa dos habitantes, 1830" [Map of inhabitants, 1830], fogo 30, Maria Custódia de Alvarenga; "Lista geral dos habitantes, 6.ª Companhia, 1829" [General List of Inhabitants, 6th Company, 1829], fogo 1, Custódio Ferreira Braga. 2.º Distrito de Juiz de Paz da Vara de Santo Antônio de Parahybuna do município da mesma, quarteirão n.º 2, Aesp-SM, maços de população, Jacarehy, Santa Branca, Parahybuna, 1835, Stack 2, Case 86, Order 86, fogo 38, Manoel da Cunha de Azeredo Coutinho Souza Chichorro. See also Lauderdale Graham, 2002, p. 50-62; and Richard Graham, 2008, p. 19-39, especially 21-24.

35. Ottoni e Ottoni, 1978, I – Quadro genealógico.

36. Ferreira, 1998, p. 71-3; 103; *Annuario genealogico brasileiro*, 1939 [Genealogical Brazilian Annual, 1939], p. 318-9.

37. "Corte de Apelação, processo-crime n. 583, Amélia, mina, escrava de Domingos José Dias Guerreiro, réu, Rio de Janeiro, 1854" [Appeals Court, Criminal case n. 583, Amélia, Mina slave of Domingos José Dias Guerreiro, defendant, Rio de Janeiro, 1854], AN-RJ, Stack 84, Gal. C., f. 1-39. Soares (2005) elaborates on this case in detail, p. 210-2.

38. "Divórcio, 1857," transcript.

39. With respect to prostitution in Rio de Janeiro, see Lauderdale Graham, 1991 (especially p. 671-679) and 1996, p. 53-66.

Bibliography

Andrade, Maria José de Souza. *A mão de obra escrava em Salvador, 1811-1860*. [Slave Labor in Salvador]. São Paulo: Corrupio; Brasília: CNPq, 1988.

Annuario genealogico brasileiro, [Brazilian Genealogical Annual], I.º Ano. São Paulo: Empreza Graphica da Revista dos Tribunaes, 1939.

Avé-Lallemant, Robert. *Viagens pelas províncias da Bahia, Pernambuco, Alagoas e Sergipe (1859)*. [Travels Through the Provinces of Bahia, Pernambuco, Alagoas, and Sergipe (1859)]. Trans. Eduardo de Lima Castro. São Paulo: Itatiaia/Edusp, 1980.

Barata, Carlos Eduardo de Almeida; Bueno, Antônio da. *Dicionário das famílias brasileiras*. [Dictionary of Brazilian Families]. São Paulo: Ibero-Americana, 1999.

Bergad, Laird W. *Slavery and the demographic and economic history of Minas Gerais, Brazil, 1720-1888*. Cambridge: Cambridge University Press, 1999.

Chagas, Paulo Pinheiro. *Teófilo Ottoni – Ministro do povo*. [Teófilo Ottoni – Minister of the People]. 2. ed. rev. Rio de Janeiro: Livraria São José, 1956.

Clarke, William H. *Travels and explorations in Yorubaland, 1854-1858*. Ibadan: Ibadan University Press, 1972.

Faria, Sheila Siqueira de Castro. *Sinhás pretas, damas mercadoras – As pretas minas nas cidades do Rio de Janeiro e de São João del Rey, 1700-1850*. [Black Mistresses, Merchant Ladies – Black Mina Women in the Cities of Rio de Janeiro and São Jão del Rey, 1700-1850]. 2004. Thesis (Livre-Docência em História do Brasil). Universidade Federal Fluminense, Niterói, Rio de Janeiro.

Ferreira, Laís Ottoni Barbosa. *Os Ottoni – Descendentes e colaterais*. [The Ottonis – Descendents and Collaterals]. Rio de Janeiro: L. O. B. Ferreira, 1998.

Graham, Richard. "Os números e o historiador não quantitativo." [Numbers and the Non-Quantitative Historian]. *Locus – Revista de História*, v. 4, n. 1, 2008.

Johnson, Samuel. [1921] *The history of the Yorubas – From the earliest times to the beginning of the British Protectorate*. London: Routledge & Kegan Paul, 1966.

Lander, Richard; Lander, John. *Journal of an expedition to explore the course and termination of the Niger with a narrative of a voyage down that river to its termination*, 2 v. New York: Harper and Brothers, 1837.

Lauderdale Graham, Sandra. "Slavery's impasse – Slave prostitutes, small-time mistresses, and the Brazilian law of 1871." *Comparative Studies in Society and History*, v. 33, n. 4, Oct. 1991.

_____. "O impasse da escravatura – Prostitutas escravas, suas senhoras e a lei brasileira de 1871." [The Impasse of Slavery – Slave Prostitutes, their Madams, and Brazilian Law of 1871]. Acervo, v. 9, n. 1-2, Jan.-Dec. 1996.

_____. *Caetana diz não – Histórias de mulheres da sociedade escravista brasileira*. [Caetana said no – Histories of Women in Brazilian Slave Society]. São Paulo: Companhia das Letras, 2002.

_____. "Being Yoruba in nineteenth-century Rio de Janeiro." *Slavery & Abolition*, v. 32, n. 1, Mar. 2011. *Afro-Ásia* (in press).

_____. "Ser mina no Rio de Janeiro do século xix." [To be a Mina in Rio de Janeiro of the 19th Century]. *Revista Afro-Ásia*, Salvador, n. 45, 2012, p. 25-65.

Malheiro, Agostinho Marques Perdigão. [1866-1867] *A escravidão no Brasil – Ensaio histórico-jurídico-social.* [Slavery in Brazil – a Historical-Juridical-Social Analysis]. Petrópolis: Vozes, 1967.

Otoni, Cristiano Benedito. *Autobiografia.* [Autobiography]. Brasília: Editora da UnB, 1983.

Ottoni, Cristiano Benedito; Ottoni, Bárbara Balbina de Araújo Maia. *Cartas aos netos.* [Letters to Grandchildren]. Rio de Janeiro: Ministério da Justiça, Arquivo Nacional, 1978.

Ottoni, José Elói. "Memória sobre o estado atual da capitania de Minas Gerais (1798)." [Memoir about the Current State of the Captaincy of Minas Gerais (1798)]. *Anais da Biblioteca Nacional*, n. 30, 1908.

Ottoni, Teófilo Benedito. *Discursos parlamentares.* [Parliamentary Discourses]. Introd. e ed. Paulo Pinheiro Chagas. Brasília: Câmara dos Deputados, 1979.

Scully, William. Brazil – *Its provinces and chief cities; the manners and customs of the people; agricultural, commercial, and other statistics.* London: Trübner & Co., 1868.

Soares, Carlos Eugênio Líbano. "A 'nação' da mercancia – Condição feminina e as africanas da Costa da Mina, 1835-1900." [The "Nation" of Commerce – The Feminine Condition and African Women from the Mina Coast, 1835-1900]. In: Farias, Juliana Barreto; Soares, Carlos Eugênio Líbano; Gomes, Flávio dos Santos. *No labirinto das nações – Africanos e identidades no Rio de Janeiro.* [In the Labyrinth of Nations – Africans and Identities in Rio de Janeiro]. Rio de Janeiro: Arquivo Nacional, 2005.

10

"WITH HER, HE LIVED LIKE A DOG LIVES WITH A CAT": EMANCIPATION, MATERNITY, AND GENDER ON THE SOUTHERN BORDER

Paulo Roberto Staudi Moreira

> *Reading, one comes to know almost everything. I also read. Something you will know however. Now I am not so sure. And so, you will have to read it another way. As, it doesn't work the same for everyone, each one invents his own, whatever that is to you, there are some who go their entire lives reading without ever getting more than the text, they remain stuck on the page, not realizing that the words are just stones placed to cross the current of a river, if they are there it is so that we can reach the other side; the other side is what matters. Unless, unless, which, unless such rivers don't have two shores, but many, that anyone who reads might be, she, her own riverbank, and what might be hers, and only hers, is the riverbank that she will have to reach.*
>
> —José Saramago, A caverna, p. 77.

It was two o'clock in the morning on March 21, 1870 when the "Brazilian citizen" João Pereira Soares was "awakened from his sleep," in his farmhouse, on the right bank of the Imbahá River, in the municipality of Uruguaiana.[1] The one responsible for disturbing the sleep of the farmer Soares was the *catarinense* (person from Santa Catarina) Francisco José de Medeiros, 58 years old, resident of the surrounding area of Imbahá, who at the time was staying in the house of the plaintiff, where he made "his bed in the barn of the ranch." Francisco went to tell Soares that he noticed suspicious movement and had observed the emancipated black man Antônio and another individual, who he had not recognized, driving the slave Rosa and her five children (Eugênio, Francisco, Fláubio, Domingos, and one in her arms) to a *mangueira*.[2]

Informed about the theft of his slaves and knowing the proximity of his farm to the border with Uruguay, Soares tried to move quickly. Although possible, always desired, and sometimes achieved, the escape of southern slaves across the border in search of protection in the bordering countries, where slavery was no longer in effect, was not easy.

Before mounting his horse, Soares ordered Francisco to go to the house of his close friend, Anastácio Silveira Gularte (from the same province, married, 30 years old, resident of the coast of Imbahá, illiterate), and call him to help in the capture of his slaves that had been "stolen." Later, Soares mounted his horse and went to wake up his "watchman"[3] Pedro Fagundes (born in Comarca de Missões, married, 42 years old), to leave with him in pursuit of the "thieves" of his slaves.

Half a league ahead, Soares and Fagundes found the stolen "property" near the pass of Imbahá: "Rosa who had brought two little children and another man who brought three small *crioulos*, whom he [Pedro Fagundes] testifies that he ran down, however he could not hold them because he had gotten too far into the bush, he was able, however, to catch the horse." The freed black man Antônio—appointed as the defendant in the trial—was not found at the time of the seizure. However, the following day the farmer, João Pereira Soares, was able to arrest him and filed a complaint against him in the local police precinct of Uruguaiana, asking him to be convicted by Article 257 of the Criminal Code: "Taking another's property against the will of its owner, for himself or for another. Penalty: imprisonment with labor for two months to four years; and a fine of five to 20 percent of the value stolen."

Soares did not indicate how the arrest proceeded, but Antônio declared that he was in a bush searching for wood for a house and, in turn, he was arrested. In his inquiry, he called himself Antônio Mina, confirmed being free, leaving out who his father was and his age ("however he appears to be about 60 years old"). He stated that he was married, a farmer, African from Iguá (port on the Costa da Mina) and illiterate. He had been a slave of Soares and his family, and at the time of the crime, had some crops on the land of a neighbor of his former owners, Ms. Joaquina Fonseca; actually, she was the sister of his former owner's wife. The letter of complete emancipation of Antônio had been issued in Imbahá on March 8, 1869, signed by João Pereira Soares and his wife, Maria Inácia da Fonseca Soares. Antônio is described in the letter of emancipation as being from the coast, 56 years old, and his owner, illiterate, had not signed the document that had freed the captive. Vicente Osório Rodrigues signed the letter on behalf of the mistress, with Augusto Peres de Farias and Zeferino de Ávila Rodrigues as witnesses.[4]

The letter was composed on March 8, 1869; however, it was only registered in the notary's office more than two years later on August 28, 1871, five days after Antônio was released. As the letter was conditional, and apparently free, it must not have been with the owner, but with Antônio or someone he trusted. We say "apparently" free because we know of some cases in which the letter did not stipulate a condition of service or payment, but there was some type of "indemnity" to the owner for the property that left his roster of material goods. The friction in the court perhaps made Antônio think that the legitimacy of his emancipation was at risk.

The theft of the slaves occurred in the middle of the night between Sunday and Monday and the defendant argued that on Sunday he had been in Vila de Uruguaiana, selling melons and other fruits from his crops, presenting as a witness Domingos Barbier, who had bought them. Later, Antônio returned to the ranch of Ms. Joaquina Fonseca, where his crops were; he rested there, since the next day he had to look at his plantings because he was told the cattle had ruined them. Antônio denied during the whole trial to having participated in the crime, despite all of the contrary evidence, and among his claims a particularly naïve sounding one: he could not cross the Uruguay river because "he doesn't know how to swim."

The case narrated here occurred on the Brazilian southern border, in the municipality of Uruguaiana, along the banks of the Uruguay river. Uruguaiana was founded in 1823, when the Chapel of Uruguay was created, the name given probably for its proximity to the river of the same name, and in 1846 became a town. The Vila de Uruguaiana bordered the province of Corrientes on the Argentine side, and the department of Salto, an eastern state of Uruguay. The Arroyo Imbahá, frequently mentioned in this case, situated two leagues from the town, was a tributary of the Uruguay river and was characterized as a traditional location of contraband; as such, it was also an escape route for criminals and slaves.

At least since the army's invasion of the eastern front led by the Portuguese general Lecor in 1816, and upon the request of the directorate of Buenos Aires, who was frightened by the caudillo Gervasio Artigas, the Portuguese conceded the lands between the rivers Quaraí and Arapeí. The ranchers from Rio Grande do Sul who settled there continued to support their ranches through slave labor, which caused no problems until the Guerra Grande (Great War) (1843-1851), when the easterners found themselves facing the inevitable: that they would be required to free their captives in order to strengthen the war effort. The Uruguayan abolitionist laws of 1842 and 1846 created a serious diplomatic problem: what to do with the slaves belonging to the Brazilian ranchers settled on the eastern front and how to deal with the children of these captives who had been born on *solo livre* (free soil)? In the Argentine case, abolition demanded reiterated laws, until slavery was finally extinct in 1853.

Of course, before these dates Argentineans and Uruguayans, whenever possible, supported fugitive slaves as a way of destabilizing the expansionist ambitions of the Brazilian empire. However, after 1846 in Uruguay and after 1853 in Argentina, the situation became even more tense, when the flow of black people on both sides of the border was heavy. Slaves belonging to owners from Rio Grande do Sul tried their luck escaping across the border; black Uruguayans were kidnapped and enslaved in Brazilian territory, captains of *gaúcho* farmers (inhabitants of the *pampas* in South America, especially Argentina and southern Brazil) worked on their ranches on the Uruguayan side under the guise of conditional emancipation and contracts for peonage etc. Notwithstanding the hostility that was normal in the southern lands, whose society was consistently involved in internal civil wars (such the decade of 1835-1845, a time during which there was a revolt in the southern states of Brazil, also known as the Guerra dos Farroupilhas, or the War of the Wretches) or in disputes with neighboring countries.[5] In August of 1865, for example, the city of Uruguaiana was invaded by Paraguayan troops; the city was undefended as the brigadier David Canabarro retreated with his forces seeing as he did not have sufficient troops to confront the enemy.[6]

However, let us return to the case of the escape of Rosa and her children. Complaint filed and defendant arrested, the documents indicate a theft perpetrated by a freed slave, with the intention of obtaining personal monetary earnings. The first impression of the case begins to change with the testimony of one of the "stolen" slaves as a witness: the little *crioulo* Eugênio, son of Rosa, 12 years old. Eugênio states that "Father Antônio" hid in the room of his mother, next to the kitchen, and from there, in the middle of the night, hauled a "bundle of clothes behind the pigsty and from there, on the back of a *picaço*[7] horse, led the witness to the edge of the woods." The accomplice of "Father Antônio" was a *crioulo* named João, who, according to Eugênio, stopped for a while in the house of Antônio Pedro de Miranda e Castro, customs forwarding agent, resident of Vila de Uruguaiana. According to the testimony of Rosa's eldest child, near the location where they were captured, "Father Antônio" separated from them saying "see you later."

Antônio, who throughout the trial insisted on his absolute innocence, had to watch in anguish a second testimony, even more awkward for his affirmation of having done nothing. Called to testify was the slave Rosa, *crioula*, single, 39 years old. Rosa clarified and removed any uncertainty that could have been clouding the reality of what occurred. Asked about what she knew: she "responded that her master, having freed the defendant and wanting also to give a letter of freedom to the witness, her mistress opposed this, and as the witness had already given eleven offspring, she believed that this was an injustice done against her by her mistress, who even declined the price of the witness' freedom."

"WITH HER, HE LIVED LIKE A DOG LIVES WITH A CAT"

So, after having raised 11 children, which increased the capital of her master, Rosa thought that she deserved freedom. Antônio and Rosa were partners, members of the harsh reality of a family of slaves; however, only the first had received emancipation as compensation for his good services. The slave couple, denied freedom without burden or condition, still tried to buy emancipation, which was denied to them. It was necessary to reformulate their family plans, and conversing on the same ranch from which they had escaped, they decided, "since they refused her freedom, even if they had paid for it," they needed to search for other solutions. The defendant hid in her room one night, "until the doors were closed," and from there, escaped with her children. According to Rosa, they were not going to Corrientes, but they "came to this village to see if they might find someone to buy her and her children."

Pressed by these testimonies that put his declaration of innocence in doubt, Antônio Mina was questioned again about the relationship he maintained with the captive *crioula*, Rosa. He had to admit that he knew her and the she was his partner, "and with her has always lived like a dog with a cat, that is, always at odds with each other."

Although admitting to knowing her and maintaining a close and personal relationship, despite not living together, Antônio testified that "he never cared about Rosa's freedom," that they never discussed this, and if by chance they had spoken about it, he "would have sought to persuade her to flee." Emancipated in 1869, he shared with Rosa that the hope of freedom was not a mere concession from the owners, but a conquest. When asked by the judicial authorities if he was "esteemed" by his former owners, Antônio responded, "that he was, for how much he had served them."

With the complaint filed, the evidence presented, and the witnesses heard, the police chief of Uruguaiana, Joaquim do Nascimento Costa da Cunha e Lima,[8] considered it just that Antônio Mina was convicted by Article 257, with Article 269 of the Criminal Code of the Empire ("theft with violence to a person, or items, was a penalty of one to eight years in the galleys") and in Decree no. 138, of October 15, 1837 ("being extensive, the offenses against the law, for the crime of the theft of slaves, the penalty and the established classifications were more severe than for those of mere theft"). With the case concluded in the police jurisdiction, it was sent to the judge of the district of Alegrete to continue the trial. In December of 1870 a jury session, presided by the judge Evaristo de Araújo e Cintra, was opened, with the lawyer Matias Teixeira de Almeida named to defend Antônio.

The lawyer Matias, in his argument, based the defense on the penalty imposed on Antônio; in finding the mischaracterization of the crime of theft—after all, the defendant would not have wished to steal the slaves for himself: "When it was proved that the defendant helped the slave Rosa and her children escape, which he denies, he had just contributed to helping this slave put into effect her project of removing herself and her children from captivity, going to enjoy freedom in another country were slavery was not permitted." Judge Cintra sympathized with the declarations of the lawyer Matias and in his sentence, absolved the defendant: "Certainly, there was the taking of something against the will of its owner, but what he took, he had no intention of making his own property; nor did he take it for someone else, seeing as his intention was to bring these slaves to the Republic of Uruguay, in attempt to recuperate their freedom, which the master denied them."[9]

Antônio's ordeal seemed to be ending; however, the interim prosecutor José Sérgio de Oliveira appealed to the Superior Court of Appeals in Rio de Janeiro, which, in meeting on May 19, 1871, confirmed the decision of the judge. We should not be surprised with Antônio's pardon, a freed black African man accused of stealing slaves. Between the crime supposedly committed in March of 1870 and the definitive charter for release, issued on August 23, 1871, we see him enduring an embittering year and five months of imprisonment. At 60 years of age, would he have conditions to reorganize his abandoned crops? Could it be that some of his partners that he had counted on as witnesses of his innocence (the emancipated black men Pedro and João, and the slaves Henriqueta and Benedito), who were never called to testify, had gotten to save at least part of his estate?

This case, told in such a succinct form, seems to limit itself to a simple anecdote or "account," without any relevance to the understanding of the complexity of slave society of the nineteenth century. However, we tried to look at it more closely for it to reveal to us the historical reality of southern slavery, in its agrarian and frontier dimension. *Crioula* Rosa and Antônio Mina, as well as the children created from this union, which certainly lasted several years, composed a family of slaves. We don't have information on the rest of the slaves João Pereira Soares owned; however, the difference in origin between the couple—she, *crioula* and he, *africano*—doesn't seem to have impeded the course of their relationship (despite being described by Antônio as that of a "dog with a cat").

João Pereira Soares passed away on June 13, 1893 in Uruguaiana without registering a will, and leaving just three children: Quilídia Soares de Farias (married to the lieutenant-colonel Ceciliano de Farias Correia, 30 years old), João Batista Soares (30 years old) and Manoel Antônio Soares (28 years old). In the inventory list made, the good with the highest value was a piece of land located in the *sesmaria* (lands granted by the Portuguese empire for agricultural use) of Imbahá, "which was listed as having" about five *contos de réis*.[10] (One *conto* is equal to one thousand *mil-réis*, or, 1,000,000 *réis*.)

This story from 1870, which occurred in Uruguaiana, integrates dimensions of slave life such as familiarity, emancipation, escape, and the strategic use of the frontier space, contemplating the necessity of daily political decisions "made in extreme conditions of uncertainty." After all, "during the life of each one, appearing cyclically, are problems, uncertainties, choices; ultimately, the politics of daily life whose center is the strategic use of social norms." Addressing the action of slaves from this perspective, highlighting constant doubts in the complete execution of plans, often very precarious, and decision-making in situations of nearly complete inferiority of power, it is a presupposition that brings us closer to the historiographical lens of the life of these human beings that the slave system wanted to transform into mere commodities. "In between stable or emerging regulatory systems, groups and people act with their own significant strategy, able to leave lasting marks on political reality; although they are not able to stop the dominating forms, they are able to condition and modify them" (Levi, 2000, p. 45).

Frustrated by thwarted hopes and failed attempts at emancipation, Antônio and Rosa opted for escape, using the border in their plans for obtaining freedom. The uniform testimonies in the trial can further deepen the analysis. Upon testifying, Rosa not only contradicts Antônio's version of the story, but she also introduces a detail that went unnoticed by the interrogators: she declares that she was not going with her children towards the border, but to Vila Uruguaiana, where they sought someone who would want to buy them. Decree no. 1,695 of September 15, 1869, which prohibited the sale of slaves through bids and public display also determined in its second article: "In all slave sales, private or judicial, it is prohibited, under the penalty of nullity, to separate husband and wife, or child from father or mother, except children older than 15 years of age."

As it was initially stated, Rosa brought her five children with her, the youngest being "still breastfed" and the oldest being 12 years old. The escape route and the place where they were apprehended bring us to doubt that they were not headed for the other side of the border. But, perhaps, the strategy was to place Rosa and her children in a secure place, while Antônio dealt with getting a sponsor to negotiate the purchase and subsequent emancipation of his partner. The mysterious accomplice of Antônio (the *crioulo* João, who was never found) was riding a horse that was captured when it fled into the woods and had a marking that was unrecognized by the local farmers. Could it be that João was Antônio's contact on the other side of the border, someone who guaranteed a secured place for Rosa and her children?

Cited in the trial as the owner of the house where João "stopped," Antônio Pedro de Miranda e Castro, customs agent, resident of Vila Uruguaiana, could have been able to be the black couple's contact for obtaining sponsorship. We know the importance of sponsorship ties to resolve problems among owners and captives in colonial and imperial society. It was typical among slaves to seek sponsors who mediated the procurement of emancipation, negotiated the return after an escape, or even the sale to "better" owners. To go in search of a sponsor was to get a protector who negotiated a solution to some problem, who in general dealt with negotiations with the owner for the sale of the captive or his return to the owner. The sponsor sought by these slaves had to be a white man with more power (or at least equal to) that of the owner of his so-called "beneficiary," because he had to be able to act as an intermediary between the parties. In the case of return to the plantation, the sponsor had to work out with the master of his protégé the punishments that would be administered if necessary, since many of the "sponsored" slaves had committed some error, whether it was theft, escape, or something similar.

What is certain is that successful emancipations and escapes, like revolts and *quilombos* (colonies of escaped slaves), required networks of support for those who put themselves at risk in these plans to obtain freedom. It is likely that Antônio Pedro de Miranda e Castro had served as protector for the slaves who wanted to buy their own freedom, and despite not having much information about him, a document produced two years after the imprisonment of Antôno Mina makes us believe that he maintained a close relationship with the local black community. On July 8, 1872, Pedro adopted and raised the innocent Adélia, who was under his care, born on October 18, 1869. Adélia was the natural daughter of the slave Felicidade (de Antônio Simões Pires), baptized as free and sponsored in the baptismal font by the baron of Ijuí and his wife. Adelia's freedom was guaranteed by the payment of 200 thousand *réis* by a committee commemorating the return of the baron of Paraguay. This committee was composed of father Francisco Alves Barroso, Fernando Vieira de Carvalho, Antônio Pedroso de Albuquerque Sobrinho and Pedro Fortunato Ortiz.[11]

The escape of Rosa, her five children, and her partner Antônio Mina, taking on the border as the choice for their resistance, shows us how that space was capable of being crossed and makes clear the difficulty that it presented. We notice that sometimes our imagination sees the border as being composed of large territories void of populations. However, recent studies—principally those directed towards agrarian history—have demonstrated that the scenario was not quite like this. Large, medium, and small establishments existed together, being first populated not only by owners and their workers (slaves and free men), but also by *agregados* (people who have become a part of a family, be they relatives or not, or a poor farmer who lives on land with permission of the owner providing services caring for the land) and squatters (Farinatti, 2010). Soares, upon being alerted to the escape (theft) of his captives, immediately mobilized an *agregado* (who was also a friend) and his guard/herdsman, and was able to rapidly begin the search for his captives in places where crossing the river of Uruguay was known to be possible.

Rosa's mistress, upon denying her the emancipation that had already been granted to Rosa's partner Antônio, opted to keep one half of the couple in captivity not only to control the children who were still slaves, but the dependent freed man himself. The fact of her being Maria Fonseca Soares, wife of João Pereira Soares, denying Rosa's emancipation while seemingly accepting Antônio's liberation, makes us think that this mistress had a certain "dose" of power in the management of the farm and the roster of slaves. The *sesmaria* of Imbahá originally belonged to her family, not to Soares, and the couple came to obtain the land as an inheritance from her parents, Manoel Joaquim da Fonseca and Inácia Ferreira da Fonseca.[12]

The African, Antônio, was represented by a good lawyer; Matias Teixeira de Almeida was well known in the region, working for various causes, representing mainly major landowners. In 1852 he acted as the district attorney of Alegrete. However, we are mistaken in calling him "lawyer" since he did not have formal training as such. He was a *rábula* (someone who practices law without a diploma or degree), a professional whose knowledge was based on the forensic practice of legal advising (Flores 2007).[13] Even with a good "provisional" lawyer, none of the four individuals selected by Antônio as witnesses were called to testify. Additionally, the trader Domingos Barbier, who had bought the farm goods from Antônio on the day of the crime, was not summoned to court.

If the four black witnesses selected by the African defendant were known for belonging to the local black community and were members of the flocks of slaves belonging to important masters, Barbier was an even more prominent member of this border society. He was Italian, from Sardinia, and he had resided in Uruguaiana for many years. In 1855, he gave his testimony as a witness in a trial that occurred in the district of Alegrete, when a subject named Inácio Carvalho had too much to drink in Barbier's establishment and had asked Maximiano José Pedro to take him to the home of Liutenent Mariano, where he usually stopped. En route, the horses and harnesses of the drunken individual mysteriously disappeared. In 1855, Barbier was 33, single and a businessman.[14]

The woman who owned the lands where Antônio lived and where his crops were, had very close ties with Antônio's former owners. Dona Joaquina Fonseca, as cited by Antônio Mina, called herself Joaquina Ferreira da Fonseca, and she was the widow of Silvano Rodrigues Soares. It was a double kinship; Joaquina was the sister of the mistress of Antônio and Rosa, and Silvano was the brother of João Pereira Soares. Silvano had been a city councilman in Uruguaiana in 1858 and his will had been listed in 1867, with the executrix being the widow. Silvano and Mrs. Joaquina were owners of a farm made up of more or less a half a league of land, in the *sesmaria* between Imbahá and Touro Passo (valued at seven million and five hundred thousand *réis*).[15]

Wills are valuable sources for a variety of themes, including questions of health and sickness. For example, in the calculation of debts that the deceased, wealthy Silvano Soares had left, José João Fanqueiro, who had a barbershop, appeared requesting reimbursement for the expenses generated for treating said deceased. According to the bill for 196 *réis* presented by the barber, Fanqueiro had traveled to the farm of the deceased and conforming with what Dr. Bayley claimed, he had done two applications of European bleeders, four *réis* for each one, with 19 leeches in one application and 30 in the other. In the same will, also presented were a public deed and promise of sale of lands in the sector of Salto, in Uruguay, for 14 *contos* de réis (or the equivalent of seven thousand silver *patacões*, a currency of the day), made by the brothers of the deceased (Fidêncio Pereira Soares) on December 12, 1863. This will prove a common practice: the owners had land on both sides of the border. Almost

32 percent of the total goods willed were concentrated on the lot of slaves, which was made up of five captives: two Africans (João, 50 years old; Pedro, 55 years old) and three *crioulos* (Benedito, 41 years old; Tomás, 25 years old; Anacleta, 34 years old).

Notably, the four members of the local black community who were selected by Antônio as witnesses of his innocence were linked to this lot. Whether they had really seen Antônio at the house of Joaquina da Fonseca, or whether they had been close enough to Antônio to lie in his favor, the following were mentioned (but never called to testify): the emancipated blacks Pedro and João, and the slaves Henriqueta and Benedito. The slave João, as we saw, was African and was 50 years old. At the time of the will, he was assessed at 500 thousand *réis* and, as was custom (and later legalized by the law of September 28, 1871), he presented the money for his freedom, which was accepted by the heirs. The widow Joaquina Ferreira da Fonseca then gave him a letter of freedom on November 18, 1869 (notarized on December 20), confirming receipt of the amount agreed.[16] If Antônio mentions the African Pedro, 55 years old in 1870, as emancipated, the letter of emancipation must not have been notarized, but was more likely one of those oral agreements that occurred between captives and their illiterate maters. Benedito was not African like Antônio, but they shared a certain age affinity, as he was around 41 years old.

It is possible that whoever annotated what Antônio said made an error. Perhaps he had cited as witnesses, slaves Pedro and Benedito, and emancipated João and Henriqueta. As we saw, the first two appear in the mentioned will, that of Silvano Rodrigues Soares. João also, at the time, presented savings with the value of his assessment. And Henriqueta? According to church documents, we find some clues that indicate who Henriqueta was (friend and accomplice? of Antônio), what brought them together, and which networks of friends and relatives they shared.[17] On October 24, 1846 the innocent Manuel was formally baptized, born on October 12 of that same year, slave of Manuel Joaquim da Fonseca, who was the father of the wife of João Pereira Soares, master of Antônio. The godparents of the innocent Manuel were two slaves: an Angolan man whose name is crossed out and Henriqueta, slave of Silvano Rodrigues Soares. Five years later on May 11, 1851, it was the innocent Belarmino's turn, son of an anonymous father and Zeferina, slaves of Inácia Ferreira da Fonseca, wife of Manuel Joaquim and mother of the wife of the owner of the African Antônio. The sponsor of the baptized (Belarmino) was Tomás Anastácio, who we don't know if he was a slave or a free man, and the slave Henriqueta, who appears without any indication of who her master was.

We know mainly by the baptism of the child Manuel in 1846 that in among Silvano Rodrigues Soares' slaves there was a captive named Henriqueta, but she doesn't appear in his inventory of 1867. The mystery of her disappearance faded when we found an emancipation granted by Silvano Soares. On February 28, 1860, Silvano Rodrigues Soares composed a letter of emancipation *granting* freedom to the black African woman from Costa da Mina, Maria Henriqueta de São José, 40 years old.[18] We use the word "granting" ironically since Henriqueta, after working years for her master, still had to pay a *conto* of *réis* to buy her freedom.

It was not for nothing that Antônio trusted that Henriqueta would testify in his favor. She shared with him the experience of enslavement in Africa and of the transatlantic diaspora. Additionally, they were both from Costa da Mina. Antônio was defined in the emancipation letter as "from the coast," but in his record, he had classified himself as *Mina*. Both belonged to the same age group, between 50 and 60 years old in 1870 and they probably came from the Bight of Benin, a place from whence various ethno-cultural groups came:

> ...they are divided into various linguistic groups, among them are those who speak the Ewé language, enslaved as a consequence of the wars carried out by the kingdom of Daomé (Dahomey). These people of the Ewé tongue (sometimes called Jeje) cannot be confused with those of the Yorubá tongue (currently Nigeria and part of the current Daomé). The people of the Yorubá tongue trafficked to Brazil in the 18th and 19th century (here called Nagôs) are in large part from Daomé—Mina-Jeje and Mina-Nagô (Soares, 2000, p. 19).

We do not know what differences the two brought from the African continent; however, we do know that these differences did not impede cultural dialogues or ethnic reinventions. It would be a stretch of the historical imagination to believe that they had come together in the crossing of the Calunga Grande, companions of the Atlantic passage, on the same voyage. However, even driven in different ships, they shared the unrest of arriving in a strange land, the hard task of covering up homesickness and reducing the memory of the uprooting, wrapped in kinship and affectivity; they were invested in making, if not the same ties, at least some familiar to those that were distinct in the lands of their origin.

The important part of the connections forged among captives can be seen in church documents, especially in baptism registries. Ties are confirmed around the baptismal font, with the holy oils not only blessing the entrance of the one being baptized into the world of Christianity, but also anointing the formation of a network of spiritual relatives and potential allies. Observing upon whom fell the choice of sponsoring children and adults can give us a good point of analysis about the existing socio-familial networks and the relationships in which they invested in order to acquire and accumulate relational capital.

With this objective, we searched the church registries of Uruguaiana, stage of that unsuccessful escape towards the border undertaken by Antônio's family: Rosa, and her five children. We admit that our task was not unfruitful; however a bitter taste of frustration was left in the end. Let us be reminded that Rosa justified her ambition for emancipation as having *given eleven offspring to her owners*. Of these, just five were with her at the time of escape: Eugênio, Francisco, Fláubio, Domingos, and an infant. Eugênio perhaps the oldest being 12 years old. We planned to locate the baptisms of Rosa's children and to see what they told us about her relationships and kinships. Unfortunately, we found just one record of baptism related to her children. On June 16, 1862, Francisco was born, son of Rosa, both slaves of João Soares Pereira. However, five months later, on November 28, Francisco was baptized in the parish of Santa Ana de Uruguaiana by the vicar João Vicente Fernandes,[19] having as godparents the slave Antônio and free woman Henriqueta—who we already know. Henriqueta was free from the emancipation granted in 1860 and Antônio was still a slave, keeping in mind that he would break the shackles of captivity just seven years later in 1869. However, Rosa's son being sponsored by Antônio imposes on us a conundrum, since we know that according to the *Constituições Primeiras do Arcebispado da Bahia* (First Constitutions of the Archbishop of Bahia), the father could not be chosen for this role:

> Conforming to the disposition of Santo Concílio Tridentino, we order that in the baptism there is not more than one godfather and one godmother, and not permitted are two godfathers and two godmothers; such sponsors are selected by the father or mother, or the person who is responsible for the child; and being an adult, he chooses. We mandate that the priests do not take other sponsors other than those aforementioned, named, and chosen, being people already baptized; the godfather should not be less than fourteen years old, and the godmother not less than twelve years old, except with our special permission. The mother and father cannot be godparents of the baptized, nor can unbelievers, heretics, or the excommunicated, interdicts, deafs, mutes, and those that ignore the principles of our Holy Faith; not friars, nuns, ruling canons, or any other religious teacher (except military orders) can be chosen, nor by proxy (in Brügger, 2007, p. 283).

Unable to appear in the church registry of his child as the father because he had not married Rosa under Christian sacraments (which was a ritual of great importance, even for the African population) perhaps Antônio had resolved to appear as the godfather? If this had happened, either the vicar was not familiar enough with the black community of the border to identify the familial arrangements of the parish, or he was Antônio's accomplice in concealing it. Let us be reminded that Rosa's son, Eugênio, identified Antônio as his father in his testimony, proving the relationship that unified them. Perhaps Antônio had not been Rosa's only companion throughout her life. A woman who was black and determined, principally if we consider the stirring statement that she gave, which made clear her opinion of the captivity she had experienced and the plans she had for the future, Rosa did not hesitate to state in the court what she believed to be just, even though this weakened Antônio's pleas of innocence.

Or perhaps the relationship of the two had seen good moments and turbulent moments, with separations and emotional relapses, which would justify the phrase of that African man, almost in a tone of alleviation: "and with her he has lived like a dog does with a cat, that is, always at odds with each other."

Rosa's demand to be emancipated in return for the offspring she gave was not lacking in foundation. Doing a quick search for the emancipations registered in the notaries of the interior of Rio Grande do Sul, made available in the project done by Apers, we found dozens of letters with such justification. Repeated research on emancipations has demonstrated how women appear in most of the letters of freedom. Of the 10,055 letters of manumission registered in notaries of Porto Alegre, around 56 percent were for women. Entertaining intimate relationships (of various forms) with their masters, many of these women performed domestic services and must have been seduced with promises of freedom, not only to avoid possible revenge, but also to incentivize the production of offspring that increased the estate of their masters. Still, it is evident that the number of emancipations of women could not have been so considerably superior to those of men; after all their freedom corresponded to a loss of natural reproduction among slaves; upon freeing a woman, her womb was also freed—from then on, the offspring she had no longer belonged to the master. Aware of this, masters opted to emancipate women who had already created slave children and were no longer of childbearing age.

The master João Francisco da Silva, resident of Rio Pardo, gave a letter of emancipation to the African woman Mariana, from Benguela, who embodies the situation of various women like Rosa and the significance, not only patrimonial, but also political, of her reproductive ability. The letter was given by her master on August 3, 1825, for Mariana having:

> ...served me for more than 20 years with good will and helped to raise my children, and moreover for her having given 10 offspring, all of whom are living, and I have endowed them to my children, for these considerations and good services she is worthy of better luck and for this reason, from here forth, I give full and general freedom, gratu-

itously and of my free and spontaneous will without estrangement of any person (Rio Grande do Sul, 2006).

The word "gratuitously" is, in this type of document, a fallacy, a con. Twenty years of "good work" and the production of ten offspring, of which all of them surviving, make up capital (social, financial, relational) difficult to be measured. Especially in border zones, good management (in terms of investment and maintenance) in the composition of networks and socio-familial hierarchies was essential. According to what the historian João Fragoso presents (2003), referring to the old regime, but whose content very well concerns analysis for a good part of nineteenth century Brazil:

> The strategies of the groups were based on reciprocity, gifts, and countergifts. That was present in marriages—it is enough to consider dowries—such as in the distribution of gifts: service in royal offices and appointments to military posts. These practices established links with nobles and with sub alternative colonial groups; needless to say, reciprocity did not signify equality, particularly in the old regime (p. 27-8).

The 11 offspring raised by the *crioula* Rosa gave her the hope that her owners were *fair* enough to allow her to surpass the limits of the plantation. The children of Rosa that did not go with her in the scurry towards the border probably had not reached maturity, they were sold or served as dowry to solidify the matrimonial ties of the children of the owners. At almost 40 years old, with a body debilitated by the backbreaking work as a captive (even though domestic) and by the 11 children she produced, and as a mistress of an African man about 60 years old, it was unlikely that Rosa dreamed about procreating in freedom. Most likely, the plans of the couple were to obtain emancipation without onus or conditions and invest the savings they had and what they would accumulate in the future of freedom by at least some of the children they had while in captivity. The lady Maria Inácia da Fonseca Soares, however, stripped them of these desires.

Now, we slightly digress, before returning to the relationship of Rosa and Maria Inácia. As we saw when we referred to the church documents, other primary sources of the period can be consulted to illuminate bonds of various types. If we return to Antônio Mina's letter of emancipation from 1869, we will see that, in addition to the names of the beneficiary captive and the kind masters, we have three more individuals who are not introduced. Since the Maria Inácia was illiterate, signing on her behalf were Vicente Osório Rodrigues and as his witness, Zeferino de Ávila Rodrigues. João Pereira Soares signed for himself and as his witness, signed Augusto Peres de Farias.

Augusto was a witness in the trial against the freed man Antônio. He was 26 years old, native of Serro Largo, an eastern state of Uruguay, lived in Imbahá, married to the cousin of João Pereira Soares, in whose fields he lived. That is, he was absolutely a partial witness, given that he was dependent on and related to the master that was said to be harmed by the escape (or theft) of Rosa and her five minor children.

Scouring the baptism registries of Uruguaiana, behind the clues about the family of Rosa, we found one of the other witnesses of the letter that resulted in the captivity of Antônio. Zeferino de Ávila Rodrigues was born on August 14, 1846, son of Firmino Rodrigues de Ávila and Maria Inácia da Fonseca, both from Alegrete. Sixteen days after his birth, Zeferino was baptized in Cúria de Uruguaiana, having as sponsors his maternal grandparents, Manuel Joaquim da Fonseca (from Vacaria) and Inácia Francisca Ferreira (from Cachoeira). That is, we discovered that before marrying João Pereira Soares, the mistress and tormentor of Rosa had already been married once with a man named Firmino Rodrigues de Ávila; going after the documents of the deceased man, we embarked on another journey in the archives. Firmino had passed "from the present life" on July 24, 1856, without a will; his patrimony had been listed in 1857 and through it, we know that this wealthy deceased man had a flock of six slaves, which contains our female character:

Name	Age	Valuation	Other Characteristics
Luciano	50 years old	300$	
José Dionísio	16 years old	500$	
Rosa	26 years old	550$	
Martinha	8 years old	250$	
Eva	4 years old	150$	
Dionísio	16 years old	1:600$	Herder[20]

In general terms, this group seems to be balanced in terms of gender, with three men and three women, but, if we focus just on the group of adult captives, we will see that Rosa was the only woman of childbearing age. The *post-mortem* inventories are great sources, though it is rare that they give detailed facts about the familial relations of the assessed *merchandise*. However, this does not prevent us from imagining that Rosa, being the only adult woman of the bunch, is likely the mother of Martinha, 8 years old, and Eva 4 years old. But who was Rosa's companion in 1857? If Rosa's relationship was with someone within that group, it certainly wouldn't have been José Dionísio or Dionísio because they were not old enough to father two offspring of the *crioula* Rosa. We could bet, however, that it was Luciano.

The death of owners, or of one of them, always roused tensions in the black community. Negotiations with masters were cut, possibilities of the sale of part of the captive family were pressing. Savings were quickly put together to try and prevent relatives from being separated, who were sold as payment of debts owed by the deceased masters or given as inheritances to distant heirs. The couple, Firmino Rodrigues de Ávila and Maria Inácia da Fonseca, had, at the time of the passing of her husband, five minor children: Florinda (13 years old), Zeferino (11 years old), Vitalino (8 years old), Franklim (5 years old) and Inácia (2 years old).

Name	Age	Valuation	Heirs
Luciano	50 years old	300$	For the widow
José Dionísio	16 years old	500$	Divided into three shares of 166$ for Zeferino, Franklim and Inácia
Rosa	26 years old	550$	For the widow
Martinha	8 years old	250$	For Florinda
Eva	4 years old	150$	Vitalino
Dionísio	16 years old	1:600$	Divided among the orphans[21]

We can see from the distribution presented in the table of the "livestock" that Maria Inácia opted to keep what we guess to be the slave couple, with Rosa being of childbearing age and still able to produce offspring.

In an official letter dated March 8, 1862, six years after the passing of Firmino, João Pereira Soares indicates that he is married to Maria Inácia, her second marriage, that he is guardian of her children, and as such, administrator of her goods. On February 24 of the following year, João Pereira asks for the public sale of the livestock belonging to the fatherless children and requests that the judge also include in this lot the *pardo* José Dionísio, 16 years old, herder, because he suspected that the slave was planning to escape "and not wanting by any means to run the risk of this escape, that can be easily executed through the position of this municipality neighboring foreign republics."

We mention this excerpt to call attention not only to the latent possibility of slave escapes through the border, which the inhabitants of the southern province knew very well, but also to demonstrate how the owners could use these paths to freedom for their own benefit. That is, João Pereira wanted to publicly sell a good that did not belong to him, but to the orphans of Firmino Rodrigues de Ávila, and an efficient method that he came up with to convince the judicial authority was *to play on the consensus about the potential of the border as a strategy for slave escape.* This *consensus* was based on an old tradition of slave escape, but this case in particular was a false pretense, a trick played by the master of José Dionísio. We know this because it was during the time of the *vacas magras* (a figure of speech literally meaning "thin cows") in 1862, with droughts, fall of the price of cattle, etc. The judge accepted the master's argument, and three times José Dionísio went to the auction without finding a buyer. Years later, when one of sons adopted by João Pereira Soares, Zeferino, reached legal age and wanted to receive part of his paternal inheritance, there was José Dionísio. His possible escape, his plans of undertaking a dangerous (and perhaps successful) journey to the land of the Spanish doesn't seem to have been more than a clever speculation of the master.

We ask the readers for just one more moment of digression before closing this essay. It will be the last, and for good reason, attempt to put our lens closer to the *crioula* Rosa, to see her in more detail. We decided to try our luck and go after the inventory of the parents of Maria da Fonseca, she who denied Rosa's emancipation, perhaps to better understand the relationship between these two women, Rosa and Maria, slave and mistress. Maria Inácia, as we saw, was the daughter of Manuel Joaquim da Fonseca and Inácia Ferreira da Fonseca. Her father passed away in 1848 and her mother in 1851. In the will, dictated in the same year of his death, her father was said to have been born in the province of São Pedro do Rio Grande do Sul 58 years prior, who found himself "bedridden but in his right mind," who was married under the blessings of the church with Inácia Ferreira and who was the legitimate son of Manuel Joaquim da Fonseca and his wife Maria Barbosa.[22]

The parents of Maria Inácia were, however, very wealthy in terms of their estate and legacy. They owned about three thousand heads of cattle, composed of domesticated and wild oxen for breeding (788), young tamed bulls (12), tamed oxen (17), steers (200), wild mares (777), tamed mares (49), newly trained horses (40), horses (82), tamed and wild mules (11), and sheep (700). Among the real estate, what stood out was the stage for the escape of Antônio and Rosa, a plot of uncultivated land on the coast of the Imbahá Creek, part of the lower Uruguay river, that is, bordering with the Eastern State of Uruguay, valued at 12 *contos* of *réis*.

The black community under ownership of these masters was made up of ten members, *large and small*, "and outside of these there was one more mulatto named Ludovino who fled." In his will, Maria Inácia's father inserted a clause asking that listed captives not be divided, but that they should remain with his widow: "I declare and ask of all my children that the existing slaves in this testament, upon my death, if they can, remain with my wife to be divided in the second inventory." We see that the community was:

Name	*Characteristics*	*Valuation*
Felipe	Mina, field worker, 50 years old	200$
José	Cabinda, herder, 24 years old	600$
Joaquim	Mina, field worker, 28 years old	500$
Pedro	Congo, herder, 24 years old	600$
José Maria	Angola, field worker, 20 years old	400$
Benedito	Crioulo, herder, 20 years old	600$
Dionísio	Crioulo, 8 years old	200$
Manuel	Crioulo, 2 years old	80$
Zeferina	Crioula, 28 years old	500$
Teresa	Crioula, 26 years old	400$

These ten black individuals composed a disparate group in terms of distribution among the sexes: eight were men and only two were women. If we isolate only the adults, the difference diminishes a little, being six men and just two women. The presence of Africans in this community under captivity was considerable: five of the six adult men were from the transatlantic trade. Two were from Atlantic West Africa (coincidentally they were both fieldsmen) and three from Central Africa (Congo, Angola, and Cabinda). Of course, this black community was not limited to these individuals in captivity; they associated themselves with the world of other plantations and even with free and freed individuals. The fact that most Africans enslaved and commercialized through the Atlantic were men was an extremely important variable in the matrimonial market of the time. The African Diaspora made its victims not only reinvent their cul-

"WITH HER, HE LIVED LIKE A DOG LIVES WITH A CAT"

tures, but their affections, creating dialogues and finding similarities with partners who they found to be in conditions like their own.

Still, the detail that interests us most in this will and inventory is the declaration of the gifts given by this wealthy and provident couple to their children. Cautious and aware that their sons and daughters needed some help in the beginning of their married lives, Manuel Joaquim da Fonseca and Inácia Ferreira da Fonseca resolved to give them goods that they considered to be important. This practice was mentioned and detailed in the inventory, because the gifts acted as advances of the inheritance and should have been discounted at the time of fulfillment. The widow communicated that the heirs had already received the following:

Child	*Spouse*	*Gift (dowry)*
Januário Ferreira da Fonseca	Married to Leonor de Ávila	• Pedro, slave (Congo, 14 years old) – 600$; • 700 breeding cattle (reses chucras de criar) and 10 tame horses; • In money, in different times, 1:190$800 and more 200$
Remualdo Ferreira da Fonseca	Married to Joana de Tal	• 300 breeding cattle and 10 tame horses
Joaquina Ferreira da Fonseca	Married to Silvano Rodrigues Soares	• Henriqueta, slave (Mina, 30 years old)
Carlota Manoela da Fonseca	Married to José Machado Leão	• Cecília, slave (Conga, 30 years old) • 500$;
Maria Ferreira da Fonseca	Married to Firmino de Ávila	• Rosa, slave (16 years old) – 700$;
Gertrudes Ferreira da Fonseca	Married to Alberto Pereira de Lima	• Catarina (Mina, 15 years old) – 700$;
Inácio Manoel da Fonseca	Single, 16 years old	

We don't want to belabor the point, but we would like to highlight that in the table, some names already well known to us appear transcribed in bold. Joaquina Fonseca, owner of the lands where Antônio had his crops in 1870, received as a gift the African *Mina* woman Henriqueta. If there was a process of an attempt—almost desperate—for these individuals to make themselves similar in captivity so they could be recognized as allies, relatives, lovers, friends, Antônio and Henriqueta, without a doubt, were examples of this, being close to each other from the beginning. The cultural, linguistic (Ewé or Yorubá) and religious symmetry—of both—in addition to the experience of the diaspora, allowed them to be deemed, in 1870, as accomplices and in partnership.

Also in the table is Maria Ferreira, married first to Firmino Rodrigues de Ávila (died in 1857) and later to João Pereira Soares. She received as a marriage dowry, none other than the *crioula* slave Rosa. And, if Rosa was approximately 39 in 1870 and 26 in 1857, we can suppose that she had been born around 1831. If Maria Ferreira had a 13-year-old son in the will of her first husband in 1857, then she must have married around 1844. The age difference between these two women must not have been very large. When Rosa served as a dowry, she must have been about 13 years old and her owner not much older.

Looking closely, the table presented shows us a pattern: daughters received female slaves and men received, principally, cattle. Perhaps the logic was to provide a captive woman of childbearing age to begin breeding a flock of slaves, but also to give women who were leaving their father's house for the first time a form of support—a captive woman who accompanied them from their youth. Of course, these slaves mentioned could have been purchased with the objective of becoming the dowry of daughters and sons; however, what is more likely is that they were a part of the future flock of the couple. We can then imagine that Rosa had grown up in an environment almost completely African, and possibly was the child of one of these women who survived the suffering of the slave ship and, arriving here, drew, from who knows where, the energy and spirit needed to reorganize their lives (sexual, familial, and emotional), as best as they could. The difference in the presumed age of the African Antônio, around 60 years old, and the *crioula* Rosa, 39 years old, was about 21 years, perhaps indicative that he had a privileged socio-community position which is evidenced by the fact that he could emancipate himself and build his house and crops in neighboring land. Rosa associated with the peak of the hierarchy of the plantation and of the local black community.

It is hard to find Rosa at this intersection of borders she inhabited; from the border between slavery and freedom that she faced from birth, all the way to the delicate and cruel situation of having had and lost children, which characterized her motherhood. Rosa and Maria, slave and mistress, had *connected* lives; it is unknown from exactly when, but they were certainly in proximity with each other for dozens of years. Rosa's reproductive strategies depended on keeping some of her children close (Slenes, 1999, p. 200-4). However, these plans were imagined in terms of their possibilities and idiosyncrasies in a game of what was possible and what was desired. Slaves who, in plans of bettering their life in captivity and obtaining emancipation, became so important that their masters avoided freeing them or their complete families.

We could say that Rosa's emancipation may have been used in a dispute in the internal politics of this nuclear seigniorial family. The goods belonged to the couple, but a good part of the inheritance came from the family of the mistress. That is, perhaps not freeing Rosa had been a part of a micro-political game of the mistress asserting her power upon her husband. In Antônio's emancipation letter, a relative of Mr. João Pereira Soares and the son of Mrs. Maria Inácia da Fonseca Soares signed as witnesses. It was clearly a lordly, noble family, though not necessarily inseparable.

In any case, it was not exclusively a fight between a mistress and her slave. Let us be reminded that they both shared the same domestic space of the house. What feelings permeated this intimacy of gender? After so many years of being supported by her slave, perhaps Maria wondered how would she be able to live without her. On the other hand, Rosa must have felt a profound hatred when she realized that the years in which she dressed and fed her mistress, having and losing children, that made her owners rich and helped them build networks and alliances, were not sufficient for her to be worthy of enjoying some years of complete freedom with some of her children and her lover.

It was a part of the politics of seigniorial rule to bargain with the slave family, keeping the emancipated family members nearby (if possible) in order to provide services and obedience. We reviewed the notary books of Uruguaiana through the end of the slavery period and we encountered nothing on Rosa and her children. Had this escape condemned Rosa and her offspring to remain in captivity without any chances of obtaining emancipation? It is common that we fall in love with individuals who fleetingly appear in our research and, in general, this passion ends up as frustration because we don't know the fate that befell them. However, the little that we know and have tried to recount here seems to give us a little of the dimension of the complex relationships created among captives and masters in the slave world and near the southern border in the 19th century.

Notes

1. Arquivo Público do Estado do Rio Grande do Sul (APERS) [Public Archive of the State of Rio Grande do Sul], Uruguaiana, 1° Cartório Cível e Crime [Archives of Civil and Criminal Cases], bundle 70, no. 2604.

2. A *mangueira* is "a large corral of wire, stone and wood, attached to the house of the ranch, which encloses the cattle for tagging, curing of worms, castration, sorting, etc" (Bossle, 2003, p. 320).

3. *Posteiro*: a close friend of the ranch, who living on the outer edge or border of the field, is in the best position to guard the property and impede the invasion of strangers. He also cares for the fences and cattle, helps with rodeos, and performs other tasks" (Bossle, 2003, p. 411).

4. APERS, Livro de Tabelionato n. 8, Transmissões e Notas, f. 111-2r.

5. See Caratti, 2010; Petiz, 2006.

6. Uruguaiana was recaptured on September 18, 1865, in a siege organized by Brazilian, Argentine, and Uruguayan troops. The date remained symbolic in the mind of the local inhabitants. On September 18, 1870, Dr. Joaquim do Nascimento Costa da Cunha e Lima gave a letter of emancipation to Sebastião, 12 years old, in honor of the "5th anniversary of the surrender of Uruguaiana." The letter, however, was not without fee or condition: "being only required to accompany me for 9 years, being a minor [...] and incapable of governing and caring for himself." PERS, 1.° Tabelionato de Uruguaiana, Livro 8 de Transmissões e Notas, p. 60v.

7. *Picaço*: "said to be a horse with dark or black hair with a white forehead and hooves (some or all)" (Bossle, 2003, p. 395).

8. Cunha e Lima received a bachelor's degree in Social and Judicial Sciences from the School of Law of Recife (Faculdade de Direito de Recife). On July 25, 1859 in Paraíba do Norte, he gave a letter of emancipation to Silvério, not registering it until 10/26/1868 in Alegrete. The letter was granted in retribution for the good service provided, "love, zeal and fidelity, and sincere friendship with which he has given me: (Alegrete, 2.o Tabelionato, Livros Notariais de Regis- tros Diversos, Livro 1, 1859 a 1877, p. 30r, Catálogo do APERS, p. 52).

9. A clarification about the judicial process in this case is fitting. Probably due to the still fragile situation of the imperial borders and to avoid unnecessary delays, Lei n. 566 [Law 566] was enacted on July 2, 1850, regulated in the same year on October 7th by regulation no. 707. This legislation took from the purview of the jury some penal infractions such as counterfeiting, theft, homicide, resistance, and removal of prisoners. It was up to the municipal court to determine guilt, pronouncing the accused to be brought to trial by the judge. Only in 1871, with Law no. 2,033 (of September 20th) and the Decree no. 4824 (of November 22nd), did the jury regain to its power over such crimes.

10. APERS, 2.º Cartório Cível de Uruguaiana, Inventariante: Maria Fonseca Soares, 1893, bundle 1, document 38.

11. APERS, Tabelionato de Uruguaiana, Livro 9 de Transmissões de Notas [Notary of Uruguaiana, Book 9 of the Transmission of Notaries], p. 27. In 1861 Antônio Pedro de Miranda e Castro was working in the Alfândega de Uruguaiana (customs office). On that date, the Commisão de Inspeção [inspection commission] was sent from Porto Alegre to investigate the "poor state of oversight" it was in. Miranda e Castro was one of the questioned, acting as a discharge official, performing duties of the 3rd clerk (Flores, 2007, p. 130-1). The employees of customs offices are little studied, but they make up very interesting types of socio-professionals. Fulfilling their duties on the borders, conversing and interacting with Brazilians and *correntinos* [from Argentina], Orientals and Castilians, smugglers and soldiers, they obtained information on both sides of the lines: political-partisan situations, aggressions, slavery and trafficking restrictive laws etc. Because of this, it was not rare that there were elements that raised the suspicion of authorities. On December 8, 1861 in Santa Ana de Uruguaiana, Manoel was baptized; born on October 5th of the prior year, son of Joaquina, slave of Joaquina Francisca da Silva. His godparents were: Antônio Pedro de Mirana e Castro, Emília, in addition to a freed woman whose name was erased.

12. APERS, Tabelionato de Uruguaiana, 12.º Livro de Transmissões e Notas [Notary of Uruguaiana, Book 9 of the Transmission of Notaries], p. 344 and 351.

13. Matias was a friend and ally of Ribeiro de Almeida, a powerful border clan. On December 7, 1869, he and Claudiana Maria Teixeira sponsored the *crioula*

slave Zeferino, born on June 28 of that same year, natural daughter of the *parda* Eufêmia, slave of the lieutenant-colonel Feliciano Ribeiro de Almeida. Arquivo Histórico da Cúria Metropolitana de Porto Alegre (AHCMPA), Book 2 of baptisms of saves of the Igreja do Rosário church, f. 100.

14. APERS, Comarca de Alegrete [Judiciary District of Alegrete], 1.ª Vara Cível e Crime [Civil and Criminal Jurisdiction], Box 009.0300, Case no. 2367. Two years later, in 1857, Barbier's business place was broken into and two foreigners were indicated as defendants: Domingos Baru Agote (native of the city of Paraná, Entre Rios) and Pedro Celestino (from Estado Oriental). APERS, Comarca de Alegrete, 1.ª Vara Cível e Crime, Box 009.0299, Case no. 2332.

15. APERS, Comarca de Alegrete, [Judiciary District of Alegrete], Inventory no. 202, 1.º/1/1867.

16. APERS, 1.º Tabelionato de Uruguaiana, Livro 7 de Transmissões e Notas (1847 to 1854), f. 57v.

17. The church authorities are still a little hesitant to open their archives freely to historians. With the exception, in the case of Rio Grande do Sul, the Cúria Metropolitana de Porto Alegre. In the case of the church registries of Uruguaiana, there are many obstacles to reach the manuscripts deteriorated by time and poor conservation. However, the solidarity among historians *moves mountains*! I kindly thank Marcelo Matheus, Jonas Vargas and Leandro Fontella for providing the photos of the deaths and baptisms in the surveyed region.

18. APERS, Tabelionato de Uruguaiana, Livro 4 de Transmissões e Notas, f. 3r, letter registered on March 6, 1860.

19. Native of São Paulo, Freguesia da Sé, legitimate son of José Vicente de Jesus and Maria Francisca Fernandes. Ordained in São Paulo on September 21, 1830. Parish priest and Vicar of Vara de Lages from 1831 to 1846, later transferred to Cruz Alta and, finally to Uruguaiana where he remained from 1848 to 1863. He passed away in Porto Alegre on July 16, 1863 from cardiac illness at 63 years old. (Rubert, 1994, p. 123).

20. APERS, 1.º Cartório de Órfãos de Uruguaiana, Inventário n.º 101, Inventoried: Firmino Rodrigues de Ávila, Executrix: Maria Inácia da Fonseca: 1857.

21. Two of the couple's daughters did not survive: Florinda passed on 12/29/1860 and Inácia on 12/25/1865.

22. APERS, 1.º Cartório de Órfãos de Uruguaiana, Inventário n.º 39, Inventoried: Manoel Joaquim da Fonseca, Executrix: Ignácia Ferreira da Fonseca, Date: 1/1/1848.

Bibliography

Bossle, Batista. *Dicionário gaúcho brasileiro.* [Brazilian Gaucho Dictionary]. Porto Alegre: Artes e Ofícios, 2003.

Brügger, Silvia. *Minas patriarcal: família e sociedade (São João Del Rei – séculos 18th e 19th).* [Patriarchal Mines: Family and Society (São João del Rei –18th and 19th Centuries]. São Paulo: Annablume, 2007.

Caratti, Jônatas Marques. *O solo da liberdade: as trajetórias da preta Faustina e do pardo Anacleto pela fronteira rio-grandense em tempos do processo abolicionista uruguaio (1842-1862).* [The Soil of Liberty: Pathways of the Black Woman Faustina and the Mulatto Anacleto through the Rio Grande do Sul Borderlands During the Times of the Uruguayan Abolitionist Period (1842-1862)]. 2010. Masters Thesis (História) – Universidade do Vale do Rio dos Sinos (Unisinos), São Leopoldo, RS.

Farinatti, Luiz Augusto Ebling. *Confins meridionais: famílias de elite e sociedade agrária na Fronteira Sul do Brasil (1825-1865).* [Southern Borders: Families of the Elite and Agrarian Society of the Southern Border of Brazil (1825-1865)]. Santa Maria: Ed. da UFSM, 2010.

Flores, Mariana Flores da Cunha Thompson. *Contrabando e contrabandistas na fronteira oeste do Rio Grande do Sul – 1851-1864.* [Contraband and Traffickers in the Eastern Border of Rio Grande do Sul – 1851-1864]. Masters Thesis (História) – Universidade Federal do Rio Grande do Sul (UFRGS), Porto Alegre, 2007.

Fragoso, João Luís. "A nobreza vive em bandos: a economia política das melhores famílias da terra do Rio de Janeiro, século XVII. Algumas notas de pesquisa." [Nobility Lives in Gangs: Political Economy of the Best Families of the land of Rio de Janeiro, 18th Century. Some Research Notes]. Tempo, Niterói, UFF, v. 8, n. 15, Jul.-Dec. 2003.

Levi, Giovanni. *A herança imaterial.* [Immaterial Inheritance] Rio de Janeiro: Civilização Brasileira, 2000.

Petiz, Silmei de Sant'Anna. *Buscando a liberdade. As fugas de escravos da São Pedro para o além-fronteira (1815-1851).* [Searching for Freedom. Slave Escapes of São Pedro Beyond the Border (1815-1851)] Passo Fundo: Ed. de Passo Fundo, 2006.

Rio Grande Do Sul. Secretaria de Administração e Recursos Humanos. Departamento de Arquivo Público. Documentos da escravidão. Catálogo Seletivo de cartas de liberdade. Acervo dos Tabelionatos de municípios do interior do Rio Grande do Sul. [Secretary of Administration and Human Resources. Department of Public Archives. Documents of Slavery. Selective Catalog of Freedom Papers. Collection of Municipal Notaries of the Interior of Rio Grande do Sul]. Porto Alegre: Corag, 2006, v. II.

Rubert, Arlindo. *História da Igreja no Rio Grande do Sul.* [History of the Church in Rio Grande do Sul]. Porto Alegre: EDIPUCRS, 1994, v. II.

Slenes, Robert. *Na senzala, uma flor: esperanças e recordações na formação da família escrava no sudeste do Brasil, século XIX.* [On the Plantation, a Flower: Hopes and Memories in the Formation of Slave Families in the Southeast of Brazil, 19th Century]. Rio de Janeiro: Nova Fronteira, 1999.

Soares, Mariza de Carvalho. *Devotos da cor. Identidade étnica, religiosidade e escravidão no Rio de Janeiro, século* XVIII. [Devotees of Color. Ethnic Identity, Religiosity, and Slavery in Rio de Janeiro, 18th Century]. Rio de Janeiro: Civilização Brasileira, 2000.

11

GENDER RELATIONS IN THE DAILY LIFE OF
BLACK WOMEN IN 19TH CENTURY BAHIA

Isabel Cristina Ferreira Dos Reis

Domingas and Jacó; Augusta, Ubaldina and Carlos Hermes da Purificação: characters with complicated stories in Bahia in the second half of the 19th century. I call special attention to the story of women who faced a daily fight for survival and sought ways to defend themselves from exploitation and subjugation under the system of slavery, in addition to such unequal relations between men and women in the society of their time. Being a woman, and black, in a slave society made the existence of these women more difficult and complex because they were always subject to all sorts of assaults and bad conditions.

The emotional relationship between Domingas and Jacó

The freed African woman Domingas was found dead inside her house in the city of Muritiba, a term for the town of Cachoeira, in the Recôncavo Baiano. The principal suspect of the crime was Jacó, her "lover" of 16 years.[1] Jacó was a *Nagô* (Yoruba) African, he was more than 40 years old and lived doing farm service in the company of his master, captain Carlos Pereira da Mota, for more than 20 years. The suspicion fell upon on the lover of the deceased woman because on the night of December 30, 1861, days before the crime, some people claimed to have heard him say that "he would kill the woman and then cut out her tongue." The day after these threats, Domingas went to a neighbor's house saying that she had escaped being killed by Jacó. After these events, the body of the African woman was found in a state of decomposition on the morning of January 7, 1862 in her home, "a house with a straw roof, mud walls with a window and two doors, one in front and the other leading to the backyard...."[2] The coroner's report indicated that the corpse was on the floor of the bedroom. It was stated that the door to the backyard was open, with the key in the inside lock, which led the experts to believe that the assailant had left through that door, after having fought with the woman; the woman was determined to be killed by "strangling."

The description of the house and the belongings of the African woman, as well as her daily life full of much work, provide an idea of how blacks who left captivity lived. The belongings of Domingas were listed by the investigators as two "trunks," a larger one and a smaller one. The larger trunk was open and contained all the clothes belonging to the woman, "good and bad";[3] the smaller was closed and was broken open by a deputy, who found in it a "bulk of new shirts" and some fabric that was considered useless. In the living room of the woman's house, there were approximately 20 melons, about a "yoke" of green bananas, and 1,600 *réis* (currency of the time) in coins in a corner, buried in the dirt. There was also a large amount of sheet tobacco: "an *arroba*" (a unit of measurement used during the time, equivalent to 32 lbs).

Domingas, like an infinite number of African and African-descent women of her time, was an entrepreneur; she owned a small house with rooms and was able to save a little money which she amassed from her "sales"—in the trial these appear to be melons, bananas, sheet tobacco, lard, *aipim* (cassava or manioc root), beans, and "other things" not explicitly named—working Saturdays and Sundays, rain or shine. The daily life of work for a freed black woman is a particularly important aspect to observe throughout Brazilian history. Different from what happened with the majority of white women, especially from the middle class and high society of the time, black women always had to find ways to make their subsistence viable.

In the 19th century, slavery in urban centers—and even in a small town like Muritiba—was distinguished by the amount of male and female workers for hire, those working the commercialization of products and the offering of services. Africans and *crioulos* (blacks born into captivity in Brazil) of both sexes and different legal statuses filled the day-to-day of the main towns and cities of the provinces of the empire, and were seen in the streets, squares, and alleys with their baskets and trays, very eager to sell various products. If there were individuals of both sexes, there were predominantly, without a doubt, women; they were typical figures in this realm of activity, accompanied by their small children tied to their back, wrapped in a large variety of colored fabric.[4]

In the area of service, black women worked as wet nurses, washwomen, ironers, seamstresses, and cooks, among other occupations. Men worked as bakers, shoemakers, carpenters, tailors, cooks, coachmen, coopers, sailors, masons, chair carriers, caulkers, goldsmiths, etc.[5] These were the ways in which many enslaved people could pay for their emancipation, with the savings accumulated from doing such work. Once freed, they continued as workers, guaranteeing they could continue to sustain their families.

Through the information made available by the deponents in the trial of Domingas' death, it is clear that she worked for hire, creating a small business from the products found in her house. Although negligible, the money found among her belongings was the result of her savings and could have been something she was reserving to purchase of the emancipation of her partner.

Eight people were called to testify in the trial of her murder. The first to be called was her neighbor Marciano Francisco Martins, who said that "on one day in December" he heard "disruption" and, shortly thereafter, Domingas appeared, wanting to file a complaint against someone. Right behind her was Jacó; however, Marciano refused to listen to either one of them. When the couple was returning to the place from whence they came, Marciano heard Jacó proclaim the following: "If you want to buy me tomorrow, go to the house of my owner."[6] On the 31st, Domingas showed Marciano her swollen and scraped forehead and knee, saying that Jacó caused the injuries. The reason for the tussle between the couple stemmed from the promise made by the woman to buy the emancipation of her "lover."

During the hearing of the witnesses, the representative of the defendant, lieutenant Joaquim Pereira Teixeira, appeared to attempt to suggest other causes for the death of the African woman, such as the possibility of her having died due to some illness. Before the hypothesis of Domingas having been murdered was even presented, the lieutenant argued that the suspect of the crime could be someone else, not Jacó, since the good behavior of Domingas' companion was ratified by all of the deponents in the trial. Effectively, the witnesses were unanimous in acknowledging that Jacó was a "peaceful" man, which was favorable for the defense of the accused.

Balbino José de Sena, for example, affirmed that he heard Jacó ask forgiveness from various neighbors for certain things that he said. There was someone who said that they had never seen Jacó cause disorder with strangers, as well as completely ignoring who could have been Domingas' killer. However, some witnesses admitted to knowing that between the couple, "there were scuffles." The deponents also revealed that Domingas complained "more or less" of some "ailment," or "secret disease," of pains in the body that, "when they attacked her she was all twisted up," lasting for a few hours. Regarding enmities of the African woman, Marciano Francisco Martins testified that "he had heard about, more or less" someone complaining about Domingas.

Domingas' house was located across from the house belonging to Inácia Moreira da Conceição, and even so, she claimed to know nothing of these "scuffles" between the couple. From her house, the neighbor had seen Jacó and Domingas together in the window of the house of the deceased on January 1, "in the complete harmony they had always lived in."[7] Inácia also said that on Saturday afternoon, January 4, she saw the freed woman arrive on the street where she sold her goods, very happy, even singing. As that afternoon was very rainy and stormy, Inácia did not see her any more that day, nor the following Sunday and Monday. On Tuesday, the 7th, around two o'clock in the afternoon, Jacó passed in front of Inácia's house on a horse. At that time, she called him to mention the great "stench" that was coming from the house of his "lover." Jacó then responded to her that perhaps it was because of the sheep that she kept inside the house. Despite this being a possible situation, in the trial, there was no other reference to this animal raised inside Domingas' house.

It seems that this couple lived, as it would be said in contemporary and very colloquial terms, a bit of a love/hate relationship. (The original phrase translates as "between slaps and kisses," indicating an on again/off again tempestuous quality to the relationship). This is evidenced by Bernardino José de Sena's statement that, on January 2nd, Domingas appeared complaining about Jacó because he had hit her on her head and back with a stick. Bernardino said that he failed to see the "offenses" Domingas claimed and gave a description—a nearly idyllic scene—of the following day, a Friday, when he saw Domingas pass by,

> …with her trough on her head, selling lard and other things, and on Saturday morning he also saw her pass by the door, selling *aipim*, and in the afternoon on the same day, when there was a growling thunderstorm, he saw her return singing very happily, which according to the alleged witness, was Sunday, and Monday he didn't see her again and then on Tuesday, the seventh of the same month, she was found dead....[8]

Another of Domingas' neighbors, Teodora Maria de Oliveira, contrary to what Inácia claimed, affirmed that she saw the fight between the couple the day before and even heard Jacó say to his lover "that the next day she was going to buy him from his master." The day following the fight, Teodora saw Domingas doing her "business" until Saturday night, when the African woman disappeared, only reappearing again on Tuesday, January 7, the day she was found dead. Bernardino José de Sena, who witnessed the deputy break into Domingas' house, suspected that after her death, the woman had been robbed because many of the things he hoped to find in her house were not found, such as troughs with lard and beans. Given Jacó's expectation of being emancipated with Domingas' savings, it can also be speculated that the amount of money found inside the house of the African woman was paltry. Perhaps it was left to cover up a theft?

The testimony of Antônio de Cerqueira do Carmo, a 60-year old man, provoked controversy upon affirming that he heard from the freed man Albano Joaquim Pereira that Jacó had sworn to cut out Domingas' tongue, "kill her and lay her tongue under her body."[9] On the day of Domingas' burial, Antônio had found Jacó accompanying the "group" that carried the corpse of the woman. When he asked him why he had committed that crime, Jacó gave the response that it was all "untrue" what they wanted to blame on him, that "he had only given her [Domingas] a few smacks"—which actually denotes that giving "smacks" to women was a fact of life that was not typically censored, especially when it came to a black woman. On account of the statement given by Antônio, the ex-slave Albano was invited to testify, but in court he denied having heard Jacó threaten Domingas with death and assured that what he told Antônio was only what he had heard from other people. The two witnesses, Antônio and Albano, were later summoned for a reconciliation of their testimonies, confirming what they had said before.

For the above reasons, it would not be imprudent to suppose that Jacó was, in fact, the perpetrator, motivated by the delay or even abandonment of his companion in buying his freedom. It is very likely that, in the activity in which he was employed, Jacó did not have conditions to get the necessary resources to emancipate himself, and for this reason, he was counting on the help of his partner. He, however, flatly denied committing the crime and affirmed that at the time, he was in the bed at his master's house, "sick with stomach pains." Unfortunately, the trial does not contain the testimony of his master, corroborating or not, the enslaved man's alibi.

Jacó's new representative, Felipe Néri Teles, made his defense arguing it to be evident, from the interrogation of the accused, that he was not a criminal, because there was no compromising proof or any indication that he was the killer. For the representative, the eight witnesses called upon in the trial affirmed nothing against the accused that would constitute proof of the facts presented. The accusation placed upon Jacó, in the opinion of his defender, was only based on the fact of him being the "lover" of the victim, which should have served as support for his defense, seeing that,

> ...living with her for 16 years, and not having science of fact of something extraordinary between them [?], for the minor disagreements which appeared between them not being enough to induce the accused to perpetrate a crime of murder, especially with Domingas being his closest friend, the African man Jacó not having committed the smallest crime during his time here in her residence, being completely calm, exactly as the witnesses in the trial affirmed.[10]

In spite of the allegations made by the defender, the complaint was upheld. The examination of the corpse, the interrogation of Jacó and the testimonies of the witnesses were considered sufficient to indict the accused, and his arrest was ordered. The owner of the slave appealed the decision with the district judge of the province.

Curiosity about how a shared life experience between a freed woman and a man subject to the regime of captivity was so enduring was satisfied through Jacó's second interrogation. He revealed that he lived in the area for 25 years and that the relationship of the couple, as we already discovered, lasted 16 years. He even said that he went to his "lover's" house on Sundays and at night when he didn't have work to do for his master, which indicates that he had permission from his owner to meet with Domingas. Despite so many years living together, it appears that the couple did not have children, since this fact was not mentioned in the trial. There is also no indication that Domingas had belonged to the same master as Jacó.

The interrogation of the defendant proceeded with explanations about the "illness" that befell him at the time of Domingas' death, with headaches and "spasms" piercing his side, and about the symptoms of Domingas' sickness, described as pain in her bones; "ailments" they both suffered from for some time. Jacó admitted to having "exchanged some words" with the victim in the month of December of the previous year and not having gone to his lover's house that Monday because he was sick. However, he was not able to free himself from being convicted of the crime. On May 16, 1862 he was given the sentence: penalty of "perpetual galleys" (a life sentence of hard labor) and payment for the costs of the trial, which in virtue of his enslaved condition, had to be paid by his owner.

The history of the couple Domingas and Jacó makes it clear that emotional relationships and family ties grew in importance for individuals who had experienced life trajectories profoundly marked by subjugation and exploitation. For those who were not able to solidify family or community ties, the situation became very precarious. Solidarity and mutual support were indispensable elements and could contribute to Africans and African-descendants conquering a life with some dignity or obtaining help in moments of great hardship. The support of close friends and relatives was fundamental, especially for those who became sick or incapacitated, or those who reached old age, situations in which they didn't have enough strength to work and support themselves. Based on the information contained in the criminal trial, we can gather that there was an agreement between the couple, namely, the promise of Domingas to buy Jacó's emancipation. Everything indicates that this was behind the disagreements between the two, resulting in the violent death of the African woman.

Augusta's savings and Ubaldina's wedding

We can confirm that this story began in 1872, opening with a criminal trial; however, certainly it deals with a much older story, involving a distant history fed by dreams, projects, and commitment to making them happen. The case occurred in the capital of the province of Bahia and the protagonists were two women born in captivity: sisters Augusta and Ubaldina.

Regarding the *parda* (mixed race or mulatta) Augusta, I have little information. I only know that she belonged to the powerful magistrate João José de Almeida Couto.[11] However her sister, Ubaldina Ana da Conceição, was 24 years old, native of the city of Santo Amaro (in Recôncavo Baiano) but lived in Freguesia da Sé in the center of Salvador, and belonged to Joaquim Domingos Lopes. I believe that, like Augusta, Ubaldina had also been born in Santo Amaro. The sisters, having been sent to Salvador, had the luck of remaining close to each other, even though they belonged to different owners.

I do not have any details available about their interactions in Salvador, nor the frequency with which they contacted each other. Still, it would not be too much to suppose that they interacted daily, considering the wide mobility and autonomy that typically permeated the lives of enslaved residents of urban centers such as Salvador in the second half of the 19th century. The story of Augusta and Ubaldina came to us by way of a criminal trial of embezzlement filed against Carlos Hermes da Putrificação on November 19, 1872. In the trial, there is no more information about the owners of the slaves; they remained on the sidelines, not even testifying. Even though Augusta's master was the plaintiff, attorneys always represented him.

It just so happened that Augusta, having created a small savings of 600 thousand *réis*, asked her master to collect it at the Caixa Econômica, with the intention of "winning some prize." Augusta was trying to use the savings "in benefit of her freedom." Her sister, knowing that Augusta had this amount of money, mentioned it to Carlos Hermes da Purificação, with whom she "entertained relations." Aware that the money existed, Carlos Hermes formulated a "gimmick" to get it. He convinced Ubaldina to ask her sister for the money, to use it for her emancipation; once done, he would marry her—Ubaldina. It was as such that Augusta, Carlos Hermes, and Ubaldina made an agreement. Carlos' proposal seemed reasonable; it was important that Ubaldina was emancipated before marrying because that way, the couple could live autonomously, without exploitation, interference, or impositions from the owner of the captive woman, and more importantly, the offspring of the couple would not be born from the womb of a slave.

Upon deciding to give her savings to Carlos Hermes, Augusta considered that, to benefit her sister, "it would make her happy as if she had lost nothing, seeing as later she would be reimbursed for her money." She imagined she would be able to wait a little longer to reach her so desired freedom, because she found herself "under a gentle and smooth rule."[12] I do not have any information available about the style of interaction between Augusta's sister and her owner—if the treatment given by Ubaldina's owner influenced her sister's decision or not. Further, as a matter of common sense, facing the need to count on the support of her owners in this feud, it would not have been wise for the sisters to express any type of complaint about the treatment from their masters at the time. What was evident was Augusta's satisfaction in being able to contribute to her sister being freed and getting married.

As is commonly known, in spite of the purchase of emancipation being a common practice for some time, only starting from the Law n. 2.040 of September 1871 (*Lei do Ventre Livre*), was the legal right given to the enslaved person to accumulate "savings" through donations, endowments, inheritances, and what they obtained with the consent of their owner, through their work and savings.[13] From then on, captives widely used this resource to buy their own freedom or the manumission of friends and relatives, even though it was against the wishes of their masters. The story of the two sisters Augusta and Ubaldina shows that the task of the slave to possess savings not only involved personal aspirations, projects, and expectations, but those of friends and relatives as well.

Accumulating savings was a difficult task because it often required some years of arduous work. The enslaved person had to get an income higher than that demanded by their owner from their daily work, which was not a small amount. One of the options for many was to work with nearly no break in order to gain these savings, which could have been saved for a variety of different uses.[14] Augusta, aiming to fulfill the request of her sister, delayed her personal goal, and on January 11, 1872, gave the amount she had available to Carlos Hermes da Purificação, who promised to emancipate, and later marry, her sister. And who was this person?

He was a *pardo* (mixed race) man, single, 29 years old, native of Salvador and also resident of Freguesia da Sé "for nearly six years," and was a cigar maker. In her testimony, Ubaldina said that she had known him since he started to live in the store in her master's house, on Ajuda street, and that Carlos spoke to her "always in a way expressing his desire to make her happy."[15] On a certain occasion, Ubaldina said to him that she was trying to borrow from her sister an amount of 600 thousand *réis*, which she had in the Caixa Econômica, for the purpose of buying her emancipation. Carlos Hermes then told her to get the money and give it to him, "because with this amount not only would he be able to free her…, but if she were free, he would marry her."[16] Trusting the good intentions of this man, Augusta, using her mistress as an intermediary, convinced the magistrate João José de Almeida Couto to grant her wish of taking the money from the Caixa Econômica and giving it to Ubaldina who, in turn, would give it to Carlos Hermes. It seems that the abolitionist societies in the province of Bahia mainly emancipated women and children. The fact that the candidate for emancipation possessed some savings to complement their value was of great importance, hence Carlos Hermes' promise appealing to such, and the faith the sisters had in giving the money to him.

In possession of the money, Carlos Hermes continued to deceive the sisters "with a thousand imaginary excuses" however, and never fulfilling his promise to acquire Ubaldina's emancipation, much less the much desired marriage. According to Ubaldina, Carlos Hermes alleged that her owner was demanding an amount higher than that which they had available to pay for her emancipation, and that he still had not gotten any assistance from the "Sociedade Libertadora."[17] In different parts of the trial, it seems that the version divulged by the defendant claimed he needed more money to complete the value demanded by Ubaldina's owner. This value, however, was never revealed by the defendant or any other person questioned.

Some time later, Carlos Hermes wrote a letter to Augusta, in which he confessed that the 600 thousand *réis* disappeared from his house; and he said that he did not know how this happened. Before that happening, Carlos Hermes, who was always calling on Ubaldina, disappeared. In the letter, he wrote the following:

> Mrs. Augusta
>
> To your good health. First, I present to you the disgrace that happened to me. I do not know the day or the time, but when I went to look for your money, I did not find it, I searched all over the house, from corner to corner and I cannot blame anyone, because every day, all day, there are people here. What I can do in this case is serve someone as a slave to pay you, because even if I should lose my life, the shame

that has befallen me will never leave me because of having caused such great harm; surely even with the bad reputation that is on me madam will not deem me capable of causing such tragedies, according [to] the friendship that reigns between myself and your sister. Perhaps you can rest easy in the knowledge that I sleep with the door open, because God is very just and shall show that my conscience is clear; however I am here, ready to suffer whatever madam wishes, because your indignation is justified, if I listen the counsel I have been given. How can they tell me, now that this shame will never pass, I having felt the desire to commit such a foolish act, I don't have the nerve to face you, perhaps one day I can, but I don't have the life for business.

Your servant—Carlos.[18]

Due to the circumstances, Carlos Hermes was immediately sought by the authorities but was nowhere to be found. In his residence, "a store, on the street behind the jail," in the neighborhood, no one had any news of him and he was reported missing until he was found and arrested months later on April 20, 1873.

The testimonies of the six witnesses called upon in the trial proved the defendant's involvement in the alleged crime. There was even someone who revealed to have had access to a letter that the defendant sent to Augusta alerting her about the disappearance of the money. José Duarte Ferreira—married, 56 years old, "native of Bahia," resident of Freguesia de Santana, who worked as an "attorney at law"—said that leaving the house of the defendant, where he went several times to question him about what happened, he met a Portuguese man, whose name omitted and whom he questioned about what he was doing there. Upon telling him what had happened, the Portuguese man said "that must be why the defendant had such extraordinary expenses; it made the Portuguese man wonder, how he was able to host frequent gatherings, always riding in a chair" (similar to a litter, carried by two servants).[19] Also, João Antônio de Cerqueira Lima—single, 31 years old, "native of Bahia," resident of Freguesia de São Pedro who "made a living in business"—said in his statement that Carlos Hermes, instead of using Augusta's money as promised, "was squandering the money on clothes made of cashmere, holding gatherings and always riding in a chair; all of this the witness heard in the theatre of São João where he is employed, and where those people talked...."²⁰ From the statements, I can imagine the ordinary Carlos Hermes da Purificação as a typical *bon vivant* and *malandro* (scoundrel), realizing his dreams of conspicuous consumption, parading in high quality woven garments up and down the steep streets of the center of Salvador in a "chair," as did those who belonged to the middle class and the members of the local elite, all with the money stolen from these two poor enslaved women.

Malaquias José dos Reis, widow, 49 years old, native of Salvador, resident of Freguesia de Santana and "forum attorney," was another important witness in the case. He said that, between January and February of the previous year, that is, 1872, the defendant went to his house looking for him, in order to know how he should proceed (and how much money he would need) if he wanted to solicit the Sociedade Libertadora 7 de Setembro (The 7th of September Liberation Society) to "bid" for the emancipation of Augusta's sister, slave of magistrate Couto, whom he intended to marry. Carlos Hermes had also declared at the time that he had received from Augusta an amount of 600 thousand *réis* for such a purpose. Malaquias then responded that he must submit a petition to the organization and the amount that the entity would be able to bid would be between 200 and 400 thousand *réis*.²¹ Some days later, Malaquias asked the secretary of the Sociedade Libertadora if a petition from Carlos Hermes da Purificação had appeared, to which the secretary responded, no. Malaquias ended up not knowing if this petition was presented at some later time. After a few months, Malaquias got news that Carlos Hermes had misappropriated the money received from Augusta; indignant with the action of the defendant, Malaquias went to his house. In this encounter, Carlos repeated what other people said about the disappearance of the money belonging to the sisters. The complainants' lawyer questioned Malaquias to see if he knew the defendant was running up expenses greater than his possessions and the witness responded that after he found out what happened he asked some people about the behavior of the defendant; he learned that "he had played the women, made a mockery, in short."²²

With the questioning of the witnesses concluded—there was unanimous agreement that Carlos Hermes' was the perpetrator in the matter—the case was upheld, with the arrest of the defendant ordered on February 26, 1873. As mentioned, after various attempts, Carlos Hermes da Purificação was arrested on April 20 of the same year. Finally arrested and questioned, he tried to trick the authorities because he admitted to knowing Augusta for more than three years; however, he said he did not know nor had ever seen Ubaldina. Regarding Augusta's money, he confessed to having received it to "set up" a cigar store, but unfortunately the money had been stolen. The defendant even had the audacity to claim that "he was suspicious that Augusta herself, his lover, had been the thief to incriminate him."[23] When asked about how he would explain the content of the letter in the case file—which he read and recognized as being written by him—he responded that it was written at Augusta's suggestion, so that she could show it to her master.

Everything leads us to believe that the defendant blatantly lied in his statement. Even so, Carlos Hermes was not able to escape the accusations that hung over him. Brought to trial, he ended up convicted, on October 13, 1873, to four years of prison with hard labor, payment of a fine of 20 percent of the value unduly misappropriated, and the costs of the trial. On the same date of the sentence, his defender, the professor Firmo José Alberto appealed to the Superior Court of Appeals. On February 24, 1874, in extensive deliberations, the lawyer of the sisters, Augusto Ferreira França, argued strongly in defense of maintaining the sentence which convicted Carlos Hermes, emphasizing that he:

> Deceived the unsuspecting women with tricks, hopes, and in this way obtained their fortune; received the money for a certain purpose and appropriated it, completely dissipating it; the [appellant] deprived the [plaintiff] and her sister of the desired emancipation, the golden and cheerful dream of every slave, and her most rightful aspiration; and brought upon them a true fraud.[24]

Submitted to a new trial, the defendant was once again questioned, at which time he reaffirmed that he received the money from Augusta, in the form of a loan, to "setup a business" and, trying to modify his version of events, he added that on one occasion, having been drinking, he ended up losing the money, which was found and returned to him by a woman. He had, however, lost it again, or perhaps it had been stolen from him. Carlos Hermes maintained the claim that Augusta was his lover and he also maintained the first version about the writing of the letter, because that way, he showed Augusta's owner that the money was not lost, since he promised to pay it.

With the second trial on July 7, 1874, the defendant was able to get his sentence reduced from four years to three years and three months of prison with hard labor; the payment of the fine of 20 percent of the value stolen and the costs of the trial were maintained. Unsatisfied, the defendant's lawyer appealed the sentence again; however, he was unsuccessful. On October 6, 1874, the trial was concluded in which Carlos Hermes was convicted for taking from Augusta, via "fraudulent contrivance," the amount of 600 thousand *réis*.

It is undeniable that for Augusta and Ubaldina, to have their savings stolen was a great loss. I consider it difficult, however, to measure the level of frustration from their aspirations in the context of family life. Ubaldina had abandoned the hope of becoming free and married, and Augusta was not able to support a loved one or herself.

In this text we have shared two extraordinary stories that deal with gender relations in the daily life of black women subjected to the slave system in 19th century Bahia; as such we sought to narrate their feelings, objectives, and hopes.[25] The stories of Augusta, Ubaldina, and Domingas exist among so many other tales of black women of the past who, in spite of their strategies and capacity for overcoming obstacles, were subjected to all sorts of violence, violence which did not only come from their masters. They are stories of strong women, often generous and supportive, who had to face the inhumanity of slavery, the government, and oppression from men.

Notes

1. See the criminal trial that deals with the murder of the African Domingas in Arquivo Público do Estado da Bahia (Apeb), Secção de Arquivo Colonial e

Provincial, Judiciário, Núcleo: Tribunal de Justiça, Série: Homicídio, Classificação: 11/388/01, Cachoeira, 1862 (88 pages).

2. The spelling was updated to current standards.

3. The spelling was updated to current standards.

4. See the topic in Mattoso, 1982; Andrade, 1988; Dias, 1985; Soares, 1994 and 1996, in addition to other texts and relevant authors.

5. See more on the theme in Andrade, 1988; Mattoso, 1982; Reis, 2000, among others.

6. Italics from the document. The spelling was updated to current standards.

7. Apeb, Núcleo: Tribunal de Justiça (Judiciário) [Justice Court], Série: Homicídio [Series: Homicide], Classificação [Classification]: 11/388/01, Cachoeira, 1862, p. 21. The spelling was updated to current standards.

8. Apeb, Secção de Arquivo Colonial e Provincial [Colonial and Provincial Archive], Judiciário [Judiciary], Núcleo:Tribunal de Justiça [Center: Justice Court], Série: Homicídio [Series: Homicide], Classificação [Classification]: 11/388/01, Cachoeira, 1862. (88 pages), p. 26-26v. The spelling was updated to current standards.

9. The spelling was updated to current standards.

10. Apeb, Secção de Arquivo Colonial e Provincial, [Colonial and Provincial Archive], Judiciário [Judiciary], Núcleo: Tribunal de Justiça [Center: Justice Court], Série: Homicídio [Series: Homicide], Classificação [Classification]: 11/388/01, Cachoeira, 1862. (88 pages), p. 44-44v. The spelling was updated to current standards.

11. The magistrate João José de Almeida Couto, future Barão do Desterro [Baron of Exile], temporarily occupied the presidency of the province of Bahia at various times between 1870 and 1873. See more about him in Wildberger, 1949, p. 583-8.

12. Apeb, Núcleo: Tribunal de Justiça [Justice Court], Série: Estelionato [Series: Fraud], Classificação [Classification]: 07/243/05, Salvador. Parties: Complainant: Augusta (slave) and/or parties: Carlos Hermes da Purificação, bundle 2360, 1872. (125 pages), p. 2v.

13. Article 49 of Chapter II of the law of Ventre Livre states in regard to personal savings and the slave's right to emancipation: "the savings of the slave will be left in the hands of the master or the owner, if he consents, save the circumstances of Article 53, earning interest of 6 percent annually; and moreover, may with prior permission of the orphan's court, be collected by the same master or owner of the tax stations, or some savings or deposit bank that is well-trusted." Pessoa, 1875, p. 73. (The spelling was updated to current standards.)

14. See, for example, Xavier, 1996. In the chapter entitled "Vidas em contrato" (Lives under contract), the author emphasizes the long path to be walked by the captive in order to achieve emancipation, and for the freed slave to reaffirm it. Xavier shows that they "used various strategies, creating and taking advantage of opportunities that might arise" (see especially p. 71).
15. Núcleo: Tribunal de Justiça [Justice Court], Série: Estelionato [Series: Fraud], Classificação [Classification]: 07/243/05, Salvador. Parties: Complainant: Augusta (slave) and/or parties: Carlos Hermes da Purificação, bundle 2360, 1872. (125 pages), p. 31.
16. Idem.
17. According to Jailton Brito, the Sociedade Libertadora 7 de Setembro arose in 1869 and was probably the most important abolitionist association of Bahia. Active between 1869 and 1875, it freed around 500 captives. The association also produced a circular starting from March 15, 1871, the periodical *O Abolicionista*, which had 24 editions. In 1871, there were 512 members, 497 males and 15 females. Brito, Jailton, apud Fonseca, 1988, p. 244-8.
18. Letter written by Carlos Hermes da Purificação himself. It is a piece of paper found attached to the case. The spelling has been updated to current standards.
19. Apeb, Núcleo: Tribunal de Justiça [Justice Court], Série: Estelionato [Series: Fraud], Classificação [Classification]: 07/243/05, Salvador, maço 2360, 1872. (125 pages), p. 30. The spelling has been updated to current standards.
20. Idem, p. 35v.
21. Apeb, Núcleo: Tribunal de Justiça [Justice Court], Série: Estelionato [Series: Fraud], Classificação [Classification]: 07/243/05, Salvador, maço 2360, 1872. (125 pages), p. 37. The spelling has been updated to current standards.
22. Idem, p. 37v.
23. Idem, p. 72v.
24. Idem, p. 83v. The spelling has been updated to current standards.
25. The two stories told in this text are a part of my doctoral thesis, see Reis, 2007.

Bibliography

Andrade, Maria José de Souza. *A mão de obra escrava em Salvador, 1811-1860*. [Slave Labor in Salvador, 1811-1860]. São Paulo: Corrupio, 1988.

Dias, Maria Odila da Silva. "Nas fímbrias da escravidão urbana: negras de tabuleiro e de ganho." *Estudos Econômicos*, São Paulo, v. 15, Special Issue, p. 89-109, 1985.

Fonseca, Luís Anselmo da. *A escravidão, o clero e o abolicionismo*. [Slavery, Clergy, and Abolitionism]. Apresentação de Leonardo Dantas Silva. Ed. facsimilar. Recife/Brasília: Fundação Joaquim Nabuco, Massangana/CNPq, Comissão de Eventos Históricos, 1988.

Mattoso, Kátia M. de Queirós. *Ser escravo no Brasil*. [To be a Slave in Brazil]. 3. ed. São Paulo: Brasiliense, 1982.

Pessoa, Miguel Thomaz. *Manual do elemento servil*. [Manual of the Servile Sector]. Rio de Janeiro: Eduardo & Henrique Laemmert, 1875.

Reis, Isabel Cristina Ferreira dos. *A família negra no tempo da escravidão: Bahia, 1850-1888*. [The Black Family in the Time of Slavery: Bahia, 1850-1888]. 2007. Diss. (Doctorate in History) – Instituto de Filosofia e Ciências Humanas (IFCH), Universidade Estadual de Campinas (Unicamp), Campinas, São Paulo.

Reis, João José. "De olho no canto: trabalho de rua na Bahia na véspera da abolição." [An Eye on the Angle: Street Work in Bahia on the eve of Abolition]. *Afro-Ásia*, Salvador, n. 24, p. 199-242, 2000.

Soares, Cecília Moreira. *A mulher negra na Bahia no século* XIX. [The Black Woman in Bahia in the 19th Century]. 1994. Masters Thesis (History) – Faculdade de Filosofia e Ciências Humanas, Universidade Federal da Bahia (UFBA), Salvador, Bahia.

____. "As ganhadeiras: mulher e resistência negra em Salvador no século XIX." [Female Day Laborers: Women and Resistance in Salvador in the 19th Century]. *Afro-Ásia*, Salvador, n. 17, p. 57-71, 1996.

Wildberger, Arnold. *Os presidentes da província da Bahia, efetivos e interinos, 1824-1899*. [Presidents of the Province of Bahia, Permanent and Provisional, 1824-1899]. Salvador: Tipografia Beneditina, 1949.

Xavier, Regina Célia Lima. *A conquista da liberdade. Libertos em Campinas na segunda metade do século* XIX. [Achieving Liberty. Freedmen in Campinas in the Second Half of the 19th Century]. Campinas: Área de Publicações CMU/Unicamp, 1996.

12

TO GRANDMA VITORINA, WITH LOVE. RIO DE JANEIRO, AROUND 1870

Sandra Sofia Machado Koutsoukos

The photo of the nurse

The little yellowed photo that I present (on the following page) shows a young black woman with a small white girl in her lap, captured in the photography studio of Carneiro & Gaspar, in Rio de Janeiro. The year is uncertain; however, it can be placed with certainty in the period between 1866 and 1875, because this was the period in which the studio in question operated in the Brazilian capital. In the caption of the photo reads a brief note in pencil: "Grandma Vitorina, who did all the banquets and dinners of Vicente P. S. Porto ([Pereira da Silva], with Maria Elisa, [married with] Bernardo Magalhães." We do not know if Vitorina was a slave woman, a freed woman, or if she had been born free. However, we can sense that she lived with or worked for the Porto family for many years, enough to earn the affectionate nickname "grandma Vitorina." At the time of the photo, she was perhaps just one more of the many nurses captured in studios, a theme in vogue in the second half of the 19th century as much in Brazil as abroad, which enabled *self-representation* of the master's family: the photo of the child with her nurse, a portrait that would very well come to compose the range of "themes" of the album of the white family.

The surviving albums of the white families of the 19th century include few domestic workers. Among the few photos that exist, the majority are portraits of nurses (wet nurses or dry-nurses) with the white children they cared for. As far as it may be assumed, the wet nurses and the dry nurses, free or enslaved, were brought to the studios principally by the wishes of the owners who wanted a photo of the nurse, who, with such affection and dedication (and also obedience and fidelity towards her owners), was raising their child (and for who they could even have a true fondness for; or at the very least, sincere gratitude). They wanted to thank the nurse, offering her a beautiful photo with the child nurtured by her (maybe the first and only photo that the nurse would have); or maybe they were even wanting a photo of the child, who would not sit still in any other lap, except that of the one with whom she was closest—*her* wet nurse, or *her* dry nurse. If these were not the motives, what might the motive be?

Image of "Grandma Vitorina" with Maria Elisa. Photography from the studio of Carneiro & Gaspar. Rio de Janeiro [1866—1875]. Collection Roberto Menezes de Moraes, Niterói. Photo provided by the collector." [1]

Usually in the photography studios of the second half of the 19th century, the nurses were placed in erect poses, elegantly dressed, some even dressed in luxury, in European fashion, or in African fashion, with fine cloths, shawls, sometimes wearing jewelry, well-groomed hair or turbans, seated in chairs with ornate backrests, and having, in general, the child in her lap, or by her side.[2] Such were the simple depictions in terms of the setting, so that the attention of the viewer is not taken away from the point: the child and the nurse captured in a form that was intended to be *positive*.[3] This type of photo attempted to convey the idea of intimacy, harmony, and affection (also common in the studio-produced photos of mothers with their children), in a period in which the use of nurses was being systematically condemned by medical doctors and by moralists. Some even sought to devalue, to a certain extent, this type of work, while incentivizing the image of the "new white mother," who should be dedicated to nursing her children and caring for them herself. Next, in spite of the apparent contradiction of the situation, the nurses captured in photography studios (whose photos were preserved together with the photos of the of the families they served) would have been those that were considered "good nurses"—that is, those who had supposedly filled the numerous prerequisites demanded in the process of choosing a nurse (also methodically listed by medical doctors)—those who had managed to free themselves from the many suspicions about nurses that fell upon them from the master families, winning some sort of trust, and being seen as well-wishing, or even as an asset.[4]

The reasoning of medical doctors in the 19th century[5]

In the newspapers of the 19th century, it is possible to find numerous announcements for rentals, sales, purchases, and requests for nurses. Such announcements could be found next to the offers of other slaves, of furnishings of "the latest style recently arrived from France," England, or from Porto, pianos with the "best voices," offers of wines, cheese, cloth, dresses, hats for masters and gentlemen, calico and muslin for slave clothing, of auctions of large and small properties, of carriages, quills, books, jewelry, cookware sets, among other miscellaneous items. The ads for nurses followed a certain pattern, with a small, direct text, many times with the expression, "wet nurse" highlighted, in capital letters, or in bold. To help in the selection of the "merchandise" or, that is, in the purchase or rental of a slave, the ad was phrased in such a way that the nurse being offered was a "piece" to be examined, the details of which the interested buyer should pay attention, in order to avoid the risk of "bad deals."[6]

In Brazil, beginning in the mid-19th century, with the constant epidemics of yellow fever and cholera that ravaged the cities, hygienist doctors increased the pressure for white babies to be breastfed by their own mothers. In addition to the attempt of the doctors to create a "new mother," or a "sanitary mother," in the 1880s some suggestions for the regulation of the service of chambermaids and wet nurses (free or slave) arose,[7] with constant medical exams in clinics that were set up for this, aiming to give more assurance to employers that their children, in case they didn't have any other option other than to be fed by wet nurses, would be more protected against a range of sicknesses and *germs* of "suspicious diseases," that the doctors believed the nurses could potentially transmit to them.[8]

It was not commonplace in Brazil for children to be sent to be raised in the houses of the nurses. Instead, the small ones usually remained in the houses of their birth parents and, in a way, under their surveillance. This fact was highly praised by Brazilian doctors in general, who criticized the practice still common in Europe and the United States during that period: that parents allowed the child to be "raised" in the nurse's house, which was usually on the countryside, by means of an arranged monthly payment.[9] The doctors believed that children would be subjected to poor treatment, negligence, and additionally subjected to a lack of affection. The formation of a bond between the child and the family, most importantly between the child and its mother, was also considered essential even if the mother herself was not in charge of breastfeeding her child. Another point that was criticized concerned the possibility of the nurse taking more than one child to raise in her house, in addition to her own; this meant a smaller portion of milk for each child, as well as the premature introduction of foods for which the body was not ready—because it was expected of the nurse that she always brought the baby back "chubby."

On the other hand, the rental of a captive wet nurse yielded a good monthly payment to the owner that had a slave nurse to rent. In some ads of sale or rental, the owner insisted on stressing that the nurse didn't have any "defects or diseases." A nurse with "good manners" (which was also understood as "obedient") that was also "affectionate and trustworthy," could be a guarantee that the baby would be in good hands. Sometimes the fact was highlighted that she had "given birth recently," that is, the milk was new. Other times, it was highlighted that the milk was "the first birth," which for many hygienist doctors signified the purest milk, but also indicated that the nurse candidate was possibly inexperienced in dealing with babies. Some health professionals defended the choice of the "multiparous" woman (mother of more than one child), who, in addition to offering the advantage of maybe being more experienced dealing with a baby, by having had other children, they also had stronger and more abundant milk. The nurse to be rented could be offered "with or without a small black handmaid." Lucky was she who breastfed two at the same time: her own baby and the baby of the master—which, in spite of excessive and tiring work, was offset by the fact that they didn't find themselves separated from their children. But the option, by the masters, of allowing the child of the nurse to be raised together with their own child, feeding from the same breasts, was rare. Rarer still was that they were motivated by the love of the nurse for her own child; when this happened, it was an attempt not to "spoil" the milk of the nursing mother in order to avoid her transmitting feelings of "contrariness" to the child of the master through her milk, or even mistreating the child. On the other hand, ensuring the breastfeeding of the black baby increased the chances of the master's baby surviving.

In addition to the direct access that the doctors had to many families (especially in urban centers), another form of pressuring and trying to change the course of the history of the breastfeeding in Brazil was the publication of texts in periodicals that explored stories that increased the guilt and fear of mothers that didn't breastfeed their own children. One of these periodicals was *The Family Mother*, a magazine published every two weeks in the city of Rio de Janeiro, between 1879 and 1888, which followed the publication of a French journal, by a certain Dr. Brochard.[10] The principal editor of the magazine was Dr. Carlos Costa, "specialist in children's diseases"; however, other doctors eventually wrote additional texts. *The Family Mother* had a part titled "The Medical Lecture," always written by Dr. Carlos Costa, in which he took advantage of the space to magnify the benefits of maternal milk, attacked the use of wet nurses, highlighted the "dangers" arising from using such, and once again, repeated the dominant discourse published in the theses of his colleagues. The magazine advised that a doctor should be consulted to examine the nurse, in case her employment was unavoidable, giving instructions about dealing with animal milk, its preservation, the preparation and cleaning of supplies. He presented tips on how to identify and treat infant sicknesses, as well as ways of dealing with children, their hygiene, their toys, their trips, their education, their relationship with family, etc. There was even the exploration of a series of texts that spoke about "maternal love," supposedly innate in various animals, including some that breastfed their offspring, such as whales. In the stories of the magazine, even snakes cared for their young.

In July of 1882, *The Family Mother* published the story of a young mother that wanted to breastfeed her own newborn son, but was being pressured by her own mother to arrange a nurse, because the grandmother of the baby "feared" for the health of the girl. After the consultation, the doctor could convince the family that the breastfeeding done by the mother was the best for her as well as the baby. The health professional even guided the young mother on the work she had before her and agreed to accompany the development of the baby personally. In the end, the doctor highlighted: "Praise the heavens if all mothers behaved like you. Many innocents would be saved."[11]

In *Protection and Obedience*, Sandra Graham observes that the public debate that had taken hold in Brazil starting from the mid-19th century had not only raised (higher) suspicions about the wet nurse as a threatening figure and possible transmitter of physical and moral sickness, but had also begun to modify the image that women had of themselves as mothers. Graham (1992 p. 144) argues that in the old theses from the mid-19th century, the doctors were more tolerant with the women who didn't breastfeed their children.[12] The periodicals, such as *The Family Mother*, came to fulfill their mission of arriving directly in the family reach and influencing, with their stories, the ladies so that they fulfilled their maternal role, regardless of the sacrifice necessary for such.

Blame and *fear* were important factors in the attempt to create a "new mother," the "sanitary mother," exalted by doctors of medicine during the period. The principal factor was the necessity of developing a greater affection between the mothers and their small children, which was believed to be able to guarantee them greater chances of survival during infancy, since those "new mothers" would become allies of the doctors responsible for the health of the children. For a long time, however, and for many families with great wealth, the choice to breastfeed or not lay not only within the woman's purview, but a decision made by the couple and sometimes even the rest of the family.[13] However, the mother's role as breast feeder, in addition to protecting the life of the children, fulfilled another role in society of that period: to behave as a woman in a disciplined universe, controlling her social feminine behavior.

A relationship of "affection"?

Before returning to the presented photo of the nurse Vitorina, let's consider the matter that may help explain the production of that type of photo and its subsequent packaging and storing in the album of the white family—the "affection." The issue of affection involves the discussion of "paternalism," understood as a network of reciprocal duties and rights; that is, the masters offer "protection" (sustenance, food, clothes, shelter, and treatment of sicknesses), "respect" and "justice" (even when punished), and in turn, they demanded obedience, work (dedication), and loyalty (gratitude).[14] It was a circle of exchanges, since, in turn, the nurse must also protect the master's baby. Sandra Graham (1992, p. 61) addresses a little bit of this circle of exchanges and expectations in this way:

> Personal servants—housekeepers and wet nurses—could aspire to be compensated with affection or trust. During their work, these maids frequently passed through the spaces of the house exclusive to the family members and maintained contact with them daily. Through the infinite little attentions that that they gave to their employers they could closely witness the leisure and richness that belonged to a class of which they, being poor servants, would remain forever and always removed. Even so, they reasonably identified themselves with the families they belonged to. To be a maid or nurse brought tangible compensation—understood as such by both sides—in return for a valued service: they could receive attire or finery that signified a special *status*, for example, a silk scarf to tie in their hair or a pair of slippers; a day trip, or sometimes, even a long trip....

Who knows, maybe some of the nurses also received their portrait with the children that they were breastfeeding (or had breastfed), taken in a photography studio as a gesture of attention, affection, or nostalgia? Graham (1992, p. 61) adds, referring to the figure of the old nurse in the end of the 19th century:

> As slaves were decreasing in number and were not substituted by others in the homes of Rio de Janeiro, the personal handmaids that served their whole life and were linked to the patron family by strong ties of loyalty and privilege were gradually disappearing. However, the favorite handmaids continued to exist, in a slightly different form. The free woman, the dry nurse of various children of a family, could maintain a place in the house, as an elder and respected figure that deserved affection and care, well after the children had grown up.

Or, for some, would the figure of the elder have been a growing "burden," from which they didn't have the courage or methods to free themselves? After all, after the fulfilled duty (sometimes, successively, with more than one child of the family) and, with the passing of years, already being the old and sick nurse, "useless" for any type of service, would she not be considered a "burden," to which the family now owed protection, care, and *even* affection?

The following story explores some of the contradictions of the relationship between the masters and the nurses. In his work, *His-*

torical Chronicles of Colonial Rio, Nireu Oliveira Cavalcanti (2004, p. 187-9) tells the story that he found in a litigation in the National Archive of Rio de Janeiro, titled: "The wet nurse. Slavery and its contradictions." The story takes place in the year 1803; in it, a couple, after the birth of their first child, rented a wet nurse slave of Mina origin, called Joaquina, for 3,200 *réis* (currency of the time) monthly. Joaquina proved to be dedicated to the child, which caused the couple to continue renting her until the child was weaned. When the second child of the couple was born, the parents hurried to rent the same slave again, but her owner wanted to keep her, alleging that Joaquina was also good at domestic work. After some negotiation, the owner agreed to sell the slave for 102,400 *réis*; however, she must have had some esteem for the girl, for she established an "infallible condition" that 3 years after that date of sale, she would be "an emancipated slave and free, without any obligation to serve her masters, only if she wants to." The agreement was made, because the new masters also liked the girl and the way she dedicated herself with "affection and pleasure" to their children.

After a while, aware of the fact that she would be free after three years from the sale, Joaquina slowly became "disobedient" and "petulant," responding in a cross manner to her mistress, who on one occasion became enraged at a response from the nurse that she *punched her*. From there, the story gets heated: after the punch, Joaquina advanced upon her mistress and gave her bites, scratches, and shoves, and "spoke many offensive words." The neighbors had to separate the fight, and the witnesses declared that they had to take the 6-month old baby from the grips of Joaquina, as she had bitten the baby as well. A doctor was called to attest to the injuries suffered by the mother and the child (and it appears that he ignored the punch imprinted on the face of Joaquina). From there, the masters didn't know what to do with the slave, because they didn't want to send her to prison and take the loss of remaining without her help and losing the value paid for it; on the other hand, given the clause of the sale contract, they also could not sell her for the value they had paid. The couple decided then to avenge themselves of the slave, hiring a lawyer to try to annul the conditional emancipation of Joaquina. The judicial battle occurred between the lawyers of the new masters and the lawyer contracted by the old owner of Joaquina (who, apparently, remained on the side of the ex-slave). In the end, the contract remained as it was, because it was concluded that the annulment would only fit if Joaquina had attacked her old owner, who was the one who conditioned the emancipation. Defeated, the masters of the slave had to decide what to do, or in what way they could live with her until Joaquina was freed.[15]

What stands out as most interesting here is that the nurse was "loved" while her dedication lasted. Apparently, starting from the moment in which she realized that, whether dedicated and faithful or not, her freedom was guaranteed, she changed her attitude, just as the attitude of the masters changed. At first, they were so thankful with the care that Joaquina dedicated to their children that they *even* agreed with the freedom of the slave, three years after the date of sale. They had agreed with the condition by thinking that the nurse deserved it; however, facing the "ingratitude" of Joaquina, their "affection" for her gave way to a feeling of revenge, which they would have liked to have seen manifest in the restitution of their power over the freedom of the slave. If this freedom had been conditional based on the quality of the services provided as a wet nurse, the story would have been another; if that had been the case, perhaps these feelings of gratitude and appreciation would have stayed in the memory of the family. While she had been grateful, obedient, and dedicated, Joaquina was loved, protected, and compensated. With the balance of the changed situation, however, in the place of "affection" arose feelings of deception, anger, and revenge.

In *Machado de Assis Historian*, Sidney Chaloub (2003, p. 134-5) highlights that the paternalism of the masters and the relationships of the dependence of the free or slave domestic workers frequently provoked situations of violence and humiliation. The masters could demonstrate "esteem" that they had for their dependents, but their situation of superiority sometimes provoked suffering and humiliation. Even though the dependents, free or slave, were to a certain extent "appreciated," they knew, however, their situation of social inferiority. Even when treated with the respect they deserved as people of the "family," if they tried to express their own thoughts and feelings contrary or unfit in the view of the masters, they would suddenly be seen as "ungrateful," "insolent," "underhanded," or "audacious." Nevertheless, there were many cases of slaves that clung to the families and remained with them of their own free will, even after abolition; and not just for necessity of protection (shelter, clothes, food, treatment of sicknesses, and "support" in old age), but for feeling at home in the house (or in the ex-slave quarters) of the masters, or for feeling like a part of the white families that they had belonged.

From the relationship between the masters and the nurses, it can be said that the nurses pictured in the photography studios had won the "right," not only to appear in the photo, but additionally by having their photos kept by the families that they served, they were able to overcome at least some suspicions that these situations aroused, becoming in some way, and to some extent, cherished members of the household. How much manipulation and calculation there was in each case, on the part of each one involved, as well as how much reciprocal "affection" was given or not, or even humiliation and pain, or happiness, it is impossible to measure exactly. But, we can certainly guess that there was a good dose of almost all of those ingredients.

Vitorina in the photography studio

In an image, the presence of certain "objects" usually prompts an association of ideas—like this, the book would indicate the culture and the possible erudition of the pictured, the dog would indicate loyalty, jewelry would signify wealth, flowers would mean delicacy, etc. In the case in question, the presence of the white child would evidence that the black woman was a wet nurse, or a dry nurse, and the black woman, next to the small white child, told that that child had been breastfed by that nurse.

The photos of the nurses certainly portray a moment in their lives and of the children; they could even record a rite of passage, like a child that had finally been weaned, or of a christening, or any other important date. In my research, I didn't see any nurse in a photo portraying the death of a child; these generally photographed in the mother's lap, or photographed alone, like "angels" (often, angels with open eyes). In addition to the use of the image as an item of remembrance, when it was framed and placed on furniture, hung on walls or stored in albums, boxes, or drawers, it was also was an item of exchange when it was offered, often with dedication to friends, relatives, and acquaintances. I put here another question: if the employers had offered these images to the nurses, were the copies of those images sent to relatives and distant friends to show the value of their status, their position, within the families they served? I believe that it is very possible.

The family album is a chronicle with gaps, because it doesn't record everything that happens in the life of the characters, but only what they want to be recorded and stored, as noted by Schapochnik (1998, p. 457).[16] If this is so, then great importance may have been given to the nurses over the rest of the household. They, after all, for the fulfillment of their role, had to be capable of great dedication and self-sacrifice. It was the figure of the nurse with which the baby identified best, the smell of her milk that stimulated the child's hunger, her lap in which the child snuggled, her songs and stories that put it to sleep. Once again, the child that she had breastfed and raised would have guarded her memory with affection.

Let us finally return to the photo of Vitorina with the girl Maria Elisa. It appears Vitorina had fulfilled her role well as a nurse, as well as an excellent cook, without deceiving the Porto family; on the contrary, her dinners remained tastefully marked in the memory of the family and her photo was maintained with affection in the middle of the collection of stored photos. Serving *with obedience* for many years, the nurse/cook must have been very well liked by "her" white family who maybe she had grown old with and earned the affectionate nickname "granny Vitorina." Maybe we can go a little further and say that in her "nurse photo," still young and well dressed like a maid of a wealthy household, with corsage buttoned to her neck and the impeccable white collar of the blouse framing her face and neck (following the European fashion used by many women of the society during that time), Vitorina looked at the photographer with a certain pride. The luxury presented wasn't excessive, but the clothing buttoned to the neck and the long sleeves show the "importance" of the position she occupied. In general, the clothes in which the nurse is shown can display, in public, the wealth of the house to which she belonged, as well as her somewhat privileged position before the other slaves of the house. However, many times, the *mise-en-scène* hid the sad story of the separation of the nurse from her own child. A story that wasn't told, only assumed. The reference to the existence of a nurse obviously brings the idea of the existence of two children: the master's child, raised by her, and the black child, fruit of her womb, of which we know little or nothing about. We don't have any information about the natural child, or children, of Vitorina. If she really had nursed the girl in the photo, her last natural child would have been that same age.[17]

Vitorina's dedication earned her the "right" to be called "granny" by the Porto family and their descendants. I reiterate, the nickname, affectionate even, allows us to believe that she had lived a selfless life of obedience, of dedication. Yes, this must have been her story. Had she demonstrated any sign of revolt or feelings of social injustice, the story would have been different. Her image probably would not even have been kept with such care. Or, if it had (because, after all, it is also an image of the girl), the nurse would not have been named in the verse of the photo, much less with the term "granny" preceding her name.

Ultimately, my argument here is: as with many other nurses, Vitorina gained her spot in the affection (in the heart), in the album, and in the history of that family, because she had always served with dedication, obedience, and silence (humility).

To conclude, I turn to the novel *O mulato* by Aluísio Azevedo, published in 1881, in which the author describes the capacity for selflessness (for lack of any other option) of the wet nurse Mônica. She had raised the little girl of the novel, devoting to her the love that she had not been able to give her own children, who had been sold and sent far way (Azevedo, 2005, v.1, p. 327):

> Mônica, about 50 years old, was fat, healthy, and very neat; large breasts drooping inside of her collar. Around her neck, she had a string with a metal cross, a coin of 200 *réis*, a tonka bean, a dog tooth, and a seal embedded in gold. Since she had nursed Ana Rosa, she had

dedicated to her a doting motherly love, a disinterested and passive dedication. Iaiá had always been her idol, her only 'care,' because her own children were taken from her and sold to the South. She would never come back from the well, where she spent her days washing, without bringing back fruits and butterflies, which, for the little girl, were the best pleasures in life. She called her 'her daughter, her captive' and every night, and every morning, when she arrived or left for work, she gave her a blessing.... If Ana Rosa caused any trouble in the house that displeased the black mother, she would reprimand her immediately, with authority; provided, however, that the accusation or the complaint came from another, if it were from her father or grandmother, they were soon punished by the girl and she turned against them the most.

After being freed, as must have happened with many other nurses, Mônica remained in the house of her masters, diligently caring for Iaiá better than before, but more captive than ever (Azevedo, 2005, v.1, p. 327).

Notes

1. Researcher Marcelo Eduardo Leite notified me of the existence of this photo in the collection of Roberto Menezes de Morães, in Niterói. Shortly after, the collector himself clarified for me that Vicente Porto was a Brazilian railroad businessman in the 19th century and that there were two copies of this photo amid the document collection of the Porto family.

2. During my doctorate research, I found a little over 30 images of nurses. I presented 28 of these images in Koutsoukos, 2007.

3. On this topic, see Leite, 2000.

4. In chapter 2 of my book *Negros no estúdio do fotógrafo* (Koutsoukos, 2010), I discuss at length the discourse of the theses of the doctors of medicine on the topic of "wet nurses," showing what they defended and what they opposed, as well as the norms that they imposed for the nurse to be considered "good." I also explore some of the contradictions that can be seen in the difficulty of the job of the nurses and in the proclaimed "affection" that was involved in the master/nurse/child relationship. To deal with such a complex and fascinating topic, I cross-referenced photographic accounts with the ads and newspaper texts of the period, the medicine theses (a good number of them are currently still conserved in the library Academia Imperial de Medicina in Rio de Janeiro), memoirs, the chroniclers of the time, and the few books that deal with breastfeeding in history.

5. I also discuss the topic in Koutsoukos, 2009.

6. Manuals such as that of Imbert, I.B.A., *Manual do fazendeiro ou tratado doméstico sobre as enfermidades*, 1839, gave advice on the purchase of a "piece." Cited in Schwarcz, 1996.

7. For example, "Posturas Municipais da Capital para o serviço de criados e amas de leite decretadas sobre proposta do Chefe de Polícia Manuel Juvenal Rodrigues da Silva—Juiz de Direito." São Paulo: Tipografia a vapor de Jorge Seckler & Co., 1886. No Arquivo Nacional, série Justiça, Gifi 5B, 543.

8. On the topic, among others, see Castilho, 1882, p. 14.

9. On history of breastfeeding in the United States and Europe, see Fildes, 1988.

10. *A mãe de família. Jornal científico, literário e ilustrado*. Publicado quinzenalmente, Rio de Janeiro, Tipografia dos Editores Lombaerts & Comp., 1879 to 1888.

11. Text edited by Dr. P. Blanche, A mãe de família..., July 1882. In a text published in 1905, in *Brasil Médico*, Dr. Antônio Fernandes Figueira commented: "The largest blame in the situation goes to *(penitent me)* the doctors. In case after case, in the living situation of families, we have given way to the suggestions of relatives who consider breastfeeding a task that is almost despicable. In the shameful days of slavery, the job was expected of the wretched captives, whether the poor little fellow that they had brought into existence suffered or not.... Rich women, who absolutely refuse to breastfeed, it is advised that you use a nurse for your child before animal milk. The nurses however, will be disappearing, and the wealthy people will better understand what they must do...." Figueira, 1905, p. 19-20.

12. In the 1890s, also in the city of Rio de Janeiro, another magazine appeared, specifically directed at the valorization of maternity as something that brought satisfaction: *O quinze de novembro do sexo feminino* (1892-1896).

13. On the topic, see Golden, 2001, p. 13. Regarding breastfeeding in the United States in the 18th and 19th centuries, the author further comments that for the poorest families in which the work of the woman represented part of the subsistence economy, sending the child to the house of a nurse meant the possibility of a mother returning to work and that, often, this decision was imposed on the woman by her husband or another family member.

14. On the topic, among others, see Chalhoub, 1990.

15. Arquivo Nacional do Rio de Janeiro (ANRJ) Corte de Apelação: maço 215, no 215, gal. C. (cited in Cavalcanti, 2004, p. 187-9).

16. I wrote a short text on family albums in the end of chapter 1 of *Negros no estúdio do fotógrafo* (Koutsoukos, 2010).

17. In her master's thesis, Rafaela de Andrade Deiab (2006) did an analysis on the figure of the black mother in Brazilian literary texts and she explored the no-

tion of "the unhappy slave mother," but "fulfilled wet nurse," following the trail of authors in the late 19th century and the early 20th century, such as Mello de Moraes Filho (abolitionist poet) and Augusto dos Anjos (poet), among others.

Bibliography

A mãe de família. *Jornal científico, literário e ilustrado.* [Scientific Journal, Literary and Illustrated]. Published bimonthly, Rio de Janeiro, Tipografia dos Editores Lombaerts & Comp., 1879 to 1888.

Azevedo, Aluísio. "O mulato." [The Mulatto]. In: Aluísio Azevedo. *Ficção completa em dois volumes.* [Complete Fiction in Two Volumes]. Rio de Janeiro: Nova Aguilar, 2005, v. 1.

Castilho, Ildefonso Archer de. *Higiene da primeira infância.* [Hygiene of Early Childhood]. Doctoral Diss. Faculdade de Medicina do Rio de Janeiro. Rio de Janeiro: Tipografia Universal de H. Laemmert & Co., 1882.

Cavalcanti, Nireu Oliveira. *Crônicas históricas do Rio colonial.* [Historical Chronicles of Colonial Rio]. Rio de Janeiro, Faperj e Civilização Brasileira, 2004.

Chalhoub, Sidney. *Machado de Assis historiador.* [Machado de Assis, Historian]. São Paulo: Companhia das Letras, 2003.

Deiab, Rafaela de Andrade. *A mãe-preta na literatura brasileira: a ambiguidade como construção social (1880-1950).* [The Black Mother in Brazilian Literature: Ambiguity as a Social Construction (1880-1950)]. 2006. Master's Thesis—Departamento de Antropologia da Faculdade de Filosofia, Letras e Ciências Humanas (FFLCH). Universidade de São Paulo (USP), São Paulo.

Figueira, Antonio Fernandes. "Bases científicas da alimentação da criança. Suas consequências sociais." [Scientific Bases for Childhood Nutrition. Social Consequences]. *Brasil–Médico*, Rio de Janeiro, 1905, p. 19-20.

Fildes, Valerie. *Wet Nursing. A History from Antiquity to the Present.* Oxford, New York: Basil Blackwell Inc., 1988.

Golden, Janet. *A Social History of Wet Nursing in America. From Breast to Bottle.* Columbus: Ohio State University Press, 2001.

Graham, Sandra Lauderdale. *Proteção e obediência. Criadas e patrões no Rio de Janeiro (1860-1910).* [Protection and Obedience. Servants and Bosses in Rio de Janeiro (1860-1910)]. São Paulo: Companhia das Letras, 1992.

Koutsoukos, Sandra Sofia Machado. "Amas na fotografia brasileira da segunda metade do século XIX." [Wetnurses in Brazilian Photography in the Second Half of the 19th Century]. *Revista Studium*, Projetos Especiais, Representação imagética das

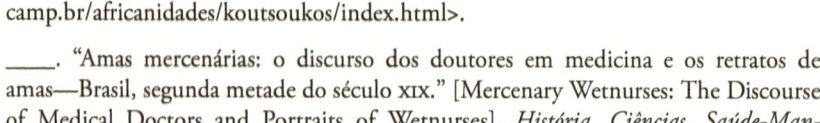

africanidades no Brasil," November 2007. Accessible at: <http://www.studium.iar.unicamp.br/africanidades/koutsoukos/index.html>.

_____. "Amas mercenárias: o discurso dos doutores em medicina e os retratos de amas—Brasil, segunda metade do século XIX." [Mercenary Wetnurses: The Discourse of Medical Doctors and Portraits of Wetnurses]. *História, Ciências, Saúde-Manguinhos*, [History, Sciences, Health-Manguinhos]. Rio de Janeiro, v. 16, n. 2, Apr./Jun. 2009.

_____. *Negros no estúdio do fotógrafo*. [Blacks in the Photography Studio]. Campinas: Editora da Unicamp, 2010.

Leite, Miriam Moreira. *Retratos de família*. [Family portraits]. São Paulo: Edusp, 2000.

Schapochnik, Nelson. "Cartões-postais, álbuns de família e ícones da intimidade." In: Sevcenko, Nicolau. (Org. and introd.). *História da vida privada no Brasil. República: da belle époque à era do rádio*. [History of Private Life in Brazil. Republic: from the Belle Epoque to the Era of Radio]. São Paulo: Companhia das Letras, 1998.

Schwarcz, Lilia Moritz. "Ser peça, ser coisa." In: Schwarcz, Lilia Moritz; Reis, Letícia Vidor de Souza. (Orgs.) *Negras imagens: ensaios sobre cultura e escravidão no Brasil*. [Black images: Essays on Culture and Slavery in Brazil]. São Paulo: Edusp e Estação Ciência, 1996.

13

BETWEEN TWO BENEDICTS: STORIES OF WET
NURSES IN THE DECLINE OF SLAVERY

Maria Helena P. T. Machado

The relationship between slave wet nurses and the seigniorial babies who they took care of was, and still is, one of the most difficult aspects to assess in slave relations. The widespread practice of turning over small children to be nursed by captives was frequent in all slave societies of the Americas. The black nurse wrapping in her arms a rosy and well-nourished white child was a recurring theme in the representations of slavery in painting, photography, and literary descriptions, wherever slavery existed. However, in any of the American slave societies, the black mother or the *mammy*, as the wet nurse or nanny was called in the North American southern slave society, arose as a central image of sentimentalized domestic slavery.

A series of reasons justified the diffusion of the practice which was then called, at least in Brazil, *mercenary breastfeeding*. The poor health of the mother due to contagious or debilitating illness; consecutive and early age births, resulting in puerperal complications; malnutrition; post-partum depression; the absence of a culture which valued breastfeeding; and perhaps, above all, the belief that white women, for being a "lymphatic" type, were too fragile to breastfeed, producing milk that was weak and insufficient to nurture babies, all seem to have been the principal reasons explaining the rarity of natural breastfeeding by women from families who owned slaves or could rent them for nursing.

Throughout the second half of the 19th century, the emergence of a medical discourse regarding "scientific maternity" selected the mother and maternal nursing as central issues. Using as a theme the supposed natural fragility of the woman and her biologic fate as mother and nurturer, whose natural realm was in the domesticity of the home and the raising of offspring, the medical studies translated the modern anxieties of the literate classes who longed to insert Brazilian society into the ideological parameters derived from the ascension of the middle classes from industrialized countries.[1] It is clear that these studies referred only to women of wealthy classes who could be preserved from contact with the external world. Since poor women, especially blacks, captives, or those freed from slavery who had to leave the house in search of work, or who, according to the point of view of the dominant beliefs, didn't even own homes, were not a part of this universe, a web of racialized and exclusionary knowledge that justified the emerging forms of social control was imposed upon them.[2]

In Brazil, one of the central themes in the development of the study of "scientific maternity" was the disapproval of the presence of the slave, especially the slave woman, in the household. This critique synthesized—in a disapproving manner—the figure of the wet nurse and mercenary breastfeeding. However, in spite of the growing condemnation of the presence of domestic slaves in the family environment, the Brazilian reality of the second half of the 19th century, even in cities, retained slavery or forms derived from it. As a consequence, thousands of women—slaves, freed, being freed, and recently freed—frequented the domestic environment as wet nurses, nannies and maids, filling all the roles belonging to the idealized woman/mother in the medical studies.

Certainly such studies were not safe from incurring a series of contradictions. Thus, although medical theses, which became important vehicles for valuing breastfeeding in the second half of the 19th century, generally blamed the "vanity" and "futility" of well-bred white women as the reasons for rejecting natural breastfeeding, the truth is that these same doctors easily listed various conditions in which natural breastfeeding would not be recommended, not for the mother or the child, who would receive contaminated milk or milk with little nutrients. The weakness of nerves, the shape of the breast, family diseases, physical weakness of the mother, among many others, arose as sufficient motives to advise against breastfeeding—understood as a great maternal sacrifice. Even though black women nurses seemed to be characterized by innumerous physical and intrinsic moral defects, in addition to being contaminated by sicknesses and bad habits, they were considered producers of abundant and nutritious milk because they had a "sanguine" type or because they were described as robust women.[3]

Beginning in the mid-19th century, the invention of the bottle, patented in 1841 by C. Windship, and the pacifier, patented in 1845 by Elijah Pratt, linked to the discovery of the pasteurization of milk, in 1859, and sterilization in 1886, artificial feeding became more safe for newborns deprived of natural breastfeeding.[4] Next to these innovations in 1867, the first industrialized formula for feeding newborns was discovered in Europe, and quickly became popular in the United States as well, making the wet nurse an obsolete figure destined to disappear.[5]

We know little regarding the introduction of these modern discoveries in Brazilian society; however, everything suggests a late entry of the hygienic procedures related to artificial nursing. This is what is suggested by the famous theses of the medical universities of the time, which—as it seems—were poorly informed about the discoveries of artificial nursing of babies.[6] Notably, the writings of doctors regarding nursing—which increased in the second half of the 19th century—always highlighted the increasing concerns about sanitary conditions and the evils of breastfeeding done by nurses, whether slaves or simply black women. But these concerns show them to be out of touch with the new discoveries in artificial feeding. For example, a medical thesis from 1873 about breastfeeding in Rio de Janeiro references artificial breastfeeding as that which substitutes the milk of the woman, usually milk from a cow, "and is given to a child through a jar or any instrument designated for this purpose" (Milward, 1873, p. 2). The absence of the word "bottle" here is clearly evident, perhaps suggesting its little use in the society of the time in Rio de Janeiro. In the same thesis from 1873, upon discussing artificial feeding, the student stated definitively that it was befitting that "milk was never brought to a boil, otherwise it will lose the aroma and air it normally contains and will become more difficult to digest." And that was when the pasteurization of milk had already been around for more than 10 years. Another doctoral candidate, in 1874, not only confirmed that milk should never be boiled, he also proposed feeding a weaned child with donkey milk, which should be sucked directly from the animal![7] Let us be reminded that such practices, found in European societies until the first half of the 19th century, had already been forgotten due to the introduction of relatively safe artificial feeding. Of course issues regarding the shape, cleaning, and ease of replacement and handling of bottles were resolved only later.[8]

Examples of a vision hardly in tune with the novelties of artificial feeding abound in the works of Brazilian doctors, also indicating the lack of a more modern vision of breastfeeding. I note here that in Europe and the United States, in spite of the spread of medical discourse directed towards the valorization of breastfeeding, the social trend, in reality, was the popularization of artificial feeding. Despite the medical discourse surrounding breastfeeding, at the core of which new standards of bourgeoisie domesticity were encrypted, from the 1870s forward in European countries and the United States, the incline was towards the popularization of feeding newborns with bottles and industrialized formulas. In Brazilian society, although one could find ads for artificial nursing for babies by the end of the 1870s in Rio de Janeiro, there seems to be a consensus that until the beginning of the first decades of the republic, these products were not adopted on a considerable scale.[9] In addition, natural breastfeeding itself and support for "scientific maternity" seems to have remained throughout this period in Brazilian society more in discourse than practice.[10]

More ideological practice began to present the possibilities of the creation of a field of monopolized knowledge as a producer of a certain national vision. More so than practical and rational texts, the writings about breastfeeding that came from medical schools and other Brazilian institutions made sense when interpreted in the narrow scope of the exposition, meaning little in practical terms. Also, the public was not expected to read them or consider them as guides for daily life. They were just reverberations that reached literate society, creating a new vocabulary. As it seems, if the doctors were able to spread greater worry among the elite about the health of nurses, their advice in terms of changes in informal social practices meant little. In this context, it is not surprising that throughout the second half of the 19th century, among the dominant classes of urbanized Brazilian society, maternal breastfeeding remained rare, artificial feeding was still dismissed, and the practice of using slaves as wet nurses continued to spread.

As a result, the second half of the 19th century saw a preservation of the wet nurse culture, which entangled relationships of proximity, dependence, and intimacy, prevalent in the violence of slavery. As it could be noted, the extreme dependence that natural nursing caused in infants prior to the introduction of the bottle and modified powder milk linked the deep intimacy that this action established between the nurse and the child and the formation of symbolic kinship—with the "mother's milk" creating a link between the natural mother and her child. This concept, intersecting with slave relations marked by paternalism, generated a complex web of sentimental and economic motives, as well as power relations in this type of relationship.

However, obviously, in order to produce milk the nurses had to first give birth to their own children, who were also dependent on breastfeeding to survive. Even so, the representation of the black nurse nursing the white child continued to be produced profusely in books, magazines, and other media, emerging so full of intimacy but at the same time, so banal that looking at such images, even today, it is very rare that we question the fate of their own children or the tensions that hid behind that idealized scene. In Brazil, for example, the photographs of nurses richly adorned with their white babies in their lap are still frequent and published uncritically, often promoting nostalgic versions of a Brazilian society sentimental for a sweet and familiar slavery.[11]

A question as uncomfortable as it is unanswerable due to the scarcity of documents and accounts of the fate of the children of slave wet nurses—and to a certain extent, freed women pressed by the need to find work—keeps us at a distance from what we all know: the sentimental scene of the nurse with the white child in her arms completely elides a chaotic and tense universe of social relations that unfolded in the intimacy of homes, in which the possibilities of survival for these children—white and black—were at risk. The offspring of the wet nurse, in her presence or absence, were always a constant point of tension and negotiation.

A small and rare fragment of the dramatic tensions that developed in the intimacy of the home, in which black children and white children fought over the breast of the black woman as the sole form of survival comes up, for example, in the memoirs of the former slave of a property in Georgia (USA), William McWhorter, recorded by the Federal Writers Project. In 1938 when William, 78 years old, recalled the stories that had been told about life on the pre-civil war southern plantation and told about the dramatic life events of one of his aunts, a wet nurse in a neighboring property:

> My aunt Mary belonged to Mr. John Craddock and when his wife died leaving a small baby—little Miss Lucy—aunt Mary was nursing her baby, a newborn, so her master John made her nurse his infant as well. If aunt Mary was feeding her own baby and Miss Lucy started to cry, Mr. John would take her baby from her lap, turn him upside down and beat him in order to make Aunt Mary feed his baby first. Aunt Mary could not say anything, but my mom told me that she always saw aunt Mary cry so much that her tears ran down her cheeks.[12]

This brutal competition between white and black infants for access to vital food, we can see equally in literary and visual representations that circulated throughout North American society—even more prolific in terms of its production of sources—and it can be noted that, focusing on black children and white children, contemporaries struggled to find arguments that justified the abandonment of the former and overprotection of the latter. As indicated by Kimberly

Wallace-Sanders, the terrible tensions that hid behind the image of the *mammy*—stereotypical figure of domestic and harmonious southern American slavery torn between caring for her children and the master's children—appear recorded in numerous sources, written and non-written, which raise concerns regarding the existing intrinsic differences between white children and black children. In these representations, white children are described as beautiful, fragile, and needing constant attention; and the black children appear in picturesque scenes as strong and robust, playing by themselves with a constant smile on their lips.

As the author exemplifies, the children's book *Mammy's Baby* (1890) contained verses in which the white child, left alone for only a moment, cries in complete confusion. Then in the following verse presents the black baby, which, left alone among tables and chairs, laughs entertained and "never needs attention" (Wallace-Sanders, 2008, p. 26). Such representations would be forms of rationalizing the tragedies experienced by the nurses who found themselves obligated to totally or partially abandon their children to care for their masters' children, and the tragedies experienced by the families who had to live with the emotional tension provoked by such circumstance.

There were many reasons that could explain the very common situation of the nurse and her child. Separated from the mother at birth, turned over to a baby hatch or some third party, or even dying during labor or shortly after, it was difficult for a nurse to keep her child with her, and this did occur. The situation required constant vigilance of the nurse's behavior from the masters because she obviously tended to neglect the child in her care in favor of her own child. Upon analyzing the female labor market in 19th century Rio de Janeiro, Bárbara Canedo Martins indicates that in 92 percent of the newspaper ads that offered the services of slave wet nurses, they did not appear accompanied by their children.[13] However, the seigniorial families knew, and the medical theses confirmed, that the separation of the nurse and her newborn child could cause problems in her ability to execute her duties. In the opinion of some, keeping the child with the nurse made her milk healthier, keeping in mind that it was believed that separation from the child and the resulting sadness ruined the quality of her milk in addition to compromising her goodwill towards the infant under her care. In this sense, some medical theses advised keeping the child with its mother as a strategy to guarantee the quality of the milk, as suggested by Sandra Koutsoukos (2009, p. 307-8).

However, under this circumstance, it certainly created a hierarchy among the necessities of both children, the nurse and the family that employed her. The availability of milk and the order of priority defined who nursed first, which could mean that the child of the nurse did not receive sufficient food, a situation that certainly persisted until artificial feeding became safe.

Ambrosina's story and the maternity of the nurse[14]

In this context, the case of the nurse Ambrosina, accused of suffocating the little boy Benedito, 2 months old, comes up as a very significant document. The case, which occurred in the city of Taubaté in 1886—in the final throes of slavery—produced a lengthy document through which the historian opens a small gap for a glimpse into the nearly invisible aspects of the domestic tensions provoked by the presence of a wet nurse with her child during the decline of slavery. If on one hand the hygienist discourse instilled intense distrust of the nurse among the literate elite, on the other hand, the disintegration of slavery itself—with its promises of freedom—made rented nurses such as Ambrosina unwilling to submit herself to a situation that put the survival of the child who accompanied her at risk, ironically also named Benedito.

Additionally, the outcome of the short life of Benedito allows us to closely follow the terrible trauma of what the death of a small child meant to a family. We know that as a way to circumvent the deep trauma that the death of a child caused in any family, contemporaries dedicated themselves to throwing lavish and festive burials, which in almost every way were the opposite of those for adults. The processions for children were held during the day, contrary to those for adults, which were held at night; and in the mother's absence—whose presence was forbidden at the burial—they became public events in which passersby and even foreign travelers participated. However, although in their external, ostentatious and festive presentations, death and funeral rites of small children throughout the 19th century aimed to focus on positive aspects, if not, at least on the acceptance of the inevitable, such events did erase the troubles experienced in private.[15] The case of Benedito is proof of this; his death was a great burden on the family.

Ambrosina's story, as she reveals according to the analysis of the criminal trial, shows us a very realistic dimension of the inherent conflicts from the nurse and her child cohabitating alongside the seigniorial family. Moreover, Ambrosina was the slave of Dr. Alexandre Coelho, native resident of Mogi-Mirim, no age listed, single, maid, illiterate, and legitimate daughter of Abraão and Eva (slaves of the late Manuel Gurgel). She comes up in the trial as the figure of a woman full of ill will, angry, and incapable of having compassion for little Benedito, who depended on her to survive.

As recounted in the trial, Benedito Filadelfo de Castro—municipal judge of Mogi-Mirim—after the birth of his son Benedito, was forced to go stay in Taubaté, in the house of his mother and brother—who was the city vicar—due to the mother's inability to care for the newborn and his older brother. We know nothing of the origin of this inability; however, from the facts relayed in the document, which notes that the children had been housed in a room far from their mother, and that during the night, the father locked the door to the master bedroom to prevent the mother from escaping, it can be assumed that it was severe post-partum depression and possibly mental illness. The way the family prevented the mother coming in contact with her children suggests that she was a risk to the children.

In his move to Taubaté, the judge brought with him two slaves: the black woman Isabel, 19 years old, nanny to his older son; and Ambrosina—nurse to the newborn Benedito—along with her son. Ambrosina agreed to go to said city under the condition that she would be able to return as soon as the judge found another nurse for the child. However, to her despair, Dr. Filadelfo seemed unable to fulfill his promise. Since they arrived in the city, two months had already passed and no other nurse appeared to take Ambrosina's place. According to the declaration made by the child's grandmother, knowing "black Ambrosina's bad precedents, they tried to find a nurse; they encountered some delays because it is difficult to choose a nurse in good moral and physical condition, or, if you will, moral and hygienic." It can be assumed that Ambrosina met some of the requirements doctors recommended; she was the daughter of married parents and she still lived in the city where she grew up. She must have been considered more trustworthy in terms of health and moral habit than an unknown slave, that is, one recently acquired or rented in the commission houses in Rio de Janeiro during the time. Such qualities, however, were unable to mask a rawer reality: Ambrosina was very opposed to fulfilling her role as a wet nurse, always seeming to be upset and in a bad mood. One of the reasons for the family's apparent lack of action could have been the mother's illness, which may have demanded all of the family's attention, making it impossible to search for a replacement nurse for little Benedito.

In one statement among many made by the child's grandmother, burdened with dealing with the domestic issues, she describes the complicated situation that manifested in their household since the inhabitants had to deal with the "bad ways" of the difficult Ambrosina. In her statement, Ms. Gertrudes Placidina de Castro declared that:

> …she always noticed from the time Ambrosina came to the city, her ill will towards the boy, always seeming annoyed when she was asked to nurse the child. This was how Ambrosina behaved, so the deponent, dedicating much love to the child, avoided asking Ambrosina to breastfeed because she would get angry and this was very displeasing to the deponent. She also said that Ambrosina would never nurse the child on her own—even when the child cried—she only did it when they ordered her to do so.[16]

Other witnesses also confirmed Ambrosina's lack of willingness to do her work related to the child under her care. A neighbor, Ms. Teresa Luzia de Jesus Nogueira, a farmer and occasional resident of the city, claimed that whenever she was there, "Ambrosina usually spent the day in her house." I suppose to keep the child far from a dangerous mother, but she always kept watch on what the nurse did. She feared that something would happen to the child given that the nurse was not trustworthy because on one occasion, a week before Benedito's death, when they were both at her house, she heard an unusual cry from the child:

> as if suffocated, she found him at the point of needing to be shaken to breathe, after some time in this state of asphyxiation, he cried as ordinary children cry, noting on the part of the accused on this occasion the surprise at the state of the child, as if she didn't count on the help of… this deponent.[17]

The picture outlined here is very suggestive: that of a helpless newborn child with an incapacitated mother and an impatient and undedicated nurse. What would have brought Ambrosina to act in such a manner? The other side of the trauma is revealed when we hear the statement of the nurse herself. However, even so, the reader must be cautious, which is the difficulty that we have when we hear the voice of Ambrosina. Ruthless, evil, incapable of having any compassion, and even monster were adjectives used by witnesses, the prosecutor, lawyers, and judges when they described her. Additionally, little Benedito, helpless, mistreated, and certainly starving, captures all the attention and sympathy during the time and also from the reader today. However, because we can hear the nurse, we must move beyond the defense arguments she presents as the defendant in the trial. Among other superficial or imaginative arguments, Ambrosina, in order to justify the claim that Filadelfo de Castro's family did not like her, claimed that the witnesses lied and that all of this was the result of a hex that had been placed on her. For example, when asked if she had some motive that might place blame for the murder charge on her, Ambrosina responded:

> …that she suspected an old black woman of the house, Maria, had done some harm to the little boy Benedito, trying to compromise and oust her [Ambrosina], who did not like Maria.[18]

Only when we get beyond this level of argument are we then able to assess the great story that unfolded between Ambrosina and her two Beneditos. In her initial statement, she asserted her innocence in the crime. Actually, at the time "she responded that she indeed breastfed Benedito, the two-month old son of Dr. Filadelfo de Castro who died earlier today, but she did not have the slightest guilt nor did she play any part in the event...."[19] Upon telling the final night of little Benedito, which was spent in the room where she, her son, the nanny Isabel and Dr. Filadelfo's two children slept, Ambrosina reconstructs the intimacy of a bedroom organized by the standards prior to gentrification, privacy, and hygienic standards proposed by medical discourses on sanitation:

> she responded that she indeed breastfed Benedito, the two-month old son of Dr. Filadelfo de Castro, who died earlier today, but she was not the least bit guilty nor did she play any part in the event, seeing as she was sleeping in a room in the house of the very reverend city vicar, with her own son Benedito, the slave Isabel, and Dr. Filadelfo de Castro's two small children, namely Antônio, and Benedito, who died. She slept on a straw mat on the floor with her son Benedito, near a sofa where Dr. Filadelfo's slave Isabel slept along with Dr. Filadelfo's two children....

Similarly, the use of the space and the bedroom furniture where the slaves and children slept is telling of the social relations that were very distant from the modernizing social ideas propagated by the educated discourse from hygiene. According to "Ambrozina [sic], little Benedito slept at the foot of the bed of the nurse Izabel [sic] along with his older brother Antônio. Three people, being an adult slave woman, a small child, and a newborn, slept together on a sofa, while the nurse slept with her child on a mat on the floor." In other passages, Ambrosina confirms that, eventually, sleeping on the floor was she, her son, and little Benedito.

> ...the defendant always came when Isabel called for help when the child she was raising cried; she would breastfeed the child or care for him, afterwards returning the child to Isabel to sleep; that is what happened in the early hours of this morning in which the defendant nursed the crying child and returned him to Isabel to sleep, placing him at the foot of Isabel's bed as usual; at sunrise she woke up to take care of her usual duties, leaving the boy quiet in the bed, convinced that he was sleeping, it never crossed her mind that he was dead and when the respondent, at the backyard well washing the child's diapers, had been called by Ms. Gertrudes—mother of Dr.

Filadelfo—telling her the child was dead, implicating the defendant, to which she claimed, in her defense, that she was ignorant of such a thing.

Ambrosina added, noting the trouble that she experienced, divided between the two Beneditos that:

> She did not know how to explain the fact that because she is innocent and ignores how the event happened and cannot blame it on anyone; she also said that she cherished the boy so much that her own child only nursed at night, drinking from a bottle during the day so that she did not lack milk for the child.[20]

What was happening to the black Benedito being kept on the bottle? Was the milk being given to him boiled first? If not, we can suppose that little black Benedito was suffering from frequent indigestion, diarrhea, and dehydration, potentially fatal problems at that age. Such a situation, a terrible competition for vital nourishment, seems equally suggested by the child's grandmother who takes Ambrosina's unavailability to nurse little white Benedito as ill will.

However, she does not leave out the other Benedito—sometimes called "the Little Creole"—who we actually know very little about. Through the testimonies we are only told that the little black Benedito was an arm baby of nursing age. Nothing was recorded about his physical state, if he was healthy or not, if he cried from hunger and lack of care like the little white Benedito did almost all the time. Actually, as Ms. Gertrudes Placidina tells the story, black Benedito was not deprived of necessities and perhaps was as hungry as white Benedito. To appease the nanny, Ms. Gertrudes allowed her to nurse her own child first and only afterward, the white Benedito. However, we can ask how long did black Benedito nurse, whether he was taken from the breast before he was satisfied, if he cried or not, and moreover, if he could count on the attention of his mother when he cried.

She further states that on the 16th, returning from the convent around 8 p.m., upon entering the house, she found the boy crying and Ambrosina was with her own son in her lap listening impassively to that cry, which caused the deponent to call for Ambrosina and order her to nurse the Benedito who died. Ambrosina angrily came and picked up Benedito and nursed him from the same right breast, which did not have any milk, as the deponent observed; however, as Ambrosina's child was crying a lot, the deponent ordered Ambrosina first to nurse him to calm him down and return to nursing Benedito. When Ambrosina tried to pull the boy from her body, the deponent saw that Ambrosina's left breast was losing the milk that it held, which made the deponent notice that Ambrosina had saved the milk from the left breast for her son. The deponent made Ambrosina give part of this milk to the boy that the she (the deponent) had just taken from her arms.[21]

How to resolve this economizing of breast milk which two newborn children depended on for survival? Certainly, the trouble that Ambrosina experienced was intense and devastating, resulting in emotional crises, threats to do crazy things, and mainly, a lot of tension as seen from the testimonies that narrated the days up until the death. Ambrosina had threatened to kill her own child in order to leave the house. When asked about such statement, she responded that:

> ...once, she had said as a mere joke, to the witness Vicência that she was going to hit the boy's head—her son, that is—but she said that she had said this with no intention of doing it when being called to breastfeed one of the two children, shortly after finishing nursing the other, because she [Ambrosina] was burdened with breastfeeding her son and Dr. Filadelfo de Castro's son at the same time.[22]

As the authorities proved, the child's death was caused by suffocation. The finding of a diaper with blood stains led to the retracing of what happened in the bedroom on the morning the child died. As suggested by the expert, the nurse Ambrosina put a "dummy" in the child's mouth, described as a method nurses and mothers use to subside small tantrums. The dummy was basically a diaper torn down the middle to form a roll for the child to suck on. This predecessor of the pacifier certainly presented many risks. In Benedito's case, the dummy was either put too far into his mouth or Benedito had sucked on it too hard because it became lodged in his throat, stopping respiration.[23]

Vicência, Ms. Gertrude's slave, said on that morning, minutes before daybreak:

> ...she, the deponent was still in her bedroom, which is near to where Ambrosina slept, when she was called by Ms. Gertrudes who had told her to go see what was making Benedito cry as if he were suffocating; and when she, the deponent went to the room that Ambrosina and the boy were in, put her hand on the door latch to open it but could not because it was locked with the key from the inside, the deponent then called Ambrosina and asked her what was wrong with the boy. She responded that it was nothing, and that she was nursing him, and at that moment the boy stopped crying so the deponent left. Later, Ambrosina came out of the room with her son and when Ms. Gertrudes asked about the boy, Ambrosina said that he was still sleeping; Ms. Gertrudes noted that Ambrosina had covered the boy's mouth and Ambrosina denied she had done this. After some time, Dr. Filadelfo came from breakfast in the dining room and passing by the room with the boy in it, he found him dead; he called for his mother Ms. Gertrudes who confirmed the boy was dead and called for Ambrosina who was in the backyard. Ambrosina responded with exclamation, declaring that she had not killed the boy.

The testimony suggests that on the morning of the fateful day, Ambrosina—who had already spent the night with the child in her arms—tired and sleepless, but mainly without milk, or trying to save some for her own son, allowed white Benedito to cry. Admonished by the slave Vicência at the behest of the child's grandmother, Ambrosina—perhaps filled with rage and impatience—put the dummy in little Benedito's mouth and allowed him to choke to death.

We know nothing with respect to Ambrosina and her son's fate beyond what appears in the criminal trial. Accused of murdering white Benedito, Ambrosina endured many months in prison. The trial also does not inform us if, during this time, she could nurse her son Benedito, or if he was separated from her. Acquitted by the jury in 1886 due to lack of evidence, Ambrosina still remained in custody due to the appeal immediately submitted by the municipal judge of Taubaté. Everything indicates that she must have continued fighting against the ruling.

Although this might be, in terms of violence and crudeness, a unique case, it allows us to penetrate the depths of domestic slavery.

After all, nothing brings us to suppose that the problems described here were exceptional. In addition, Ambrosina's case does not fail to raise some broader concerns. In the decline of slavery, as so many other illusions fed by slaveholders and their supporters, that which was understood as the nurse's dedicated and loyal love for the white child for which she cared was often detrimental to her own child; it may have begun as another sweet illusion, undone by the proverbial ingratitude of the former slaves. Provided with more autonomy, it can be assumed that prospective wet nurses actively sought to prioritize raising their own children, making them less available to feed the imaginations of a proprietary class of slaves accustomed to the brutal practices of domination. The fact that many today still allow themselves to get wrapped up in the apparent sweetness of the slave relations represented by the captive nurse and her white baby proves that the innermost fantasies of a kind slaveholding past and of a racial democracy spontaneously constructed still persist.

Notes

1. Maria Martha Luna de Freire, *Mulheres, mães e médicos. Discurso maternalista no Brasil.* [Women, Mothers,and Doctors. Maternalist Discourse in Brazil]. Rio de Janeiro: Ed. da FGV, 2009, p. 97-146.

2. For example, see my article "Corpo, gênero e identidade no limiar da Abolição: o caso de Benedicta Maria Albina da Ilha ou Benedicta, escrava (Sudeste, 1880) [Body, Gender, and Identity in the Threshold of Abolition: the Case of Benedicta Maria Albina of the Island or Benedictia Slave (Southeast 1880)], Revista Afro-Ásia, n. 42, 2010, p. 157-193.

3. On the theme of breastfeeding in 19th century Rio society, see: Carneiro, 2006, principally chapters 2 and 3. The discussion of the medical theses regarding natural, mercenary and artificial breastfeeding is an extensive topic that does not fit in this essay; however, on the feminine types and breastfeeding, see, for example, the medical theses of Meirelles, 1847, p. 8 and 9, and of Moreira Sampaio, 1873, p. 22. Regarding the factors that caused a mother's inability to breastfeed, see an example in Sampaio, 1873, p. 10.

4. On the invention of the bottle, see: <http://www.breastfeeding-mom.com/baby-bottles.html>, visited 15/5/2011. On the pasteurization and sterilization of milk, see Viangre, Diniz and Costa, 2001, p. 340-5.

5. Levenstein, 1988, p. 122-3.

6. For an assessment of medical theses on breastfeeding, see Chapters 2 and 3 from Carneiro, 2006.

7. Cunha, 1873, p. 37; Reis, 1874, p. 14-5 and Milward, 1873.

8. Júnia Sales Pereira, "História da pediatria no Brasil do final do século XIX a meados do século XX," [History of Pediatrics in Brazil at the end of the 19th Century], Doctoral Dissertation in History, Universidade Federal de Minas Gerais, 2006, p. 179-181.

9. For an argument on artificial nursing, see Júnia Sales Pereira, *op.cit.*, p.165-187, especially p.174, where you can see an ad from 1879 for products for artificial nursing.

10. M.M.L. de Freire (2009), *op.cit.*, p. 210-243 and *Mulheres, mães e médicos. Discurso maternalista* in women's magazines (Rio de Janeiro and São Paulo, 1920s), Doctoral Dissertation, Programa de Pós-Graduação em História das Ciências e da Saúde, Casa Oswaldo Cruz, Fiocruz, 2006, chapter 2, especially p. 48-9.

11. For example, see Ermakoff, 2004, especially p. 98-103. For a critical view of this reality, see Koutsoukos, 2010 (part 2) and 2009, p. 305-24; Martins, 2006, Chapters 3 and 4.

12. See interview with McWhorter, *Born in Slavery: Federal Writers Project, 1936-1938*. This excerpt is also cited in Wallace-Sanders, 2008, p. 36.

13. Martins, 2006, p. 61.

14. This item is based on the criminal trial of 1887: Cidade de Taubaté. Tribunal do Júri. A Justiça: Autora, Ambrosina, escrava de Alexandre Florindo Coelho: Ré. Departamento Arquivo Histórico Felix Guisard Filho, Taubaté (DMPAH). I thank Ms. Lia Carolina Prado Alves Mariotto for her kind help and reproduction of the document.

15. On the theme of infant death, see Vailati, 2010.

16. Depoimento de [Testimony of] Ms. Gertrudes Placidina de Castro, f. 16 v-19 v.

17. Depoimento de [Testimony of] Teresa Luzia de Jesus Nogueira, f. 47.

18. Interrogatório da ré [Interrogation of the defendant] Ambrosina, f. 90-93 v.

19. Depoimento da escrava [Testimony of the slave] Ambrosina, fls. 5 verso e 6.

20. Depoimento da escrava [Testimony of the slave] Ambrosina, f. 5 v-6.

21. Depoimento de [Testimony of] Ms. Gertrudes Placidina de Castro, f. 16 v-19 v.

22. Interrogatório da ré [Interrogation of the defendant] Ambrosina, f. 90-93 v.

23. Forensic examination of the diaper found among Ambrosina's belongings, f. 40-44 v.

Bibliography

Born in Slavery: Federal Writers Project, 1936-1938. Manuscript Division, Library of Congress. Disponível em: <http://memory.loc.gov/ammem/snhtml/>. Accessed: 10 May 2011.

Carneiro, Maria Elizabeth Ribeiro. *Procura-se: uma preta com muito bom leite, prendada e carinhosa: uma cartografia das ama de leite na sociedade carioca, 1850-1888*. [Wanted: A black woman with good milk, agreeable, and affectionate: a cartography of wet nurses in the society of Rio de Janeiro, 1850-1888]. 2006. Diss. (Doctorate in History). Universidade de Brasília (UnB), Brasília, DF.

Cunha, Augusto Álvares da. *Do aleitamento natural, artificial e misto e particularmente do mercenário em relação às condições em que ele se acha no Rio de Janeiro*. [On natural breastfeeding, artificial nursing, mixed, and particularly the hired wet nurse and the conditions in which she finds herself in Rio de Janeiro]. Diss. Faculdade de Medicina do Rio de Janeiro. Rio de Janeiro: Tipografia do Acadêmica, 1873.

Ermakoff, George. *O negro na fotografia brasileira do século XIX*. [Blacks in Brazilian Photography in the 19th Century]. Rio de Janeiro: George Ermakoff Casa Editorial, 2004.

Koutsoukos, Sandra Sofia Machado. "Amas mercenárias: o discurso dos doutores em medicina e os retratos de amas – Brasil, segunda metade do século XIX." [Mercenary wet nurses: the discourse of medical doctors and portrayals of wet nurses – Brazil, second half of the 19th century]. *História, Ciência e Saúde*. Manguinhos, v. 16, n. 2, Rio de Janeiro, 2009, p. 305-24.

_____. *Negros no estúdio fotográfico*. [Blacks in the Photographic Studio]. Campinas: Unicamp, 2010.

Levenstein, Harvey. *Revolution at the Table: The Transformation of the American Diet*. New York: Oxford University Press, 1988.

Martins, Bárbara Canedo Ruiz. *Amas-de-leite e mercado de trabalho feminino: descortinando práticas e sujeitos (Rio de Janeiro, 1830-1890)*. [Wet nurses and the feminine labor market: revealing practices and subjects (Rio de Janeiro, 1830-1890)]. 2006. Thesis (Masters) – Instituto de Ciências Humanas e Filosofia (IFCS). Universidade Federal do Rio de Janeiro (UFRJ), Rio de Janeiro.

Meirelles, Zeferino Justino da Silva. *Vantagens do aleitamento maternal*. [Advantages of natural breastfeeding]. Diss. Faculdade de Medicina do Rio de Janeiro. Rio de Janeiro: Tipografia do Diário, 1847.

Milward, Cornélio Emílio das Neves. *Do aleitamento natural, artificial e misto e particularmente do mercenário em relação às condições em que ele se acha no Rio de Janeiro*. [On natural breastfeeding, artificial nursing, mixed, and particularly the hired wet nurse and the conditions in which she finds herself in Rio de Janeiro]. Diss. Faculdade de Medicina do Rio de Janeiro. Rio de Janeiro: Tipografia do Apóstolo, 1873. Disponível em: <http://www.siaapm.cultura.mg.gov.br/acervo/teses/TM-0156.pdf>. Acessed: 20 Sep. 2012.

Reis, Celso Eugênio dos. *Do aleitamento natural, artificial e misto e particularmente do mercenário em relação às condições em que ele se acha no Rio de Janeiro.* [On natural breastfeeding, artificial nursing, mixed, and particularly the hired wet nurse and the conditions in which she finds herself in Rio de Janeiro]. Diss. Faculdade de Medicina do Rio de Janeiro. Rio de Janeiro: Tipografia Oliveira e Silva, 1874.

Sampaio, Francisco Moreira. *Do aleitamento natural, artificial e misto e particularmente do mercenário em relação às condições em que ele se acha no Rio de Janeiro.* [On natural breastfeeding, artificial nursing, mixed, and particularly the hired wet nurse and the conditions in which she finds herself in Rio de Janeiro]. Diss. Faculdade de Medicina do Rio de Janeiro. Rio de Janeiro: Tipografia do Diário, 1873.

Vailati, Luiz Lima. *A morte menina: infância e morte infantil no Brasil do Oitocentos (Rio de Janeiro e São Paulo).* [Girl death: Childhood and infant death in Brazil in the 1800s (Rio de Janeiro and São Paulo)]. São Paulo: Alameda, 2010.

Viangre, Roberto Diniz; Diniz, Edna M. A.; Costa, Flávio A. Vaz. "Leite humano: um pouco de sua história." [Human milk: a little of her history]. *Pediatria*, São Paulo, n. 203, 2001, p. 340-5.

Wallace-Sanders, Kimberly. *Mammy: A Century of Race, Gender, and Southern Memory.* Ann Arbor: University of Michigan Press, 2008.

14

THE "LIVRO DE OURO" (GOLDEN BOOK),
EMANCIPATION FUND AND ENSLAVED WOMEN:
GENDER, ABOLITION, AND THE MEANINGS OF
FREEDOM IN THE COURT, 1880s[1]

Camilla Cowling

In March of 1886, Maria Rosa, a freed woman, sent a letter to the empress of Brazil, Ms. Teresa Cristina, asking that her daughter, Ludovina, be freed in a slave emancipation ceremony that would be happening in the next few days in the empire's capital. Nine of those ceremonies happened in Rio de Janeiro between 1885 and 1887, all depending on the presence and support of the imperial family. In the ceremonies, Princess Isabel generally gave letters of freedom to the slaves, but, as that specific ceremony to which Maria Rosa was referring was to celebrate the empress' birthday, it would be Teresa Cristina herself giving away the letters. The freed woman's request on behalf of her daughter emphasized that she was "a poor freed black woman," "mother of an unhappy child who was always sick to the point of bleeding from the mouth, and with three minor children still under the bondage of captivity." Perhaps aware of being sent to a woman who was often praised as the "Brazilian mother," the petition sought to emphasize the aspect of Maria Rosa being a *mother asking for help for her daughter*, establishing a subtle link between the two women who, although belonging to extreme opposite ends of the social hierarchy of Brazil during the period, had maternity in common:

"this is what this poor mother begs of Your Majesty's Magnanimity, also wishing you opulent birthdays for many years, always accompanied by the happiness that you and your noble family so deserve."[2]

In the ceremonies to which Maria Rosa referred, slaves were freed and their masters were compensated by an emancipation fund called the *Livro de Ouro* (Golden Book), established by the Câmara Municipal (City Council) in 1884. The ceremonies always occurred on the birthdays of the imperial family or on Independence Day. They were lavish events, watched by the members of the imperial family as well as by council members, ministers, and other local and national "dignitaries."

Despite the spectacle of the ceremonies, the results of the *Livro de Ouro* were insignificant in numerical terms because the fund freed 797 people in total, representing only 3 percent of the decrease in the city's slave population in this period (from 24,615 in 1884 to 7,488 in 1887). Even so, it is interesting to investigate its function because it opens a new window on the process of the abolition of slavery in the tumultuous imperial capital which, during the time, was the stage for intense abolitionist campaigns and fights among the Câmara Municipal and the conservatism of the government of Barão de Cotegipe (August 1885 to March 1888) about the issue of slavery. Women represented 76 percent of the people freed from the fund, and from the beginning, the councilmembers explicitly prioritized them for emancipation. Where did this interest in freeing women come from? Could it be that they had a deciding role in their own freedom? What were the expectations of freedom created by various participants—from the councilmembers to the imperial family, all the way to enslaved and freed women such as Maria Rosa?[3]

The Municipal Emancipation Fund and the "logic of the free womb"

The councilmen never discussed the motives of the decision to free women. They seemed to find that the motive was obvious. Why? In 1871, seeing a gradual end to slavery, the Rio Branco law declared that children born to slave women were already "free." That is, there was a link between the womb and the legal status of the child. Such association had existed for a long time. In Brazil as in other slave societies of the Americas, a legal principle (of Roman origin) called, in Latin, *partus sequiter ventrem* was followed, which meant that the legal status of the individual came from the womb. Until 1871, however, the child of a slave mother and a free father was considered a slave. In 1871 this principle was, on one hand, inverted, allowing the children of slave women to be "free." On the other hand, the legal connection between the womb (or, technically, the enslaved mother) and the legal status of the child still remained. As such, the Rio Branco law established a national emancipation fund to free slaves, which, for this fund, women with children were prioritized. In the 1880s, when abolitionist movements arose in the country, various local funds for emancipation were created, private and municipal; they customarily gave priority to women with children or young women (probably expectant mothers). Soon, when the members of the Câmara Municipal at Court contemplated the establishment of a similar fund, there were already many precedents in place that linked the process of emancipation to the womb, leaving the councilmen to simply follow what we would call the "logic of the free womb."[4]

Such logic did not operate only on the plane of abstract legal ideas or in elite debates on the process of emancipation. It also influenced the daily life of enslaved people and of their free or freed families. Generally, families prioritized the manumission of the woman because children that would be born, would be born free. Furthermore, women themselves always stood out in the fight for the emancipation of their children, whether it was saving money to free them or claiming their freedom through legal proceedings in the courts. To assure that the legal provisions were complied with, the "Lei do Ventre Livre" (The Law of the Free Womb) of 1871 depended, in good part, on the legal or personal initiatives taken by mothers of children who were born "free."[5]

Feminine abolitionism?

In addition to this "logic of the free womb," the presence of women—both women being freed and women in the audience, as well as members of the imperial family—reflected an abolitionist "fashion" of the time. The discourse of councilmen at these events appealed to the emotions of the listeners, invoking emotional images of the suffering of enslaved mothers, which reflected the "feminized" culture of abolitionism in Brazil in the 1880s that also characterized the clubs, meetings, and abolitionist press. There was a tendency to appeal to the "mistresses," in search of supposedly feminine reactions such as benevolence, kindness, and emotional attachment. And, although most of the highlighted abolitionists were male, women very actively participated in the abolitionist movement.[6]

In August of 1886, the famous opera singer Nadina Bulicioff visited the Court. After charming the public with her voice, she remained on the stage with a "commission of mistresses" and the distinguished abolitionist, José do Patrocínio. Through her own resources and donations made by the "mistresses" of the city, the artist freed six slaves, and she, herself, delivered their letters of freedom. Instantly, she became the heroine for the abolitionist public in Rio de Janeiro. The abolitionist newspaper *Revista Illustrada* from August 20, 1886 described the event as follows:

> ...Bulicioff was extraordinarily moved seeing before her the poor women, for whom she was a redeemer, and as such, giving them letters of freedom, hugged and kissed the women being freed... they all trembled.... The scene was full of mistresses.... Her Majesty, the Empress, cried; in the stands, the handkerchiefs... were wet with spontaneous tears that the woes of the slaves drew from the viewers (p. 6).

In events such as that one, the women played an important role, symbolically. The women being freed were "poor women," serving as objects of compassion for the women in the audience who, in turn, were the subject of a "feminine" rhetoric full of emotion and ideas of "charity." Such rhetoric also reached the women of the imperial family. The image being constructed of Princess Isabel as a "redeemer," was, after all, hyper-feminine. In the municipal ceremonies, the Princess, as well as her mother, Teresa Cristina, gave out letters of emancipation and were called the "mother of slaves," being praised for their "charity," "piety," and "heart." When councilman

João Pereira Lopes addressed the Princess in the ceremony celebrated on her birthday in July 1886, he exclaimed:

> Madam, when... in the sweet companionship of family ye shall receive in your arms dear children, welcome them to your breast; there, where pure and holy love rests, this—sublime love—called maternal love... imprint on them delirious and perfumed kisses from a loving mother... do not yet forget the millions of children, as Brazilian as us, your children also, who... lie in captivity, spread throughout the entire South American continent![7]

Similar to the letter written by Maria Rosa addressed to the empress, Pereira Lopes linked the women of the imperial family to the slaves. The most effective method to express this link was through the notion of maternity, at the time seen as the most essential part of feminine identity. In many other examples of the time, abolitionist writers used the same technique. The theme of women separated from their children due to slavery, for example, had become common ground for abolitionists. The first article of the series from the debut of the newspaper *O Abolicionista* pointed out "the ads for the purchase and sale of humans..., the rental of mothers, separated from their children, as maids for other children...," saying that such facts were "reasons for humiliation for every Brazilian." The *Gazeta da Tarde* constantly denounced that, despite a provision of the Rio Branco law against the separate sale of mother and children, this practice was still occurring. The mother/child relationship was placed, for abolitionist purposes, as a powerful experience that encompassed all human beings, free or slave; that is, a notion that equaled (rhetorically, at least) appellee and appellant.[8]

As such, maternity and the "feminine" became relevant within abolitionist discourse of the time. But, could it be that these ideas had some impact or relevance for the struggles of women such as Maria Rosa?

Enslaved women's search for freedom

The organization of ceremonies served to create a visual representation that would be written in historical memory, through which emancipation would be seen purely as a "gift." But, a search in the municipal archives makes it clear that the history of the operation of the emancipation funds such as the "Livro de Ouro" were not so simple. The list of people to be freed did not only depend on the initiatives of the councilmen, nor on the efforts of the masters of the enslaved people. On the contrary: the slaves and their relatives also took various initiatives to achieve emancipation for themselves. Through the frequent ceremonies and the ads about the fund in the principal newspapers of the capital, the slaves and their families knew about the existence of the fund and the opportunities for emancipation that it offered.

Many people emancipated by the "Livro de Ouro" contributed a good portion of their own price for emancipation. Regulation of the fund prioritized the emancipation of women who had their own savings. The councilmen did not give detailed information about the contributions made by people freed through the "Livro de Ouro." However, a list compiled in 1880 of six people emancipated through the national emancipation fund (Fundo Nacional de Emanicipação), which was similar to the Rio de Janeiro municipal fund and was administered in part by the same councilmen of Rio de Janeiro, it had five women who had saved about 450 thousand *réis* (currency of the time) each, which was almost the equivalent of the average price of a slave freed by the imperial national emancipation fund. In another similar fund, in Recife, the freed women contributed 71 percent of the total price of their own restitution. The slaves to be freed not only had to give over money; they also had to enter into a complex bargaining process participating directly in negotiations between the city council and their masters and/or mistresses. In November of 1887, a young black Creole woman, named Josefa, made an offer to the councilmen: she would contribute 100 thousand *réis* if the council gave the rest, which would be an amount of 200 thousand *réis*, composing her total price of 300 thousand *réis*. After a process of negotiation, she was emancipated for a value of 150 thousand *réis*, of which her savings represented two-thirds.[9]

Other women, such as Maria Rosa, used the concept of maternity in their requests, fitting themselves into the "logic of the free womb" and in the "feminine" rhetoric of charity and empathy that were common in discourse during the time. In June of 1885, a freed couple, Manuel Caetano Alves de Oliveira and Benedita Caetana, wrote a letter, through a scribe, to the Câmara Municipal asking for help to free their daughter Paulina. Manuel and Benedita lived far from the capital, in the town of Resende. However, despite the distance and illiteracy (like the majority of slaves), they knew of the fund's existence. Offering a contribution of 150 thousand *réis* that they had saved, they asked that the "Livro de Ouro" bear the rest of the cost for Paulina's freedom. In addition to offering money, the request used emotional rhetoric based on Benedita's experiences as a suffering mother:

> ...and see the freed woman Benedita end her final and sad days without [the] hope of getting her just goal that excited her until now, she comes with a tortured heart in a final attempt, begging Your Excellency the alms of completing, through the blessed Livro de Ouro, the amount... for the freedom of her daughter....

The letter asked that the councilmen had "commiseration of the pain and desperateness of a woeful mother." Despite the request having been written in the name of both the father and the mother, the scribe (or perhaps the couple themselves) opted to highlight the mother's suffering—perhaps assuming that this was the best way to win the empathy of the listeners—a strategy similar to that which was used in another petition that reached the council, in October of 1885, in the name of Rita, a young *parda* (mixed race) woman. Her situation was very difficult: her master, Manuel José Dias Corrêa, had imprisoned her in the Casa de Detenção (detention house) as a punishment for some error or disagreement, but she was "far along in a pregnancy, that is, the last period." The letter asked that the councilmen, showing "benevolent protection" and "charity," include Rita in the list of slaves to be emancipated in the next freeing ceremony. And if Rita were free, what would she do after? We will discuss this in the next section—the issue of the meanings of feminine liberty, seen quite differently by the councilmen and by women such as Rita and so many others who sought freedom for themselves and their children.[10]

"Enlightened mothers" or *"gifted servants"*?

While the councilmen prioritized the freedom of women and children, they also took some initiatives for the sons and daughters of these women who were technically "free" after 1871 and became known as *ingênuos* (innocents). Upon founding some schools and charitable or social institutions in the municipality, they traced connections among these activities and the process of emancipation. Thinking about the future of the *ingênuos*, the councilmen also discussed the role of the children's mothers and, thus, the social role of former slave women.

One of the most interesting debates in this direction happened when the councilmen established a school for *ingênua* girls. The proposal for the creation of an institution was made in 1884 by Teresa Pizarro Filha, one among many female professors who took care of the education of the girls in the Court. The Câmara Municipal agreed with the proposal, and the school Escola Isabel was founded. In the report of councilman Torquato José Fernandes Couto, on behalf of the school, it was argued that abolition implied the necessity of educating the former slaves, "instructing them, teaching them to work, moralizing them, and instilling in them work ethic," because "otherwise, the freed man and the *ingênuo* will be a social danger." Using arguments common among the elite that contemplated the end of slavery, he said: "[T]he thought that rules the slave when he becomes free is the denial of work." Speaking specifically on the issue of domestic service, a point of anxiety among the elite in favor of abolition, he highlighted the lack of training of the domestic servants in Brazil. For Fernandes Couto, such unpreparedness was due to the absence of certain familial habits. "In Europe, there are families that from generation to generation have given themselves to domesticity—the parents teaching their children from the experience they have gained; among us domesticity has been exercised by slaves." The *ingênuos* did not escape the "vices" of slavery because "they are naturally in contact with their parents, who pass on to them their habits and imperfect way of thinking."[11]

Couto took on the idea that the girls would learn little—or only negative examples—from their parents. The Escola Isabel was a boarding school, separating the children from their parents. It is difficult to imagine the reaction of the enslaved or freed mothers who, frequently, worked and sacrificed much to achieve their own freedom and the right to bring their children with them. Could it be that they wanted their daughters to be educated far from their families, to be raised as maids for elite families? Actually, the lessons the girls learned included academic subjects that mothers and fathers could not teach; however, they almost always learned domestic tasks such as washing and ironing clothes, cooking and preparing desserts and drinks that their own mothers, also usually domestic servants, could teach them.

After founding the school, Couto's colleagues began to express their doubts. In December of 1884, a report prepared by three councilmen complained that the *ingênuas* were being taught separately from the other girls who also studied in Escola Isabel. According to the councilmen, this was unacceptable "in an age that preaches equality, in which schools are founded to graduate free citizens and enlightened mothers of families." They also said that "the instruction given to the unfortunate *ingênua* girls… is clearly a separate instruction, not to prepare future mothers of families, but to prepare skilled servants; not to enlighten the spirit nor to form the character of the *ingênua*, but to make her feel that her aspirations cannot go beyond the limits of domestic service."

For such elite men of the 1880s, these were the sentiments relating to the freedom of these girls in post-abolitionist society. On one hand, the elite were anxious about the continuation of domestic service after abolition, using racist "scientific" notions of the time about the vagrancy of former slaves in general, and especially the social and moral "contamination" represented by the idea of black women who breastfed white children and served in the "midst" of white families. On the other hand, the notions of "equality" that were referenced did not signify, especially for women, "citizenship," but the possibility of being mothers of future "citizens," something exclusive like the role of being a mother was reserved for women of the elite. (Even for most freed men, the possibility of active "citizenship" through voting had disappeared as a result of the electoral reform of 1880 that required voters be literate in a society that did little to educate those freed from captivity.)[12]

Many mistresses owning slaves who sought freedom through the "Livro de Ouro" emancipation fund also participated in this debate on the thoughts and motives of freedom for women. Council member Couto perhaps liked the September 1887 request of Ms. Rufina de Sousa Vilar asking for the compensated freedom of her slave Marcelina. To support her argument, Ms. Rufina noted that Marcelina was "black, robust, wise, young, and skilled in all domestic services, especially in the kitchen." It seems that she was assuring the reader that Marcelina, once emancipated, would continue to do the same work as before. Since the councilmen had already criticized Escola Isabel, perhaps they sympathized with the request made by Ms. Maria Carmina Caldas Reis for the manumission of her slave Idalina, *parda*, specifying that Idalina was "a very talented maid, 18 years old," and that "the requested freedom directly competes for the greatest joy of the little *parda* Idalina because, already being asked in marriage, she desires freedom to be able to marry with dignity...." The implication was that for a girl like Idalina, freedom offered the possibility of becoming a "respectable" wife and mother. The comparison between the description of Idalina, *parda* and with prospects of marriage, and the black Marcelina, "robust," "hardworking," and "young," also reminds us that the notions the elite held regarding freedom for enslaved women depended, in good measure, on subtle racialized distinctions.[13]

The councilmen represented the elite of the time. Their discourse expressed two basic interpretations of freedom for former slaves: that of serving as domestic servants or, in a more liberal, idealized vision, that of achieving the exclusive status of "mother," something that had always only existed for women of the elite. However, they also needed to deal with the fact that many poor women in Brazil, enslaved or free, had to balance work and maternity in their lives. As such, in April of 1888, councilman Couto supported the proposal to found nurseries in the city because they "allowed, mainly mothers, to work for the well-being of the family without apprehensions about the care of their children." However, if these were the concerns of the councilmen, what were the views of freedom held by the women who sought it assiduously through the "Livro de Ouro"?[14]

"Views of freedom" held by formerly enslaved women

In the third emancipation ceremony, celebrated by city council on December 2, 1885, city councilman Cláudio da Silva made a speech in which he reminded the public that, in a few moments, "more than one-hundred and thirty-three new citizens" would receive their letters of freedom from the hands of Princess Isabel, becoming "free men." Actually, 113 (85 percent) of these "free men" were women. Differently than men, they did not have the remote possibility of being active citizens. In any case, it is unlikely that the women being freed who were listening to the long speech of the councilman were concerned with the exact definitions of citizenship. What, then, was their meaning of freedom? Their initiatives, after the end of the ceremonies and letters received, suggest some possibilities.[15]

After the ceremony of March 1886, presided over by Empress Teresa Cristina, the police chief of the Court, João Coelho Bastos, wrote to the Câmara Municipal denouncing an attempt made by the artisan Jerônimo José de Melo to take a *parda* woman named Gabriela to Nova Friburgo, "by violent means." Gabriela had been Melo's slave; however, she had been freed in the ceremony. Thus, she could resist the attempt to be taken from the city, being protected by the same "slaver" police that was slandered tirelessly by the abolitionist press. The newspapers denounced police who persecuted people of color suspected of being runaway slaves, despite many of them being legally free. However, here, Bastos called Melo's attempt to take Gabriela from the city "criminal," and he prevented it from happening. For Gabriela, freedom meant more control over her own mobility and the chance to stay in the city where she had networks of friends and family members.[16]

Melo was also the owner of two other women. In the same ceremony of 1886, he received compensation for Maria, a *parda*, 18 years old, who had an *ingênuo* child. For Maria, liberty offered the same opportunity as it did for Gabriela, that is, the chance to control her own mobility. But, as a mother, it also meant the possibility of avoiding yet another separation from her son, which was still common during the time despite being forbidden by the law of Rio Branco. Similarly, young Rita—pregnant and imprisoned in the Casa de Detenção—must have thought about freedom as a way to save the life of her child and to have a chance to stay with him. For these women, freedom significantly limited the rights that Melo had over them—rights that, for many owners of slave women, included sexual rights. The dispute between Melo and Gabriela reveals how difficult it was for the artisan to get accustomed to this new situation. After all, just a few years before, he had imprisoned another one of his slaves, Martinha, simply for "saying obscenities."[17]

Other women freed through the "Livro de Ouro" experienced many difficulties in achieving, in practical terms, the freedom they had formally received. In September of 1885, according to the abolitionist newspaper *A Gazeta da Tarde*, the district police of Espírito Santo detained a black woman, Ana, "at the request of a foreign mistress" who claimed the detained woman was her slave. Furthermore, according to the newspaper, "Ana resisted the arrest and declared that she retained authority over her person, that they could not arrest her, that she was free [and] she belonged to the number of slaves freed on September 7; that she had received her title of citizen from the hands of the imperial princess, that she did not have the letter with her, but she would go get it." The newspaper reported, however, that the woman's protests were ignored. Ana remained arrested and suffered a dehumanizing experience—and especially defeminizing—her head was shaved; a common practice of the "slaver" police that was condemned by the abolitionist press. The police defended their actions saying that Ana, a black woman (*preta*), had somehow gotten the letter of freedom that belonged to another Ana, a *parda* (mixed race) woman. We cannot confirm the correct version of the story, but at least it remains evident that freed women had serious difficulty in keeping the freedom that they had legally received.[18]

Ana's example further suggests a series of fights and disagreements that happened in the process of emancipation; very different from the view of a harmonious and hierarchical abolition based on generosity and gratefulness that the elites wanted to create. Thus, for example, the *parda* Rosa, 19 years old, resisted the attempts of one such Delfino Lerma, who said that she owed him 700 thousand *réis* for "expenses paid by him for her to obtain her freedom," wanting "Rosa to give him the salary she received as a maid, which she refused to do."

Next, even though we do not have access to the words of the women being freed, we can glimpse into some meanings of freedom for them. The study of the "Livro de Ouro" fund, in conjunction with other investigations, shows that such women used their new free status to avoid separation from their children; to gain more autonomy in their work conditions, residence, and salary; or to defend themselves against physical and sexual acts of violence. Although their appeals and communication sometimes used concepts of womanhood that were recognized by the councilmen and the elite in general, their perspectives on freedom were much more complex, based on their own experiences of slavery and freedom.[19]

Gender and the paths to abolition in Brazil

The "Livro de Ouro" emancipation fund, although inefficient in terms of number, created a new perspective on the process of the abolition of slavery in the city of Rio de Janeiro and, by extension, across the country. The activities and the reception of the fund indicate how the womb became a fundamental concept linked to slavery and to emancipation, as much in the laws as in the ways of thinking for the elite and for enslaved women and men. The development of a "feminine" abolitionist language provided a discursive space for emotional arguments in favor of the freedom of women and children. The operations of the fund also help us to understand the meanings of feminine freedom, seen from different points of view. Prioritizing women and children for freedom, the councilmen used their own racialized concepts of gender and citizenship, seeing freed women as domestic servants or imagining them reaching the status of "mothers of families"—generally a status reserved for the elite. The meanings of freedom for the women themselves were more rich and complex.

They worked as much to define the meanings of freedom as they did to achieve freedom in their lives. If the councilmen tried to create an image of emancipation as a gift, the actions of the women themselves prove that abolition was a process that was challenged in many aspects and was built mutually, albeit in profoundly unequal way.

We cannot conclude without first asking what happened with Maria Rosa's story, the freed woman who wrote the letter to the empress. Actually, she was successful: Ludovina, her daughter, was freed in the ceremony celebrated some days after the delivery of the letter. Interestingly, Maria Rosa already knew that Ludovina's owner was one of the councilmen of the Câmara Municipal that was actively freeing slaves. He freed Ludovina just before the ceremony, perhaps because of the embarrassment that Maria Rosa's letter caused him. What remains to be seen are the meanings of freedom that the mother, daughter, and grandchildren gave to their lives from that point forward.

Notes

1. I thank the archivists and employees of the Arquivo Geral da Cidade do Rio de Janeiro (AGCRJ) and the Fundação Biblioteca Nacional (FN); the Institute for the Study of Slavery, University of Nottingham, United Kingdom, and the Leverhulme Trust, United Kingdom; and María del Carmen Baerga, Celso Castilho, Astrid Cubano, Keila Grinberg, Hebe Mattos, Jessica Millward, Mariza Soares e Giovana Xavier, for commentary and help. Parts of the chapter were published in English in Cowling, 2010.

2. AGCRJ, fundo Escravidão: Emancipação [Slavery Fund: Emancipation] (E:E), Book 6.1.41, 6 March 1886, p. 35; Schwarcz, 2003, p. 94. Maria Rosa's petition was signed as if she had written it herself, however, what is more likely is that a scribe or someone she knew who was literate had written it, like other letters from enslaved or freed people discussed in this chapter; this is because most these people, during the time, were illiterate. (The spelling has been updated to current standards)

3. Boletim da Câmara Municipal (Boletim) [Newsletter of the Municipal Council], 29 July 1885, p. 29; 10 September 1885, p. 115-7; Gazeta de Notícias, 2 December 1885, p. 1; Boletim, 18 March 1886, p. 122; AGCRJ, E: E, Book 6.1.41, p. 44; Boletim, 2 December 1887, p. 69; Conrad, 1972, p. 285; Castilho and Cowling, 2010.

4. I thank professor Hebe Mattos, who used the term "free womb logic" in discussion of my research at Universidade Federal Fluminense (UFF) in 2004. Since then, this has become a useful expression to reflect upon the relations between the black woman, the womb, and slavery. See also: Castilho and Cowling, 2010; Cowling, 2010, p. 287-8; Dauwe, 2004, p. 76-7, 82, 100-1, 108.

5. Chalhoub, 1990, p. 123-30, and 2003, Chapter 4; Cowling, 2007; Faria, 2001, p. 289-329; Grinberg, 1994; Pena, 2001; Soares, 2001/2002.

6. Kittleson, 2005.

7. João Pereira Lopes' speech at the municipal freedom ceremony on July 29 (birthday of Princess Isabel), Boletim, 5 August 1886, p. 6. (The spelling has been updated to current standards). Daibert Júnior, 2004.

8. "A Nossa Missão," O abolicionista: órgão da Sociedade Brasileira contra a escravidão, 1 (1º November 1880), p. 1; Abreu, 1996.

9. Boletim, 2 June 1885, p.102-3; "Relação dos escravos, que neste Juízo de Órfãos da Segunda Vara apresentaram e têm quantia para pecúlio...." ["List of slaves that appeared before the Orphan's Judge of the Second Court and have the amount for payment...."], AGCRJ, E: E, Book 6.2.1, 21 August 1880, p. 9; Conrad, 1972, p. 302; Castilho and Cowling, 2010, p. 103, 108; Josefa to the president and councilmen of Câmara Municipal, AGCRJ, E: E, Book 6.2.9, no date, approx. November of 1887, p. 161-2; Boletim, 2 December 1887.

10. Manoel Alves d'Oliveira and Benedita Caetana to the president and the councilmen of Câmara Municipal, AGCRJ, E: E, Book 6.2.6, 20 June 1885, p. 20, 28; Francisco Pinto da Silva, on behalf of Rita, to the president and councilmen of Câmara Municipal, AGCRJ, E: E, Book 6.1.61, 12 October 1885, p. 45.

11. Report of councilman Fernandes Couto, Boletim, 13 March 1884, p.123-4. On education, see Schueler, 2007, p. 212-9, 243. For perspectives of the elite on domesticity of black children, see Cunha, 2007.

12. Dr. Luiz de Moura, H.A. de Carvalho and Dr. Pinto Guedes. Education committee report on municipal schools. Boletim, 18 December 1884, p. 153-4; Chalhoub, 2006; Graham, 1991; Schwarcz, 1993.

13. D. Rufina de Souza Villar to the president and councilmen of Câmara Municipal, AGCRJ, E: E, Book 6.1.17, 30 August 1887, p. 90; D. Maria Carmina Caldas Reys to the president and councilmen of Câmara Municipal, AGCRJ, E: E, Book 6.1.17, 31 August 1887, p. 81.

14. Boletim, 5 April 1888, p. 9-10.

15. Boletim, 3 December 1885, p. 132; *Gazeta de Notícias*, 2 December 1885, p. 1.

16. João Coelho Bastos to the secretary of Câmara Municipal, AGCRJ, E: E, Book 6.1.61, 17 March 1886, p. 59; "Serafim, escravo," *Gazeta da Tarde*, 20 October 1885, p. 1; *Revista Illustrada*, 30 November 1885, p. 4-5; Chalhoub, in print.

17. "Casas de maternidade," *Gazeta da Tarde*, 4 September 1885, p. 1; Frank, 2007, p. 317.

18. "Polícia negreira," *Gazeta da Tarde*, 23 October 1885, p. 1. See three letters from João Coelho Bastos to the president of Câmara Municipal, dated 31 October, 17 November, and 12 December 1885, AGCRJ, E: E, Book 6.1.61, 27, p. 27, 30-1; *Gazeta da Tarde*, 24 May 1886, p. 2; Boletim, 18 March 1886, p. 122; Albuquerque, 2009, p. 113-23.

19. *Gazeta da Tarde*, 22 October 1886, p. 1; Caulfield, 2000, p. 130-3; Abreu, 1989, p. 160-63; Farias, 2010; Farias, Soares and Gomes, 2005, mainly Chapter 5.

Bibliography

Abreu, Martha Esteves. *Meninas perdidas: os populares e o cotidiano do amor no Rio de Janeiro da belle époque*. [Lost Girls: Popular and Quotidian Love in Rio de Janeiro of the Belle Epoque]. Rio de Janeiro: Paz e Terra, 1989, p. 160-3.

____. "Slave mothers and freed children: emancipation and female space in debates on the Free Womb Law, Rio de Janeiro, 1871." *Journal of Latin American Studies*, v. 28, n. 3, p. 567-80, 1996.

Albuquerque, Wlamyra. *O jogo de dissimulação: abolição e cidadania negra no Brasil*. [The Game of Dissimulation: Abolition and Black Citizenship in Brazil]. São Paulo: Companhia das Letras, 2009.

Castilho, Celso; Cowling, Camillia. "Funding freedom, popularizing politics: abolitionism and local emancipation funds in 1880s Brazil." *Luso-Brazilian Review*, Madison, University of Wisconsin, v. 47, n. 1, p. 89-120, 2010.

Caulfield, Sueann. *In Defense of Honor: Sexual morality, modernity and nation in early twentieth-century Brazil*. Durham: Duke University Press, 2000.

Chalhoub, Sidney. *Visões da liberdade: uma história das últimas décadas da escravidão na Corte*. [Visions of Liberty: A History of the Last Decades of Slavery at Court]. São Paulo: Companhia das Letras, 1990.

____. *Machado de Assis, historiador*. [Machado de Assis, Historian]. São Paulo: Companhia das Letras, 2003.

____. "The politics of silence: race and citizenship in nineteenth-century Brazil." *Slavery & Abolition*, n. 27, p. 81-4, 2006.

____. "Precariedade estrutural: o problema da liberdade no Brasil escravista (século XIX)." [Structural Precarity: The Problem of Freedom in Brazil's Slavocracy]. *História Social: Revista dos Pós-graduandos em História da Unicamp*, n. 19, p. 33-62, 2010.

Conrad, Robert. *The Destruction of Brazilian Slavery 1850-1888*. Berkeley: University of California Press, 1972.

Cowling, Camillia. "Matrices of freedom: women of colour, gender and the ending of slavery in Havana and Rio de Janeiro. 2007." Tese (Doutorado) – Universidade de Nottingham, UK.

____. "Debating womanhood, defining freedom: the abolition of slavery in 1880s Rio de Janeiro." *Gender & History*, n. 22, p. 284-301, ago. 2010.

Cunha, Olívia Maria Gomes da. "Criadas para servir: domesticidade, intimidade e retribuição." [Raised to Serve: Domesticity, Intimacy, and Retribution]. In Cunha, Olívia Maria Gomes da; Gomes, Flávio dos Santos. (Orgs.). *Quase-cidadão: histórias e antropologias da pós-emancipação no Brasil*. [Almost-Citizen: Histories and Anthropologies of Post-Emancipation Brazil]. Rio de Janeiro: Editora da FGV, 2007, p. 377-417.

Daibert Júnior, Robert. *Isabel: A redentora dos escravos. A Princesa entre olhares negros e brancos (1846-1980)*. [Isabel: The Redeemer of Slaves. The Princess Between Black and White Viewpoints (1846-1980)]. Bauru: Editora da Universidade do Sagrado Coração, 2004.

Dauwe, Fabiano. A libertação gradual e a saída viável: os múltiplos sentidos da liberdade pelo fundo de emancipação de escravos. [Gradual Liberation and the Viable Exit: Multiple Meanings of Freedom from the Depths of the Freedom of Slaves]. 2004. Thesis (Masters in History) – Universidade Federal Fluminense (UFF), Niterói, Rio de Janeiro.

Faria, Sheila. "Sinhás pretas: acumulação de pecúlio e transmissão de bens de mulheres forras no sudeste escravista (sécs. XVIII e XIX)." [Black Mistresses: Accumulation of Property and the Transmission of Women's Wealth in the Southeastern Slavocracy (19th and 19th Centuries)]. In Silva, Francisco Teixeira da Silva; Mattos, Hebe Maria; Cardoso, Ciro Flamarion. (Orgs.). *Escritos sobre história e educação: homenagem a Maria Yedda Leite Linhares*. [Writings on History and Education: Homage to Maria Yedda Leite Linhares]. Rio de Janeiro: Faperj/ Mauad, 2001, p. 289-329.

Farias, Juliana Barreto. "Greve nas marinhas: protestos, tradições e identidades entre pequenos lavradores, quitandeiras e pombeiros no Rio de Janeiro, século XIX." [Strike in the Navy: Protests, Traditions, and Identities Between Landowners, Female Street Vendors, and Traders in Rio de Janeiro in the 19th Century]. *Revista Art Cultura*, 2010.

Farias, Juliana Barreto; Soares, Carlos Eugênio Líbano; Gomes, Flávio dos Santos. *No labirinto das nações: africanos e identidades no Rio de Janeiro, século XIX*. [In the Labyrinth of Nations: Africans and Identities in Rio de Janeiro, 19th Century]. Rio de Janeiro: Arquivo Nacional, 2005.

Frank, Zephyr. "Layers, flows and intersections: Jeronymo José de Mello and artisan life in Rio de Janeiro, 1840s- 1880s." *Journal of Social History*, v. 41, n. 2, p. 317, 2007.

Graham, Sandra Lauderdale. "A abolição na cidade: amas-secas, contaminação e controle." [Abolition in the City: Nannies, Contamination, and Control]. In Andrade, Manuel Correia de; Fernandes, Eliane Moury. (Orgs.). *Atualidade e abolição*. [Actuality and Abolition]. Recife: Massangana, 1991, p. 75-90.

Grinberg, Keila. *Liberata: A lei da ambiguidade: as ações de liberdade da Corte de Apelação do Rio de Janeiro no século* XIX. [Liberated: The Law of Ambiguity: Freedom Lawsuits in the Appellate Courts in Rio de Janeiro in the 19th Century]. Rio de Janeiro: Relume Dumará, 1994.

Kittleson, Roger. "Women and notions of Womanhood in brazilian abolitionism." In Scully, Pamela; Paton, Diana. (Orgs.). *Gender and slave emancipation in the Atlantic World*. Durham: Duke University Press, 2005, p. 99-120.

Pena, Eduardo Spiller. *Pajens da Casa Imperial: jurisconsultos, escravidão e a lei de 1871*. [Attendants in the Imperial House: Legal Advisors, Slavery and the Law of 1871]. Campinas: Unicamp, 2001.

Schueler, Alessandra Frota Martínez. Culturas escolares e experiências docentes na cidade do Rio de Janeiro (1854-1889). [Scholarly Cultures and Professional Experiences in the City of Rio de Janeiro (1854-1889)]. 2007. Diss. (Doctorate) – Universidade Federal Fluminense (UFF). Niterói, Rio de Janeiro.

Schwarcz, Lilia Moritz. *O espetáculo das raças: cientistas, instituições e a questão racial no Brasil*. [The Spectacle of Races: Scientists, Institutions,and the Racial Question in Brazil]. São Paulo: Companhia das Letras, 1993.

_____. *As barbas do Imperador: D. Pedro* II, *um monarca nos trópicos*. [The Emperor's Beard: Dom Pedro II, a Monarch in the Tropics]. São Paulo: Companhia das Letras, 2003.

Soares, Carlos Eugênio Líbano. "Comércio, nação e gênero: as negras minas quitandeiras no Rio de Janeiro, 1835-1900." [Commerce, Nation, and Gender: Black Women Street Vendors in Rio de Janeiro, 1835-1900]. Escritos sobre história e educação, p. 402-13. *Revista de Mestrado em História*, Vassouras, v. 4, n. 1, p. 55-78, 2001/2002.

15

TEODORA DIAS DA CUNHA: CONSTRUCTING A PLACE FOR HERSELF IN THE WORLD OF WRITING AND SLAVERY

Maria Cristina Cortez Wissenbach

> *Where they passed, the earth was devastated...But the words had fallen from the boots of the Barbarians, the beards, the helmets, the horseshoes, like pebbles, the luminous words, that remained here shining brightly... We came out losing... We came out winning... They took gold and they left us gold... They took everything and they left us everything...They left us words.*
>
> Pablo Neruda, Confesso que vivi, p. 51-2

When I started long ago with my research of criminal records that involved slaves and freed slaves from the city of São Paulo in the second half of the 19th century, I came across some manuscripts that accompanied the investigation of a robbery. Among them, I found a set of letters written at the behest of the African Teodora Dias da Cunha: domestic slave and resident of the city at the end of the 1860s. The location of them, by the simple fact that they were not sent to whom they rightly belonged, confirmed an obligation to make them public which, in that moment, I set to fulfill within the limits of my possibilities as a social historian (Wissenbach, 2009). In this essay, I would like to revisit them, and beyond the explicit central content, add to their interpretation other analytical perspectives that pertain to studies on the history of writing practices among subaltern social groups, generally regarded as illiterate, as well as its appropriation in the context of the history of the Atlantic world of the 19th century.

First, I present the principal characters of this plot according to the evidence brought by the criminal trial of 1867-1872 and by the correspondence to which all of them were directly or indirectly linked.[1] I begin with Teodora, or better yet, Teodora Dias da Cunha, as she makes a point to call herself in much of the trial. I revisit her identification made right in the beginning of the interrogation she underwent in January of 1867, in which she declines her origin, the name of her father, and the fact of being married:

> She responds to being called Teodora, ignoring her age, that seems to be 50 to 60 years, married to Luis, who she believes was be sold in Campinas, daughter of the carpenter Balanger, ignoring her maternal name, both from the Congolese coast, native of the coast, slave of the offended party, a cook, doesn't know how to read or write (PC 1492, p. 45).

African by birth, possibly coming from one of the various Atlantic ports from Central-Western Africa and from one of the territories subject to the Congo kingdom, the circumstances and the trajectories of the enslavement of Teodora are known only in part. When she was brought to Brazil, she was first taken to the rural zone of São Paulo, most likely near Limeira, where she lived for an unspecified time as the slave of João Rodrigo da Cunha, from who she took the surname, being his family at the time. Around 1862, she was put up for sale in Campinas and sold in São Paulo by a merchant that she called Marciano Quina. Already in the city, separated from her husband and son, serving as the domestic slave of the clergyman José da Terra Pinheiro, resident of the street Liberdade, her domestic duties took her to the streets daily, to fetch water from the fountains of the city, or to buy goods from the grocery stores. On one of these trips, she met the slave, Claro Antônio dos Santos, the name with which he signed the documents he authored. A stonemason, Creole native of the countryside of Paraná, a slave for hire belonging to the clergyman Fidélis Álvares Sigmaringa de Morais, and resident of the coast of São Gonçalo, he was sought by Teodora precisely for the fact that he knew how to read and write. At the time of the trial in which he was indicted as defendant, he was on the run, being arrested only in 1872, four years after the conclusion of the first trial. Initially, we have indirect information about him given by Teodora:

> She responded that one time coming from a grocery store on São Gonçalo street, in a house in the back of Remédios, which was being floored by Claro, she saw that he was writing; and for this reason, giving him six *vinténs* [former coins], the respondent asked that he write a letter to her husband and son, and that she would request others as well (PC 1492, p. 47).

In another interrogation, when asked about the place where she met the slave, she responded:

> Seeing him repairing the floorboards in the courtyard of his house in Remédios with a paper in hand at the moment that the defendant passed by on the street to do her shopping. When asked if she was accustomed to going to the house of Canon Fidélis, she responded that she went occasionally. To do what? She responded, to be taught how to read and write with paper. How many letters did you have Claro write? She responded, five, having given six *vinténs* for the postage; the slave Claro not having [sent] the letters according to what his comrades told her (PC 1492, p. 205).

The letters were attached to the records of the district of São Paulo and are currently found deposited in the Public Archive of the State of São Paulo (Arquivo Público do Estado de São Paulo). In the police investigation, they served as evidence that Teodora participated in the robbery committed by Claro and his partner Pedro in the house of her master, the robbery in which a locked basket that contained money (more than 800 thousand *reis*), clothes, and objects was taken. During the investigation, as pleadings proceeded, the letters were found scattered in various locations: in the house of Maria Doce and her daughter, concubine of the defendant Claro, on the street of Liberdade, "to the right as you go to Pelourinho," where he probably hid or had a rented room, amongst the belongings of Teodora, and finally, in the hands of his master, the clergyman, Terra.

Of the seven letters contained within the trial, five of them were written by Claro, and two others were written by a scribe, about whom there is no information in the proceedings. They were found addressed to multiple recipients, the majority of which never received them since they were confiscated by the authorities. Folded in the shape of the envelope, containing the respective addresses, four were to be sent to Teodora's husband, Luís da Cunha, whose whereabouts she didn't know, or only guessed; one to her master, the clergyman José da Terra Pinheiro, incidentally, the only one who received and read it; one to the son of Inocêncio, whose fate the slave also ignored, and the seventh would be sent to the brother of the ex-owner of her husband, in the attempt to discover the whereabouts of the latter.

During the proceedings, before the crime was to be tried by the Tribunal Jury of São Paulo, the judge dismissed Teodora's indictment and ordered her to be released and returned to her master. Thus, we don't know the final outcome of her story. However, through the words dictated by the slave to the two scribes, it is possible to recover parts of the trajectory of her enslavements, the contingencies that were imposed, the efforts and the greater goals of this African woman, as well as her dreams.

The general meaning of the content of the letters is expressly clear and determined; there is no doubt as to her greater meaning. Broadly and through various strategies and resources available, Teodora sought to recompose her family, which had been dismantled by their sale,[2] to obtain her freedom and that of her husband, and return to Africa.

The first letter addressed to Luís is not dated, but based on the facts that it contains, it had to have been one of the first ones. In it, there is essential information about Teodora's struggles: before a separation that didn't seem too distant in time, she told her husband the whereabouts that she had followed after her sale, inquired about his fate and evoked, with all of the arguments possible, the promise that they made together whose fulfillment depended expressly on him. Here I present the complete letter in its striking terms:

My husband, Mr. Luis

> Much shall I esteem that this will find you in good health for my wish is that you send me word, to tell me where you are living. The one

who took me away was a young rich boy from the plains; the man calls himself Marciano Quina/ I made a promise in Congo, you don't remember the promise you and I made to each other/ you don't remember that you/ father sold you to be reminded of the promise/ he let me know at night but I was sleeping/ The Queen has made a habit of making promises and not keeping them and now she is imprisoned by evil and for this she asks the saints to help/ and for this you see that the Queen is the greatest in the world and she is imprisoned by evil/ and she cannot save herself because Saint Benedict lost her in the sea/ she can't be saved/ for this I do not risk the saints/ I hope to one day fulfill my promise, even if I should be with white hair/ my lord you said that the letter of release from slavery was false/ the union of this couple/ we also need to bring the couple together/ make money/ to pay for our freedom papers/ I want us to be together as a couple not to make money afterward/ but to pay the ones who are lords over us/ I'll end up just like the Queen (PC 1492, p. 37).

The second letter was directed also to her husband, being, as it seems, one of the first. By the peculiar writing and style, it was evidently written by Claro, unlike the first, whose author is unknown:
My husband Luis, São Paulo

> I esteem that Vance is in good health/ I am here in the city/ I am writing to you to remind Vance of the promise we made to each other/ I need to find you/ I have sent several mementos to you/ Gather some money there/ If you can come here to speak with me, please do/ if not, can you please send me a response and keep saving money there/ If I can arrange it myself here, I will send you the money.

> From your wife, Theodora, who was sold like cattle to the clergymen, Terra (PC 1492 p. 36).

After that, it is possible to highlight still a third one, which, presented in its entirety, complements the information that can be obtained through them. Maybe it is one of the most expressive: addressed to the master with whom Teodora resided in São Paulo, denotes that, in spite of the physical proximity, writing was the method chosen by the slave to communicate her wishes and issues, imagining it possible to include in it the whole load of feelings. In this letter, in a narrative equally shocking in which dreams and reality merge and mix, the arguments of a pervasive devotion that runs rampant in the direction

of her priest master, are evidenced by the words which the slave used as she sought to find in him an ally for carrying out her plans:
My Master:

> I had a warning in the night/ it came and spoke to me to fulfill the promise that I vowed to return to my land/ this conga [sic] that speaks to me says that if I die here I will not fulfill the promise that not even I could see. Vance didn't fulfill this promise because my father was guilty of selling me/ because God does not want us to be apart, me from my black Angolan/ My lord, Vance promised to collect one hundred/ for this I want retaliation / because you allowed me time off on Sundays to go collect alms to give to you, master / I already have 4 thousand *reis* and Vance already has nine thousand in his hand/ Your slave, Tiodora (PC 1492, p. 193).

Dominating the overall tone of the whole collection of letters produced by Teodora, Claro, and the anonymous scribe, the emancipation is placed as Teodora's most pressing goal; she presented this achievement as a religious obligation that transcended purely Catholic beliefs. The quest for emancipation signified the fulfillment of a promise that she had made in the Congo, of which the responsibility was shared with her husband and with her master, swearing to fulfill it "even if she is with white hair." The nest egg that she was saving, the organization of her daily life, as well as her attention to the movement and interactions that were developing were efforts that revolved around this wish of "uniting the couple." The return to Africa, on the other hand, was the realization of freedom in clear form, or in terms used by the African, the horizon of possibilities in reversing the impact of the diaspora—"or to end up just like the queen," the queen that Saint Benedict lost at sea. In this interpretative direction, and making use of the of the elements of the central African cosmology, once the sea, one of the Bantu divinities, not only stood between the two sides of the Atlantic, but also separated the world of the living and the world of the dead, the desire to return changed the idea of death to a return to their world. Without a doubt, it is these yearnings that Teodora shared with other slave partners, as well as the central African people who lived as she did, the forced crossing across the Americas and the enslavement and the longing to return to the land of their belonging, as emphasized by Slenes (1991-1992, p. 53-5).

On a separate note, considering the analyzed documents as expression of the letter-writing practice that existed among slaves, it is possible to establish some of the characteristics, notably those that relate to a particular writing. In the first place, transcribing the letter *ipsis litteris* highlights the fact that in its making, there is an obvious formalism and respect to a given protocol that, without a shadow of a doubt, the scribe Claro insisted on following (The below translation is an approximation because of the variations in spelling, grammar, and syntax):

> *Il^{mo} Inos Senço*
>
> *em São Paulo 20 de novembor de 1866*
>
> *Meo filho eu hetima muito e a sua saude como para mim dezeio noto bem pa voes/ me mandra scrita como vai de saude/ no mais eu bosto a minha benção/ Deos te abeso para tempo/ te dezeio como para mim dese noto bem/ para*
>
> *Sou a tua maite a dora no mais a Deos*
>
> *[Sobrescrito]*
>
> *Il^{mo} Nosenso*
>
> *Numa falzenda de pasto na*
>
> *Bipopara*
>
> *Jundiahi* (PC 1492, p. 194).
>
> Most Illustrious Inos Senço [sic]
>
> In São Paulo, 20th of November of the year 1866
>
> My son, I greatly esteem you, and for your health I desire only the best report/ please send word of your good health/ in any case I send my blessings/ May God be with you forever/ I desire for you as for myself only good reports/ for
>
> I am your beloved forever in God,
>
> [Address to]:
>
> My Lord Nosenco [sic]
>
> On a cattle farm in
>
> Bipopara

Jundiahi (PC 1492, p. 194).

In the letters, it is evident that the writing is neither perfect nor does it follow educated or scholarly standards, which were distant not only for the scribe slave Claro, but also for most the population of the city and Brazilian society of the age. Stressing that the inaccuracies and the "flaws" of the discourse didn't take away from the overall thoughts in the writing of Claro and Teodora or what they wanted to express, we note that the syllables and letters were exchanged, words were swallowed and some become almost incomprehensible to the current reader. But, above all—and what seems significant—the letters reveal an oral communication that flows freely and pervades the rhythm of the written words, linking thoughts with swiftness. Spoken, they probably make resounding oral communication (or oration, as the scholars of oral tradition wish) of the society then, with its rhythms and rhymes, sequences and expressed links in a speed almost as intense as the desires of Teodora and her anxiousness to provide information in as little of a space as possible (once again, this translation is an approximation):

> ...*eu vos iscrevo pa Vnce se lembrar daquela promeça que nois fizemos eu heidi prócura por vose mandou muita lembrança pa vose e ajunta hum dinheiro la sepuder vim falar commigo venha senão puder me manda a reposta e dinheiro va juntando la mesmo se czo eu maranjar por aqui mando propia la. Dessa Vosça Mulher theodoria escrava do connio terra que fui vindida na vacaria...* (PC 1492, p. 36)

> ...I write to you to remind you of that promise that we made to each other/ I heidi [sic] to find you/ I sent so many mementos to you so you could save money, if you could/ come speak with me, come/ if you cannot, please send me an answer and save some money there/ if I can manage it here I'll send it to you there. From your wife, Theodoria [sic], slave of the clergyman Terra, who was sold at the cattleyard.... (PC 1492, p. 36)

Or, in this other passage, in which the rhythm and the linking are imposed in the repetitions, in the accents, in the use of the same words for different thoughts (approximate translation):

> ...*para mi fazer o favor de vi por o nata falla com migo sem falta mi falta 198 reis para minha liberdade no mais mi mande a repota desta para o*

> *senhor demicianno na cidade de solcrava* sem falta no mais *eu itou pagando como huma icrava deste pader mavado no mais* a Deus a Deus *a te hum dia que* Deus *me ajunde com sua garça divina mizeicódia no mais sou a sua mulhe tiodora dias da cunha* (PC 1492, p. 90, grifos meus).

> ...for me to do the favor of seeing you put the cream/ speak to me *without fail/ I'm only short 198 reis* for my freedom/ apart from this, send me an answer so that my master can give me cianno [sic] in the city of solcrava [sic] *without failing, and what's more*, I'm paying like a slave this wicked priest/ no longer *to God to God* to you/ one day *God* will help me/ with his divine merciful grace/ above all, I am your wife, tiodora dias da cunha [sic] (PC 1492, p. 90, author's emphasis).

Evaluating written Portuguese in Luanda, Rita Chaves (2005, p.31) found that the changes in syntax and, beyond this, ellipses, repetitions, and any other "inaccuracies" reshaped "the Portuguese language" and evoke an orality of which the written Angolan is a contributor. As such, notably linked to this aspect, the letters transmit the qualities of Teodora as an African storyteller for whom reality did not outweigh dreams, and these, in turn, appeared in her foreboding thought. (Approximate translation below).

> *Eu tive hum avizo de noute vinha eme falava dizendo que cumpriçe a promeça que promiti de vortar para minha terra esta conga que fala comigo dis que ceu moredo a qui não compraei pormeça que nem eu enxú....* (PC 1492, p. 193).

> I had a warning last night/ M came to me saying he would fulfill the promise he made to me to return to my homeland/ this conga [sic] that spoke with me said if I die here I won't fulfill the promise that even I can't *enxú* [sic].... (PC 1492, p. 193).

As Hampâté Bâ (2003, p. 15) recalls in his childhood memories, for Africans, the dreams in their absolute materiality are parts of experienced reality and bring news "like a postman who had come to deliver a letter to the addressee." Then, we are faced with an illiterate African that constructed a place for herself in the world of writing—organizing ideas, clarifying thoughts, dictating desires and intentions, feelings, and sensations—and from their use, she elaborated various strategies to achieve her plans. All of this gains even more relevance when considering that exchanging letters or corresponding involves exposing oneself, sharing experiences of daily life:

> ...the act of writing personal/intimate letters consists of confronting established codes, and from them, constructing/inventing a place for yourself, through words. Exchanging letters, corresponding, are forms of exposing yourself, sharing experiences of daily and/or professional life and, especially 'putting your ideas in order, clarifying and recalling thoughts, sensations, and feelings' (Cunha, 2002).

Thus, in transposing this interpretation to the unique experiences of the slaves, it is possible to say that, even being *da rossa* (an expression meaning "from the backwoods or deep forest") and not knowing the "customs of the cities" (PC 1492, p. 197), Teodora dominated significant parts of the codes of the everyday, educated universe, understanding the relevance of writing and making use of it as something more. By purchasing letters, dictating her words, the African put herself into a set of values generally seen as an attribute of the world of the elite. Much like a nineteenth-century version of the plot in the film *Central do Brasil*, she was a part of a society in which, according to the words of Daniel Fabre (1985, p. 33), "some read, others listen, or simply see, but all of them approach writing well or poorly, all realize and experience its presence." We will return to this.

In the annals of history of Brazilian slavery and of the populations of Africans and Afro-descendants in Brazil, direct testimonies left by these social groups were either rare or extremely rare. But, even though hard to find, when found they play a significant role in historiographical revisions, because they introduce evidence to reveal the perceptions that both slaves and freed slaves had of their experiences, the way they perceived relations with masters, and the meaning of their own condition. We can take as an example, *Tratado de paz dos escravos relados*, from the Santana mill in Ilhéus, found by Stuart Schwartz (1977, p. 79-81) and dated from the end of the 18th century. Its expressiveness was recognized mainly by presenting the notions that the captives had on the nature of the work they did as well as its pacing and rhythm, on the relationships they maintained with each other, and the disagreements among the inhabitants of the plantation and among the various ethnic groups. They also stated the list of the demands they made to return to work: among other things, the recognition of holidays, the right to garden and gain their own profits, and to sell their products at the Sunday market. And especially, the right to free time that restored the humanity they demanded: "We will be able to play, rest, and sing at any time we want, with nothing stopping us and no permission necessary."

Because of their rarity, Teodora's letters can also be considered remarkable documents. Their content, however, refers to the everyday dilemmas experienced by a very wide range of the enslaved and introduces perceptions of slavery and of their paths possibly shared by other comrades. Part of the historical quality of the documents discussed here arises from the very uniqueness of the judiciary source which, when evaluated with a focus on the history of minority groups, has proven to be exemplary. Beginning with the simple fact that, in the search for the facts of the crime, the police and judicial authorities incorporated her speech, her sayings, and her characteristic expressions, as well as her visions. "If João da Várzea had come with 'garoas' [drizzle, mist], that would be one less slave that Nhô Gole had!"[3]

Amid other documentary evidence, the criminal trial that involved Claro and Teodora offered significant elements to understanding the context of slavery in São Paulo, in the second half of the 19th century. It indicated the forms of organization of slave work, the interactions and the encounters in the streets of the 19th century city, as well as the social exchanges between domestic slaves and slaves for hire. It revealed the dramas experienced by the enslaved, and the wounds of their enslavement—families destroyed, unfamiliar places, unsent letters, the uncertain nature of slave lives and, with respect to city life, the suspicion caused when slaves exhibited behavior and habits seen as unusual (for example, knowing how to read and write and corresponding with distant relatives). From this case, it was also possible to reach a middle ground existing between individual experiences and the broader context of slave society: on one hand, retracing the circumstances of urban slavery, and on the other, the hopes of a slave who longed for the mending of her family, obtaining freedom, and returning to Africa.

The analyses of the writing practices of common people and the formation of their own spaces, made by them, in the world of literacy, as well as of the issue of the dynamics of literacy, also allows sensing another complexity inherent in the interpretation of the letters of Teodora and Claro, especially so because the rarity of the documents we are studying does not necessarily affirm the rarity of literate slaves. Gradually, historiography unveils a practice that was spreading,[4] such as the processes of these groups becoming literate in the imperial world and the beginnings of the Republic.[5] Moreover, one should consider the presence of written words composing charms, rites, and spells, present in the violent day-to-day of slaves and freed slaves (Wissenbach, 2002).

In the framework of 19th century São Paulo, the letters of Teodora and Claro must be understood in an urban society in which they were symbols expressive of the world of the literate: with the Academy of Law, founded in the first half of the century and dominating the landscape of the central area, with its students, who came from various parts of Brazil, circulated through the streets, and rented the houses of the inhabitants and whose lives were accompanied by the captives growing up in the same household. In the case of the two slaves, the approximation to the universe of the literate took place surely because they belonged to clerical masters, these usually taking greater care with the instruction of their captives (Piratininga Jr., 1991). Furthermore, this was essentially a society in transformation because of the substantial changes in slave relations that were introduced by the end of the Atlantic slave trade (1850) and by the approval of successive emancipation laws. Ultimately, historical trials existed which put the relations between masters and slaves in different terms and prepared for the overthrow of the slave system.

Symbolically, it is not possible to ignore that the same urban environment produced a figure as expressive and prominent in the abolitionist movement as Luís Gonzaga Pinto da Gama. Without a doubt, the two slaves were very close, socially and physically, to the latter; they met or crossed the same streets of São Paulo at the end of the 1860s. It was he, furthermore, one of the experts, who carried out the examination of *corpus delicti* in the house of the clergyman

Terra, certainly encountering Teodora on this occasion. According to history, the trajectory of Luís Gama is distinguished: sold as a slave in Bahia and brought to São Paulo, it was here that he was progressively raised by a student of the School of Law who instructed him, and after being freed, became a clerk in the delegacy of São Paulo and protégé of the managing director (Francisco Maria de Souza Furtado de Mendonça), also professor of the Law School. In exemplary fashion, it is possible to observe through him the historical conditions of the 19th century, which allowed an ex-slave to become a paralegal, a writer, and an advocate of the abolitionist struggles (Souza, 2001; Azevedo, 2012).

Lastly, and within the frameworks of the organization of slave labor in the cities, the skills of Claro Antônio dos Santos, as we will see, the dexterity with writing and the prominence in the world of slaves and freed slaves of the city cannot be dissociated from the condition of slave for hire.

Female, African, and captive, at the center of Teodora's relations are three figures by which it is possible to scale her historical personality: her husband, her master, and the scribe responsible for writing most of her letters. Before each one of them, especially the first two, she is positioned differently, using distinct arguments in order to make them aware of, and gain their assistance in, the achievement of her goals. Perhaps we should consider that the projects that she had in mind were loftier than her chances of achieving them. In the letters this can be seen in the repetition of the arguments, and the recurrence of the theme; similarly, before those in charge of interrogating her—also possibly intimidating male figures from the precinct of São Paulo—the African Teodora made it clear what the gap was that existed between the price of her emancipation and that which she had managed to save, sometimes with her work, and sometimes begging at Sunday masses.[6] The dialogue between her and the police authority during the investigation indicated how much the pursuit of liberty and the building of wealth were viewed with suspicion by society, since they were only legitimized after 1871.

> – Asked if she didn't tell her master that she wished to save money for her freedom?—She responded yes. —How much money had you gathered?—She replied with 37 thousand *reis*.—Where is it?—In her box—Where did this money come from?—She replied that it came from her work of carrying water to sell for three *vinténs* when there were many soldiers.—If she requested letters to be written to her husband and son and by whom?—She replied that she asked Claro to write them (PC 1492, p. 198-9).

To compensate for all of this, she resorted to various arguments and strategies that mixed very concrete mediums with dreams that came from the force of a figure from an ancestral entity—"This conga that speaks to me"—identified as a queen who São Benedito had lost in the sea.

The relationship with Luís da Cunha wasn't just an amorous one, because the slave continued demanding, in all written communication, that her husband gather and send money and return to Africa with her. In broad historical terms, Teodora's immediate needs denote the importance of family in the life of slaves, notably as a means of affirming struggles and substantiating a sense of belonging. As Joseph Miller (2011, p. 22) provocatively states, "nothing more heartbreaking to African slaves than the feeling of being alone."

The attitude of the slave towards her master is also clarified: even referring to him as this "wicked priest," in the letters, the idea prevails that he has obligations to her and part of his responsibility is for her to be freed: "… I already have four thousand *reis* and you already have nine thousand *reis* in your hand." Meanwhile, what is most moving in the manner which Teodora devises the master's obligations are the ambiguous arguments of guilt that influence a minister of God: "you are guilty of me being sold because God doesn't want the conga [sic] woman separated from her black Angolan man." Alongside the express ethnic similarities that appear here between a woman from the Congo and a black man from Angola, once again, the religious appeal drives the argument; and in the search for allies, it expresses the slaveholding relationship in other terms. The use of the word "father" assigned to her first master, who sold the couple (Teodora and Luís), is another element to be considered.

The ties with Claro were equally complex. Despite the suspicion of that falls on Teodora, since she would have opened the doors of her master's house to her slave partners, the notion prevails throughout the body of the criminal proceedings that the African woman was a naïve victim of a cunning and independent individual, the leader of a gang that regularly committed crimes of theft. And, it is possible that because of this, the indictment of Teodora as a defendant of the trial had been considered unjust by the court of law. Viewed from a historical perspective, however, the relationship references the frameworks of a sociability allowed to slaves in an urban context, and within this, the possible exchanges between differentiated workers and across a heterogeneous social hierarchy that distinguished urban slaves among themselves. Claro's dexterity and skills, as well as the privileges he had at his disposal, were noticed and considered by the slave who saw him as a potential ally, or better, one more she sought to enlist in her plans.

> The slave calls himself Claro, he is tall, rugged, of the Fula/Fulani people (Bronze-colored; belonging to a Nigerian-Congolese family), he has signs of smallpox, is around 39 years old, a good carpenter and was purchased on the 13th of April 1853 by Mr. Luis Alves de Sa. in a letter of order written by Francisco Álvares de Sa. of Xiririca, brother of Luís and owner of the slave (PC 1492, p. 43).

It was in these terms, the clergyman Fidélis Sigmaringa de Morais described the characteristics of the slave, one of the defendants in the trial, but at the time a fugitive. Years later, his profile would be completed during his arrest. In the interrogation, he confirmed being Creole, son of Antônio and Remígia, both slaves, being 42 years old, married, a carpenter by profession, native of Poço Grande in the province of Paraná, resident of Cadeia square, in the house of the master. Previously, his personality had already been traced, considering that he was in a large part of the testimonies of those involved in the trial: he was cunning and independent; he had property and lovers, despite being married; he maintained a significant degree of mobility, which facilitated his escape; even though he lived with a master, he had a rented room in the house of the mother of his mistress and, on the run, he had been seen sometimes in the region of São Bernardo, where a friend lived, sometimes in Santos along with his mistress, where they were said to be hidden, sometimes even in the region of Paraná, close to the place where he had served as a slave and where he was finally arrested. Besides the fact of being literate, handling paper, pencil, and pen, he made a point to display them in the streets, perhaps to assert himself socially and to distinguish himself from his associates. Acting "as if he were free," before he escaped he prepared an inventory of goods, with their respective values, leaving them in the care of his partner, during a time in which the possessions of slaves were still not recognized by the law or they were only recognized through common law.

In the same place where the authorities found some of Teodora's letters, a list of his belongings and a letter addressed to a woman charging her for a service rendered in the value of 100 thousand *réis* were also confiscated, the latter having the letterhead of the law school. His signature was, without a doubt, elaborate, and revealed the personality of the scribe. Transcribed below are his assets:

> São Paulo, 21st of February 1864
>
> Most Illustrious sir,
>
> One more black silk waistcoat 6$000
>
> One aforementioned silk sun hat 8$000
>
> One more cap 7$000
>
> One aforementioned white wool shawl 9$000
>
> One aforementioned pair of black silk pants 12$000
>
> One aforementioned pair of black cashmere pants 20$000
>
> One aforementioned pair of canvas pants 9$000
>
> Aforementioned wool blazer 6$000
>
> Aforementioned red wool shirt 5$000
>
> 4 thin muslin shirts 24$000
>
> Shirt of baize (coarse felt-like wool) 3$000 One more aforementioned shirt rack 1$000
>
> Another knife holster 3$000

Another hat 3$000

9$2000

To the municipal palace, by my order, I assign this power of attorney to Mr. Francisco Benedito de Assis

Claro Antonio dos Santos (PC 1492, p. 198-9).

In his work on the issue of literacy and its effects on the cognitive process in the literate, Jack Goody (1988) explains that the list form, or roster, is one of the first manifestations of storing information that accompanies the learning of letters and the characteristic phases of a system of pre-literate writing or of a limited literacy.[7] In Claro's case, however, in spite of claiming in court that he knew how to read and write very poorly, various versions of his writing were found as part of the trial proceedings; they were related to both the defense of his interests and attending to Teodora's plans. In addition to making his assertion of limited skill a relative one, the same criminal trial that collected Teodora's letters, turning them into a historical source, also brought attention to the manuscripts authored by Claro. Produced in different ways and for different reasons, their letters denote that the slave experiences in the cities were neither similar nor homogenous. At the very least, we can say that the hope for freedom, the methods of attaining freedom, and the aspirations of the slaves were not singular. It can be assumed that since he already lived "as if he were free," formal freedom was not as pressing for the slave, Claro, as it was for Teodora.

Considering the value of writing in terms of the slave society of Brazil, it is necessary to first remember that "the letter" held a significant symbolism that cannot be discounted. In a broader sense, it amounted principally to the letter of freedom that the slaves exhibited as a materialization of their greatest conquest and new condition. Possession of this document constituted one of the principal emblems that ultimately separated free men from slaves. On the other hand, considering the importance of the appropriation of writing as a symbol of *status* to be exhibited and as a display of dominion over a code of the whites, as indicated in the analysis of the historical figure, Claro, the social terms associated with it came from a system of cultural references marked by the slave experience as well as an African influence. Displaying the scope of these references, it is appropriate to note the fact that in the lexicon of the spoken tongues of Brazil, or in the Portuguese spoken in Angola, the term *mukanda*, which can be translated as "letter," had a wide range of meaning. In the *quilombo* community of Cafundó, in the language that its residents called African or *cupópia*, the word *mukanda* appears not only to have corresponded to "letter" as it also seemed to confer qualities of rural labor tools to the art of writing; for example, the term for "pen" (*caneta*) is *tenhora de mukanda*, which translated literally means "a writing hoe" (Fry and Vogt, 1996).

Specifically observing the intense presence of lexicons coming from African languages in Brazilian Portuguese, studies on the history of language in Brazil have revealed processes of *quimbundização* (Kimbundi-zation) and *umbundização* (Umbund-ization) (This is a reference to the main languages of Angola: Kimbundu and Umbundu and signifies making the Portuguese language more like these two languages). This is similar to what occurred in the spoken Portuguese of Angola. In her dictionary of African words incorporated into Bahian Portuguese, Yeda Pessoa de Castro (2001) quantifies a wealth of words brought by the Bantu languages that are generally classified as *brasilerismos* (Brazilian-isms) by the more traditional lexicographers. According to her dictionary of Bahian sayings (but also Brazilian), it is possible to verify that they borrow most commonly from words of the African languages related to affection, sexuality, or even the violence of life—or that is, perhaps, everything that had resonance in the experience of Africans brought by the slave trade and to their descendants. On the other hand, in one dialogue that cannot be left out, as indicated long ago by Pierre Verger, the polysemy of the term "letter" presented in the context of Brazilian slavery can be evaluated in contrast to the context of African societies in the pre-colonial era. Historically, the term *mukanda* meant many things: "letter" among "indigenous objects" listed by Capelo and Ivens (Tavares 2008, p.165), "passes" (such as letters of freedom), "notes," "decrees" and "work contracts" signed by the expedition of Henrique de Carvalho between 1884 and 1888 (Santos, 2010, p.184-5). In its broadest sense, according to Victor Turner (2005, p. 205), *mukanda* is the name given by the Ndembus, Chokwes, and other Central-Western Bantu peoples to the rites of circumcision that mark the transition from youth into adulthood: "the *mukanda* is to treat the novice for him to become strong and gain power."

Words and meanings that equalize experiences, reaching the point of being recorded in the experiences and letters of the African Congo woman, Teodora Dias da Cunha, addressed to her husband, a black man from Angola, Luís da Cunha.

Notes

1. Archive of the state of São Paulo. A Justiça versus Claro e Pedro, slaves of the clergyman Fidélis Alves Sigmaringa de Morais. Processo 1492, de 1867-1872, Box 80, order 3980, hereafter PC 1492, following the reference page.

2. The individual sale of married slaves was prohibited by Decree n. 1.695, of 1869, artigo 2º. *Coleção das leis do Império do Brasil*, Tipografia Nacional, 1869, p. 129-30. On the contingent nature of slave merchandise, see Miller, 2011, p. 17-64.

3. See Wissenbach, 2009, p. 125; Schwartz, 2001, p. 21-57, 119-21.

4. See Reis, 2003; Goody, 1986, p. 318-43.

5. See Silva, 2002; Fonseca, 2002; Lobo e Oliveira, 2007.

6. For more on the context of emancipation in the 19th century and its contingencies, see Florentino, 2002, p. 9-40.

7. See also Santos, 2006.

Bibliography

Azevedo, Elciene. *O direito dos escravos. Lutas jurídicas e abolicionismo na província de São Paulo*. [The Rights of Slaves. Juridical Struggles and Abolitionism in the Province of São Paulo]. Campinas: Editora Unicamp, 2010.

Bâ, Amadou Hampâté. *Amkoullel, o menino fula*. [Amkoullel, the Fulani Boy]. São Paulo: Palas Athena; Casa das Áfricas, 2003.

Castro, Yeda Pessoa de. *Falares africanos na Bahia. Um vocabulário afro-brasileiro*. [African Speech in Bahia. An Afro-Brazilian Vocabulary]. Rio de Janeiro: Topbooks, Academia Brasileira de Letras, 2001.

Chaves, Rita. "José Luandino Vieira: consciência nacional e desassossego." [José Luandino Vieira: National Consciousness and Disquietude]. In *Angola e Moçambique. Experiência colonial e territórios literários*. [Angola and Mozambique. Colonial Experience and Literary Territories]. Cotia: Ateliê Editorial, 2005.

Cunha, Maria Teresa Santos. "A escrita epistolar e a história da educação." [The Letter Writer and the History of Education]. Pôster, XXV Reunião da Anped, 2002. Available at: <http://www.anped.org.br/reunioes/25/posteres/mariateresasantoscunhap02.rtf>. Accessed 2 May 2011.

Fabre, Daniel. "Le Livre et sa magia." [The Book and its Magic]. In Chartier, Roger. *Practiques de la lecture*. Paris: Éditions Rivages, 1985.

Florentino, Manolo. "Alforrias e etnicidade no Rio de Janeiro oitocentista: notas de pesquisa." [Liberation and Ethnicity in 19th Century Rio de Janeiro: Research Notes]. *Topoi*, n. 12, p. 9-40, 2002.

Fonseca, Marcus Vinicius. "Educação e escravidão: um desafio para a análise historiográfica." [Education and Slavery: A Challenge for Historiographical Analysis]. *Revista Brasileira de História da Educação*, n. 4, p. 123-44, 2002.

Fry, Peter; Vogt, Carlos (e colaboração de Slenes, Robert). *A África no Brasil: Cafundó*. [África in Brazil: Far Away Place]. São Paulo/Campinas: Companhia das Letras Ed. da Unicamp, 1996.

Goody, Jack. "Writing, religion and revolt in Bahia." *Visible Language*, n. 20, p. 318-43, 1986.

_____. *Domesticação do pensamento selvagem*. Lisboa: Presença, 1988.

Lobo, Tânia; Oliveira, Klebson. "Escrita liberta: letramento de negros forros na Bahia do século XIX." [Freed Writing: The Writing of Free Blacks in 19th Century Bahia]. In castilho, Ataliba. *Descrição, história e aquisição do português brasileiro*. [Description, History, and Acquisition of Brazilian Portuguese]. Campinas: Pontes; Fapesp, 2007, p. 437-60.

Miller, Joseph C. "Restauração, reinvenção e recordação: recuperando identidades sob a escravização na África e face à escravidão no Brasil." [Restoration, Reinvention, and Recording: Recuperating Identities Under the Enslavement of África and Facing Slavery in Brazil]. *Revista de História*, n. 164, p. 17-64, 2011.

Neruda, Pablo. *Confesso que vivi—Memórias*. [I Confess that I Lived—Memories]. 4. ed. Rio de Janeiro: Difel, 1977.

Piratininga jr., Luiz Gonzaga. *Dietário dos escravos de São Bento*. [The diets of Slaves in São Bento]. São Paulo: Hucitec; Prefeitura de São Caetano do Sul, 1991.

Reis, João José. *Rebelião escrava no Brasil. A história do levante dos malês na Bahia em 1835*. [Slave Rebellion in Brazil. A History of the Muslim Revolt in Bahia in 1835]. São Paulo: Companhia das Letras, 2003.

Santos, Catarina Madeira. "Escrever o poder. Os autos de vassalagem e a vulgarização da escrita entre as elites africanas Ndembu." [Writing Power. Acts of Servitude and the Vulgarization of Writing Among Ndembu African Elites]. *Revista de História*, n. 155, p. 81-95, 2006.

; Tavares, Ana Paula. *Africae Monumenta. A apropriação da escrita pelos africanos*. [Monumental África. The Appropriation of Writing by Africans]. Lisboa: IICT, MCES, 2002.

Santos, Elaine Ribeiro dos. *Barganhando sobrevivências: os trabalhadores centro-africanos da expedição de Henrique de Carvalho à Lunda (1884-1888)*. [Bartering Survivals: Central-African Workers of the Henrique de Carvalho á Lunda Expedition (1884-1888)]. 2010. Thesis (Masters in History)—Faculdade de Filosofia, Letras e Ciências Humanas (FFLCH) da Universidade de São Paulo (USP), São Paulo.

Schwartz, Stuart. "Resistance and Accommodation in 18th century Brazil." *Hispanic American Historical Review*, v. 57, n. 1, p. 79-81, 1977.

. "A historiografia recente da escravidão brasileira." [Recent Historiography of Brazilian Slavery]. In *Escravos, roceiros e rebeldes*. [Slaves, Farmers, and Rebels]. Bauru: Edusc, 2001.

Silva, Adriana Maria Paulo da. "A escola de Pretextato dos Passos e Silva." [The School of Pretexto of Passos and Silva]. *Revista Brasileira de História da Educa- ção*, n. 4, p. 145-66, 2002.

Slenes, Robert W. "'Malungo, N´goma vem!' África coberta e descoberta no Brasil." ["Hey Comrade/Brother, N'Goma is coming!" África, Covered and Uncovered in Brazil]. *Revista USP*, n. 12, p. 53-5, 1991-92.

Souza, Maria Cecília C. C. de. "O preto no branco: a trajetória de escritor de Luiz Gama." [The Black Man in the White Man: the Trajectory of Writer Luiz Gama]. In Vidal, Diana Gonçalves. (Org.). *Brasil 500 anos*. [Brazil 500 Years]. São Paulo: Edusp, 2001, p. 97-116.

Tavares, Ana Paula. "A escrita em Angola: comunicação e ruído entre as diferentes sociedades em presença." [Writing in Angola: Communication and Tumult Among the Different Present Societies]. In Heintze, Beatrix; Jones, Adam. (Eds.). *Angola on move. Transports, routes, communications and history*. Frankfurt am Main: Verlag Otto Lembeck, 2008.

Turner, Victor. *Floresta de símbolos—Aspectos do ritual ndembu*. [Forests of Symbols—Aspects of Ndembu Ritual]. Trad. Paulo Gabriel Hilu da Rocha Pinto. Niterói: Editora da UFF, 2005.

Wissenbach, Maria Cristina Cortez. "Cartas, procurações, escapulários e patuás." [Letters, Powers of Attorney, Monastic Scapulars, and Amulets]. *Revista Brasileira de História da Educação*, n. 4, p. 145-66, 2002.

_____. *Sonhos africanos, vivências ladinas. Escravos e forros em São Paulo (1850-1880)*. [African Dreams, Cunning Lives. Slaves and Freedmen in São Paulo (1850-1880)]. 2. ed. São Paulo: Hucitec, 2009.

16

WOMEN OF THE HOUSE: BLACK WOMEN AND DOMESTIC WORK IN THE IMPERIAL COURT

Flavia Fernandes de Souza

Reflecting on the theme of gender relations and slavery in the history of Brazil implies, above all, consideration of the experiences of black women in the world of work. Black women—slave or free, Brazilian, or African—played a role in the work spaces of rural and urban environments and took care of the most varied production activities in different moments of history. Among the jobs they held over time, domestic work is the most recognized. Actually, domestic work was the principal sector that placed women in the world of work during the formation of Brazilian society. As in many past civilizations and other cultures, the work needed for the organization and maintenance of homes tended to be done by the female sex.

One of the factors that can be attributed to explaining the significant participation of women in performing domestic work is the existence of slavery in the historical process of Portuguese colonization in America. First by means of exploiting the workforce of indigenous peoples, and later Africans and their descendants, domestic slavery was one of the principal uses of slave labor. During the entire colonial period, slaves were fundamental figures in humble homes and wealthy homes alike, in both the country and the city. Since that time, female slaves have stood out as the majority among the servants of colonial houses.

With the gradual spread of slave labor from the intercontinental African slave trade during the colonial period, black slaves, particularly women, became regular and indispensable figures in domestic jobs. Due to aversion to the manual labor typical of slave societies and the demands of the colonial economy itself—still very dependent on human labor—many enslaved women were placed into homes. The work these women did was not limited to the completion of tasks such as cleaning or caring for residences. Their duties also included tasks that were a part of the total economic output for the household. As recalled by Leila Mezan Algranti (1997, v.1, p. 43), it was up to these women to perform activities related to domestic production such as food, clothing, and making of equipment and tools for work.

In the imperial era, domestic slavery remained an accepted practice used in different social classes and was a widespread phenomenon in urban spaces, and the importance of slave servants in domestic spaces was not restricted to work. Since slavery structured the economy and society from colonization, the presence of slaves in nineteenth-century homes was also an indicator of social status. The number of domestic slaves indicated the degree of wealth, power, and prestige of a certain family. Furthermore, with slave ownership being socially accessible, rich as well as middle-class families could have captives to do domestic work in their homes in the city.

The number of slaves varied widely, depending on the social conditions of the families and the urban homes. According to Luiz Carlos Soares (2007, p.107-8), between 1810 and 1849 in Rio de Janeiro, for example, the number of slaves ranged between one and two in poor families, five and six in medium-sized families with few possessions, and ten or more in wealthy families. In rich homes, the total number of enslaved servants reached 20 or more individuals. Starting in the 1850s, with the beginning of the process of the gradual reduction of urban slaves, owners began to use fewer and fewer captives in their residences. However, during this period, slaves remained an indispensable presence within most families who owned at least six or seven captives dedicated to domestic work.

This generalized use of slaves in urban households appeared often in the stories told by travelers who were in Brazil in the 19th century. In observing the characteristics of the slave practices in Brazil, some foreigners described, in various forms, domestic slavery. One European observer who shared some of these observations was the well-known French painter and artist Jean Baptiste Debret (1768-1848). In his works, a large part done in the 1820s, we can find interesting images that portray scenes of daily life marked by the presence of slaves in homes, with a focus on female domestic slaves.

In the archives of the painter, black women of diverse conditions and origins—i.e. African and African-descendant, slave or free, are portrayed in the daily toil of domestic work (Debret, 1978, t.1, v. 2, p. 182-6, 195-9, 253-7). It is not by chance that he was inspired by the reality of the Imperial Court and that Debret produced lithographs of that nature. After all, as another traveler, German painter and artist Johann-Moritz Rugendas (1802-58), affirmed, "a large part of the slave population of Rio de Janeiro [found] itself employed in domestic work" (Rugendas, 1979, p. 269).

In fact, in Rio de Janeiro—which became the principal slave city of the Americas with an enormous group of Africans—domestic slaves formed the largest contingent of the captive population. Even without the content of the manifests created in the first half of the nineteenth century, studies done with the aid of various sources prove the predominance of slave labor in domestic work. This fact is even supported by the information presented in the 1872 Census of the Brazilian Empire, which was completed during a time when there was an accelerated reduction of the number of captives in the city. According to this survey, of the 48,939 slaves living in Rio de Janeiro, including both rural and urban areas, 46.67 percent (22,843 slaves) worked inside of residences. In the case of urban parishes, where the population indices were higher, of the 37,567 existing captives in 1872, 55.43 percent (20,825 slaves) worked as "house servants."[1]

Consequently, in terms of occupational distribution, most of the slave population in Rio de Janeiro found itself in "domestic services." In this scenario, characterized by the presence of slaves in the home, women were always in the majority. According to the analysis of the data from the census of 1872 done for the Município Neutro,[2] of the 22,843 domestic slaves, 14,185 (62.09 percent) were females. It is worth noting that this number represented 58.97 percent of the female slaves in the city, which together totaled 24,053.

Table 1: Slave population in domestic services in the municipality of Rio de Janeiro in 1872

Neighborhoods	Men	Women	Total
Urban	8,098	12,727	20,825
Rural	560	1,458	2,018
Total	8,658	14,185	22,843

Source: *Recenseamento do Império do Brasil de 1872.*

Although they shared the same legal and social condition, slave women could have very diverse experiences in terms of exploitation of their labor. In Rio de Janeiro, not all domestic slaves served in the houses of slave-owners and their families. Some of them were also "for hire," that is, they were slaves who lived "for themselves" and offered their services to those interested; with their services, they earned compensation which had to be passed on to their owners in the form of a determined daily value (per diem wages). Or, as with the majority, domestic slaves were hired to work for third parties (renters), to perform services offered by their masters (lessors).

The renting of slaves was, as a rule, a practice that yielded profits for their owners. While they kept the income earned by renting the servant, the renters were obligated to sustain and care for the captive during the period of the rental. It was common in these cases that some owners taught or required teaching of "domestic duties" to their slaves so they could generate income by renting out their labor force. Regarding this phenomenon, English traveler John Luccock, who was in the Imperial Court between 1808 and 1818, affirmed that:

> ...every house of means had slaves to whom they taught some or most common skills of life, and they not only performed these specialties for the families they belonged to; they were also rented out, by their masters, to people who were not as well off.... (Luccock, 1975, p. 72).

In the second half of the 19th century, the transactions related to the rental of domestic slaves became even more common in the city. This growth was due to the progressive increase of the price of captives after the official end of the traffic in Africans in 1850. From that point, many owners turned to renting their slaves to maintain the use of their slave workforce. Above all this indicates that at this moment, direct social relationship between domestic work and the practice of renting began to be established. As Emília Viotti da Costa (1998, p. 96-7) affirms, "the term itself began to signify domestic hire." According to this historian, various news ads from the 1870s and 1880s show the expression "for rent" was frequently used synonymously with "domestic servants."

The ad sections in the large periodicals in the capital of the empire, which had become important resources for the slave trade, were privileged spaces for announcement of requests related to domestic work. So much so that beginning in the 1870s, the requests for these services, found in well-known daily papers such as *Jornal do Commercio*, began to constitute 70 percent of the total announcements for work that were published. However, even before the second half of the nineteenth century, the offers and requests for domestic slaves—principally for captives—already comprised the majority of slavery ads.

> For sale, a beautiful light brown-skinned woman, 20 years old, pleasant, perfect maid, knows how to sew perfectly, she cuts all of her owner's clothes and makes the most delicate lace possible; she is outstanding in ironing, cooking, baking various types of sweets, setting and serving a table; she knows how to wash tulle and even silk stockings with lye and soap; in short, she has all of the qualities to make a perfect maid; Rua Larga de S. Joaquim n.94. (*Jornal do Commercio*, 27 Jan. 1835).
>
> Seeking a good wet nurse, brown-skinned, first or second delivery; a housemaid with a reserved demeanor who knows how to sew and iron perfectly, no defects, no schemes, and no diseases; Rua do Cano n.42 (*Jornal do Commercio* 14 Apr. 1835).

> Seeking to rent on Rua do Lavradio n. 84, a black woman who knows how to wash, iron, cook, and shop; no more than 8$R monthly. Needed in the same house, a loving little black girl to care for a child; no more than 6$R monthly rent. (*Jornal do Commercio*, 21 Jan. 1835).

It is worth highlighting that the ads sections in some periodicals were also used for agents that worked in the slave market, especially starting in the 1840s. Such dealers worked as the intermediaries in the operations associated with the purchase, sale, or rental of their own captives, or for third parties; through taxes they were paid by those interested in their services. In general, the majority of slaves sold by these agents (in establishments called "agencies" or "commission houses") were employed as domestic servants. According to the observations of the French traveler Charles Expilly (1814-86), who was in Brazil in the beginning of the 1850s, these firms were held by small-scale slaveholders. Owning between two and four captives, some owners kept one slave to serve their families and put the rest in houses or agencies to rent (Expilly 1862, p. 171-207).

With the progressive decline of slavery in the final decades of the century, such establishments started to broker freed workers for domestic service. In the capital, in the 1870s, 1880s, and 1890s, there were a significant number of agencies that made announcements in *Almanak Laemmert* and only worked booking servants to work in residences, business, and service establishments.[3] Usually, such rental houses did not have a good reputation in the city. There were frequent allegations that the agencies acted in bad faith with owners and renters, exploiting their clients or arranging schemes with hired workers. Still, these establishments functioned until the end of the century, managing many workers and often announcing their requests in daily papers.

> People needing staff for domestic service can place their order in the *Agência Central de Empregos* on Rua da Candelária n. 26. (*Jornal do Commercio*, 3 Mar. 1874).
>
> Anyone in need of good nannies, maids, waitresses; and expert cooks, laundresses, and ironers; and all staff available for domestic service will want to send their booking request to Rua do Senhor do Passos n. 145, loft. (*Jornal do Commercio*, 14 Feb. 1888).

> Male and female servants for rent for all domestic services; Rua Larga de S. Joaquim n. 137, *Empresa de Serviços Domésticos*. (*Jornal do Commercio*, 14 Jul. 1888).

Women constituted the largest part of the workers brokered in these businesses, and the composition of the group of servants rented through this mechanism materialized the changes that were in progress in the last decades of the nineteenth century. Starting in the second half of the 19th century, slaves were no longer predominant, in numerical terms, among the women who worked in domestic service. From then forward, the number of freed and free women working as "servant girls," often next to slave women, increased. According to the data from the 1872 census of the Município Neutro, of the 38,463 total working Brazilian and foreign women classified in the "domestic service" category, 63.12 percent (or 24,278 women) were free. This trend was evident in most the parishes of Rio de Janeiro, where the number of free women who reported working in the sector was considerably higher than that of slaves.

Table 2: Distribution of female domestic workers in the parishes of Rio de Janeiro in 1872

Parish	Free Brazilian	Slaves Foreign
Sacramento	1,564	710
São José	886	512
Candelária	204	89
Santa Rita	702	658
Sant'Ana	2,765	1,419
Santo Antônio	2,280	1,687
Espírito Santo	2,031	780
Engenho Velho	1,514	409
São Cristóvão	1,259	283
Glória	1,053	713
Lagoa	491	85
Campo Grande	288	5
Jacarepaguá	427	39
Ilha do Governador	138	1
Paquetá	59	20
Guaratiba	264	9
Inhaúma	379	119
Irajá	337	57
Santa Cruz	42	0
Total	16,683	7,595

Source: Recenseamento do Império do Brasil de 1872.

It seems that in Rio de Janeiro, in the context of the last decades of the nineteenth century, a large portion of women who were engaged in some type of paid activity worked in domestic service. According to the study done by Sandra Graham (1992, p. 17-8, 208), servants made up about 70 percent of all the women working in the city during that period. In this sense, the provision of domestic service seems to have constituted an important work space for free and freed women, especially in the final period of slavery, a fact that certainly contributed to making this occupation one of the largest in Rio de Janeiro in the last years of the nineteenth century, since it had a large concentration of workers.

In the censuses that followed that of 1872, that is, the general censuses of 1890 and 1906, the data presented for the "domestic service" category in the then federal capital were exceptionally high compared to the other sectors. So, in these censuses completed in the post-abolition period, the percentage relative to the world of domestic service comprised about 14 percent of the working population recorded and classified in different occupational fields. This percentage was higher than those represented by other sectors that also included large groups of workers, such as "manufacturing" and "trade." The numbers corresponding to domestic work are only second to those registered in the categories of "without profession" or in jobs "poorly defined" or "unknown."

Soon afterward, in the city of Rio de Janeiro at the end of the nineteenth century, domestic service was a sphere of the work world that included thousands of workers who were mainly female, in addition to being a professional area that had a concentrated percentage of workers of African descent, as suggested by the data in the "racial" classification boxes of the 1890 census. According to this census, the 74,785 individuals who declared working in domestic services, more than half (52.75 percent or 39,453) were classified as "black" or "mixed" (Hahner, 1993, p. 117). In other words, in Rio de Janeiro, black and mixed-race women fundamentally performed domestic work.

The presence of these women in the world of work by way of paid domestic labor can be explained by the analysis of different factors, some of which highlight the relationships in slavery—as it was discussed, many slave women were placed as "servant girls"—and work arrangements that involved the "rental of domestic service" after gaining freedom. Facing the limited options for ex-slaves to join the "free market of work," many freed women sought to perform domestic services—even if they were poorly compensated, as Henrique

Espada Lima (2005) noted in his recent article. In the daily ads, it is possible to find hints that many women found themselves in this situation.

> If you need a freed black woman, to care for children, very loving, contact Rua Nova do Livramento n. 83. (*Jornal do Commercio*, 16 Feb. 1864).
>
> Seeking to rent a colored woman, free, child or elderly, for small tasks in home; Rua de Santa Luzia n. 42. (*Jornal do Commercio*, 12 Feb. 1864).

Another factor that can explain why domestic service was a highly-sought occupation by poor, free women is that such activities were related to the tasks they did daily in their own homes. According to Eni de Mesquita Samara (1997, p. 41-48), during the nineteenth century, in different regions of the empire, the majority of working women occupied jobs that were considered typical of the female sex, such as paid domestic work. After all, this service involved tasks related to the cleaning and tidying of spaces, food production, washing and treatment of clothes and caring for children, in addition to innumerous complementary activities that were generally completed by women, such as the sale of food products or services such as alterations and embroidery, that extended from work completed in their own homes.

Many of these women that offered domestic services, worked from childhood until they were seniors. In the case of enslaved workers, this phenomenon was associated with slave practices of exploiting the labor of minors and the elderly because, in accordance with the demands of the slave economic and social order, captives could not be "useless weight" for their owners. In the case of freed workers, obviously, the placement of children and elderly in the workforce stemmed from the needs imposed by the precarious living conditions of the poor. Many adult women assumed the role of breadwinners for the livelihood of their families in the 19th century; girls and older women took to work as a means of survival. Moreover, some employers preferred to rent these types of workers, since children or "women of age" were generally considered the cheapest labor. It was not a coincidence that many girls were introduced to domestic environments to be "trainees"; in exchange, they were exploited for their labor.

> Seeking an older woman to take care of a house and two children, offering moderate rent; Rua do Alcântara, n. 68D, loja. (*Jornal do Commercio*, 10 Mar. 1874).
>
> Seeking a little black girl to care for a child and do a few house chores; Rua do Hospício, n.74. (*Jornal do Commercio*, 8 May 1878).
>
> Seeking to take in a little girl, 8-10 years of age, to teach domestic service; Rua do Machado Coelho, n. 12. (*Jornal do Commercio*, 10 Sep. 1886).

In general, domestic servants completed diverse tasks in the spaces in which they worked, inside of homes or even in some business and service establishments (cafés, small restaurants, bakeries, hotels, guesthouses, inns, etc.). Even though the use of servants for "all duties," principally in families who didn't have the means to maintain many employees, it was common that the servants did specific tasks that varied according to different domestic environments. This phenomenon was related to the division and distribution of jobs for slaves in homes and translated to the existence of distinct levels of specialization of hired labor in domestic services.

As Sandra Graham (1992, p. 31 and 45) highlights, servant girls had their job roles defined according to the activities they did, which were broken down by the areas where they worked. Servants, therefore, were distributed by the chores done inside of the home—designated by the Portuguese expression "indoors"—and by those services done outside of indoor spaces—called "outdoors" or "street service." However, it is important to note that this spatial division of the functions fulfilled by servants, designed from the existence of rigid boundaries between the "home" and the "street," was not always respected. Olívia Maria Gomes da Cunha (2007, p. 379) highlights this aspect, that the domestic spaces were constantly redefined by the subjects who used them. In this way, the "servant girls" could perform a vast range of tasks that could change at the will of their masters.

For that matter, it is likely that many domestic workers found themselves in situations similar to those of the character Bertoleza from the romance novel *O cortiço* (1890), by Aluísio de Azevedo (1857-1913). Slave of the Portuguese trader João Romão, Bertoleza had the triple role of "clerk, servant, and lover." As Azevedo (1996, p.12) defined, Bertoleza "toiled": she kept house, cooked for quarry workers, served as a tavern counter clerk, and sold groceries in addition to washing and caring for the clothes of her lover.

In reality, there were innumerable servants that performed activities that placed them between homes and external spaces. Certainly, this was the case of washwomen, ironers and steamers, water carriers, and servants who sold products or did shopping, even some seamstresses and embroiderers. In general, these servants worked as much within the range of the house of their masters or bosses as they did in the streets to complete the tasks they were assigned. As such, most these servants frequented public spaces such as streets, markets, and fountains, typical of cities like the Imperial Court.

Some of these diverse types and levels of specialization of certain servants, such as washwomen and water carriers, arose from the precariousness of the availability of urban services. Lacking infrastructure, domestic workers headed to different spaces in the city to complete their work. In some cases, the service could be completed inside of the home, as was done at the end of the century with the collective washing of clothes in the slums. Other tasks completed by servants were not directly linked to the domestic space. In these circumstances, one could find, for example, slaves who divided their time between the house of their master and the practice of small food trade. Another example was the seamstresses who, in addition to working in the houses of their masters, did complementary work such as being employed in sewing workshops.

The specializations of the servants who worked in interior spaces of the residences or in business and service establishments were varied. This variety included governesses, maids, chaperones, cooks, waitresses, housekeepers, those responsible for cleaning, chambermaids, room servants, dry nurses, and wet nurses (these last two were dedicated to the care of children). Some of these specializations suggested distinct levels. As Sandra Graham (1992 p. 46-7) differentiated, the cooks, for example, could be "trivial" (that is, prepared only to take care of the daily stovetop cooking) or of "oven and stove" (knowledgeable in the use of wood, coal, or clay stoves and in the preparation of more elaborate dishes). Beyond this there were the specialized cooks, or as they said during that time, "masters of their art," who made pastas, delicacies, and sweets.

When enslaved, some of these "servant girls" who worked in internal spaces could receive preferential treatment relative to the other captives. Gilberto Freyre (1980, p. 489) noted the existence of a certain hierarchy among slaves, in which domestic slaves were at the top, and even among them, there were distinctions of status. In some documents from the time, such as images, traveler reports or literary texts, it is possible to see that certain slaves (who were maids or squires) had small privileges. These captives would receive clothes and food of the best quality and enjoy certain benefits due to their proximity to their masters. Examples of this occurred in situations in which some slaves would accompany their masters on different occasions (such as travel, tours, church services, parties, and plays), or if they received some type of teaching, albeit rudimentary. Moreover, some domestic slaves were treated with some respect and affection by the families they lived with or were born into—being that in many cases, they were bastard children of their masters.

However, even under the guise of "earnings" generated by proximity and familiarity, such convivial relations established between owners and slaves were always constituted by the logic of social dominance. To understand the power relations—the authority, dependency, and hierarchy—domestic slavery involved, at the same time, "granting of privileges" and the existence of abusive practices and physical and moral violence against slaves. As Sidney Chalhoub observes, various criminal trials in the 1870s and 1880s involving captives "recorded despicable stories about the treatment of slaves by their masters." According to the author, many of those documents showed the testimony of domestic slaves concerning the cruel practices of beatings and humiliation that were seen as unfair, but were justified by the master under the pretense that it was necessary to impose punishment on disobedient slaves. Perhaps they had been so excessive and widespread in the city throughout the nineteenth century that it led the Câmara Municipal da Corte (city council) to try to regulate the surveillance of masters in the treatment of their slaves. The Código de Posturas of 1838 (laws regarding the use of public space, public hygiene, and other issues commonly seen as zoning laws), for example, instructed responsible authorities be vigilant about overseeing "bad treatment and cruelty that was customarily practiced with slaves, indicating methods to prevent such practices, and giving all parts to the council" (Chalhoub 1990, p. 201).

Therefore, one cannot lose sight of the complexity of the work relationships established in the domestic spheres, those relating to enslaved women as well as free women. Upon entering a domestic environment to provide their services, the maids were involving themselves in a turbulent web of social relations generated amid private control conferred by the "sovereign will of a master" to his dependents, subordinates, and slaves. That is because in the Brazilian society of the 19th century, the politics and ideology of paternalistic dominance and social control imposed upon enslaved workers played a fundamental role in the establishment of social relations, as Chalhoub observed most recently (2003, p. 44-64). In the world of work, where this process tended to manifest in a more evident form, the relationships among servants and their owners/employers could be even more crossed by the complex involvements generated by power relations such as the ethnic or racial context and especially gender.

As the relations between owners and slaves or between employees and employers were characterized by the provision of personal services and intimacy—often derived from the cohabitation of servants that lived with their masters—such practices of domination could be manifested through the granting of favors or the exploitation of labor. On one hand, as Sandra Graham (1992, p. 15-16, 108) analyzed, for many women, domestic work could signify protection. According to the author, the servants performed services and were obedient and, in turn, received the protection of their employers. Such support could take the form of basic care, like food, clothing, housing, treatment in the case of sickness or even help in raising their children. In fact, they could even be mechanisms for substituting monetary payment of the salaries of free workers, which was still perceived by employers as just a "reward." In part, domestic service was often considered in terms of the personal relationships between the family of the owners and the servants, as the relationships could be characterized by links of belonging, complicity, affection, or friendships generated from daily life.

In this scenario, the attributes demanded of the servants were not only about the quality of work to be done, but also the characteristics related to the person's character or behavior. In other words, attributes that were much more necessary to the establishment of a type of personal relationship than the performance of a job, in addition to being "qualities" that were expected of women in general, having to do with the ideals and conceptions of the feminine created during the 19th century. It would be very common for ads of nineteenth century newspapers related to requests for servants to present demands for moral attributes. Among these it was common to search for women who were humble, faithful, diligent, honest, obedient, or simply with "good behavior" and the absence of "defects." In some cases, such "prerequisites" of morality could be proven by "guarantors" who attested to the behavior of the servants.

On the other hand, however, the intimacy created in the routine of the services performed by the servants could suggest other meanings. The proximity of living with the master/employer and his family involved excessive work, poor treatment, suspicions and accusations, constant surveillance, unjust punishment, and all sorts of physical, sexual, and moral violence. In general, the private and personal nature of domestic work made the servants, like households and dependents, subordinate to the power exercised by the masters of the family unit and to the conflicting games and negotiations that were inherent in them. In the absence of laws that regulated work relations and by the very deficiency of the guarantee of civil rights—that in the 19th century was still based on the old Philippine Laws—the work relations tended to be oriented towards the values and practices of paternalism and slavery. Amidst such relations, domestic servants were subject to difficult work circumstances and life in the private sphere of the "home."

In that case, working as a servant could involve similar situations—often worse—as described by the writer Júlia Lopes de Almeida (1862-1934) in the chronicle entitled "Os criados" (1896). In citing the thought of a French columnist with whom she agreed, Almeida defined the following form of life of the domestic servants (Almeida, 1905, p. 119-26):

> ...Getting up at dawn, going to bed late, standing all day, save for the two or three hours of rest, living in eternal squalor: the dust, the dishwater, and the bathwater; eating leftovers, only having a few hours free each month, of which fatigue prevents enjoyment... Not to mention the physical and emotional pain! Enduring eighteen hours of the whims of an entire family, hearing the cruel teasing of children, the impertinences of the wife, the rudeness of the master, the bitter comments and demands of the senile grandparents... and that is not all. You must bear the insulting suspicions, closed cabinets, the set of keys taken with superiority, cutlery officially counted in front of the maids at night, after the family has secretly assured itself, underhandedly, that nothing is missing; an endless series of phrases with double meaning, sideways glances, and more horrible suffering in the heart than a stab in the flesh.

At the end of the 19th century, a moment of crisis for traditional forms of social domination, the sphere of work constituted by "servants" witnessed significant transformations. Because of the decline and end of slavery and the development of the historical process of the passage from slave work to free work and salary, the relations sewn into the domestic environment saw changes in the form of contracts and in the conditions of treatment and control of workers. It was not by chance that beginning in the 1880s domestic service became the subject of worry for many public authorities of the empire, principally for the representatives of municipal powers. At that time, in various municipalities of the country, projects for regulation of services provided by servants were proposed and approved.

In the city of Rio de Janeiro, the municipal representatives also took initiative to regulate domestic service. During the 1880s and 1890s, councilmembers and stewards presented and debated different designs to fit the activities of domestic servants into certain rules. In general, those normative texts had a structure oriented towards the control of workers, which, from the perspective of public representatives, should have been rigorously characterized—by the use of records and ID booklets—and supervised by competent bodies such as the police and the city council. Some proposals for regulation even predicted the standards for contracts and agreements for the provision of services, such as the work relations established between domestic workers and their employers. In that case, rules were included for the hiring and firing of servants and the guidelines relative to the rights and duties of masters and servants.

The resources produced in this process sought to justify the initiatives for the regulation by means of arguments that characterized domestic service as a social problem requiring the representatives in power to create a solution. Seen as a necessity, regulation should place limits on a sector that was supposedly found to be "careless," "disorganized," and "demoralized." In the opinion of ruling groups, reasons for this situation were related to the fact that the servants were mostly "dishonest," "immoral," "defective" people who committed all types of crimes against their employers. The approval of serious regulation, from the perspective of some, however, would be a fundamental measure to put an end to the "difficulties" that were common in domestic work, at the same time it would help combat "vagrancy" in the city.

As indicated in the analyses of the debates on regulation of domestic work in Rio de Janeiro, which involved arguments both in favor and against, what seemed to be at stake were the fears and hopes surrounding the end of slavery. It was believed at the time that the crumbling of slave relations would create, among other imperatives, the need to maintain ex-slaves in jobs. In what was referred to as the sphere of domestic service, the transformations stemming from the abolition of slavery gained specific features, and as such presented the possibility of employers losing their private power of control and the exchange of favors in relation to their employees. After all, with the possession of freedom, they would be more prepared to negotiate work conditions.

In fact, in the city of Rio de Janeiro, the proposals of regulation were strongly rejected by domestic workers and their representatives. As councilman José do Patrocínio (1853-1905) affirmed in 1889, the approval of a regulation for this sector, in the format that was being implemented, would put domestic servants in the "worst situation." That is because, in his opinion, such regulations gave "more guarantees to the employers than to the servants" in establishing "certain inequalities" in work relations. According to Patrocínio, the regulation was nothing but "a new law of disguised slavery" that dealt with the services and obligations that the servants would be subject to, but forgetting the balance that existed in the relationships of the employers with their servants.[4]

Generally speaking, even though initiatives had been taken and some projects had become municipal ordinances—as in 1896 with the creation of the general registration of domestic service—the process of regulation was not successful in the 19th century. It appears that the approved regulation did not have the effects desired by its legislators. Much resistance came not only from domestic workers, but also from employer sectors. Those resisting, in some cases, saw regulation as an interference of public power in the private domain. As a result of this process, a number of issues were raised at that time or debated by public authorities for decades afterward without ever reaching a consensus. For example, that was what occurred in the case of trying to define the nature of relations established between employers and domestic servants and the notion of contracting services as an impersonal relationship between equal individuals, as Cunha (2007, p. 396-403) points out.

However, the analysis of these attempts at regulating domestic service reveals many aspects of the history of this sphere of work in Brazilian society. The rising crisis and the end of traditional forms of social dominance, the issue of regulating domestic service, in terms of the end of the 19th century, indicate the existence of contiguous social and symbolic relations between slavery and domestic work in the history of Brazil.

Notes

1. Recenseamento do Império do Brasil de 1872. [Census of the Empireof Brazil of 1872] Available at: http://biblioteca.ibge.gov.br/

2. "Município Neutro" was the oficial term used to refer to the city of Rio de Janeiro. This also became known as "Corte/Court, " according to the Constituição de 1824, it was the political headquarters of the Brazilian empire and the oficial residence of sovereign Brazilians.
3. Administrative, commercial and industrial Almanac of Rio de Janeiro (1870, 1875, 1880, 1885, 1888, 1890, 1895 and 1900.
4. AGCRJ. Bulletin of the Câmara Municipal of the Court of 1889, p. 111.

Bibliography

Algranti, Leila Mezan. "Famílias e vida doméstica." [Families and Domestic Life]. In Souza, Laura de Mello e. (Org.). *História da vida privada no Brasil: cotidiano e vida privada na América portuguesa.* [History of Private Life in Brazil: The Quotidian and Private Life in Portuguese America]. São Paulo: Companhia das Letras, 1997, v. 1, p. 83-154.

Almeida, Julia Lopes de. "Os criados." In *O livro das noivas.* [The Book of Brides]. 2. ed. Primeira edição de 1896. Rio de Janeiro: F. Alves, 1905, p. 119-26.

Azevedo, Aluísio. *O cortiço.* [The Beehive/Ghetto]. 32. ed. Primeira edição de 1890. Rio de Janeiro: Ediouro, 1996.

Carvalho, Marcus F. M. de. "A imprensa na formação do mercado de trabalho feminino no século XIX." [The Press in the Formation of the Female Working Class in the 19th Century]. In Neves, Lúcia Maria B.; Morel, Marco; Ferreira, Tânia Maria B. da C. (Orgs.). *História e imprensa: representações culturais e práticas de poder.* [History of the Press: Cultural Representations and Practices of Power]. Rio de Janeiro: Faperj, 2006, p. 176-99.

Chalhoub, Sidney. *Visões da liberdade: uma história das últimas décadas da escravidão na corte.* [Visions of Liberty: A History of the last Decades of Slavery at Court]. São Paulo: Companhia das Letras, 1990.

_____. *Machado de Assis: historiador.* São Paulo: Companhia das Letras, 2003.

Costa, Emília Viotti da. *Da senzala à colônia.* [From the Slave Quarters to the Settlement]. 4. ed. São Paulo: Unesp, 1998.

Cunha, Olívia Maria Gomes da. "Criadas para servir: domesticidade, intimidade e retribuição. "[Raised to Serve: Domesticity, Intimacy, and Retribution]." In GOMES, Flávio dos Santos (Orgs.). *Quase-cidadão: histórias e antropologias da pós-emancipação no Brasil.* [Almost-Citizen: Histories and Anthropologies of Post-Emancipation Brazil]. Rio de Janeiro: Editora da FGV, 2007, p. 377-418.

Debret, Jean Baptiste. *Viagem pitoresca e histórica ao Brasil.* [Pictoral and Historic Travels Through Brazil]. Primeira edição em francês de 1834-1839. Trad. e notas de Sérgio Milliet. Belo Horizonte: Itatiaia; São Paulo: USP, 1978, t. 1, v. 2.

Expilly, Charles. *Le Brésil tel qu'il est*. Paris: Arnauld de Vresse, Libraires-Éditeurs, 1862.

Freyre, Gilberto. *Casa-grande e senzala: introdução à história da sociedade patriarcal no Brasil*. [The Masters and the Slaves: A Study in the Development of Brazilian Society]. 20. ed. São Paulo: Círculo do Livro, 1980.

Graham, Sandra Lauderdale. *Proteção e obediência: criadas e seus patrões no Rio de Janeiro (1860-1910)*. [Protection and Obedience: Servants andtheir Masters in Rio de Janeiro (1860-1910)]. São Paulo: Companhia das Letras, 1992.

Hahner, June Edith. *Pobreza e política: os pobres urbanos no Brasil (1870-1920)*. [Poverty and Politics: the Urban Poor in Brazil]. Brasília: UnB, 1993.

Lima, Henrique Espada. "Sob o domínio da precariedade: escravidão e os significados da liberdade de trabalho no século XIX." [Under the Dominion of Precarity: Slavery and Meanings of Freedom of Work in the 19th Century]. *Topoi*, Rio de Janeiro, v. 6, n. 11, p. 289-326, Jul.-Dec. 2005.

Luccock, John. *Notas sobre o Rio de Janeiro e as partes meridionais do Brasil*. [Notes on Rio de Janeiro and Southern Parts of Brazil]. Primeira edição em inglês de 1820. Trad. Milton da Silva Rodrigues. Belo Horizonte: Itatiaia; São Paulo: USP, 1975.

Rugendas, Johann-Moritz. *Viagem pitoresca através do Brasil*. [Pictoral Travels Through Brazil]. Primeira edição em alemão de 1835. Trad. Sérgio Milliet. Belo Horizonte: Itatiaia; São Paulo: USP, 1979.

Samara, Eni de Mesquita. "Mão de obra feminina, oportunidades e mercado de trabalho no Brasil do século XIX." [Feminine Labor, Opportunities and the labor market in Brazil in the 19th Century]. In Samara, Eni de Mesquita (Org.). *As ideias e os números do gênero: Argentina, Brasil e Chile no século XIX*. [Ideas and Numbers of Gender: Argentina, Brazil,and Chile in the 19th Century]. São Paulo: Hucitec, 1997, p. 23-61.

Soares, Luiz Carlos. *O "povo de Cam" na capital do Brasil: a escravidão urbana no Rio de Janeiro do século XIX*. ["Canaanites" in the Capital of Brazil: Urban Slavery in Rio de Janeiro in the 19th Century]. Rio de Janeiro: 7 Letras, 2007.

17

ZIZINHA GUIMARÃES: BETWEEN HISTORY AND MEMORY

Petrônio Domingues

> —*Mommy! Mommy!*
> —*What is it my child?*
> —*We ["women of color"] are nothing in this life*
> Lima Barreto, Clara dos Anjos, p. 196.

On December 2, 1964, the *Sergipe Jornal* announced on its front page a passing. "Professor Eufrozina Amélia Guimarães passed away at 6 p.m. yesterday," from "arteriosclerosis that she had been suffering from for some months, keeping her confined to the bed and needing serious medical care from her doctor, Dr. Francisco Rollemberg." According to the newspaper, Ms. Zizinha left an entire generation of "distinguished" students, shaped with constant zeal and dedication, marking her "indelible spirit, always refined and youthful." The article affirms that "it is not only the city of Laranjeiras that mourns today, but the whole state of Sergipe mourns the brave professor who knew how to transform her students into eminent citizens of the Brazil of today."[1] The *Gazeta de Sergipe* also announced that the "The beloved professor D. Eufrozina Guimarães has passed away in the city of Laranjeiras where she resided." Popularly known as Zizinha Guimarães, she "taught a generation of

Sergipeans and was a person who enjoyed great prestige among those who were fortunate enough to pass through her classrooms."[2]

On December 3, the periodicals *Sergipe Jornal* and *Gazeta de Sergipe* and some memorial records published the funeral ceremony details. With the accompaniment of friends, godchildren, admirers, civil and military authorities, former students and onlookers, as well as all of the schools of Laranjeiras, the burial procession of Zizinha Guimarães began at 4 p.m. at the house in which she lived, covering parts of several city streets until reaching the cemetery, Cemitério da Misericórdia. Fulfilling her wish, the coffin was carried by her godchildren, and followed by her former students. Before the burial, various authorities made speeches, many of which were former students, "all praising that professor who changed all of their lives." Dr. Henrique Neto, legal advisor of the legislative assembly and representative of the governor, spoke first, sharing his memories, his pain, and his "gratitude, wishing for Dona Zizinha to rest in peace." He also pointed out that the government would "pay homage" to the "mourned master," for her "sixty-two long years of educational work." The deputy Fernando Franco asserted, "she remained in the memory of us all." Even Dr. Temístocles Diniz "affirmed that she was the greatest public figure of all time in Laranjeiras."

In addition to those former students, general Antônio Leite, resident of Rio de Janeiro whom she called "my little father," appeared at the ceremony as well. Also present was Ms. Alda Mesquite Teixeira who, accompanied by her husband Oviêdo Teixeira, in a gesture of acknowledging the merits of her former professor, wished to honor her one last time at her burial. In summary, all of the former students of Ms. Zizinha appeared at the time of her final farewell. "We acknowledge," said the *Sergipe Jornal*, "the merits of this worldly teacher who magnified Sergipe through her teaching.... This is the professor that we revere in this moment." The coffin was placed in the grave by Teotônio Mesquita, Temístocles Diniz, Hercílio Cruz, Mário Lobão, Mário Policiano, and Francisco Bragança. Amid "tears and sadness, Ms. Zizinha left this world to find in heaven, the fruits of her goodness, her dedication to education, and her faithfulness to God and her homeland. Friendship, affection, and love were ever present yesterday afternoon in the posthumous homage the residents of Laranjeiras gave to that professor."[3]

It is clear that Zizinha Guimarães was a prominent figure in Sergipe, respected by the government and by the sectors of civil society as a talented professor and businesswoman who shaped generations of Sergipean students. Her funeral on the afternoon of December 2, 1964 was crowded and mobilized a multitude in a spontaneous feeling of unity. Reportedly, the Sagrado Coração de Jesus Philharmonic Orchestra led the procession, in which people of all social classes and ethno-racial backgrounds marched, gloomy and bereaved, to the intense sounds of the percussion. The emotional tone of speeches at her graveside marked the event, but who was this woman whose death was reported in the principal vehicles of communication in Sergipe? Who was this woman whose interment ceremony included representatives from entities of civil society and from municipal and state governments? This chapter seeks to map and examine some aspects of the trajectory of Zizinha Guimarães. Far from conclusive pages, the intent here is to begin to weave the threads of history and the memory of a woman who faced (and sought to overcome) various obstacles of her time.

From Eufrozina to Zizinha Guimarães

Eufrozina Amélia Guimarães was born in Alto do Bonfim, in the city of Laranjeiras, in the state of Sergipe on December 26, 1872.[4] Information on her family is limited. It is known that her father Manuel Ferreira de Oliveira Guimarães was a white tailor, and her mother Amélia da Silva Guimarães was a free black woman, and that she had two siblings: Ofélia de Oliveira Guimarães and Antônio Vespasiano Guimarães. With this background, Eufrozina Guimarães faced a series of difficulties in her childhood, sometimes from the scarcity of family resources, sometimes for her race. Being *parda* (biracial)—as it was declared in her baptism registry—in the middle of a world of slavery was not easy; and, in Laranjeiras, the situation was even more complicated. Located in the valley of Cotinguiba, in the central area of the state, 23 kilometers from the capital Aracaju, the city was known in the 19th century for its sugar production, the institution of slavery and for its socioeconomic prosperity. Upon discovering the valley of Cotinguiba in 1859, the German traveler Robert Avé-Lallemant (1980, p. 332) was impressed with what he found. In Maruim, he saw beautiful homes and a "church, completely new, with two towers, beautiful, and even the streets, this expression, by and large, has become a euphemism, the small cities in the north of Brazil reflect their commercial activity and intense work."

In Laranjeiras, the picture was no different. Around 1870, the city had dozens of mills and small brandy and cigar factories; a continuous flow of sugar and other goods embarked (or landed) in its port. In 1880, the city had 12 storehouses, six in the city and six on the outskirts. Between 1880 and 1881, 128,147 sacks of sugar, 14,440 bales of cotton and 1,209 hides had been drained from them. The economic and financial development was accompanied by social progress and Laranjeiras went from being a small villa to one of the most important (and auspicious) cities of Sergipe. Decorated, in 1854, with street lamps—of light oil, which was substituted by kerosene in 1883—it was a place of opportunity and the home of politicians, bureaucrats, traders (national and foreign), priests, clerks, tailors, shoemakers, musicians, apothecaries, silversmiths, painters, barbers, journalists, lawyers, intellectuals and doctors, such as Alberto de Bragança.[5]

At the same time that this civic and social activity was occurring, Laranjeiras standardized its educational and cultural activities. When he was in the city in 1860, Dom Pedro II visited the classroom of professor Possidônia Maria de Santa Cruz Bragança and he was received with a religious hymn in French. He found that the students learned to read, write and count, in addition to "prayers," "doctrine," and "work with embroidery." The emperor watched "classes of philosophy and geography" given by professor Tito Augusto Souto de Arquimedes and visited the school of Manuel Cândido da Cunha Drumond Rocha, who taught grammar, "doctrine," and Latin, among other subjects. He went to a class of students of José Constituíno Teles and tried to watch the class of a professor who "had not been able to bring the girls together." In all, Dom Pedro II visited five teaching institutions, which indicates that Larajeiras was developing a burgeoning education system.[6]

Combined with this, the city streamlined its artistic-cultural life, with the presence of print media (circulation of newspapers), theatrical shows, literary soirees, recitals in French and an effervescent production of their "illustrious" children. It is worth mentioning two such illustrious sons of Laranjeiras: João Ribeiro (1860-1934), the polygraph who, upon moving to Rio de Janeiro, wrote many books on philology, history and folklore; and Horácio Hora (1853-90), the painter who went to Paris to perfect his technique and returned with the prestige of studying with the French masters to paint the nooks and crannies of Laranjeiras. This all gave the city pride in itself and the brilliance of its radiating culture; called an "age of gold" by Beatriz Góis Dantas (2009, v. 2, p. 185), it was a time of strong economic and cultural vitality.

In 1872, the population of Laranjeiras had 5,907 inhabitants, of which 4,247 (71.9 percent) were free and 1,660 (28.1 percent) were slaves. The religious rituals and commitments took up a large part of the time of the people, but in religion—as in society—the lines of color and social status divided the inhabitants of the city. The brotherhood of Santíssimo Sacramento, which was headquartered in the Igreja do Coração de Jesus church, and still headquartered there today, was reserved for wealthy white people; blacks were a part of the fellowship of São Benedito, housed in a small, unfinished church situated on one of the hillsides surrounding the city (Dantas, 2009, v. 2, p. 188-9). Nearly all of the opulence of Laranjeiras was based on the exploitation of slave labor. The city sheltered a large *creole* and African population (mainly *Nagô* and *Malê*). This population was not restricted to the tasks of sugar production; they also occupied places in the urban landscape: laboring in warehouses and homes (as domestic servants) and working in various trades as "slaves for hire" and "slaves for rent." As a result, it was the "field slave" who was most deprived, either by excessive daily work; abuse from masters, administrators and overseers; or by rigorous punishments to which they were subjected. Lashing was frequently given to slaves; however, there were other punishments that were more common such as the use of chains, manacles, iron neck collars, or the draconian pillory.

Sharyse Piroupo do Amaral tells the story of Lúcio, a slave in Laranjeiras in 1875, who was placed in a collar, "which he was only taken out of a week later, and he was already dead." Faced with this event, the prosecutor of Laranjeiras resolved to open a homicide trial, accusing Manuel Curvelo de Mendonça Bastos, Lúcio's owner. However, as Curvelo de Mendonça was a farming family, they were one of the richest in the region and perhaps in the whole province of Sergipe; the accused was absolved by unanimous vote. Seven years after the death of Lúcio, the Curvelo de Mendonça family was involved in a new case of mistreatment. João, a 23-year-old biracial black man, was punished with an enormous (and heavy) chain placed on his foot, a fact that shocked the abolitionist newspaper *O Libertador*. And what about Manuel, a slave, who in December 1883 was ruthlessly punished for refusing to take orders from his master? After the beating, he spent two days recovering physically, later escaping from Laranjeiras to Aracaju, where he appeared at a police station to show the marks from the beating. In the forensic examination, doctors confirmed "multiple scars on the entire back region, of different sizes" and "contusions, which produced congestion in the eyes" (Amaral, 2007, p. 96-100, 103-4, 109).

Facing such cruelties, robbery and humiliation, slaves did not remain passive or indifferent. On the contrary, they articulated diverse and creative forms of resistance. They petitioned the court in civil trials for freedom, frequented the police station to denounce mistreatment they suffered, sought refuge in the lands of other masters or even in roadside taverns, led escapes and revolts, assassinated masters and overseers, and organized slave refuges and maroon colonies. With the diminishing slave population in the 1880s—due to emancipation legislation, deaths, liberations, escapes, and the advance of the abolitionist movement—the struggles for freedom intensified until the abolition of slavery was decreed on May 13, 1888.

Causing true national commotion, abolition entered history as a quest for Brazilian society as a whole, a fact that would seal the beginning of a new era of victory for the ideals of freedom, civilization, and progress. Information from this stage of Eufrozina Guimarães' life is missing; for this reason it is not possible to know how she, at 15 years of age, received the notice of abolition. She probably participated in, or was at least an eyewitness to, the commemorations that erupted in Laranjeiras. With music, dancing, and drumming, the former slaves of plantations celebrated the day of "liberation." In the city, the commemoration celebration was extensive. With whites of "high society," freed people, and the "population of coloreds" in a jubilant state, there were civic marches, speeches from abolitionist leaders, poetry recitations, bands, and fireworks.[7]

There were no longer slaves and no longer masters. These were new times in the cities of Sergipe: time to ease tensions, renew dreams and feed hopes of a more promising future. In 1889, the Republic was established and the export of sugar from Laranjeiras and the region diminished. According to Amaral (2007, p. 259-60), it was the freedmen saying "no" to the continuation of a slaveholding past in a new form. Actually, the owners of plantations faced (and managed) a crisis in production from the last quarter of the 19th century, but it was the disintegration of the slavery system that pressed them to invest in other sectors of the economy. Far from encouraging, nothing reminiscent of Laranjeiras in its shining "age of gold." Many freedmen started to "live for themselves."[8] Others migrated to Aracaju, drawn by the opportunities for work in the growing industrial establishments—consumer goods and cotton spinning and weaving—and in the growing network of trade and services. This is how the first decades of the 20th century saw the decay of the Cotinguiba valley.

It was during these trials and tribulations that Eufrozina Guimarães learned to read and write and, at around 17 years old, she enrolled in the Colégio Inglês, where she became a student (and admirer) of the North American professor Anne Carroll. Diligent, she found a calling for "studies." She became familiar with some languages—French and Esperanto—and learned to play the piano. After basic education, she began to dedicate herself to a greater passion: the profession of teaching. As a "lay" teacher (that is, without a diploma from the regular course), she gave private classes to children from families with little means and was, little by little, gaining teaching experience. In 1894, she acquired, with her two siblings, a house of "mud and straw, on Rua da Cadeia."9 Two years later, she was named professor of public schooling. Her experience in the official school network was no small matter, in the extent that it gave her professional maturity and allowed her to have contact with different types of students. She could not stay, however, because she was discharged in 1902, due to alleged differences her father had with political leaders of the city. Eufrozina Guimarães was not discouraged. She returned to being a private teacher, gained (and captivated) a clientele, saved some resources, until she gained her license from the Administration of Public Instruction and founded, on July 4, 1904,10 the Escola Laranjeirense, the greatest accomplishment of her life (Oliveira, 1981, p. 150).

It could not have been easy for a woman, 31 years old with dark skin and humble beginnings, to make a living as a professor and institute a school (although modest) in the First Republic (1889-1930). Due to the scientific racism during this period, if we may be so bold as to call it that, based on the ideas of evolution, social Darwinism and eugenics, the elite politicians and intellectuals defined the black person as an inferior race, in biological, moral, intellectual, social, and cultural makeup. The Sergipean jurist Sílvio Romero (1977, p. 59) advocated that the "barbarism of blacks" was undisputed; after all, they had descended from the African who, "slow or stupid," influenced "negatively the formation of our people." In 1902 the engineer from Rio de Janeiro, Euclides da Cunha (2000, p. 94-5) stated: "the black does not even come close to the mid intellectual level of the Indo-European." The mulatto, less than an intermediary, would have "fallen" without the physical energy of their "savage ancestors" (blacks), and without the "elevation of their superior ancestors" (whites). In a study completed in 1905, the doctor from Maranhão, Nina Rodrigues (1976, p.4) diagnosed: "Even if we know black men or men of color of indubitable merit and deserving of esteem and respect, that does not negate the fact and the recognizable truth that, up until today, blacks could not constitute a civilized people."

Associated with barbarity, degeneration, animalism, perversion, truancy and deficiency in mental development, the Afro-descendant was the target of a series of attacks, stereotypes and negative stigmas equally from "the men of science" and in popular belief. Sílvio Romero (1977, p. 85)—who did studies in his native land in the last quarter of the 19th century—collected the following proverbs from use in daily life: "Blacks are not people"; "he has the foot of a beast, claws of an animal and cracked heels; his little finger is like the seed of a cucumber from São Paulo, his hair is prickly"; "the Blacks confesses but doesn't take communion"; "lying he is a slob, eating he is a pig, sitting he is a stump"; "the Blacks have a foul odor: resembles the devil." These ideas, however, were not only used on a scientific and popular level. Political leaders—many of which in positions with executive or legislative power—drew upon the assumptions of the so-called scientific racism to sanction government programs and public policies unfavorable to the "colored population."[11]

The result of this is that in the First Republic, black professors were uncommon. And what about black owners of schools? If the issue of race wasn't enough, Eufrozina Guimarães faced traditional gender barriers. Even though Laranjeiras had made some cultural and behavioral advances amidst the tropical *Belle Epoque*, women there were still subject to the relations of dominance/subordination to men and few worked in the public sphere—dominion of the home was their destiny. The newspapers of the city relentlessly suggested that they wished for the role of a "good mother, good wife, and good daughter."[12] The "competent" discourse of jurists, doctors, hygienists, and the religious charged the woman with the maintenance of a healthy family, in the broadest sense of the word.

To these discourses "would be added new discoveries in psychology, accentuating familiar privacy and maternal love as indispensable to the physical and emotional development of children." Marriage and maternity "were effectively constituted as the true female career. Anything that caused women to stray from this path was perceived as a deviation from the norm" (Louro, 1997, p. 454). To complicate the situation, the female sex was essentially inferior. "As impressive as the erudition and education of a woman were," affirmed the newspaper *Vida Laranjeirense* in 1930, "they remained subject to the torture of various, morbid phenomena with psychological losses the entire month, pregnancy, postpartum, menopause," finally "for the most well-kept person and health, sickness between adolescence and old age is unfailing, it is a general rule; however, in man it is an accident, the exception." The woman would be "morbid" by nature. And her "periodic morbidity has a powerful influence throughout the body and the nervous system."[13] In the press of Laranjeiras, Júlio Barreto released an epigram: "A man, in spite of everything, is always a man; a woman, no matter however much one tries, never is what she should be."[14]

As noted, the concepts, images, and representations forged (and conveyed) upon blacks and women, whether in the field of "scholarly" culture or in "popular" culture, were discreditable. Still, Eufrozina Guimarães did not wallow in the adversities of race and gender of her time and instead preferred to channel her energy into education. She saw in education a valuable, if not principal, mechanism for human emancipation. For her, school was a temple of light, wisdom and "instruction." And instruction should be celebrated, because in addition to being a universal good, it brought the ability to elicit human development and open doors (and minds) to all the activities of life. With education, the individual acquired character, moral soundness, and good principles; and above all, civilized himself, becoming cultured, respectable, and gaining recognition, regardless of gender or ethno-racial background.

The school, Escola Laranjeirense, was primary level (currently the first cycle of basic education) and the location also served as the residence of its professor, director and owner, at what is now designated as Rua Tobias Barreto, Number 12. She served students of both sexes (boys and girls) in a multi-grade class and mixed structure: there was boarding, semi-boarding, and day school. The school was private and at its peak, it had between 40 and 50 students, children from elite families of Laranjeiras and the region. Suffice it to say that Francisco de Faro Franco, son of "industrialist Col. João Gonçalves Franco, owner of Usina São João," in the municipality of Riachuelo; José de Araújo Barreto, son of "distinguished"

Mr. Esaú Muniz Barreto; and Francisco Plácido Tavares de Bragança, son of "illustrious" director of the state chemical institute (Instituto de Química Estadual) and grandson of the "respected clinician, Dr. Militão de Bragança," were students of the Escola Laranjeirense.[15] Regarding teaching, professor Eufrozina Guimarães used pedagogical tools grounded in behaviorist principles.[16] She believed that learning was an individual response to events and external stimuli. Presented with stimuli, the individual is conditioned to react, acquiring new behaviors and habits. One response produces a consequence, such as forming a word or solving a math problem. And, when the result is satisfactory, it should be rewarded. In this spirit, she regularly divulged to the press the "honor roll," with the names of the students who achieved the highest marks.[17] The intention was nothing more than to stimulate the other students to dedicate themselves diligently to their studies. Austere and refined with the methods of the age, she took paddles, knuckles, and rulers to the head as corrective methods, obliging students to learn how to behave in a "civilized" manner. At the end of the school year, she was equally accustomed to sending letters of congratulations to parents for the approval of their children,[18] as well as promoting the "honor award," a medal given to the students who stood out in the categories of "diligence," "good manners," and "the improvement of grades." In 1930, for example, the winner was Renato Franco.[19]

In his autobiography, Luiz Valença Borges (1983, p. 33) recalls events from his childhood related to the climate of expectations that filled his classes in the school, Escola Laranjeirense:

> The following day after our arrival in Laranjeiras [after the holiday break], amid the customary preparations for the return to school, my mother hurriedly prepared the final details, within the recommended time frame. At school, we were received with affection by the old and beloved Headmistress [Eufrozina Guimarães], and escorted to the classroom by the adjunct professor. The reuniting with colleagues, the hugs of affection from friends Edite Paixão and Edwirgens, reignited in us new cheer, previously unsettled by the unexpected return and our interrupted vacation. Most distracted, we were already making racket and clamor each time we saw a new colleague arrive in our classroom, quickly resulting in the entire class being severely reprimanded, and assurance that we would no longer be participating that

month in the selection of students whose names would appear on the honor roll.

In the Escola Laranjeirense, there were classes for writing, reading, times tables, grammar, arithmetic, analysis, calculus, editing, verbs, geography, the history of Brazil, natural sciences, and behavior.[20] As an extracurricular activity, Eufrozina taught piano and basic French, in spite of not being a fluent speaker in the language. She always made time for religion classes (Catholic-oriented), or to care for the cleanliness of her students, personally examining clothes, ears, nails, and teeth before the beginning of class (Fontes, 1984). Regarding teaching material, the professor used her own texts (Guimarães, no date) or others.[21] In her teaching establishment, she established a brand of creativity and patriotism. During the school year, there were various recreational activities and festive events. It was during these occasions that the students sang, danced, recited verses and participated in theatrical productions. Used as a didactic resource, plays customarily conveyed messages of faith and civility. Moreover, the students sang the national anthem every day. Events and "magnanimous" characters of national formation were celebrated. Every year on September 7, the Escola Laranjeirense commemorated Independence Day, raising the Brazilian flag and singing the national anthem.

Little by little the school was able to garner the affection of the students, parents and the community, in the 1920s and 30s becoming a renowned educational establishment in the valley of Cotinguiba. There are those who said its fame spread "becoming and equivalent to the best in the capital in higher-level education" (Borges, 1983, p. 33). Exaggerations aside, the fact is that the primary schools of that region operated in substandard facilities and the majority of them did not have proper hygiene conditions nor did they offer materials necessary for teaching. Meanwhile, the Escola Laranjeirense relayed reports of its activities to the Board of Education, stating that the building it operated in had infrastructure (desks and chairs), school supplies and satisfactory hygiene conditions. Its pedagogical activities, in this context, reverberated in the city of Laranjeiras and its academic calendar, in turn, was usually followed by the local press:

> After the traditional week of considerable examinations, this afternoon closes the school year of this well-directed educational institution led by the celebrated and dignified teacher, Ms. Eufrozina Guimarães. During the day there will be, in the elegant school of blended learning, significant festivities that will have as a perfect finishing touch, an exciting literary drama festival in our stunning cine-theatre Iris, in which almost all of the diligent male and beautiful female students of the noble establishment of instruction, will participate, having been trained by the beloved director of the most original and darling program.[22]

On an equal level to the growing visibility of the Escola Laranjeirense, the "celebrated and dignified teacher, Ms. Eufrozina Guimarães" was garnering respect, status and popularity. Conscious of this, she did not neglect her public image. Thin, medium height, and vain, she liked earrings, necklaces, ruby rings, and being in style; she wore high heels and long "princess-style" dresses and skirts when she went to the Iris Cinema, the "cinema theatre" of the city, to watch some film or theatrical performance. Elegant, she excelled in all rules of good manners and sophisticated taste. A keeper of morals and good customs, she insisted on behavior that bordered puritanical. Sociable, she carved a space in the middle of "high society," that is, she fixed herself in a network of relationships formed by people such as the mayor, councilmen, the police chief, the district judge, vicar of the head church, lawyers, doctors, traders, journalists, and "colonels" of the region. With time, her popularity passed the boundaries of her circle of friends and network of clientele. She became a public figure and was known by the nickname Zizinha Guimarães. Nevertheless, how was this possible? How was a person without a penny to her name able to leave anonymity, ascend the social web, and principally conquer the "high society" of Laranjeiras?

A Versatile Woman

Zizinha Guimarães was a versatile woman who sought to project herself on several fronts. When her school wasn't in session, she participated in events in the city, mainly those of a patriotic[23] or religious nature. On May 20, 1930, the canonization of Saint Teresa was celebrated in a solemn mass in the Igreja Nossa Senhora da Conceição church. After the mass, a "majestic procession" was formed that covered the main streets of Laranjeiras. At the front was Miss Magnólia Borges carrying the banner of the Virgem Auxiliadora and following was the Escola Laranjeirense, being led personally by its "grand director." Also appearing in the procession were the fellowships of Santa Terezinha, Pia União das Filhas de Maria and the people.[24] The following week, Zizinha Guimarães returned to the scene and sponsored the "traditional" festivals of Santa Maria Auxiliadora and Dom Bosco in the main church. There was mass, celebrated by vicar Filadelfo Oliveira and accompanied by a "harmonious chorus," formed by the students of the Escola Laranjeirense. Along the center of the "vast nave" of the church were the most "original ornaments and even more lavish lighting," a Verdi piece was recited after the consecration.[25]

Religious sentiment was another calling of this Afro-Sergipean professor. She was a practicing Roman Apostolic Catholic and frequented associations and religious fellowships when she was not supporting the head church Sagrado Coração de Jesus, going to masses, closing procession lines, orating the rosary in novenas, helping the vicar, integrating catechetical commissions, organizing church fairs or even taking on the responsibilities of the choir "Coração de Jesus." During the month of June, the worship festivals of São João Batista were characterized by their liveliness and Zizinha Guimarães' presence was obligatory, according to the newspaper *Vida Laranjeirense*:

> The city festivals held in honor of the glorious São João Batista were lively. Many fireworks, sambas, revelers, performances and other traditional entertainment, culminating in an elegant and crowded novena held in the house of our very esteemed professor Zizinha Guimarães, which involved 9 lively nights of dances e lovely family gatherings.[26]

Various "family houses," of which that of the Afro-Sergipean professor stood out, hosted the "crowded" novenas, times in which people manifested their faith and devotion, ate, drank and enjoyed themselves, and of which the pinnacle was June 25th, with a lavish festival at the Sagrado Coração de Jesus. At dawn, reveille was played by the band "União dos Artistas"; at 7 a.m., mass and general communion of the apostolate, accompanied by the "Coração de Jesus" choir under the direction of professor Zizinha Guimarães. In the afternoon there was a "great procession" and to close the event, a "Eucharistic blessing."[27]

In the first decades of the 20th century, Laranjeiras brought together a thriving and diverse wealth of popular and Afro-diasporic traditions. There, the Ninho dos Gaviões Society, one of the most popular recreational associations of the city, held dances and participated in Micareme—a carnival-like party after Lent, when carnival groups such as Laranjeirense, Botafogo and Ninho dos Gaviões paraded through their neighborhoods or through the city itself, captivating partygoers with music, skits, choreography, costumes, props and much animation.[28] There were also various *terreiros de nagô* (Candomblé religious communities) whose origins date back to the ancient Africans who crossed the Atlantic and left the veneration of the *orixás* as a legacy for their descendants. There were also several carnival folkloric groups that paraded at this time, such as *taieiras*, *cacumbis*, *cheganças*, São Gonçalo, *congos*, and *reisados*. The festival of Santos Reis covered the Christmas season and its high point was January 6th, when the black saints São Benedito and Nossa Senhora do Rosário were also celebrated. The "municipality," during that time, prepared special lighting, set up a podium in the square of the parish church and hung flags on the central streets. There were fireworks, musicians, mass and procession: all in the spirit of happiness and devotion. In the festival of 1935, all of the groups were represented in the parade, highlighting the *chegança* whose "effect was profusely heightened." Similarly, the *taieiras*, under the direction of the "popular" Belina, "were worthy of the greatest applause. And the two trios of *cacumbis*, very lively."[29]

Zizinha Guimarães moved between the scholarly and popular environments, between the diverse bodies of civil society and the power of the public, establishing connections between those "on top" and those "below," between "blacks" and "whites." Incidentally, with respect to her racial identity, she was a tightrope walker. She was aware of the disadvantages blacks had in relation to whites, because she must have experienced some problems related to her skin color; however, she did not make this a crutch or a source of insidious rebellion. Her racial identity was cosmetic, changing and continuously negotiated according to the circumstance, the people she was interacting with, and the place. She was betting that with education, work, asceticism, and perseverance, it would be possible to overcome the obstacles of life. Before demanding respect from whites, blacks believed they had to respect themselves first; that meant: learning how to read and write, mastering the rules of politesse and good manners, perfecting themselves culturally, working with resolution and honesty, having character, and being honorable and God-fearing, because whosoever walked a life of "virtue" was guaranteed a future of rewards, successes and social ascension.

The professor nurtured empathy in the masses and was even considered a great influencer of "traditions" in Laranjeiras among groups such as Ninho dos Gaviões and Laranjeirense and the *Nagô*, the fortress of the African tradition.[30] However, there is no evidence of her participation in the revelries, and that may be because she was concerned with maintaining her reputation. Her life was not a "whole, coherent and targeted set" that could or should be understood as a "unified expression of a subjective and objective intention," of an "original project";[31] however, she made herself by constructing the image of an "enlightened" person (courteous, refined and champion of morals and good customs) and, in that position, it was not advisable to adhere to the practices, symbols, rites, and Afro-diasporic cultural artifacts. If she were to be considered, for example, *xangozeira* (a venerator of Xango, an African Orixá) her good reputation would be stained or compromised.

That does not mean that Zizinha Guimarães had given up her role as a cultural agent and promoter. She dedicated herself to music, dance and theater. In the plays of the Escola Laranjeirense, she wrote scripts, rehearsed and directed the students and was still in charge of the dance and music, playing her own compositions on her piano, which was never far from her. As mentioned previously, the plays were of a pedagogical nature and generally approached historical, familiar, civic, and religious themes, with the intent to exalt the importance of traditional values, patriotism, and a bent towards the Catholic Church. Her artistic verve appeared in the important events of her school, as well as in the festivities of the city, notably the religious ones. She played the organ in the parish church, performing pieces by Chopin, Beethoven, Verdi, Carlos Gomes, Manuel Bahiense, in addition to some of her own compositions. As she had a preference for sacred music, she captured the audience with messages of the faith and love for the Coração de Jesus—the community she was a part of. She also held literary music festivals and dances in her home. Frequented by "distinct gentlemen and charming ladies of high society," the dances went until dawn to the sound of the piano, orchestra, or radiogram. The tone of the gatherings was nothing other than sociability and fraternization; however, this did not stop the young people from flirting, dating, and even arranging marriages.

In addition to her work in the education, religious, and cultural fields, Zizinha Guimarães participated in (when she wasn't leading) benevolent campaigns in the city such as the creation of the "Jardim da Infância," an orphanage to shelter abandoned and needy children;[32] support of the charity hospital; or even the renovations of the parish church.[33] With her personal dynamism, she became a reference point for social life in Laranjeiras. The name Zizinha Guimarães became synonymous with probity, virtue, and moral reserve. Her personal life, although characterized by discretion, brought an air of admiration and curiosity. Everything relating to her echoed and was discussed everywhere. "She had a slight flu," announced the newspaper *Vida Laranjeirense*, "our dear educator Ms. Zizinha Guimarães, whom we visited."[34] The press honored her and always referred to her with respect ("notable professor," "beloved educator," "genuine precept," "talented precept," "tireless and competent master"). When the *Vida Larnajeirense* defined a list of the most notable people of the city of the valley of Cotinguiba, in several areas, Zizinha Guimarães was nominated for teaching.[35] Already mature in age (around 62 years old), professionally renowned and respected by different social, political, and cultural segments of Laranjeiras, the professor received her first public tribute. In December of

1934, her students and former students prepared a "magnificent literary music festival" in the "Cine-Teatro Iris" to pay tribute:

> This afternoon in our lovely Cine-Teatro Iris, there will be a magnificent literary music festival, organized by a group of boys from the Aracaju society, in honor of the talented and esteemed professor Zizinha Guimarães. It will be a marvelous afternoon, carefully planned and the select program is divided into two charming parts.... Come one and all to the Iris cinema for this evocative and biblical afternoon.[36]

To this "magnificent literary music festival" flocked "innumerous families and people gladly from the capital and other locations in the state." On behalf of the students, the "intelligent" Francisco Tavares de Bragança took the floor and did not spare praise for his "dear master": "For you, the heartfelt messages of our affection and our gratitude, and in unison we shout: hail master, friend and mother! Three times hail our spiritual mother! Hail Zizina Guimarães!"[37] The "esteemed professor" was exalted, if not sacralized by students, former students and "countless families" from the capital and various locations in Sergipe. Her presumable qualities were addressed in the superlative: professional (master), "talented" and sensitive woman (friend) and protector (mother).

In the 1940s and 1950s, the economic decline of Laranjeiras became dire. Without its principal product generating wealth and with the consequent retraction of the network of trade and services, the city lost its lushness and glamour. This situation was aggravated by the construction of highways, which facilitated a grand exodus of the Aracaju population, the capital of the state, and other city centers. With the passage of time, Laranjeiras stagnated demographically—the population ranged from 11,350 inhabitants in 1890 to 11,158 inhabitants in 1940[38]—and suffered economically. No longer did it offer work opportunities, social progress and cultural splendor. The agenda was no longer to build, but rather destroy. The lavish mansions—ostentatious symbols of the wealthy families of yesteryear—were put up for sale with low prices. The decrepitude of the city was reflected in all areas and it was at this point that the Escola Laranjeirense showed the first signs of crisis. The number of enrolled students decreased each year. The school's income plummeted and barely covered the expenses. Without any savings, Zizinha Guimarães encountered the first financial problems.

On June 23, 1954, the newspaper *O Nordeste* published a virtually unpretentious memorandum: "The Escola Laranjeirense is preparing to celebrate, honorably, its fiftieth anniversary. All the former students of headmistress Zizinha Guimarães should attend the ceremonies because they, in part, represent them. 50 years of fruitful professorship! So much dedication and... patience, my goodness! Honors!"[39] The ironies of destiny. While the school was sinking, its owner was, paradoxically, being honored. On July 4, 1954, after 50 years of heading the school, Zizinha Guimarães was awarded with a golden anniversary plaque in a ceremony that joined former students, civil representatives and public authorities—for example, the patron was José do Faro Sobral, the mayor of the city.[40] This plaque, which she kept with love, was placed in a visible spot in her house. Times of emotions, but also of frustrations. Due to a strong flood caused by an overflow of the river Cotinguiba, the Escola Laranjeirense changed locations. The old home where the professor had enjoyed the best moments of her life and taught for decades—a townhouse built at the end of the 19th century—did not resist the impact of the water. She and her few students moved to a house located in Heráclito Diniz Gonçalves square. It was there that Zizinha Guimarães lived her last years. During this time she still worked with the Coração de Jesus Philharmonic Society, and in 1959, even allowed her space to be used for the election of the new board of the organization:

> The second day of August of nineteen fifty-nine, at eight in the evening, in the headquarters of the Escola Laranjeirense, in this city, under the leadership of professor Dona Eufrozina Guimarães, the current session for the selection of the new members of the board of the Sociedade Filarmônica Coração de Jesus was held... which are as follows: for Honorary president, the congressman Euvaldo Diniz Gonçalves; for Acting president, Mr. José de Faro Sobral, current mayor of this city; for Vice-President, Mr. Manoel Meneses dos Santos; for legal advisor, the state representative Temístocles Diniz Gonçalves.[41]

As the record of the election of the new board of the Coração de Jesus Philharmonic Society suggests, Zizinha Guimarães fed the cultural scene of Laranjeiras, weaving herself into a network of relationships made of the congressman, the state representative, and the mayor, among other important figures. The times, however, were different. She was already lacking energy. Very old, tired and almost alone, she watched her school wither and the children leave one by one. Such sadness! In the beginning of the 1960s, she became ill and unable to work. She became needy, lacking necessities, until even her students helped, offering "presents, contributing to a monthly allowance sufficient to cover her expenses." The government also helped "with a pension of Cr$10,000.00, in recognition of the merits of this professor of the generations."[42]

On March 31, 1964, a civil-military coup overthrew the democracy and implemented a dictatorship in Brazil. Zizinha Guimarães, at this point, was already living on the basis of a doctor's medical treatment and a full time caregiver. On December 18th that year, the *Sergipe Jornal* published a long interview with her: "I want to die giving Portuguese lessons, with the method of teaching that I was creating before I became sick"—this, in words "paused and cut by gasps," the declaration of Zizinha Guimarães, the "oldest and most loved professor of the state, who dedicated her entire life, in Laranjeiras, to the improved education of more than two generations." The *Sergipe Jornal* visited her and could see the grave state of her sickness that according to her doctor was "taking Dona Zizinha to her grave." Immobile in her bed, surrounded by her former female students—"now mothers"—the professor, 92 years old, still found the strength to sit up and consider the interview saying: "Ah! The *Sergipe Jornal*? They want to take a photo, is that right"?[43] Not even as a dying woman did she cease to be proud. Two weeks after the interview, after several health relapses, she passed away in her home on December 1, 1964.[44] In accordance with what she said to the *Sergipe Jornal*, she wanted her burial to be accompanied by percussion instruments: four snare drums, two drums, one bass drum, cymbals, and a muted trumpet playing the funeral march. Her wish came true.

Becoming a memory

Zizinha Guimarães did not marry or have children. Perhaps she suffered loneliness in some moment of her long life, but compensated for this lack of affection by strengthening her ties of friendship, kinship, Godparents, and especially dedicating herself "body and soul" to teaching. As it seems, she believed that teaching was an extension of motherhood—the main destiny of the woman. For this reason, each student was treated as a child and teaching as an activity of love and bestowal. She gave her self intensely to the education practice and influenced by religiousness, she perceived her craft as a ministry, a mission of God, more so than a profession. Her story dates back to a time in which women were bound to fulfill the role of mother, wife, and daughter, busying themselves with the gifts of the home (cooking, sewing, and embroidery) and hardly learned basic studies. In spite of (and perhaps, because of) that, she constructed in the classroom, and in other social spaces, her own diverse forms of dealing with gender relations. If the social institutions and the "competent" discourses, among them being journalists, doctors, and lawyers produced and reproduced degrading discourse, it is important to emphasize that the specific subjects "did not always fill, or literally follow the terms prescribed by society" (Scott, 1995, p. 88).

After her death, Zizinha Guimarães received a series of homages, through use (and overuse) of remembrance.[45] In addition to the building of her bust in public places, ceremony events, masses celebrated every December 26th—her birth date—she was quoted in public speeches, chronicles, and poetry. However, the principal tribute to her memory was in 1986. During the administration of the governor João Alves Filho—a black politician and member of the Partido Democrático Social (PDS)—discussed restoring the Escola Laranjeirense building. As the Afro-Sergipean professor did not leave any heirs, the building of the school was taken by the town of Laranjeiras and afterward given to the state. João Alves then determined that the Colégio Estadual de Primeiro e Segundo Grau (primary and high school) Professora Zizinha Guimarães would be erected in its place. Inaugurated with the Decree no. 7,882 on July 1st of that year,[46] in an event that included important authorities (João Alves

Filho, governor of Sergipe; João Gomes Cardoso Barreto, state secretary of Education and Culture; José Sizino da Rocha, the state business secretary; José Monteiro Sobral, mayor of the municipality) and the public,[47] the school signified the consecration of the memory of the professor in the valley of Cotinguiba. From that point, it became almost impossible not to hear the name Zizinha Guimarães; after all, the school that bears her name is a "place of memory"—a "testimonial mark of another time, of the illusions of eternity," where there still beats a glacial and contemplative "symbolic life" (Nora, 1993, p. 13-4). Moreover, the school is a cultural reference in the region and very popular in Laranjeiras—not to mention that today it is the only high school in the city.

Zizinha Guimarães strived to create a perfect image of herself. To this end, she sought to hone her professional skills and have exemplary, impeccable personal conduct, placing herself into a complex chain of cultural bargains, social seams, and political influences peddling and still she dealt with her racial identity. The Afro-Sergipean professor little addressed this subject through her life—so tough during her time. She was not blind to the inequality of opportunities between blacks and whites and it is possible that she had articulated some level of racial pride. However, instead of making herself a victim or revolting against the system, she preferred to believe in the universal values of education, culture, work, and righteousness—in sum, of merit. The black person who embraced these values would be, to her, sooner or later, recognized by his or her potential and works.

Currently, Zizinha Guimarães is remembered by the clientele that attend the school that bears her name, by the booklets on the cultural patrimony of Laranjeiras, by the local press,[48] by her former students who became people of influence in the political and cultural life of Sergipe, by people who maintained contact with those who studied with her, and on a smaller scale, by all those who know the history of education in the state. The group, Ninho dos Gaviões, which was one of the supporters, still parades through the streets of Laranjeiras each year and some older members keep deep in their memory the image of their professor.[49] Her musical compositions and sacred hymns are, even today, played in ceremonies of the parish church. More than "living" after death, she earned a position of highlight in the gallery of the immortals of the city that is a "nursery of Sergipean culture."

In an interview with me, Ms. Valdete Sizino da Rocha spoke of Zizinha Guimarães with enthusiasm and nostalgia for more than 40 minutes and did not hide the pride she felt for the old professor. At the end of the interview, when I questioned: "Ms. Valdete, do you have anything else to add? Feel free." To my surprise the interviewee became introspective, searching for something inside a folder. All of a sudden, she found a single sheet of paper and began to read a text previously prepared: "Today we are left with the memory and the longing of she who, in life, was known to have dignity, loyalty and kindness in all aspects without tarnishing her humble but hardworking, precious, and innovative ministry." The text was almost an epitaph and in the measure that Ms. Valdete read it, it would be moving to utter the last words: "Everything good and beautiful existed in the Escola Laranjeirense, I thank God for having given me a professor with her selfless hands, her intelligence, her teachings and love. I am who I am today thanks to Ms. Zizinha."[50]

The history of the Afro-Sergipean professor comes from being told and retold in celebratory, romanticized and sacralized narratives. It includes those who consider her "to be the greatest figure in Laranjeiras of all time." Obviously, this hyperbolic representation does not correspond to someone who existed in flesh and blood, as much as a myth. And "by being partly real, partly constructed, by being the result of a collective drafting process," the myth—to take the words of José Murilo de Carvalho (1990, p. 14)—"tells us less about itself than that what society produces." The "mythification" necessarily implies the transmutation of a real figure in order to turn it into an archetype of values or collective aspirations, and its vitality rests in the capacity to be renewed continuously by memory.

Notes

1. *Sergipe Jornal*, Aracaju, 2 Dec. 1964, p. 1.

2. *Gazeta de Sergipe*, Aracaju, 3 Dec. 1964, p. 1.

3. *Sergipe Jornal*, Aracaju, 3 Dec. 1964, p. 1; *Gazeta de Sergipe*, Aracaju, 3 Dec. 1964, p. 1, and Andrade, 1985, p. 13-4.

4. Registro de batismo [Registry of Baptisms] no. 2 (1871-77), Book 1 "a," da Igreja da Matriz Sagrado Coração de Jesus, Laranjeiras (SE).

5. See Azevedo, 1971.

6. See "Diário do Imperador D. Pedro II na sua visita a Sergipe em janeiro de 1860." [Diary of the Emperor Dom Pedro II on his Visit to Sergipe in January of 1860]. *Revista do Instituto Histórico e Geográfico de Sergipe, Aracaju*, [Journal of the Historical and Geographical Institute of Sergipe, Aracaju], v. XXI, n. 26, v. XXI, p. 72-3, 1961-65.

7. *O Laranjeirense*, Laranjeiras, 20 May 1888.

8. See Subrinho, 2000, p. 315.

9. In 1902, Eufrozina Guimarães became the sole owner of the property. See Registro de imóvel, matrícula no. 3.096, Livro 3-F, f. 285 e matrícula 3.097, Livro 3-F, f 285, Cartório do 2.º Ofício Alenir Goes Leite Vieira, Laranjeiras (SE).

10. Oliveira, 1981, p. 150.

11. See Dávila, 2006.

12. *Vida Laranjeirense*, Laranjeiras, 25 May 1930, p. 2.

13. *Vida Laranjeirense*, Laranjeiras, 17 Aug. 1930, p. 1.

14. *Vida Laranjeirense*, Laranjeiras, 5 Apr. 1931, p. 3.

15. *Vida Laranjeirense*, Laranjeiras, 25 May 1930, p. 3; 16 Dec. 1934, p. 4.

16. *Alavanca*, Laranjeiras, 1.º Jan. 1972, p. 2.

17. *Vida Laranjeirense*, Laranjeiras, 23 Jul. 1930, p. 4; *Vida Laranjeirense*, Laranjeiras, 7 Jun. 1931, p. 4.

18. *Vida Laranjeirense*, Laranjeiras, 17 May 1931, p. 2.

19. *Vida Laranjeirense*, Laranjeiras, 5 Apr. 1931, p. 2.

20. Caderneta no. 40 da Escola Laranjeirense, aluna Valdete Sizino da Rocha, curso primário, professora Eufrozina Guimarães [School Register No. 40 of the Laranjeiras School, student Valdete Sizinho da Rocha, Primary Level, Professor Eufrozina Guimarães], Laranjeiras (SE), February 1943.

21. The textbook "natural sciences," for example, was that of Acrísio Cruz, no date.

22. *Vida Laranjeirense*, Laranjeiras, 9 Dec. 1934, p. 4.

23. The Escola Laranjeirense regularly integrated the celebrations of the 7th of September sponsored by the "municipality." See *Vida Laranjeirense*, Laranjeiras, 9 Sep. 1934, p. 3.

24. *Vida Laranjeirense*, Laranjeiras, 25 May 1930, p. 1.

25. *Vida Laranjeirense*, Laranjeiras, 1 Jun. 1930, p. 3.

26. *Vida Laranjeirense*, Laranjeiras, 26 Jun. 1932, p. 1.

27. *Vida Laranjeirense*, Laranjeiras, 25 Jun. 1933, p. 1.

28. *Vida Laranjeirense*, Laranjeiras, 23 Apr. 1933, p. 1.

29. *Vida Laranjeirense*, Laranjeiras, 13 Jan. 1935, p. 5.

30. See Dantas, 1988, p. 226.

31. See Bourdieu, 2002, p. 184.

32. *Vida Laranjeirense*, Laranjeiras, 12 Jul. 1931, p. 1.

33. *Vida Laranjeirense*, Laranjeiras, 9 Dec. 1934, p. 6.

34. *Vida Laranjeirense*, Laranjeiras, 24 Aug. 1930, p. 4.

35. *Vida Laranjeirense*, Laranjeiras, 21 Oct. 1934, p. 4.

36. *Vida Laranjeirense*, Laranjeiras, 23 Dec. 1934, p. 1.

37. *Vida Laranjeirense*, Laranjeiras, 16 Dec. 1934, p. 4.

38. *Sinopse estatística do município de Laranjeiras, Estado de Sergipe: principais resultados censitários*. [Statistical Synopsis of the Municipal Province of Laranjeiras, State of Sergipe: Principal Census Results]. Rio de Janeiro: Instituto Brasileiro de Geografia e Estatística, 1948, p. 13.

39. *O Nordeste*, Aracaju, 23 Jun. 1954, p. 4.

40. *O Nordeste*, Aracaju, 17 Jul. 1954, p. 4.

41. Ata da reunião da diretoria da Sociedade da Filarmônica Coração de Jesus nesta cidade de Laranjeiras, em 2/8/1959, Livro de atas da Filarmônica Coração de Jesus, Arquivo Público Municipal de Laranjeiras. [Act of the Meeting of the Directorate of the Philharmonic Society Coração de Jesus in the City of Laranjeiras, on 2/8/1959, Book of Acts of the Philharmonic Coração de Jesus, Public Archive of the Municipal Province of Laranjeiras].

42. *Sergipe Jornal*, Aracaju, 18 Nov. 1964, p. 2.

43. *Sergipe Jornal*, Aracaju, 18 Nov. 1964, p. 2.

44. Certidão de óbito de [Certificate of Death of] Eufrozina Amélia Guimarães, Livro C, no. 20, Cartório do 2.º Ofício Alenir Goes Leite Vieira, Laranjeiras (SE).

45. On the concept of memory, its senses, meanings and implications, see Le Goff, 2003; Pollak, 1989 and 1992; Ricoeur, 2007; Nora, 1993.
46. *Diário Oficial de Sergipe*, no. 20.142, Aracaju, 2 Jul. 1986, p. 5.
47. Interview by the author with Ginaldo dos Santos, Director of the Colégio Estadual Profª Zizinha Guimarães, Laranjeiras (SE), on 6 Jun. 2011.
48. "Zizinha Guimarães," *O Liberal*, Laranjeiras, Apr. 2011, p. 10.
49. Interview by the author with Maria Gilene Andrade, communication advisor of Associação Recreativa Ninho dos Gaviões, 68 years old, Laranjeiras (SE), on 8 Jun. 2011.
50. Interview by the author with Valdete Sizino da Rocha, 83 years old, Laranjeiras (SE), on 7 Jun. 2011.

Bibliography

Amaral, Sharyse Piroupo do. *Escravidão, liberdade e resistência em Sergipe: Cotinguiba, 1860-1888*. [Slavery, Liberty and Resistance in Sergipe: Cotinguiba 1860-1888]. 2007. Diss. (Doctorate in History) – Universidade Federal da Bahia (UFBA), Salvador.

Andrade, Antônio Gomes de. "Zizinha Guimarães – espírito inovador." [Zizinha Guimarães – Innovative Spirit]. *Caderno de Cultura do Estudante*, São Cristóvão, n. 2, p. 13-4, 1985.

Avé-Lallemant, Robert. *Viagens pelas províncias da Bahia, Pernambuco, Alagoas e Sergipe (1859)*. [Travels Through the Provinces of Bahia, Pernambuco, Alagoas, and Sergipe (1859)]. Belo Horizonte: Itatiaia; São Paulo: Edusp, 1980.

Azevedo, Camerino Bragança de. *Doutor Bragança, esse varão Laranjeirense*. [Dr. Bragança, this Laranjeira Man]. [Traces of the Past]. Aracaju: s/ed., 1983.

Bourdieu, Pierre. "A ilusão biográfica." [Biographical Illusion]. In Amado, Janaína; Ferreira, Marieta de Moraes. (Orgs.). *Usos e abusos da história oral*. [Uses and Abuses of Oral History]. 5. ed. Rio de Janeiro: Editora da FGV, 2002.

Carvalho, José Murilo de. *A formação das almas: o imaginário da República no Brasil*. [The Formation of Souls: Imagining the Republico f Brazil]. São Paulo: Companhia das Letras, 1990.

Cunha, Euclides da. *Os sertões*. [Rebellion in the Backlands]. 39. ed. Rio de Janeiro: Livraria Francisco Alves; Publifolha, 2000 [1902].

Dantas, Beatriz Góis. *Vovó nagô e papai branco: usos e abusos da África no Brasil*. [Yoruba Grandpa and White Daddy: Uses and Abuses of África in Brazil]. Rio de Janeiro: Graal, 1988.

. "Laranjeiras: entre o passado e o presente." [Laranjeiras: Between the Past and the Present]. In: Nogueira, Adriana Dantas; Silva, Eder Donizeti da. (Orgs.). *O despertar do conhecimento na colina azulada: a Universidade Federal de Sergipe em Laranjeiras.* São Cristóvão: Ed. Universidade Federal de Sergipe, 2009, v. 2.

Dávila, Jerry. *Diploma da brancura: política social e racial no Brasil (1917-1945).* [A Degree in Whiteness: Social and Racial Politics in Brazil (1917-1945)]. São Paulo: Editora Unesp, 2006.

Diário Do Imperador D. Pedro II na sua visita a Sergipe em janeiro de 1860.[The Diary of Emperor Dom Pedro II on his Visit to Sergipe in January of 1860]. *Revista do Instituto Histórico e Geográ- fico de Sergipe*, Aracaju, v. XXI, n. 26, p. 72-3, 1961-65.

Fontes, Lauro Barreto. "A casa da escola da Professora Zizinha." [The School House of Professor Zizinha]. In *O vendedor de arco-íris: crônicas*. Salvador: s/ed., 1984.

Guimarães, Eufrozina. *Noções de geografia* (compilações). [Notions of Geography]. 2. ed. Laranjeiras: Escola Laranjeirense, s/d.

LeGoff, Jacques. *História e memória*. [History and Memory]. 5. ed. Campinas: Ed. da Unicamp, 2003.

Lima Barreto, Afonso Henriques de. *Clara dos Anjos*. [Clara of the Angels]. São Paulo: Brasiliense, 1956 [1923-24].

Louro, Guacira Lopes. "Mulheres na sala de aula." [Women in the Classroom]. In Del Priore, Mary. (Org.). *História das mulheres no Brasil*. [History of Women in Brazil]. 2. ed. São Paulo: Contexto, 1997.

Nina Rodrigues, Raimundo. *Os africanos no Brasil*. [Africans in Brazil]. 4. ed. São Paulo: Nacional; Brasília, INL, 1976 [1933].

Nora, Pierre. "Entre memória e história: a problemática dos lugares." [Between Memory and history: the Problematics of Place]. *Projeto História*. São Paulo, PUC, n. 10, p. 13-4, 1993.

Oliveira, Philadelpho Jonathas de. *História de Laranjeiras: registro dos fatos históricos de Laranjeiras.* [History of Laranjeiras: Registry of Historical Facts of Laranjeiras]. 2. ed. Aracaju: Subsecretaria de Cultura da Secretaria de Educação e Cultura do Estado de Sergipe, 1981 [1942].

Pollak, Michael. "Memória, esquecimento, silêncio." [Memory, Forgetting, and Silence]. *Estudos Históricos*. Rio de Janeiro, v. 2, n. 3, p. 3-15, 1989.

. "Memória e identidade social." [Memory and Social Identity]. *Estudos Históricos*. Rio de Janeiro, v. 5, n. 10, p. 200-12, 1992.

Ricoeur, Paul. *A memória, a história, o esquecimento*. [Memory, History and Forgetting]. Campinas: Ed. da Unicamp, 2007.

Romero Sílvio. *Estudos sobre a poesia popular do Brasil*. [Studies in Popular Poetry of Brazil]. 2. ed. Petrópolis: Vozes, 1977 [1888].

Scott, Joan. "Gênero: uma categoria útil de análise histórica." [Gender: a Useful Category for Historical Analysis]. *Educação e Realidade*. Porto Alegre, v. 20, n. 2, p. 88, 1995.

Sinopse Estatística do município de Laranjeiras, Estado de Sergipe: principais resultados censitários. [Statistical Synpsis of the Municipality of Laranjeiras, Sergipe State: Principal Census Results]. Rio de Janeiro: Instituto Brasileiro de Geografia e Estatística, 1948.

Subrinho, Josué Modesto dos Passos. *Reordenamento do trabalho: trabalho escravo e trabalho livre no Nordeste açucareiro, Sergipe (1850-1930)*. [Reordainment of Work: Slave Labor and Free Labor in the Northeast Sugar Plantations, Sergipe (1850-1930)]. Aracaju: Funcaju, 2000.

18

"AROUND THE WORLD" WITH WOMEN OF CAPOEIRA: GENDER AND BLACK CULTURE IN BRAZIL, 1850-1920

Antonio Liberac Cardoso Simões Pires

Many people have had the opportunity to watch *capoeira* players in the streets, public squares and in *capoeira* centers, in Brazil and in other countries. In a field study from 1995, in the city of Montpellier, in France, I observed the significant presence of female *capoeira* players, especially in *capoeira* centers, where they formed the majority.[1] The large presence of women in *capoeira* is, without a doubt, a peculiar phenomenon from the end of the second half of the 20th century. Seeing that in the last decades of the century *capoeira* entered a phase of international expansion, the *mestres* and professors—based on a characterization of the practice as art, physical education, musicality, and theatre—have treated it as a national symbol. During this time, women have adhered to the practice of *capoeira* with enthusiasm. However, those who think the females were not present in *capoeira* in previous periods are mistaken. Women were already present in the ritual of *N'golo*, which appears to be the African origin of the practice of *capoeira* that brings us to the pre-colonial period. *N'golo* is also known as the "dance of the Zebra"; it is a mixture of dance, religious theatre and an initiation ritual that developed in what is now the south of Angola. In this ritual, the warriors played and fought amongst themselves to later choose women for sexual initiation. The winners chose among women of their ethnicity: those that were seen as the most beautiful in their cultural traditions. Thus, this ritual of the Bantu of central-west Africa inspired the birth of the oldest elements of *capoeira* such as the aspects of fighting disguised as dance, movements of agility, songs, and rhythms that went on to be further developed in the African Diaspora, eventually becoming consolidated as a martial art (Desch-Obi, 2008, p. 16).

I believe that there are continuities in the practices and meaning of the cultural phenomena that arrived in the Americas through the body and soul of Africans. Certainly, *N'golo* remained, in some form, while the *capoeira* slaves left their marks, creating new meanings and new ways of practicing *capoeira*. Women who appeared in *N'golo* as the prize to be disputed among the *capoeira* warriors, remained present in the practice of *capoeira* in slaveholding Brazil, often for the same reason. Let us now elaborate the sources and the history of the elements of *capoeira* in order to understand how women participated in this process, as an invention of traditions in Brazil.

Sources and History of Capoeira

From the end of the 18th century in Rio de Janeiro,[2] the police sought to constrain the practice of *capoeira*, using it to their own advantage (Bandeira de Mello, 1904, p. 5):

> At the time of the viceroys, there was no police force, there were different regiments that provided contingents for night patrol and there were police agents—wrapped in mantles with a sword under their arm—commanded by a corporal, who roamed the streets at night....

A group of residents chose such police agents. Of each area, the agent chosen would serve for three years, having 20 men under his command. It was during this time, with hooded guards and torches to light the streets of the city, that the first accounts which mention *capoeira* arise. It was through one of the most famous police officers that *capoeira* entered the literature in the late 18th century: Major Vidigal, who in moments of deep trance would abandon his weapons to defend himself with kicks and head butts, armed with only a knife and a stick. Miguel Nunes Vidigal was his name; he was born in the old captaincy of Rio de Janeiro in Angra dos Reis, in the second half of the 18th century. Vidigal provided important services: he captured runaway slaves, removed the *quilombos* from the hill of Santa Tereza, arrested *capoeira* players and closed witchcraft and Candomblé houses.[3]

But, it was after the founding of the Civil Police in 1908, and the Military Police in 1909, that we find more frequent accounts of *capoeiras* in historical sources. From 1810 to 1821, among the 4,853 arrests made by the police in the city of Rio de Janeiro, 438 (9 percent) were accusations of the practice of *capoeira* (Algranti, 1988, p. 157). During this time, *capoeira* players formed groups and intervened in the power relations in the urban space of the city of Rio de Janeiro, in the relations between the slaves and owners, and among the slaves themselves.

However, while the state was organized by its institutions, the groups of enslaved and free workers also intensified the links of socialization. *Capoeira* activity was concerning to the authorities, who decided to adopt measures against them: "slaves arrested for this practice would be turned in to the Corrections Office to receive due punishment," as approved by the Minister of Justice at the time.

The statistics published by the North American historian Thomas Holloway in the early 1950s shows how the repression of *capoeira* groups intensified in the first half of the 19th century. The author indicates that of the 81 arrested for *capoeira* in Calabouço (the prison for slaves) between 1852 and 1858, 66 (81.5 percent) were beaten, an average of 81 lashes per person, and two received hand lashes, an average of 42 each. However, the slave owners protested various times against the excessive punishment and principally against the forced labor: practices that temporarily impeded the use of the labor for their advantage. The punishment of lashes, however, did not reach the free workers who began to appear in the police documentation, which made the repression of the *capoeira* culture more difficult and complex in the city of Rio de Janeiro (Holloway, 1989, p. 134). The organization of the *capoeira* groups strengthened in the second half of the 19th century. The *capoeira* players that were arrested and identified as belonging to a "gang" were subject to more severe punishment. The title of "gangs" became a fixture in the language of police institutions dealing with *capoeira* groups in the city of Rio de Janeiro.

In the second half of the 19th century, the number of records available on *capoeira* is overwhelming for any historian who is not accustomed to the arduous work of collection from public archives. The sources for study are varied and mention of *capoeira* groups and players appear in general literature, journalistic sources, in the Annals of the House of Representatives and principally in judicial and police documentation.

The Report of the Minister and Secretary of the Affairs of Justice in the Legislative Assembly of 1872 shows the state's levels of understanding on the importance of the activities of the *capoeira* groups. The reporter clarifies that they formed a type of society divided into neighborhoods. For the relator, the police forces found it difficult to act in a repressive and effective manner because many of them had been "members of the national guard, retired from the army or the navy, or craftsmen of the Naval arsenals" (Pires, 2010, p. 25). The presence of military men among the ranks of the *capoeira* societies largely reflects the significant participation of the *capoeira* players in the trenches of the Paraguayan war. It also reflects the deepening of the social and political relationships involving the *capoeira* groups in the city of Rio de Janeiro.

In 1878, the Report of the Minister and Secretary of the Affairs of Justice was devastating to the practice of *capoeira*. The report confirmed that any activity relating to *capoeira* should be categorized as a special crime, punishable with new penalties under the authority of the police. Foreign participants would be deported and nationals would be exiled to military colonies. There were numerous foreigners among *capoeira* participants in the 19th century. They included Portuguese, Italians, Spanish and various other nationalities. *Capoeira* groups became fundamental pieces in the political game of the monarchist regime. They formed the armed branch of the political parties during electoral disputes.[4] It is in this context that the forces of social control began to act against the *capoeira* groups.

Until 1890, at the dawn of the Republic, the practice of *capoeira* was prohibited by municipal or provincial codes and by legislative decrees, generally by ministerial request. In the 19th century *capoeira* was concentrated in the city of Rio de Janeiro; however, we can also see its presence in Salvador, Belém do Pará and Recife. Beginning in the last decade of the 19th century, *capoeira* became officially repressed and was included in article 402 of the republican penal code of 1890 which prohibited its practice, characterizing it as "movements of agility," "groups on the run," "disorderly practices," and "the use of weapons," principally being razors and knives. *Capoeira* groups were called *maltas de capoeiras* (*capoeira* gangs) and the application of the previously cited Article 402 created around 560 criminal trials in the justice system of the city of Rio de Janeiro. However, the trials generated by this law do not appear in the judicial system of Salvador, Belém do Pará, or Recife, which reveals a clear differentiation in the culture of restraining *capoeira* from city to city. The legal documentation used in Salvador and Belém do Pará, where *capoeira* groups appear, is Article 303 of the penal code of 1890, which dealt with physical offenses. We find some women participants among the defendants and victims of such offenses.

I will now describe the participation of females in the practice of *capoeira*, more specifically between 1850 and 1920, in Rio de Janeiro, Salvador, and Belém do Pará. But first, it is fitting to highlight that over the course of the 20th century, the practice of *capoeira* was removed from the penal code, undergoing social transformations related to its participants and their rituals. Under the headings of sport and arts, *capoeira* underwent a process of inclusion and incorporation into the concepts of modernity and progress. Intellectuals on the level of Coelho Neto, Luiz Murat, and Germano Haslocher placed *capoeira* on the cultural agenda, defending it as a sport. It is in this process of inventing a new tradition for *capoeira* that the proposals came for Bahian *capoeira*, giving rise to the playfulness of *capoeira* in practice (Pires, 2010, p. 139). Bahian *capoeira*, in its regional and Angolan styles, became hegemonic—bringing multiplicity into aspects of dance, sport, fighting, and art. The expansion of the practice of *capoeira* reached international borders and solidified itself in the cultural field as a symbol of Brazilian-ness, of ethnicity, becoming an object of many disciplinary approaches. The sources on *capoeira* in the 20th century are innumerable, and they constantly note the feminine presence in *capoeira*. Today, we can find women practicing *capoeira* in any *capoeira* center in the rural areas or in the Brazilian capitals, in European countries, Asia, North America, or Latin America.

Women and Capoeira in the 19th Century

As previously mentioned, between 1850 and 1920 there was a significant feminine participation in the practice of *capoeira* in Rio de Janeiro, Salvador, and Belém do Pará. According to legend, at the time when the *capoeira* gangs of the 19th century infested the cities of Rio de Janeiro, Belém, and Salvador, many women played the role of hiding weapons and giving them out during big fights between enemies. In my research, I found various documents in which women appear linked to the practice of *capoeira* since the 19th century. The Rio de Janeiro newspaper, *O Comércio*, published news on January 29, 1878, divulging the imprisonment of some of the women who fought in public places and proved to be "experts in *capoeira*" (Líbano Soares, 1999, p. 17). The specialized bibliography also shows women in the 19th century world of *capoeira* in Belém do Pará. The historians Josivaldo Pires de Oliveira and Luiz Augusto Pinheiro Leal (2009, p. 122) highlight the female presence in the practice of *capoeira* with a document regarding the "imprisonment of Jerônima, slave of Caetano Antonio de Lemos, fined for breaking the public order with the practice of *capoeira*." Another very significant document described by the authors in this respect is what I transcribe below:

> The reigning group of *capoeira* women... coming from the alley, ran into a dark-skinned woman—thin and disheveled—gesticulating and hurling insults. Soon after, another woman appeared—older—who tried to calm the skinny woman with kind words and good manners.

> What, then. The disheveled woman jumped in front of the other like a *capoeira* player (Oliveira and Pinheiro Leal, 2009, p. 150).

It clearly appears to be a fight, perhaps two working women, possibly street vendors, maybe even selling their own bodies. It was the reign of women of the streets of the city of Belém, as Pinheiro Leal stated. But what reign was this? I believe it refers to the realm of the streets, where there were micro-social powers negotiated in daily life that were revealed by clues that were not always clear, but they showed the existence of codes that interfered in the day to day dynamics in the cities. *Capoeira* was in the body of that anonymous woman, a defense weapon in body to body combat, in the game of power on the streets, among women themselves.

Another tale of women of *capoeira* in the city of Belém in the 19th century reveals the fight between a fireman and a *capoeira* woman of great courage and physical agility. The fireman was in full pursuit of a boy who was traveling with a tray on his head, a salesman, a delivery boy, perhaps a *caxinguelê*, that is, a young male practitioner of *capoeira*. A woman, seeing the scene, attacked the fireman, "when he looked as if he would use force, raising his hand to strike a blow, she surprised him; she made a small turn and a tremendous blow thundered in the face of the fireman. New display of bravado. Another *capoeira* move from the woman and…wham!"[5] The event occurred in 1893, after the approval of the penal code of 1890, when the practice of *capoeira* was criminalized throughout all of Brazil. This event did not create a criminal trial based on Article 402, but it certainly reveals the feminine presence in the world of *capoeira* in the city of Belém do Pará. The women also appear as members of *capoeira* gangs in the city of Rio de Janeiro. The work of Rugendas (1972, p. 55) masterfully reveals this aspect:

JOGAR CAPOEIRA
ou danse de la guerre

One can observe, according to the work of Rugendas (above), the presence of women in the "*capoeira* gangs." We see knives or razors, playfulness of the palms and of the *Tambor de Guerra* drum, and of course, the presence of black saleswomen. *Ô nega, o que vendes aí?*[6] ("Hey lady, what are you selling"?—*Nega* is an affectionate term for a black woman). Maybe she is selling typical regional dishes such as *angu* (Brazilian polenta), *mingau* (corn porridge) or *mungunzá* (a sweetened hot corn cereal made with cinnamon and cloves) to be heated and stirred in her pan over the fire in her cooker. Another is carrying her basket of fruits on her head. Saleswomen and slaves-for-hire were the daily companions of *capoeira* groups. It was in the world of the streets that women got involved with the culture of *capoeira*, participating in *rodas* (circular formation for playing *capoeira*), and in the drama between rival groups; they also learned to develop their "movements of agility."

Old *capoeira* chants in the public domain, produced by practitioners of *capoeira*, mention women in the 19th century: "Hey lady, what are you selling there? I am selling rice from Maranhão. Hey lady, what are you selling there? My master sent me to sell. Hey lady, what are you selling there"? Everything suggests that this old chant portrays a street saleswoman, a slave-for-hire, just as the artistic work of Mauricio Rugendas also reproduces.

The Criminalization of Capoeira and Women in the early 20th Century

At the end of the 19th century, right after the criminalization of *capoeira*, criminal processes were introduced by way of Article 402 of the penal code of 1890 in the city of Rio de Janeiro, and by way of Article 303 of the same penal code in the cities of Salvador, Belém do Pará, and possibly other locations. A vast array of journalistic documentation that dealt with *capoeira* also appears in addition to the revealing *capoeira* chants:

> *Dona Maria do Camboata,ela chega na venda e manda bota. Dona Maria do Camboata, ela disse que deu, ela disse que da. Dona Maria do Camboata, da rabo de arraia com as pernas para ar. Dona Maria do Camboata, ela chega na roda querendo joga.*[7]
>
> Miss Maria do Camboatá, she arrives to sell and says take it all. Miss Maria do Camboatá, she said she gave (fought), she said she gives (fights). Miss Maria do Camboatá, she does a *rabo de arraia* (*capoeira* move) with her legs in the air. Miss Maria do Camboatá, she arrives in the circle wanting to play.

The story being told here is that a saleswoman comes to a *capoeira roda* and puts her merchandise down and joins the game. The lyric about the move she performs suggests that Dona Maria is skilled at *capoeira*, regularly attending *rodas*.

This chant recalls the presence of a famous "*capoeira* woman" in the *rodas* of the first half of the 20th century in the city of Salvador. She became a symbol of the female presence. For her, an image of a valiant woman was created; a woman who fought with men and lived in the streets and pubs of the city of Salvador. Perhaps she was a masculinized stereotype, such as the case of the other famous woman in the *capoeira rodas* nicknamed "Maria Homem"(Maria-Man).[8] Another woman who became legendary in the city of Salvador was the "prostitute Chicão" (a masculinized augmentative ending to the common nickname Chica), the nickname of Francisca Albino dos

Santos who became famous when she attacked one of the most important *capoeira* players in that city: the famous Pedro Porreta, one of the *capoeira* leaders in the area of Pilar (Rego, 1968, p. 232).

According to the bibliographic sources regarding studies on *capoeira* in Salvador, Rio de Janeiro, and Belém in the first decades of the 20th century, women appear rarely, and with little power because of a profoundly masculinized culture.

Capoeira was a constant target of police repression in the 19th century and in the first half of the 20th century. I believe that the documentation coming from this repression clearly reveals the presence of *capoeira* among the women who were generally restricted to certain characters such as prostitutes and workers of the city streets. Furthermore, the first half of the 20th century brings mention of Salomé, a distinguished *capoeira* player. A *capoeira* chant eternalized her: "Adão, Adão, cadê Salomé Adão? Foi para a Ilha de Maré.... Adão, Adão, cadê Salomé Adão? Foi passear...." ("Adam, Adam, where is Salomé, Adam? She went to the Island of Maré. Adam, Adam, where is Salomé? She went for a walk....") (Rego, 1968, p. 136). Salomé seems to have been a woman who was able to penetrate the masculine world of *capoeira*, learning its secrets, interacting with the people and developing her *capoeira* game. When the women didn't invade this masculinized world of *capoeira*, participating in the fight, they were the motive for the fights, as in the following examples.

On December 1, 1913, in a building on the Rua do Pilar street in Salvador, there was a fight between individuals belonging to rival *capoeira* groups. Tico, Martins, and Júlio ended up fighting with razors and knives over Maria Margarida da Conceição. They were all arrested and charges were filed. They were later acquitted.[9] It is important to note the culture of *capoeira* in its distinguished elements, such as the precise use of the razor, and understanding the female place in the universe of *capoeira*. The women were disputed, loved, owned by the *capoeira* groups and players; sometimes they became the motives of feuds at work, in the prostitution houses, in the streets and in the pubs of the city.

Another case revealing these relations involves the famous *capoeira* player, Pedro Mineiro. He was arrested on August 28, 1909 for being armed with a knife and bludgeon; this also occurred in a building on Rua do Pilar street in Salvador. The fight happened because of Maria, "a woman of easy virtue." Cândido Brito, another man involved in the conflict, had booked a room with Maria, the concubine of the famous Pedro Mineiro whose name was Pedro José Vieira. It is likely that Pedro Mineiro was in love with Maria and he did not allow the sexual encounter to happen.[10] Some *capoeira* players were always involved with the world of prostitution because another conflict happened in 1910 when the same Pedro Mineiro beat Isaura Maria da Silva, a 15-year-old girl. The motive, again, was excessive jealousy.[11]

Pedro Mineiro's involvement with the prostitutes of Largo da Sé and the surrounding areas led to his death. It happened on December 26, 1926, one day after the Christmas celebrations. A group of sailors from Destroyer Piauí were having a meal in the "Galinho" bar on Saldanha street when a group of *capoeira* players invaded the place. They were the famous Pedro Mineiro, Sebastião, and Antônio, according to the newspaper *Diário de Notícias*, all "covert police," those that worked as police informants.[12] The two groups started to fight and one of the possible motives could have been the sailor who wanted to leave with Maria José, another of Pedro Mineiro's lovers, or maybe the fact that the sailor had left without paying. However, this detail is not clear in the documentation. The conflict went beyond the bar and into the streets. The sailors were Cândido, Joaquim, and Francisco—the last two dying in the fight. The ones who died were natives of Alagoas, first and second class sailors, respectively. They were all arrested and sent to the police station by the command of the ship captain of Naval Forces from Rio de Janeiro. Inside the police station, Cândido—the survivor of the conflict who fought alongside his fellow sailors—drew his revolver and shot Pedro Mineiro three times. Pedro died of these bullet wounds on January 15, 1915.[13]

This is how the saga of the famous Pedro Mineiro ended and once again the feminine presence reveals to us aspects of the relations developed by the men of *capoeira*. They built power relations into public spaces and into their productive activities. Prostitution was one of them. They had to protect their women, defend them from sex-hungry sailors, low prices, and at the same time allow the prostitutes to earn their own money (with a little left over for them). Pedro Mineiro, as revealed by his women, was part of a "secret police," maybe a monarchist, an electoral henchman, a representative of the political scenario of the Old Republic, which included figures such as the swindler, the fearless fighter, and the macho man.[14] His women on the streets had to be of the same "suit" and as such were Maria Homem, Salomé, Chicão and other *capoeira* players in the city of São Salvador.

The catalogued material regarding *capoeira*-related criminal trials based on Article 303, physical aggressions, of the penal code of 1890 in Salvador consists of 92 criminal trials with just 3 percent placing women in the position of defendant; however, with women as victims, this number increases to 10 percent.

Let's go to the description of two trials representative of the culture of *capoeira* involving women:

> Around eight o'clock she was in the window waiting for the milk man when Rufina, a friend, appeared asking if she knew about the health of a sick woman named Mariquinha, a friend; to which she responded she did not know, but she heard that she would get better; at that moment Florentina came to the window of the house where she lives—which is on the opposite side of the same street—with her lover Francisco de tal, known as Tomé, and they both started scolding the respondent with 'shameless woman, idiot, bitch, whore.'[15]

After the episode, the two women went to face each other; however, now they were not in their houses. The space of conflict had changed, for the worse; it had become more dangerous. Florentina then asked: "Didn't you say that you were brave"? With razor in hand, she attacked Adelina. The respondent arrived—covered in gashes—to the police station, the place where she confirmed that Florentina was jealous of her husband with her. The fight was "heated," according to Antônio Trindade, who was there and was one of the witnesses. He said that he saw Florentina "flip her body over."

The women learned *capoeira* from contact with the masculinized world of practitioners of the time and put it to use, as their experiences show.

Another revealing trial, because it includes the term *capoeira* in the description written by the police clerk, says the following: "That the woman invaded the stall and positioned herself [against the accused] doing the movements of one who plays *capoeira*, wanting to battle. That the accused, trying to free herself of said woman, wounded her hand on a large knife."[16] This trial began in 1900 and deals with a conflict among several laundresses. The confusion began because a towel belonged to a client of Maria Elisa do Espírito Santo, a *capoeira* woman. The problem is that she had forgotten her towel at a well. She returned to retrieve the towel thinking that it was being kept with one of her work colleagues. Previously mistrusting and suspicious of one of them, she started shouting verbal aggressions "directed at a black lady." Manuel de Santana, the defendant in the case, went towards Maria Elisa starting a fight. Maria Elisa tried to defend herself and did some *capoeira* moves, *gingando* (the basis of all *capoeira* defensive moves) to avoid the strikes of the knife, but one of them caught her, striking one of her arms. After that confusion, the "black lady" decided to return the towel. Since she was injured, Maria Elisa decided to take the towel and tie it around her wounded arm, dirtying it with blood; at the very least, it left evidence of loyalty for the owner of the towel. Certainly, her client learned of her persistence in retrieving the towel. This act may have guaranteed that she would be able to keep serving her client, and perhaps earn a little extra change. The *capoeira* woman appears as hardworking, courageous, facing the daily life of the laundresses, revealing the presence of the *capoeira* culture among the poorest working classes in Bahian society. *Capoeira*, as it appeared among the male and female sellers, artisans, and prostitutes, also came up in the middle of a very feminine activity: among the laundresses of Salvador.

The *capoeira* women in the cities of Rio de Janeiro, Belém do Pará, and Salvador appear in a similar form, that is, belonging to the same social interest groups: women who worked in the streets and maintained constant contact with the masculine universe of *capoeira*. They influenced the cultural formation of *capoeira*, being active agents and representing the fundamental aspect characterizing the practice of *capoeira*: their "agility movements." Associating themselves with *capoeira* groups, some women joined the *rodas* and learned how to use the razor.

Let's return to female *capoeira* practitioners, this time in the city of Rio de Janeiro. In a sample of 196 criminal trials from the central neighborhoods of Santo Antônio and Santana, I found just 14 that had a woman as a defendant. Among the 14 women tried through Article 402 of the penal code of 1890, one was Austrian, one Portuguese and another was from Syria; the others were Brazilian. It would be repetitive to describe the various trials involving the women on trial for *capoeira*, because most cases had to do with prostitutes and fights with razors. However, some stories reveal other social traces that are also important to understand the "way" that *capoeira* culture remained rooted in society. The case of a family of *capoeira* players is one of these examples:

> It was said: that the two accused men were causing disturbances and the three accused women were also present, being the ones alarming the neighbors and startling them with their threats and leaping gestures with their arms and legs.[17]

The family included Maria Francisca de Oliveira, Ana Antonieta de Oliveira, Antônia de Oliveira, João Pinto de Oliveira, and Marcos Martins Souza, who became a part of the family. According to the police, they were all "playing *capoeira*." It was a true *capoeira* family that trained inside their home. When the neighbors alerted the police to this practice, they were all caught in the act. They probably had some money stored because the men worked as bakers. Also, they had a stable residence. It was easy for Mr. Miguel dos Anjos Peres—who was contracted as their lawyer—to defend the *capoeira* family. Because they were employed, they were all acquitted. The lawyer dismantled the accusation alleging that the defendants were playing *capoeira* inside the house and that the law only mentioned the prohibition of *capoeira* in the streets, that is, in "public thoroughfare." Excellent argument. All that was needed at that point was to add proof of work to their case.

Ana Maria da Conceição was another woman put on trial—on February 2, 1908—based on Article 402 of the Penal Code: "Today at six o'clock in the afternoon, the driver Manuel Matoso caught Ana Maria da Conceição when she was causing disorder and doing body agility exercises on Coqueiros street, causing panic." She had been caught when she was doing "agility exercises," but she worked for the businessman Joaquim Tomás Ribeiro, a good man who was known in the city. Joaquim showed her proof of work and with this, she only stayed in jail for a few days. Ana claimed to have gone into the street to find her husband, who was playing the *jogo de bicho* (a street gambling game). He was also put on trial, but I could not find the trial in the national archive.[18]

The women were present among the *capoeira* players in various ways and the criminal trials and news about the police actions reveal that during the 19th century, and in the first decades of the 20th century, they were the target of repression focused on the practice of *capoeira*, becoming active agents in maintaining the groups and tradition of *capoeira*. The *capoeira* women were members of the gangs, they developed the agility movements and had excellent command of their weapons. With the implementation of the Republic, *capoeira* practitioners modified the cultural practice and implemented measures of social inclusion. Next, let's picture the feminine presence in this process of the invention of *capoeira* traditions.

Women and capoeira as a Sport and an Art

In a historic case related to the repression of *capoeira*, beginning with its criminalization in Article 402 of the Penal Code of 1890, intellectuals, politicians and sportsmen sought to create—redefine—*capoeira* and its practitioners. If they had been characterized as vagrants, outsiders, swindlers and bullies, a network was formed to find freedom and the construction of *capoeira* as a symbol of nationality and a contribution of black culture to the country. Newspapers and magazines started to create a positive vision of *capoeira*. *Capoeira* started to be referred to as a national martial art. This process made it possible for the practice to expand to other sectors and, as a result, resulted in further spreading within the feminine universe. It took some decades for women to penetrate this new world of *capoeira* more significantly. Strategies were created to include them, especially in Salvador where Angolan and regional *capoeira* emerged. An anonymous iconographic work reveals clues of this inventive process, as follows in the picture below.

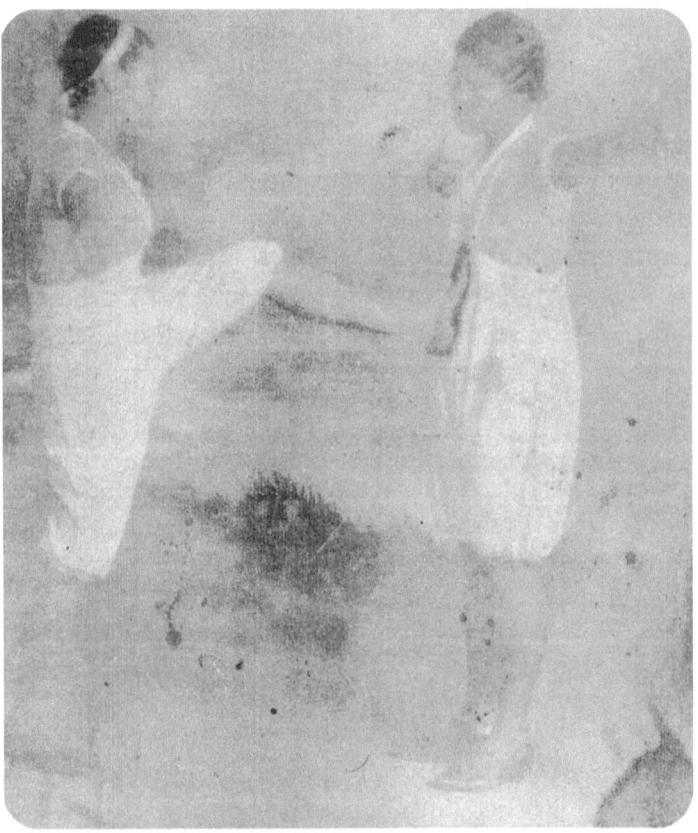

According to Jair Moura, this photographic image was put on display at Mestre Bimba's *capoeira* center (Manuel dos Reis Machado).[19] The image says a lot about technique of the pose as captured by the photo and about the intention of capturing that characteristic movement from the scenario of a *capoeira roda*. Two women in the game of *capoeira*, perhaps one of them a *chamada* (a call to the other player) coming out with a *pisão de frente* (front kick).[20] The garments are equally folkloric and indicative of the artistic show that the female *capoeira* practitioners, mainly in Bahia, were proposing to create. These cultural inventions covered the entire 20th century and incentivized transformations, adaptations, and organizations that made the social and cultural expansion of *capoeira* possible for the whole country and other places in the world. Women were extremely important for the production of new images of *capoeira*. The feminine presence helps to identify the artistic aspect of the practice of *capoeira* in its process of "social rehabilitation." Some affirm that *capoeira* tends to grow increasingly on account of female players. Today in the world of *capoeira* we can find *capoeira rodas* made up entirely of women, as well as championships and other forms of competition also directed by only women. The social group of female players has expanded and includes mainly students, artists, and intellectuals of the most diverse professional areas.

Women who participated in the world of *capoeira* in the 19th century and in the first half of the 20th century, a time in which the practitioners were under strong police and judicial repression, belonged to the marginalized groups of society of the time. As workers, outsiders, and prostitutes, they used *capoeira* to adapt themselves to the world of the streets, the oppression, the violence, and the survival strategies of daily life. Once again, they appear in the scenario of the criminal trials more so as the victims than as the defendants, the offended than the offenders, the violated than the aggressors. *Capoeira* served them as a weapon of defense, culture of negotiation, hope of survival.

Up until the present, the historiographical production regarding approaches on the issue of gender relations has hardly used *capoeira* as a theme. Studies are still rare and tend to be superficial. However, the sources related to the presence of women in the world of *capoeira* may direct studies to a series of important issues—principally with respect to cultural history of the second half of the 20th century, a period in which women migrated in large numbers to groups of *capoeira* players. We can then ask: what are the relations between men and women—pervaded by classification systems, cultures and social groups, body beauty standards, and stereotypes—constructed in a "world" of *capoeira*? The studies on "*capoeira* and gender" open windows for an analytic understanding of the concept of gender as well as making it possible to articulate the feminine experiences of racism and class inequalities. There are many sources: newspapers, magazines, television production, cinema, theatre, poetry, verbal accounts, etc.

In the most up to date scholarship, some studies of an academic nature involving the participation of women in *capoeira*—such as the works of Paula Cristina da Costa Silva, Luiza Mahin, M. J. S. Barbosa, Rosangela Araújo, and Josiane Domingues—are starting to appear. Soon we will have important works to increase our knowledge on the participation of women, specifically in the culture of *capoeira*.[21]

Notes

1. *Capoeira* Academy of the Grupo Senzala França – Mestre Sorriso and Mestre Bruzi.

2. The practice of *capoeira* occurred more often in city of Rio throughout the 19th century. Only in the 1930s of the 20th century did Bahian *capoeira* establish itself as the hegemonic form.

3. *Revista Vida Policial*, 1925, p. 17.

4. See Pires, 2010, p. 79.

5. *Diário de Notícias*, 22 Jan. 1893, p. 54.

6. *Capoeira roda* chant. Mestre Garrincha. Grupo Senzala. Rio de Janeiro, November 1990.

7. *Capoeira roda* chant. Mestre Morais. Grupo Pelourinho. Salvador, October 1990.

8. See Oliveira and Leal, 2009, p. 38.

9. Processo-crime de Aristides Santana e outros (réu) [Criminal Case of Aristides Santana and Others (Defendant)]. Year 1913, Box 24. Doc. 9, p. 3-5 – Public files of the State of Bahia – Apeb.

10. Processo-crime de Pedro Vieira "Pedro Mineiro" (réu). [Criminal Case of Pedro Vieira "Pedro Mineiro" (defendant)]. Year 1909. Box 226. Doc. 9, p. 3 – Apeb.

11. Processo-crime de Pedro José Vieira "Pedro Mineiro" (réu). [Criminal Case of Pedro Vieira "Pedro Mineiro" (defendant)]. Year 1910. Box 21. Doc. 18 – Apeb.

12. *Diário de Notícias*, Salvador, 29 Dec. 1914, p. 2.

13. See Dias, 2004, p. 64-70.

14. See Pires, 2010, p. 137.

15. Processo-crime de Florentina Maria Isabel (réu) [Criminal Case of Florentina Maria Isabel (defendant)]. Year 1914. Box 25. Doc. 7 – Apeb. The spelling has been updated to current standards.

16. Processo-crime de Manuel de Santana (réu). [Criminal Case of Manuel de Santana (defendant)]. Year 1900. Box 215. Doc. 13, p. 16.

17. Processo-crime de João Pinto de Oliveira e outros (réu) [Criminal Case of João Pinto and Others (Defendant)]. MW 586. Year 1906. AN.

18. Processo-crime de Ana Maria da Conceição (réu) [Criminal Case of Ana Maria da Conceição(defendant)]. MW 812. Year 1906. AN. The spelling has been updated to current standards.

19. Mestre Bimba was the creator of regional *capoeira* and Mestre Pastinha was the creator of Angolan *capoeira*.

20. Classification refers to the movements and rituals of *capoeira*.

21. For more information, see:
    - www.flickr.com/photos/geracao-*capoeira*/4768072730
    - www.dc.mre.gov.br/imagens-textos/revista14-mat12.pdf/view
    - www.guiaentradafranca.com.br/agendaG.php?idUrl=8186
    - www.plcs.umassd.edu/docs/.../barbosajun162006.doc
    - www.ndonline.com.br/.../encontro- -feminino-de-*capoeira*-incentiva-a-participacao-das-mulheres-no-esporte.

Bibliography

Algranti, Leila Mezan. *O feitor ausente. Estudos sobre escravidão urbana no Rio de Janeiro (1808-1822)*. [The Absent Foreman. Studies on Urban Slavery in Rio De Janeiro (1808-1822)]. São Paulo: Companhia das Letras, 2000.

Bandeira de Mello, Gustavo Moncorvo. *História da Polícia Militar do Distrito Federal*. [History of the Federal Police in the Federal District]. Rio de Janeiro: Tipografia Militar, 1904.

Desch-Obi, T. J. *Fighting for honor. The history of African martial traditions in the Atlantic world*. South Carolina: University South Carolina Press, 2008.

Dias, Adriana Albert. *A malandragem da mandiga: o cotidiano dos* capoeira* em Salvador na República Velha (1910-1925).* [The Trickery of Sorcery: Daily Life in *Capoeira* Groups of the Old Republic (1910-1925)]. 2004. Thesis. (Masters in History) – Universidade Federal da Bahia (UFBA), Salvador, BA.

Holloway, Thomas H. "O saudável Terror." [Healthy Terror]. Revista do CEAA, 16, Rio de Janeiro: 1999.

Oliveira, Josivaldo Pires de; Leal, Luiz Augusto Pinheiro. *Capoeira, identidade e gênero.* [*Capoeira*, Gender and Identity]. Salvador: Edufba, 2009.

Pires, Antônio Liberac Cardoso Simões. *Movimentos da cultura afro-brasileira.* [Afro-Brazilian Cultural Movements]. 2001. Diss. (Doctorate in History) – Universidade Estadual de Campinas (Unicamp), Campinas, SP.

___. *Culturas circulares. A formação histórica da* capoeira* contemporânea no Rio de Janeiro.* [Circular Cultures. The Historical Formation of Contemporary *Capoeira* in Rio de Janeiro]. Curitiba: Progressiva, 2010.

Rego, Waldeloir. *Capoeira de Angola.* Salvador: Itapoã, 1968.

Rugendas, João Mauricio. *Viagem pitoresca através do Brasil.* [Pictorial Journey through Brazil]. São Paulo: Martins, 1972.

Soares, Carlos Eugênio Líbano. *A negregada instituição. Os capoeiras na Corte Imperial (1850-1890).* [The Unfortunate Institution. *Capoeira* Groups in the Imperial Court (1850-1890)]. Rio de Janeiro: Access, 1999.

19

HISTORIES OF DIFFERENCES AND INEQUALITIES
REVISITED: NOTES ON GENDER, SLAVERY, RACE,
AND POST-EMANCIPATION[1]

Marcelo Paixão and Flavio Gomes

In this chapter, we seek to reflect on the past and the present of the black woman, in slavery as much as in the post-emancipation period.[2] After all, there are silences in the history of yesterday as well as that of today. As far as the role of gender and race relations in the slavery past—between the image of the *mucama* (slave mistress) and her supposedly sexual permissiveness—in the first decades after abolition, the stigmatization and eroticization of the black female body lingered. Today, there are social indicators that point to inequalities in the work place and a preponderance of females in the management of households in the greater metropolitan areas, along with many other silences. Even though studies about gender have opened new horizons and pivotal theoretical-methodological questions,[3] we still know little with respect to the historical connections between race and gender.[4] The lines of questioning about the experiences of black women in slave communities, and in the first decades of the post-emancipation period in Brazil, continue to be absent, except for these few exceptions we will be pointing out here.

Analyzing the trajectories of Africanist literature, Patrick Manning (1988) highlights the visions of an eternal Africa that were seen in the last decades by examining studies that were more concerned with complex transformations in various African societies and micro-societies; in other words, studies that took into account the social changes and dynamics unique to Africa, revealing that there were socioeconomic and demographic impacts brought about by factors other than the Atlantic slave trade, one of the principal means of contact between Africans and Europeans from the middle of the 16th century until the end of the 20th century. For a renewed approach, among the principal questions—beyond the nature of the sources and the meanings of their conclusions—there are the analyses about slavery in Africa; the impact of black commerce on pre-colonial societies; as well as a collection of demographic factors (alteration of prices, quantity, age, and gender distribution). Refuting the dichotomy between robust societies resistant to pressure and fragile societies that are easily shattered, detailed reflections emerged about regions, areas, societies, and micro-societies where diverse internal logics—such as droughts, diseases, and hunger—caused devastating impacts; this is notwithstanding that in some cases there were occurrences about normal rates of growth and recuperation.

We propose here a unique approach. First, we will look at historical studies and studies of gender and black subjectivity. We build upon the analyses of sources that can offer a glimpse at the face of the universe of the black woman in slave society, with her expectations, lived experiences, and plans. In the second part, with a base of aggregate data, we propose a historical leap and dive into the market logic in the labor market of today and of the impacts on the profile and the life of black women. Bringing together portraits of the past and the present, we suggest interrogations and perspectives about the role of history in Brazilian society.

Slavery, Black Female Subjectivity, and Historiography: Pathways and Possibilities

Contrary to what we found in the Caribbean and the United States, there are still few studies in Brazil that deal with the sociability and daily lives of enslaved women, freed women, African-born women, and Brazilian-born black women. In other societies, both in Africa and in the diaspora, women were known for their strength and spiritual power; and they developed forms of resistance, contradicting the idea that they accepted domination passively.[5] One of these bases of power can be seen in the struggle to keep the black family together, when women acted to protect the physical and psychological integrity of their children and companions, and even that of the entire community of which they were an integral part.[6] In the attempt to prevent children and spouses from being sold separately, they refused to work and threatened their masters with suicide and infanticide. Landowners especially feared being poisoned by their *mucamas*. In a world of oppression, these women built environments of self-confidence and became decisive in efforts such as helping enslaved people escape, or in obtaining information with respect to undesirable sales and transfers. Many of these women provided assistance to those interested in escaping, in addition to harboring fugitive slaves. Helping to maintain the integrity of their family groups, such as wealth and the originality of the culture they forged around them, they were the first agents of emancipation in Afro-descendent communities in the diaspora.[7]

Studies such as Bush (1985), about the experiences of enslaved women in the Americas, indicate a degree of resistance present in the daily work done on the plantations; if they did not cooperate, they were severely punished. In the rural areas, where a majority of enslaved women worked on the plantations, it was through language and music that they educated their children, reinventing cultural meanings. In the urban areas, women were already occupying important spaces in the labor market and carving out significant gender identities. In theory, during the slave trade conducted by the Portuguese in Africa in the 16th century, an anonymous ship's captain commented on the need to separate men from women in the holds of the slave ships, because, according to him, when women travel with men they incite rebellion against the ship's crew.[8]

The function of women on the plantations could represent the reconstruction and recreation of permanent original cultural aspects and, therefore, the edification of stable communities, just as Barbara Bush (1986) points out in her study of family life in the British

Caribbean. One of the distinguishing characteristics of slave culture in all of the Americas was, without a doubt, the preservation of the family unit, in all of its various meanings.[9] Being the dorsal fin of the family make-up, women held a key role in the oral transmission of the faith and values of a black community in gestation, as Bush indicates in another study (1990).

In Brazil, the few studies about enslaved women that exist emerged only in the last 30 years. In the 1980s, Maria Odila Dias (1985 and 1995) conducted a pioneering investigation, casting light on social practices and daily lives of black women, both enslaved and free, in 19th century São Paulo. Other approaches emerged in the studies of Maria Lúcia Mott (1988) and Sônia Giacomini (1988). Additionally, the classic work of Mary Karasch (2000) about urban slavery highlighted the importance of West African women in the urban labor market.[10] Luciano Figueiredo (1985, 1993, 1997, and 1998) and Liana Reis (1989) analyzed the specificities of black women who worked as *tabuleiras* (street vendors selling trays of baked goods), probably precursors to the *quitandeiras* (street vendors who sold fruits, vegetables and basic grocery items) typical of the 19th century. In the case of Salvador, Cecília Soares (1994 and 1996) problematized the central role of African women in urban commerce, just as the Atlantic dimensions of *quitandeiras* appear in the studies of Selma Pantoja Paiva (2001) and Carlos Eugênio Líbano Soares (2002 a and b; Soares and Gomes, 2007). More recently, the studies of Eduardo França (2001), Júnia Furtado (2001), and Sheila Faria (2000) recovered the link between winning freedom by means of manumission, and the power of gender relations in small business for black women (both freed and enslaved).

It is quite probable that other important research, beyond our capacity to be completely up to date, could be cited here. Even though the studies and authors we have indicated, not necessarily few in number, have importance, we insist that we need to know more deeply the lived experiences of black women in slavery and in the first decades of the post-emancipation period.[11] It is possible (and we will do this in part 1) to follow the trajectories of some important individuals in order to understand quotidian life of African-born women and Brazilian-born black women.[12] We are fundamentally interested in locating feminine voices from the past, not only voices coming from oppression, but also those in public power, in medicine, and among the educated elite.

Among these recent trends in scholarship, we can find analyses of the narratives contained in the last wills and testaments of freed women, ex-slaves, African-born women, Brazilian-born black women, and mixed-race women. Leaving aside legacies and inheritances, they speak about their own lives, their experiences with slavery, of the workplace, of their expectations, and even their affections, hopes, and memories. We will look at some testaments from Rio de Janeiro, in the regions of Irajá, Inhaúma, and Iguaçu in the 18th and 19th centuries.

What did the free black woman Sebastiana Inácia say just before her death?[13] On the 28 September 1826, she was interred in a *cova da Fábrica* (a way of burying the mortal remains of poor people or people who had no surviving relatives). She received all of the appropriate sacraments: her body buried in a white shroud of St. Francis and her soul commended to heaven by the priest, including a *dobre de sinos* (a phrase meaning a kind of lament of bells for the soul that has passed). Because she had been sick in bed with illness, two days prior to her death, in the presence of the priest and the notary, she offered her last testament. In accordance with the ritual and nature of the last testaments of the day, she revealed herself to be a "native of the *Gentio de Guiné*" (a person born in Africa) and married "in the face of the Church to Felipe Sousa, a free black man," and "from this marriage she had no children, and none from any prior marriage." Being a "sister of Our Lady of the Rosary of the Congregation of Inhaúma," she had left some debts with the sisterhood and left those debts for her husband to pay. She ordered mass prayers and freed two slaves that she possessed, "the two children, Maria and Cândido, she leaves free and liberated, as if they had been born of a free womb." For her goddaughter Maria, daughter of Isidora Maria, she bequeathed "for alms, a *dobra* (a coin from São Tomé)" and "for her goddaughter's mother Isidora, she leaves a fine sheepskin." For the "rest of her godchildren she leaves each one four *patacas* (a coin worth 40 *réis*)." As for Maria, the *crioula* (Brazilian-born black girl) from the *Engenho Velho* (the Old Mill), her goddaughter and her husband, the slave of Dona Isabel, she leaves a *dobra*, and the same amount to "Emerenciana, *crioula* goddaughter, who is also a slave to Dona Isabel, [to whom] she leaves one *dobra*." To all "the rest of her godchildren she leaves each one four *patacas*." They were all slaves of Antônio José de Souza.

The will of Rita Luísa Suzana, who passed away in October of 1834, took a similar path.[14] An African woman of the "Benguela Nation," who, in her last testament, affirmed being "Roman Catholic, native to the Costa de Leste, legally married to Pedro Antônio Álvares," also of the Costa de Leste, whose marriage did not produce children. With no direct heirs, like Sebastiana, she left her inheritance to her godchildren: two *dobras* to Bernardo, son of Bernardo João Gomes, deceased black man, to whom her inheritance and testament she would only bequeath when he should reach "the age of self-governing." As a witness, in addition to her husband, there was also Domingos da Silva, another free black man.

There are similarities to the testament of another African woman from Benguela in 1848. The years passed, but Joana Batista followed the pattern of African-born women and free black women living in the Congregation of Inhaúma. Even "being sick," she would reveal that she was "Roman Catholic," widow of Mateus José Mascarenhas, with no children. Once again, an African-born woman, married, with no children, left her wealth to relatives and godchildren. Her witnesses were Valentim Correia da Silva, "for being in her house and by virtue of the charity with she has treated me," and Gregório Pinheiro, to whom she gave as an inheritance, two *dobras*. Beyond this she distributed alms to Inácia Maria and the daughters of her relative Isabel Maria do Carmo, widow of Manuel Caetano, a black man and also her relative, and a resident of Engenho Novo. Each one would receive six *dobras* soon after she passed. For the children, the money would be "held in secure hands to be delivered only when they had reached the use of their reason." Joana's other properties included "a group of plots of land in this district" which was "rented to Antônio

Nunes for seven thousand *réis* per month, for which he has paid up to last month."

In fact, black women who left their last wills and testaments in the Congregation of Piedade de Iguaçu in the 18th century had different expectations, desires, and standards of property rights and possession. We can look at the case of Rosa Maria da Silva: she died in 1782 and "interred in a grave at the Sisterhood of the Rosary."[15] The case presents the story of a free black woman, a widow, born in Costa da Mina and baptized in the Parish of Our Lady of the Conception by Antônio Dias in Vila Rica, Minas Gerias. She possessed two spools of rope, an image of Conceição, a string of beads, and a pair of earrings. Beyond this she counted one copper pot, one copper oven, and "one manioc wheel (mill) with all of its parts." She was also the owner of slaves, with "one slave of the Mina Nation by the name of Rita, of an age that appears to be 46 years, more or less… and the two children born to that slave," and one more *crioulo* (Brazilian-born black man) by the name of Manuel, 28 years old, and another *pardo* (mixed race man) by the name of Benedito, a member of the Brotherhood, 22 years old." As far as her debts go, she made a point of registering "those two *patacas*" to a black woman named Luísa, "of whom I haven't even heard any word," but whose "witnesses consulted with those who know better than they, what to do if the woman ever appears." She registered her property, her debts, her rights, and her obligations. To the slaves Manuel and Benedito, she left "the obligation that each one, on his own, should order that the chapel and masses be recited for my soul, and for the same chapels and masses to be recited for my husband, obliging both of them to remain in service to my husband until his death; and after they shall have fulfilled all of these obligations, I shall leave them both free and liberated; beyond this I leave them the copper oven, and the manioc wheel with all of its parts, for them to divide equally among themselves." The slave, Rita, "should order that a half chapel of masses be given, and to give another half *dobla* [a coin value] for the half that belongs to me, and the rest of his value leave with my husband, who I am counting on to show himself, whose half a *dobla* should be given to my cousin Elena Maria da Silva; and when he dies, to give her the same masses for her soul." The rest of her belongings were recommended that "what belongs to my half, order another dozen masses of alms of *pataca* for the souls in purgatory as well as, on the day of my death, to give a dozen poor people alms of two *vinténs* each" (a coin of the day). Finally, she declared, "I don't owe anything else to anyone else."

Domingas Cabral de Melo, a free black woman and a widow, who died in 1778, swore that she was "*Gentia de Guiné* and baptized in the parish of the city of Luanda" and told a little more about her history when she revealed that she had come from her "land to this one at the age of 12 years, and in this same land" married Sebastião Cabral, a Ganguela man, now deceased. She had three children, all of whom had since died, leaving her with only two grandchildren, who were established as her heirs. Even though she resided in Iguaçu, she wanted to be buried in the city, in the Church of Santa Rita, with many celebratory masses for the benefit of her soul. She possessed, at the time, the slaves: José Rebolo, Maria Benguela, and "a son by the same, Luís," a copper oven for making flour, a wheel for milling manioc, a press, and "the houses where I live and all of the improvements found on the farm where" she resided. Additional belongings included "two more pairs of gold earrings, and one of diamonds."[16] As far as the "little *crioulo* named Luís," that she "was going, in diligence, to free him"; she instructed her witnesses that, if they should receive "his value in her life, she would pass on his letter of freedom; and if she died before receiving this value, he would remain enslaved."

And what does Joana Gonçalves, a free black woman who died in 1789, reveal to us? She was "native to and baptized in Ganguela," married to João Ramos, an African-born man of the Congo, deceased," with no children. Declaring herself a sister of the Sisterhood of the Rosary, she wanted her body "interred in the garments of Santo Antônio." As far as the possessions of this slave couple, we determined that João worked an additional five years "so that in this time he could give an additional five *doblas* toward his manumission," Maria also staying these same additional five years, thus giving "four *doblas* towards her manumission."

The African-born woman, Gracia Maria, "native *Gentio de Guinea*" and a widow, upon her death, left two Angolan slaves, a small flour mill and all of its accessories, an old pot, a large box for flour, two boxes, four hoes, two axes, a shotgun, a machete, and "manioc fields and rural lands." It was determined that her slave, Lucrécia, after her death, should stay on her ranch working together with her other slave in order to "harvest what has been planted under the authority of my witness." What is new in her last testament is her debts. She amassed one debt with Damião, a slave belonging to Francisco Barbosa, in the amount of 22,400 *réis*, "money that she had given to her now deceased husband for savings, and said amount was spent on his illness and burial, which amount my witness will pay with no judicial dispute." Another debt with Francisco, also a slave of Francisco Barbosa, in the amount of 14,080 *réis*, "money that was also given to my now deceased husband, which he spent, and which amount my witness will pay without judicial dispute." Of the brotherhood, in this case, the Confraternity of Nossa Senhora da Conceição, of which her husband was a member, was owed 26,430 *réis*, she also promised to pay. She also owed four thousand *réis* to the slave Lucrécia, three *dobras* of which should be discounted for her manumission. She also owed Isabel de Almeida, a free black woman, somewhere along the lines of "eleven *patacas* of money" which she had borrowed. She had debts, but she also had creditors. She was owed 38,400 *réis* from José Rodrigues, a free black man, resident of the city of Rio de Janeiro, "for a credit that he gave me for the remainder of a price of a *crioula* slave by the name of Isabel, that he, being her natural father, intended to free." In the case of non-payment, she expressly declared that the letter of manumission should not be issued and that the slave should be sold, "because this was the deal made" with José. Her witness was directed in the expectations of receiving payments as well as promissory notes on her debts. Some people were named as heirs of her possessions. To João Gomes da Conceição, a free black man, "who was my slave," she left "the small flour mill with all of its accessories," which the witness should deliver no sooner than one year after her death, once they had "made the manioc crop." One who is lucky enough, and will look beautiful when she receives a "black skirt for wearing at court," is Escolástica de Magalhães, a free black woman, resident of the city of Rio de Janeiro.

These interlacing narratives, fragments of the lives and experiences of slavery and freedom, present black women who knew slavery, some possibly even from when they were in Africa, and redefined these experiences in the diaspora. More than this, they invented slavery and freedom. They reorganized their own lives and those of their extended families. They bequeathed wealth to their children, relatives, and husbands. There are indications of goods that come from money, including items such as clothing and jewelry, items of wealth beyond land and agricultural tools for producing manioc. We did not find only stories of women submitting or exposed to oppression, that correspond to images of *mucamas*, who were sexually violated or oppressed by gender relations on the plantations. We can go even further, in the desires and plans of black women, gathering resources they have produced and which they may leave for their heirs. We confirm their views of gender solidarity and also, because the world of slavery was still present, many of them owned slaves. There are many different historical experiences of women in slavery and in the period immediately following abolition, in the cities and in the rural areas.[17] A large part of the data and contemporary statistics about workers, women, and blacks refers to other aspects (without a face) of people in the second generation after abolition. They are black women, daughters and granddaughters of the first free women in the last quarter of the 19th century.

A Contemporary Post-Abolition: Black Women and the Labor Market

To link the past and the present in a radical direct line is always dangerous, not only chronologically but also in an evolutionary sense. We lose not only the nuances and interpretive possibilities, but also the fundamental connections between people, choices, political policies, social movements, the role of intellectuals, literature, ideologies, etc. In this second part of the article, we propose an analytic counterpoint. We will begin with comments about the principal indices of the Brazilian labor market, disaggregated in groups by color or race, and sex. The idea is to verify the impacts from social models and modes of formal insertion regarding gender relations, directing a specific focus on black women.[18] In this article we have used the time period from 1995 to 2006 as a period of analysis for observation. The source of data will be the *Pesquisa Nacional por Amostra de Domicílios* (National Research on the Evidence of Domiciles—PnaD), conducted by the *Instituto Brasileiro de Geografia e Estatística* (Brazilian Institute of Geography and Statistics—IBGE), including tallies completed by the team from the *Laboratório de Análises Econômicas, Históricas, Sociais e Estatísticas das Relações Raciais* (Laboratory of Economic, Historical, Social and Statistical Analyses of Race Relations—LAESER), affiliated with the Federal University of Rio de Janeiro (UFRJ), according to their Index of Racial Inequalities (www.laeser.ie.ufrj.br). The objective of this elaboration and analysis of these indicators that follow is precisely a more detailed examination of the indicators of the labor market among the black female population. As such, the data will clearly show precisely how much the labor market is an environment quite hostile to black women.

From 1995 to 2006 the active economic population (PEA) of Brazil, not counting the resident population of rural areas in the north of Brazil, shows a total count of 20.6 million people. When we consider groups according to color or race, we can see that, among whites, this total population was 7.7 million people, and the population of black and mixed-race people was 12.6 million. Therefore, along the period of analysis, the presence of blacks in the labor market has proven to show greater dynamism than what has occurred between people of color or whites. Black women alone were counted at around 6.4 million in the labor market. Black men responded at a rate of 6.3 million people. Among white men and women, the rate of growth in the work force from 1995 to 2006 was from 2.6 to 5.1 million people, respectively.

In the same period, among men, the black PEA, in numbers of absolute workers, surpassed that of whites. Therefore, in 2006, the total number of working and unemployed blacks was 25.7 million, while whites totaled 25.6 million workers. From 1995 to 2006 the rate of participation in the labor market among white and black women grew by 7 and 4.4 percentage points respectively, whereas among white men and black men the identical indicators declined by 1.4 and 2.2 points, respectively. The PEA of employment in the entire country, except for residents of the rural north, reached a total of 20.6 million between 1995 and 2006. When these figures are disaggregated by color or race and sex, the largest area of growth was among women: 27.1 percent among white women, and 42.7 percent among black women, whereas the PEA among men, the relative growth in the number of workers was 10.2 percent among white men and 30.0 percent among black men. In total, the number of employed men increased proportionally, in the period described, by 17.1 percent among white men and by 34.9 percent among black men.

Table 1 shows us that in the PEA of working white women in 2006, the majority were salaried, with 36.8 percent of them having a *carteira assinada* (a phrase indicating that the salary is official and mechanisms are in place for social services to be accounted for and public retirement is being funded); 15.5 percent of them were salaried without a *carteira assinada*, and 7.7 percent were employed by the state. From 1995 to 2006, by these accounts, the relative weight of salaried workers with a *carteira assinada* grew 3.6 percentage points; that of salaried workers without a *carteria assinada* grew 1.7 percentage points, and that of public workers or military remained stable.

The second and more relevant form, in terms related to employment, for the PEA of employed white women, was in the area of anonymous workers. In 2006 anonymous workers represented 19.8 percent of this group, a smaller proportional rate than in 1995, at 21.4 percent. The domestic worker responded at 6.1 percent of the total of employed whites in 2006, a stable proportion since 1995 (Table 1).

In 2006 the modalities of occupations that were not waged or salaried and of labor activities for one's own consumption represented 2.6 percent and 5.3 percent of the total workers surveyed, respectively; both, when compared, had lower rates than in 1995. Yet, the condition of "employer" represents 5.6 percent of working white men in 2006 (4.5 percent in 1995) (Table 1). Still looking at Table 1, when we analyze the profile of the population of working white men, we can see that in 2006 the principal modalities of occupations were: a job in the private sector with *carteira assinada;* when joined together with public workers and the military, this population reaches 45.7 percent; self-employed was at 23.4 percent; employed in the private sector without a *carteira assinada* was at 17.2 percent; the position of employer was at 6.9 percent; and non-waged occupations were at 3.6 percent.

For the PEA of working white women, the principal modalities of occupation were: salaried employee with *carteira assinada* and public and military workers at a rate of 42.9 percent; a job with no *carteira assinada* at a rate of 13.5 percent; self-employed at a rate of 13.3 percent; domestic labor at a rate of 12.9 percent; and non-waged occupations at a rate of 7.4 percent.

Table 1: Distribution of the resident employed PEA in Brazil, in 1995 and 2006, and grouped according to sex and "person of color" or "white race" and further sorted by position of occupation (by percent).

White Workers	Men 1995	Men 2006	Women 1995	Women 2006	Total 1995	Total 2006
Employed in the private sector with a *carteira assinada*	37.3 percent	39.8 percent	27.4 percent	33.0 percent	33.2 percent	36.8 percent
Employed in the private sector without a *carteira*	16.5 percent	17.2 percent	10.0 percent	13.5 percent	13.8 percent	15.5 percent
State or federal employee or military	5.6 percent	5.9 percent	10.7 percent	9.9 percent	7.7 percent	7.7 percent
Domestic worker with a *carteira*	0.3 percent	0.3 percent	2.7 percent	3.9 percent	1.3 percent	1.9 percent
Domestic worker without a *carteira*	0.4 percent	0.4 percent	11.0 percent	9.0 percent	4.7 percent	4.2 percent
Self-employed with a college education	1.3 percent	1.9 percent	1.3 percent	0.0 percent	1.3 percent	2.0 percent
Self-employed without a college education	23.8 percent	21.5 percent	14.7 percent	13.3 percent	20.1 percent	17.8 percent
Business owner with 5 employees or less	4.0 percent	4.7 percent	1.9 percent	2.8 percent	3.2 percent	3.9 percent
Business owner with more than 5 employees	1.7 percent	2.2 percent	0.7 percent	1.0 percent	1.3 percent	1.7 percent
Labor activities in construction for one's own consumption	0.0 percent	0.1 percent	0.0 percent	0.0 percent	0.0 percent	0.1 percent
Labor activities in production for one's own consumption	1.1 percent	1.4 percent	7.0 percent	4.2 percent	3.5 percent	2.6 percent
Non-waged labor	6.6 percent	3.6 percent	12.6 percent	7.4 percent	9.1 percent	5.3 percent

Source: IBGE, micro data PnaD. Laeser Tabulations: Index of Racial Inequalities. In the year 1995, this does not include the population resident in rural areas of the North of Brazil (except Tocantins).

Table 2 shows the evolution of the distribution of the PEA of black women by position of occupation, in 1995 and 2006.[19] According to data from 2006, the principal model was the salaried employee with a *carteira assinada*, with 28.5 percent of the total employed population and a relative growth of 4.6 percentage points from 1995. The second and third most prominent models were: self-employed at 21.2 percent and salaried employee without a *carteira assinada* at 20.7 percent. In this case, since 1995 the relative importance of both modalities had opposing changes: salaried employees without a *carteira* grew by 0.7 percentage points and self-employed decreased by 1.6 percentage points.

The category of public employees and military corresponds, in 2006, to the level of 5.8 percent of the PEA of employed black women, remaining relatively stable since 1995. Similarly, in the same year, domestic labor corresponds to the level of 9.5 percent of this contingent, also remaining relatively stable since 1995. Labor activities for one's own consumption and unwaged labor had significant reductions proportionately among blacks and mixed-race persons: in the first case, from 5.1 percent to 4.8 percent, and in the second case from 11.4 percent to 7.0 percent. At the same time, the category of employer, scarce among blacks and mixed-race persons, corresponds to 1.5 percent in 1995 and 2 percent in 2006.

When we disaggregate the 2006 data on the distribution of the PEA for blacks by sex, in accordance with the division by occupation, there is significant evidence of gender inequalities. Among men, the most common occupation positions were: employed with a *carteira assinada*, together with public employees and military at 37.6 percent; autonomous workers at 24.7 percent; employed without a *carteira* at 25.2 percent; and unwaged labor at 5.7 percent. In this contingent, domestic labor corresponded to 1.1 percent of the PEA employed and category of employers to 2.5 percent. At the same time, the PEA of black women, in the same year, indicates the following relative rates: salaried employees with a *carteira assinada* in conjunction with public employees and military at 29.5 percent; domestic labor at 21.8 percent; self-employed at 16.3 percent; unwaged labor at 8.7 percent; and labor activities for one's own consumption at 10.1 percent. The category of business owner corresponds to 1.4 percent of the PEA of black and mixed race women: 1.1 percent of those with up to five employees and 0.3 percent with more than five employees (Table 2).

Table 2: Distribution of the resident employed PEA in Brazil in 1995 and 2006, grouped according to sex and "person of color" or "black race", and further sorted by position of occupation (by percent).

Black and Mixed-Race Workers	Men 1995	Men 2006	Women 1995	Women 2006	Total 1995	Total 2006
Employed in the private sector with a *carteira assinada*	27.7 percent	33.0 percent	17.8 percent	22.0 percent	23.9 percent	28.5 percent
Employed in the private sector without a *carteira*	25.9 percent	25.2 percent	10.6 percent	14.2 percent	20.0 percent	20.7 percent
State or federal employee or military	4.6 percent	4.6 percent	7.4 percent	7.5 percent	5.7 percent	5.8 percent
Domestic worker with a *carteira*	0.3 percent	0.4 percent	3.8 percent	5.2 percent	1.7 percent	2.2 percent
Domestic worker without a *carteira*	0.6 percent	0.7 percent	19.0 percent	16.6 percent	7.7 percent	7.2 percent
Self-employed with a college education	0.2 percent	0.5 percent	0.0 percent	0.4 percent	0.2 percent	0.4 percent
Self-employed without a college education	26.0 percent	24.2 percent	16.8 percent	15.9 percent	22.4 percent	20.8 percent
Business owner with 5 employees or less	1.6 percent	2.0 percent	0.6 percent	1.1 percent	1.2 percent	1.6 percent
Business owner with more than 5 employees	0.4 percent	0.5 percent	0.0 percent	0.3 percent	0.3 percent	0.4 percent
Labor activities in construction for one's own consumption	0.0 percent	0.3 percent	0.0 percent	0.0 percent	0.0 percent	0.2 percent
Labor activities in production for one's own consumption	1.9 percent	2.5 percent	10.1 percent	8.1 percent	5.1 percent	4.8 percent
Non-waged labor	10.2 percent	5.7 percent	13.4 percent	8.7 percent	11.4 percent	7.0 percent

Source: IBGE, micro data PnaD. Laeser Tabulations: Index of Racial Inequalities. In the year 1995, this does not include the population resident in rural areas of the North of Brazil (except Tocantins).

In short, this lengthy description allows for some comparisons showing evidence of the differences between color/race and gender in the distinct categories of occupation positions in the labor market. To simplify these efforts, we will only comment on the indicators respective to the PEA distributions of employed women according to the 2006 occupation positions, as shown in Tables 1 and 2:

- The category of salaried employee with *carteira assinada* was more common: among white workers (36.8 percent) than black workers (28.5 percent); among white men (39.8 percent) than black men (33 percent); and among white women (33 percent) than black women (22 percent).

- The category of salaried employee without a *carteira assinada* was more common: for black men (25.2 percent) over white men (17.2 percent). Among women, the percentage of black women was slightly higher.

- The job of public employee or military was slightly more common for white women (9.9 percent) than black women (7.5 percent) and for white men (5.9 percent) over black men (4.6 percent).

- Domestic labor included more women than men and more black women than white women. As such, one in five black women was a domestic laborer (21.8 percent). The probability of encountering a white woman in domestic labor was 8.9 percentage points less than that of a black woman.

- Self-employment was relatively common, as much among whites (19.8 percent) as among blacks (21.2 percent), the difference being that those with a university education, though quite rare, was five times more likely among whites (2 percent) than among blacks (0.4 percent).

- The category of business owner/employer was rare in both groups among color/race and gender. Nevertheless, the PEA of employed black women in this category was even less common: 2.5 percent among men, and 1.4 percent among women. Among those with more than five employees, these proportions fall to 0.5 percent for men and 0.3 percent for women. In the PEA of employed whites the category of employer occurred 6.9 percent of the time among men and 3.8 percent among women. Those with more than five employees, 2.2 percent and 1 percent, respectively.

- Labor activities for one's own consumption was a category six times more likely for a black woman (8.1 percent) than for a white man (1.4 percent). A black man is more likely to live off his own labor (2.5 percent) at a rate of 1.78 times greater than a white man (1.4 percent).

- Unwaged labor was most common among women than men. In the case of black women, the probability of encountering this position was 8.7 percent and for white women it was 7.4 percent. The PEA of male employees shows the percentage of unwaged labor at 5.7 percent of black men and 3.6 percent of white men.

Table 3 shows the relative composition, sorted by color/race and sex, the distinct modalities of occupation positions in 2006. We can see that the predominate modalities among employed white women were the categories of salaried employee with a *carteira*, public and military workers, autonomous workers with university education, and business owners. At the same time the PEA of black women had a higher rate in the modalities of employee without *carteira assinada*, domestic laborer, self-employed with no higher education, laborer (either construction or production) for one's own consumption, and unwaged laborer.

From 1995 to 2006, in the entire country, there was a net increase of 3.6 million people in the total number of unemployed people in search of work during the respective weeks that the research was completed. The biggest contributor to this increase was the female population, accounting for 68.4 percent of this total. When we disaggregate these figures by color or race and sex, blacks correspond to 60.4 percent of that increase, 22.2 percent men and 40.2 percent women. The PEA of unemployed whites alone counted for 38.3 percent, divided into 9.8 percent men and 28.5 percent women.

In 2006, 54.1 percent of the total number of unemployed persons was black, 23.9 percent men and 30.8 percent women. In 1995, blacks corresponded to 48.6 percent of the total (25.3 percent men and 23.3 percent women). Therefore, in 11 years, the relative size of the population of unemployed blacks increased, warranting special attention here as to how that occurred among black women in this group.

We can observe that, from 1995 to 2006, the unemployment rate of the PEA of blacks increased at a rate proportionally more pronounced than that of whites. In this period, the rate of increase among white men was 0.8 percentage points, compared to 1.5 percentage points for black men. In the groupings of women, the rate among whites increased by 3.1 percentage points. For black women, it was a rate of 4.5 percentage points. In other words, in this last case, the rate of increase was more than five times greater than it was for white men. Finally, comparing the average of both groups, the unemployment rate among whites went from 5.8 percent to 7.7 percent, and that of blacks from 6.2 percent to 8.7 percent.

In 2006, the monthly income from the main source of employment for white men in the entire country was, on average, R$1,164.00. This amount, in the same year, was 56.3 percent greater than the average remuneration for white women (R$744.71), 98.5 percent greater than the amount earned by black men and mixed-race men (R$586.26), and 200 percent of the income received by black women and mixed-race women (R$388.18).

What this collection of indicators reveal is that the insertion of black women in the labor market is clearly worse than for other demographic groups. This is the evidence gathered from indicators such as the position of occupation (75 percent of workers with legal guarantees, more than 20 percent employed as domestic laborers); unemployment rate (which, for black women in 2006 was more than double that of white men, in addition to having increased more than proportionally than the other demographic groups within the span of time studied); average earnings from primary source of income, of which the rate for black women was one third of the average income for white men, a little more than half that of white women, and 66 percent of the average income for black men. On the other hand, it seems abundantly clear that this reality reflects the set of discriminations lived by this demographic group at the heart of our society, in which the variable of race combines with the obstacles derived from sexism, generating a result in which the final numbers surpass the mere sum of their parts.

Table 3: Composition of the resident employed PEA in Brazil in 2006, grouped according to sex and "color/race" and further sorted by position of occupation (by percent).

	Whites		Black and mixed-race		Total*
	Men	Women	Men	Women	
Employed in the private sector with a *carteira assinada*	34.3 percent	22.8 percent	28.9 percent	13.3 percent	99.2 percent
Employed in the private sector without a *carteira*	26.7 percent	16.9 percent	40.0 percent	15.5 percent	99.2 percent
State or federal employee or military	24.7 percent	33.1 percent	19.5 percent	21.9 percent	99.2 percent
Domestic worker with a *carteira*	4.3 percent	41.6 percent	5.5 percent	48.3 percent	99.5 percent
Domestic worker without a *carteira*	1.8 percent	36.1 percent	3.3 percent	58.2 percent	99.4 percent
Self-employed with a college education	43.8 percent	36.9 percent	10.9 percent	6.1 percent	97.8 percent
Self-employed without a college education	31.4 percent	15.7 percent	36.0 percent	16.3 percent	99.3 percent
Business owner with 5 employees or less	47.3 percent	22.5 percent	20.8 percent	7.4 percent	98.0 percent
Business owner with more than 5 employees	58.8 percent	22.1 percent	12.6 percent	3.9 percent	97.4 percent
Labor activities in construction for one's own consumption	29.7 percent	3.4 percent	55.7 percent	10.4 percent	99.1 percent
Labor activities in production for one's own consumption	10.5 percent	25.7 percent	19.8 percent	43.4 percent	99.4 percent
Non-waged labor	16.8 percent	27.4 percent	27.0 percent	28.3 percent	99.6 percent

Source: IBGE, micro data PnaD. Laeser Tabulations: Index of Racial Inequalities.

* The difference between the total and 100 percent corresponds to the participation rate of Asian-descendants and indigenous populations.

How do we combine the historical experiences of the past with the data we just outlined? We need not one bit of analytic effort or sophisticated theory. The past and the present for black women are contemporaneous and true.[20] Between the victimization and symbolic production of heroes, there are complex experiences of struggle, oppression, humiliation, victory, love, pain, desires, choices, joys, and challenges. It might seem like a small thing. But it is important to recognize and make visible—in certain spaces of knowledge production and where decisions about public policy are made—the world of black women and their subjectivity of yesterday and today.[21]

Notes

1. An earlier version of this article appeared in Paixão and Gomes, 2009.
2. A useful reflection appears in Azevedo, 1988.
3. See Dias, 1984; Engel, 1989; Abreu, 1989; Graham, 1988; and Soihet, 1989.
4. See Priore, 1988 and 1993.
5. From an Africanist perspective, Pantoja reveals dimensions of power and gender, most clearly in the figure of Nzinga Mbandi, in commercial relations of traffic in the central western areas during the 17th century. See Pantoja, 2000, Chapters VI and VII.
6. Cf. Ellison, 1983.
7. Groot, 1986; Moitt, 1996; and Mullin, 1985.
8. Cf. Saunders, 1982, p. 14.
9. More recently, the historian Isabel Reis has worked with the concept of "black family" in slavery. See Reis, 1999.
10. Cf. especially Chapter 7, and see further Bakos, 1990.
11. See the Introduction to Cunha and Gomes in *Quase-cidadão*, 2007.
12. Two recent examples of attempts in historical research analyzing black female characters appear in Furtado, 2006, and Graham, 2005. An important repertory of profiles and biographies of black women of the past and present appears in Schumaher and Brazil, 2007.
13. Archive of the Metropolitan Senate of Rio de Janeiro, Notation 0632, Book of testaments and obituaries (Inhaúma), 18/9/1826, f. 54 v. The typing of the document has been updated to reflect current standards.

14. Archive of the Metropolitan Senate of Rio de Janeiro, Notation 0632, Book of testaments and obituaries (Inhaúma), 18/9/1826, f. 89. The typing of the document has been updated to reflect current standards.

15. These testaments can be found in the Book of obituaries of the Parish of *Nossa Senhora da Piedade* (Our Lady of Piety) of Iguaçu, 1777-98, Archive of the Senate of Nova Iguaçu. We would like to thank the researcher and director of the archive, Antônio de Lacerda, for recommending these testaments. The typing of these documents has also been updated to reflect current standards.

16. For the role of the religious clothing and adornments in relation to black women in the 18th century, see Escorel, 2000, and Lara, 1997.

17. In theoretical terms, we are thinking of the proposals of Scott, 1992, p. 136-201.

18. A pioneering work is that of Bairros, 1987.

19. Apart from the data being available from the 2010 Census, we consider in this article the data from the last PnaD of 2006. Analyses with graphics appear in Paixão and Gomes, 2009.

20. We are referring to the contributions of Carneiro, 2004 and 1995.

21. The studies of Márcia Lima, 1992 and 1995, are distinctly important, for thinking about temporal comparisons, among other things.

Bibliography

Abreu, Marta Esteves. *Meninas perdidas: os populares e o cotidiano do amor no Rio de Janeiro da Belle Époque*. [Lost girls: common folk and daily realities of love in Rio de Janeiro of the Belle Epoque]. Rio de Janeiro: Paz e Terra, 1989.

Azevedo, Célia Maria Marinho de. "Batismo da liberdade: os abolicionistas e o destino do negro." [Baptism of freedom: abolitionists and the fate of the black man.] *Histórias, Questões e Debates*, v. 9, n. 16, p. 38-65, Jan. 1988.

Bairros, Luiza Helena de. *Pecados no paraíso racial: o negro na força de trabalho da Bahia, 1950-1980*. [Sins in a racial paradise: the black man in the work force in Bahia, 1950-1980]. 1987. Master's Thesis (History)—Universidade Federal da Bahia/(UFBA), Salvador, BA.

Bakos, Margareth M. "Sobre a mulher escrava no Rio Grande do Sul." [On the slave woman in Rio Grande do Sul]. *Estudos Ibero-Americanos*, v. XVI, n. 7, p. 47-55, Jul.-Dec. 1990.

Bush, Bárbara. "Towards emancipation: slave women and resistance to coercive labour regimes in the British West Indian colonies, 1790-1838." In Richardson, David. *Abolition and its aftermath: the historical context, 1790-1916*. Frank Cass: University of Hull, 1985, p. 29-31.

___. "The family tree is not cut: women and cultural resistance in slave family life in the British Caribbean." In Okihiro, Gary Y. *In resistance: studies in African, Caribbean, and Afro-American history.* Amherst: University of Massachusetts Press, 1986, p. 117-31.

___. *Slave women in Caribbean society, 1650-1838.* Bloomington: Indiana University Press, 1990.

Carneiro, Sueli. "Gênero, raça e ascensão." [Gender, race, and social ascension]. *Revista Estudos Feministas*, São Paulo, v. 3, p. 301-596, 1995.

___. "A mulher negra na sociedade brasileira—O papel do movimento feminista na luta antirracista." [The black woman in Brazilian society—The role of the feminist movement in the anti-racist struggle]. In Munanga, Kabengele. (Org.). *História do negro no Brasil.* [History of blacks in Brazil]. Brasília: Fundação Cultural Palmares, 2004, p. 1-21.

Cunha, Olívia; Gomes, Flávio. *Quase-cidadão. Antropologias e histórias do pós-emancipação.* [Almost-citizen. Anthropologies and histories of post-emancipation]. Rio de Janeiro: Fundação Getulio Vargas, 2007.

Dias, Maria Odila Leite da Silva. *Quotidiano e poder em São Paulo no século* XIX. [Daily life and power in São Paulo in the 19th century]. São Paulo. Brasiliense, 1984.

___. "Nas fímbrias da escravidão urbana: negras de tabuleiro e de ganho." [At the edges of urban slavery: black women street vendors and for-hire slaves]. *Estudos Econômicos,* [Economic Studies], v. 15, n. esp., p. 167-80, 1985.

___. *Quotidiano e poder em São Paulo no século* XIX. [Daily life and power in São Paulo in the 19th century]. 2. ed. São Paulo: Brasiliense, 1995.

Ellison, Mary. "Resistance to oppression: black women's response to slavery in the United States." *Slavery & Abolition*, v. 4, n. 1, p. 56-63, May 1983.

Engel, Magali. *Meretrizes e doutores: saber médico e prostituição no Rio de Janeiro (1840-1890).* [Working women and doctors: medical knowledge and prostitution in Rio de Janeiro (1840-1980)]. São Paulo: Brasiliense, 1989.

Escorel, Sílvia. *Vestir poder e poder vestir. O tecido social e a trama cultural nas imagens do traje negro (Rio de Janeiro—século* XVIII*).* [Dressing power and power dressing: social fabric and cultural texture in the images of black dressing (Rio de Janeiro—century XVIII)] 2000. Master's Thesis (Social History). Instituto de Filosofia e Ciências Sociais (IFCS). Universidade Federal do Rio de Janeiro (UFRJ), Rio de Janeiro, RJ.

Faria, Sheila de Castro. "Mulheres forras—Riqueza e estigma social." [Free women—Wealth and social stigma]. *Tempo*, Niterói, v. 5, n. 9, p. 65-92, Jul. 2000.

Figueiredo, Luciano. *O avesso da memória: cotidiano e trabalho da mulher nas Minas Gerais no século* XVIII. [The wrong side of memory: daily life and the work of the woman in Minas Gerais in the 18th century]. Rio de Janeiro: J. Olympio; Brasília: EdUnB, 1993.

_____. *Barrocas famílias: vida familiar em Minas Gerais no século* XVIII. [Baroque families: family life in Minas Gerais in the 18th century]. Rio de Janeiro: Hucitec, 1998.

_____. "Mulheres nas Minas Gerais." [Women in Minas Gerais]. In: Priore, Mary Del (Org.). *História das mulheres no Brasil.* [History of women in Brazil]. São Paulo: Contexto/Unesp, 1997, p. 141-88.

_____. Magaldi, Ana Maria Bandeira de Mello. "Quitandas e quitutes; um estudo sobre rebeldia e transgressão femininas numa sociedade colonial." [Green grocers and sweet-sellers: a study of rebelliousness and feminine transgression in colonial society]. *Cadernos de Pesquisa*, São Paulo, n. 54, p. 50-61, 1985.

Furtado, Júnia Ferreira. "Pérolas negras. Mulheres livres de cor no Distrito Diamantino." [Black pearls. Free woman of color in the Diamantino district]. In *Diálogos oceânicos: Minas Gerais e as novas abordagens para uma história do Império Ultramarino Português.* [Oceanic dialogues: Minas Gerais and new approaches to the Portuguese Marine Empire]. Belo Horizonte: Ed. da UFMG, 2001, p. 81-126.

_____. *Chica da Silva e o contratador dos diamantes: o outro lado do mito.* [Chica da Silva and the Diamond Contractor: the other side of the myth]. 2. ed. São Paulo: Companhia das Letras, 2006.

Giacomini, Sônia Maria. *Mulher e escrava; uma introdução ao estudo da mulher negra no Brasil.* [Woman and Slave: an introduction to the study of the black woman in Brazil]. Petrópolis: Vozes, 1988.

Graham, Sandra Lauderdale. *Proteção e obediência: criadas e seus patrões no Rio de Janeiro (1860-1910).* [Protection and obedience: children and their bosses in Rio de Janeiro (1860-1910)]. São Paulo: Companhia das Letras, 1988.

_____. *Catarina diz não. Histórias de mulheres da sociedade escravista brasileira.* [Catharine says no. Histories of women in Brazilian slave society]. São Paulo: Civilização Brasileira, 2005.

Groot, Silvia W. de. "Maroon women as ancestors, priests and mediums in Suriname." *Slavery & Abolition*, v. 7, p. 160-74, Sept. 1986.

Karasch, Mary C. *Vida dos escravos no Rio de Janeiro, 1808-1850.* [Life of slaves in Rio de Janeiro, 1808-1850]. São Paulo: Companhia das Letras, 2000.

Lara, Silvia Hunold. "The signs of color: women's dress and racial relations in Salvador and Rio de Janeiro, ca. 1750-1815." *Colonial Latin American Review*, v. 6, n. 2, p. 205-24, 1997.

Lima, Márcia. "Raça, gênero e mercado de trabalho no Brasil." [Race, gender, and the labor market in Brazil]. *Estudos Afro-Asiáticos*, Rio de Janeiro, v. 23, 1993.

_____. "Trajetória educacional e realização socioeconômica das mulheres negras." [Educational trajectories and socioeconomic development of black women]. *Revista Estudos Feministas*, Rio de Janeiro, 1995.

Manning, Patrick. "Escravidão e mudança social na África." [Slavery and social change in Africa]. *Novos Estudos,* n. 21, São Paulo, p. 8-29, 1988.

Moitt, Bernard. "Slave women and resistance in the French Caribbean." In Gaspar, David B.; Hine, Darlene Clark. *More than chattel. Black women and slavery in the Americas.* Bloomington: Indiana University Press, 1996.

Mott, Maria Lúcia de Barros. *Submissão e resistência; a mulher na luta contra a escravidão.* [Submission and resistance: women and the struggle against slavery]. São Paulo: Contexto, 1988.

Mullin, Michael. "Women and the comparative study of American negro slavery." *Slavery & Abolition,* v. 6, n. 1, p. 25-40, maio 1985.

Paiva, Eduardo França. "Celebrando a alforria: amuletos e práticas culturais entre as mulheres negras e mestiças do Brasil." [Celebrating manumission: amulets and cultural practices among black and mixed-race women in Brazil]. In Jancsó, István, Kantor, Iris. (Orgs.). *Festa: cultura & sociabilidade na América Portuguesa.* [Party: culture and sociability in Portuguese America]. São Paulo: Hucitec/Edusp/Fapesp/Imprensa Oficial, 2001, v. 2, p. 505-20.

Paixão, Marcelo; Gomes, Flávio dos Santos. "História das diferenças e das desigualdades revisitadas: notas sobre gênero, escravidão, raça e pós-emancipação." [History of differences and inequalities revisited: notes on gender, slavery, race, and post-emancipation]. *Revista Estudos Feministas,* Rio de Janeiro, v. 16, 2009, p. 949-69.

Pantoja, Selma. *Nzinga Mbandi. Mulher, guerra e escravidão.* [Nzinga Mbandi. Woman, war, and slavery.] Brasília: Thesaurus, 2000.

_____. "A dimensão atlântica das quitandeiras." [The Atlantic dimension of street vendors]. In Furtado, Junia. *Diálogos oceânicos: Minas Gerais e as novas abordagens para uma história do Império Ultramarino português.* [Oceanic dialogues: Minas Gerais and new approaches to the Portuguese Marine Empire]. Belo Horizonte: Ed. da UFMG, 2001, p. 45-67.

Priore, Mary Del. *A mulher na história do Brasil.* [Woman in Brazilian history]. São Paulo: Contexto, 1988.

_____. *Ao sul da história do corpo: condição feminina, maternidades e mentalidades no Brasil Colônia.* [South of the history of the body: feminine condition, maternities, and mentalities in Colonial Brazil]. Brasília: EdUnB; Rio de Janeiro: J. Olympio, 1993.

Reis, Isabel Cristina Ferreira dos. "Uma negra que fugio, e consta que já tem dous filhos: fuga e família entre escravos na Bahia oitocentista." [One black woman who flees, it is said she already has two children, flight and family among slaves in 19th century Brazil]. *Afro-Ásia,* Salvador, p. 29-48, 1999.

Reis, Liana Maria. "Mulheres de ouro: as negras de tabuleiro nas Minas Gerais do século XVIII." [Women of gold: black women street vendors in Minas Gerais of the 18th century]. *Revista do Departamento de História,* Belo Horizonte, n. 8, 1989.

Saunders, A. C. de M. *A social history of black slaves and freedom in Portugal, 1411-1555*. Cambridge: Cambridge University Press, 1982.

Schumaher, Schuma; Brazil, Érico Vital. *Mulheres negras do Brasil*. [Black women in Brazil] Rio de Janeiro: Senac Rio, 2007.

Scott, James C. *Domination and the arts of resistance. Hidden transcripts*. New Haven: Yale University Press, 1992.

Soares, Carlos Eugênio Líbano. "Comércio, nação e gênero: as negras minas quitandeiras no Rio de Janeiro, 1835-1900." [Commerce, nation, and gender: black women grocers in Rio de Janeiro, 1835-1900]. *Revista do Mestrado de História* (Universidade Severino Sombra), Vassouras, v. 4, n. 1, 2002a, p. 55-78.

____. "Dizem as quitandeiras... Ocupações urbanas e identidades étnicas em uma cidade escravista. Rio de Janeiro, século XIX." [So say the green grocers... Urban occupations and ethnic identities in a slaveholding city. Rio de Janeiro, 19th century]. *Acervo*, Rio de Janeiro, v. 15, n. 1, 2002b, p. 3-16.

Soares, Carlos Eugênio Líbano; Gomes, Flávio dos Santos. "Negras minas no Rio de Janeiro: gênero, nação e trabalho urbano no século XIX." [Black women in Rio de Janeiro: gender, nation, and urban labor in the 19th century]. In Soares, Mariza Carvalho. (Org.). *Rotas atlânticas da Diáspora africana: da baía do Benim ao Rio de Janeiro*. [Atlantic routes in the African Diaspora: from the bay of Benin to Rio de Janeiro]. v. 1. Niterói: Eduff, 2007, p. 191-221.

Soares, Cecília Moreira. *Mulher negra na Bahia no século* XIX. [The black women in Bahia in the 19th century]. 1994. Master's thesis (History)—Universidade Federal da Bahia (UFBA), Salvador, BA.

____. "As ganhadeiras: mulher e resistência negra em Salvador no século XIX." [Women earning money: women and black resistance in Salvador in the 19th century]. *Afro-Ásia*, n. 17, p. 57-72, 1996.

Soihet, Rachel. *Condição feminina e formas de violência: mulheres pobres e ordem urbana, 1890-1920*. [Feminine condition and forms of violence: poor women and urban order, 1890-1920]. Rio de Janeiro: Forense Universitária, 1989.

INDEX

abandonment, 232, 268
abolition, 59, 124, 139, 198, 244, 256, 278, 283–84, 290–91, 294–96, 299–300, 339, 348, 391, 400
abolitionism, 243, 284, 286–87, 298, 300, 319
abolitionist press, 99, 286, 293–94
abolitionists, 286–87, 349, 414
abolitionist writers, 261, 287
absolute materiality, 309
abuse, 148, 154, 335, 347, 368
accomplices, 199, 203, 207, 219
accusations, 60, 66, 151, 153–54, 156–58, 164, 168, 188, 232, 240, 259, 337, 373, 384
activities, commercial, 135, 346
adaptations, 387
addiction, 86, 166
administration, 8, 92, 131, 156, 215, 224, 347, 350, 363
administrative structure, 5, 74, 111
adornments, 10, 138, 414
ads, 83, 95, 249–50, 259, 266, 287–88, 332, 337
adultery, 151, 154–55
adulthood, 132, 185, 209, 217, 270, 319
affection, 30, 84, 89, 218, 246, 248–50, 252–59, 318, 335, 337, 344, 353–54, 360, 362, 395
Africa, 11–12, 14–15, 37–38, 46, 49, 57, 60, 64, 161, 175, 179–80, 304, 306, 392–93, 395
    eastern, 161–62
    northern Muslim, 74

African beliefs, 47
African-born blacks, 20, 64, 74, 146, 392, 395–96, 399
African coast, 26, 37, 136, 179, 186
African commercial traditions, 167
African cosmology, central, 306, 319
African couples, 134, 152, 161
African culture, 46–47, 55
African descendants, 19–20, 22, 24, 26, 28, 30–31, 32, 63, 101, 110, 228, 234, 310, 325, 331, 350, 393
African diaspora, 33, 144, 172–73, 217, 372, 418
African drums, 45
African funeral organizations, 78
African heritage, 47, 97–98, 101, 180, 358
African identities, 143, 179
African influence, 318
African languages in Brazilian Portuguese, 318–19
African marriage, 150, 162
African martial traditions, 389
African nations, 136. *See also* nations
African origins, 45, 55, 162, 179, 371
African parents, 149
African population, 46, 210, 347
African religious traditions, 46, 57, 60, 76
Africans
    emancipated, 151, 163
    enslaved, 5, 62, 67, 149, 184
    Mina, 150–51, 155, 157, 159, 171, 218

INDEX

African slave trade, 83, 178, 184, 314, 324
African societies, 318, 392
African women, 2, 41, 131–32, 138–39, 141–42, 147, 151–53, 156–58, 162–64, 166–68, 180, 187–88, 228, 230–31, 396
   freed, 127, 131, 138, 146
   married, 162
African words, 318–19
age, child-bearing, 211, 214–15, 219
agencies, 130, 133–34, 199, 328
agents, 16, 94, 121–22, 328, 358, 372, 384–85, 393
aggressions, 188, 222, 382–83
agility, 372, 375, 377–78, 384–85
agrarian history, 204
agreements, 5, 39, 79, 120, 170, 234–35, 254, 339
   implicit, 154
   marital, 152
   oral, 207
   prenuptial, 148, 153, 169
   unanimous, 239
agriculture, 5, 110, 117, 190
ailments, 230, 233
Alagoas, 110, 112, 193, 368, 381
Alegrete, 201, 205–6, 213, 222–23
alforrias, 171–72, 320, 417
allegations, 117, 154, 156, 165, 233, 328
alleys, 229, 376
alliances, 133, 149, 173, 220
allies, 209, 219, 222, 252, 306, 314–15
allowance (monthly), 362
alms, 65, 76, 188, 289, 306, 395–96, 398
altar, 76–77, 91, 100–101
ambition, 50, 92, 181, 209
   expansionist, 198
Americas, 9, 81, 83, 261, 263, 285, 306, 323, 325, 372, 393–94, 417
amulets, 10–11, 38, 60, 321, 417
ancestors, 13, 150, 161, 350, 416
angels, 257, 369
Angola, 15, 22, 38, 63, 70, 72, 80, 217, 314, 318–21, 371, 390

Angolans, 8, 15, 46, 63, 72, 135, 161–62, 171, 207, 306, 309, 314, 375, 386, 399
anguish, 13, 199
animal breeding, 20, 110
animalization, 88, 92, 96
announcements, 248, 327–28
annulment, 146, 255
anonymity, 1, 157, 355
Aracaju, 348–49, 359–60, 365–70
Aratu mill, 25–26
Archbishop of Bahia, 146, 174, 210
archives, 1, 9, 32, 47, 78, 143, 147, 175, 213, 221, 223, 288, 319, 325, 413–14
areas
   rural, 130, 376, 393, 400–401, 404, 407
   urban, 9, 13, 137, 140, 142, 325, 393
Argentina, 198, 221–22, 342
arguments, 90, 112, 165, 180, 201, 258, 268, 273, 279, 290, 292, 304–5, 313–14, 339
arms, 23, 45, 97, 101, 196, 263, 268, 276–77, 287, 372, 383–84
arm-to-arm vaccination, 60
army, 151–52, 374
arraia (capoeira move), 379
arrests, 113, 196, 233, 239, 294, 315, 373
arroba(s), 110, 228
artificial feeding, 265–67, 270
artisans, 130, 294, 300, 358, 379, 383
artists, 76, 80, 286, 387
ascension, 30, 41, 53, 264
   social, 8–9, 13, 31, 358, 415
aspirations, 240–41, 291, 317
   collective, 365
   personal, 236
assertions, 165, 317
Atlantic
   coast, 37
   dimensions, 57, 394, 417
   ports, 302
   routes, 33, 144, 172–73, 209, 418
   slave trade, 58, 312, 392. *See also* slave trade

INDEX

West Africa, 217
  world, 80, 300, 302, 389
attorneys, 155, 235, 239, 317, 321
auctions, 216, 248
audacity, 240, 256
authorities, 36, 39–40, 43–45, 48, 50, 54–55, 140, 167, 222, 238–39, 259, 335, 344, 363, 373–74
  colonial government, 39
  familial, 185
  judicial, 200, 215, 311
  military, 344
  public, 338, 340, 361
  retained, 294
autobiography, 194, 353
autonomy, 4, 10, 30, 41, 53, 64, 92, 119, 133–34, 142, 159, 235, 278, 295
axes, 11, 399
baby, 250–51, 254, 257, 265–66, 268
  arm, 275
  black, 250, 269
  master's, 253
  nurture, 263
  old, 254
  seigniorial, 263
  small, 268
  white, 249, 267, 278
backcountry, 120–21, 368
backyard, 183, 228, 274, 277
  large, 130
Bahia, 10–13, 19–20, 22–26, 29–31, 33, 143–44, 146, 173–75, 190–91, 210, 243–44, 319–20, 387–88, 414, 418
  province of, 193, 234, 237, 242, 244, 368
  women of African descent in, 19–20, 22, 24, 26, 28, 30, 32
bailiff, 36, 55, 136–37
bakers, 229, 384
Bantu, 152, 306, 318, 372
baptismal font, 204, 209
baptism registries, 26, 115, 143, 209, 213, 345, 365
baptisms, 26, 32, 101, 143, 208–10, 223, 365, 414
barbers, 206, 346

baron, 204, 242
basket, 12, 180–81, 229, 303, 378
bass drum, 362
beads, 10, 138, 397
beauty, 73–74, 88, 95, 97–99, 101, 158
behavior, 87, 93, 95, 102, 159, 239, 311, 337, 353, 355
  good, 157, 230, 337
  licentious, 155
  nurse's, 269
  repulsive, 91
  resigned, 92
  shameless, 51
  social feminine, 252
Belém, city of, 37, 375–77, 379–80, 383
beliefs, 14, 49, 59, 89, 263
  dominant, 264
  local, 59
  popular, 350
  religious, 76
Belo Horizonte, 18, 56–57, 341–42, 368, 416–17
beneficiaries, 4, 10, 21–22, 28–30, 204
Benguelas, 135, 161, 163, 171, 211, 396
Benin, 33, 135, 144, 169, 172, 208, 418
bigamy, 146, 168
biracial, 345, 348
bishops, 47, 171, 173
black children, 184, 268–69, 297
black churches, 64, 78
black community, 68, 204–5, 207, 210, 214, 217, 220, 394
black confraternities, 67
black female body, 83, 93, 391
black hair, 91, 101, 222
black miners, 67
black/mulatto parents, 12, 16, 21
blackness, 94, 98
blacks, 5, 40, 48–49, 62–64, 74, 81, 110–11, 228–29, 262, 264, 350–52, 357–58, 400–401, 405, 408–10
  emancipated, 44, 147
  in Brazilian literature, 103, 105
  of Mina origin, 147, 153, 158, 164, 190
  unemployed, 401, 410

421

black saints, 63–64, 357
black subjectivity, 392
black Uruguayans, 198
black women, 10–12, 15–16, 35–40, 42–46, 48, 50–61, 63–67, 83–84, 93–94, 96–97, 391–92, 394, 400–402, 408–11, 413–18
  dark-skinned, 16
  emancipated, 41, 67, 77, 130, 147
  free, 59, 67, 77, 396
  old, 88, 97, 103
black women street vendors, 51, 53, 186, 300, 378, 415, 417. *See also* street vendors
blessings, 47, 209, 216, 259, 307
blood, 96, 276, 365, 383
Boa Vista, 127, 130, 134, 136–37, 143
bondage, 8, 81, 283
bonds, 4, 134, 212, 249
border, 7, 196, 198, 203–4, 206, 209–10, 212, 215, 220–22, 224
  fragile, 89
  imperial, 222
  international, 376
  porous, 95
bosses, 261, 334, 416
bottle, 261, 265–67, 275, 278
boundaries, 128, 132, 333, 355
  cultural, 128
bourgeoisie, 88, 98, 100
bracelets, 135, 138
Brazil, 11–12, 18–20, 56–57, 63–65, 80–81, 120–25, 178–81, 192–94, 261–64, 278–81, 298–300, 317–21, 340–43, 368–69, 415–18
  captaincies of, 5, 16
  slaveholding, 136, 372
  southern, 6, 198
Brazilian-born blacks, 5, 132, 134, 147, 182, 392, 395
Brazilian cities, 142, 146, 157, 168
Brazilian doctors, 249, 266
Brazilian empire, 198, 325, 341
Brazilian historiography, 19, 24, 228, 417
Brazilian literature, 92, 96, 103, 105, 261

Brazilian Portuguese, 318, 320
Brazilian slavery, 144, 172, 193, 299, 310, 318, 321, 416. *See also under* slavery
breastfeeding, 249–53, 259–60, 264–67, 276, 278–79
  artificial, 265, 278
  maternal, 267
  mercenary, 263–64
  valued, 263
bride, 151, 160, 341
brotherhoods, 80–81, 347, 397, 399
bureaucrats, 45, 346
burial, 61, 76–78, 139–41, 188, 271, 344, 362, 399
  festive, 270
business, small, 41, 163, 167, 229, 394
businessmen, 92, 94, 136, 206
business woman, 38, 137, 345
Cabindas, 135, 147, 161–62, 171, 217
  emancipated, 164, 171
cabras, 5, 16, 20–21, 111
Cachoeira, 23–24, 213, 227, 241–42
caixa, 32, 123
Calabar, 161
calundus, 45, 47, 49, 209
Câmara Municipal, 18, 43, 55, 284–85, 289–90, 293, 296–98, 336, 341
candomblé, 25, 33, 45, 140, 143–44, 173, 357
capoeira
  TABAngola, 389
  culture of, 372–73, 378, 380, 382–85, 388
  experts in, 376
  game of, 374, 378–80, 384, 386
  gangs, 375–78
  groups, 373–75, 378, 380, 384, 390
  leaders, 380
  learned, 383
  practice of, 371–77, 384–85, 387–88
  regional, 386, 389
  roda(s), 378–79, 384, 386–88
  women of, 371–72, 374, 376–80, 382–88, 390
  world of, 377, 387

422

capoeira players, 373–74, 377–78, 380–82, 384–85
  arrested, 373
  distinguished, 380
  groups of, 381, 387
captaincies, 1–2, 5–7, 13, 39, 44, 48, 63–64, 66, 122
captains, 24–25, 27, 36, 176, 198
  ship, 381
captives, 51, 109–10, 116–17, 128–30, 135, 164–67, 197–98, 203–5, 207–9, 242–43, 259, 263–64, 312–13, 324–28, 335
  adult, 110, 130, 214, 325
  former African, 142
carnival folkloric groups, 130, 144, 357
carpenters, 229, 302, 315
carteira assinada, 402–3, 405, 408–9
casamentos, 31, 172–73, 190
cases (legal), 17, 22–24, 53, 118, 146–47, 152–53, 156, 163–64, 167–68, 170, 190, 192, 223, 334–35, 384
cash, 52, 138, 180, 185
Catholic Church, 13–15, 46, 53, 59, 63, 66, 146, 151, 156–57, 159–60, 168, 358
Catholic confraternities, 163
Catholic marriage, 147, 151, 153, 160
Catholic norms, 14
Catholic rituals, 66, 76, 78
cattle, 10, 20, 197, 216, 219, 221, 305
  breeding, 218
  carts, 129
  farm, 122, 307
celebrations, 42, 65, 76, 365–66, 417
census, 130, 142, 161, 172, 325–26, 329, 331, 340, 414
  national, 110
  total population, 50
Central Africa(ns), 82, 161–62, 217, 302, 319, 321, 372
ceremonies, 48, 283–84, 287–88, 293, 296, 344, 361, 364
  funeral, 343
  interment, 345

  municipal, 286, 297
  nighttime, 45
  religious, 66
certificate, 118, 367
  baptismal, 160
chains, 8, 10, 66, 139, 347–48
chairs, 28, 139, 238–39, 248, 269, 354
chambermaids, 249, 334
chapels, 15, 64, 74, 76, 198, 397
charity, 65, 76, 286, 289, 359, 396
charms, 10–11, 88, 96–97, 99, 312. *See also* amulets
childhood, 124, 149, 281, 332, 345, 353
children, 11–13, 20–25, 27–29, 131–34, 184–87, 198–203, 209–12, 217–21, 248–60, 267–78, 284–85, 287, 289–92, 332–33, 395–98
  care of, 175, 334
  illegitimate, 20, 151, 153
  lost, 220
  master's, 269
  needy, 359
  newborn, 276
  pardo, 24, 26
  small, 137, 196, 229, 252, 263, 270–71, 274
  sponsoring, 209
cigar maker, 236
cinnamon, 96, 378
citizens, 122, 291, 293–95, 298, 343
  free, 291
city council, 147, 206, 284, 288, 293, 336, 339
Classification, 201, 242–43, 387, 389
  racial, 95
class inequalities, 388
classroom, 343, 346, 353, 363, 369
clergymen, 27, 64, 302–3, 305, 308, 312, 315, 319
clerk, 222, 313, 334, 346
clientele, 36, 47, 50, 54, 134, 167, 185, 188, 328, 350, 355, 364, 383
climate, 36, 353
  new economic, 108
cloth, 65, 135, 139, 181, 248
  acquired white, 38

black wool, 3
blue, 3, 8
expensive, 11, 140
linen, 8
thread, 3
clothes, 11–14, 41, 52, 97, 138, 189, 199, 228, 238, 252, 256, 258, 303, 332, 334–35
ironing, 291
owner's, 327
washed, 166
coachmen, 90, 130, 229
coal, 166, 335
Coast, Ivory, 169
Coast, Mina, 136, 144, 188, 194
Cocal, 60, 70, 74–80
codes, 94, 310, 317, 377
provincial, 375
coffee, 175, 177
coin, 228, 258, 303, 395, 397–98
cola nuts, 149, 181
colonial period, 9, 59–60, 63–64, 67, 72, 323–24
colonies, 18, 33, 39, 42, 171, 177, 204
maroon, 348
colonization, 177, 324
color, 18–19, 22, 26–28, 30–31, 33, 36, 39, 42, 50–51, 54, 81, 95–96, 100–102, 401–2, 416
free people of, 128, 130
free women of, 19–20, 28–31, 81, 142
person of, 404, 407
women of, 20, 22–24, 30, 36, 52, 54, 84, 98, 100–101, 343
commerce, 5, 18, 58, 173, 194, 300, 394, 418
community, 37, 48, 59–60, 65, 78, 128, 140, 149, 217, 354, 359, 393
quilombo, 318
religious, 64, 357
stable, 59, 393
companions, 4, 7, 25, 95, 134, 160, 165, 209–10, 232, 393
daily, 378
eternal, 101
female, 132

company, 21–22, 24, 26, 108, 192, 227
compassion, 271, 273, 286
compensation, 200, 253, 326
received, 293
competition, 188, 387
brutal, 268, 275
complainant, 114, 239, 242–43
complaints, 45, 47, 51–52, 54, 60, 140, 151, 166, 196, 199–200, 229, 233, 235, 259
complexion, 97, 99–100
colored, 111
darker-than-white, 84
compositions, 11, 49, 212, 329, 358–59, 412
ethnic, 49
musical, 364
comrades, 134, 140, 303, 311
concubines, 22, 42, 50, 93, 303, 381
conditions
sanitary, 265
social, 67, 89, 99, 111, 121, 186, 324, 326
conflict, 48, 92, 104, 125, 140, 153, 271, 381–83
marital, 151, 159
social, 102
confraternities, 59–60, 63–66, 68–72, 74–78, 81, 129, 139–40, 399
black, 60–61, 63, 65, 72, 77–78, 81
large, 67
congestion, produced, 348
Congo, 217–18, 302, 305–6, 314, 357, 398
Congolese, 135, 161–62, 302
consensus, 215, 266, 340
consumption, 238, 402, 405, 409–10
contingencies, 54, 304, 319
continuity, 68, 90, 134, 346, 372
contraband, 198, 224
control, social, 40, 264, 336, 375
convent, 11, 28, 141, 275
cooks, 63, 86, 92, 129–30, 159, 229, 302, 328, 334
expert, 257, 328, 335
copper, 111

cookware, 3, 11, 397
oven, 397–98
coral, 11
beaded, 3
corn porridge, 378
corpse, 228, 232–33
corruption, 83, 91
moral, 90–91
Cotinguiba, 345, 349, 354, 359, 363, 368
cotton, 110, 117, 129–30, 346, 349
warehouses, 128
council, 55, 288–89, 336
members, 284–86, 288–93, 295–97, 338, 355
countryside, 142, 189, 249, 302
couples, 7, 132–33, 138, 145–47, 149–56, 160, 162, 164–65, 205, 212, 219–20, 229–31, 233–35, 254, 305
courage, 4, 118, 253, 377
court, 36, 109, 112–14, 117–19, 124, 205, 210, 283, 285–86, 290, 293, 298, 315, 317, 341
civil, 146, 156, 181
municipal, 222
orphan's, 242
superior, 113–14, 118, 201, 240
credit, 8, 181–82, 186, 399
market, 41
negotiating, 188
creditors, 108, 112–13, 141, 181, 187, 399
creoles, 5, 79, 133, 302, 315, 347
old, 137
crime, 44, 46, 52, 54, 91, 118, 197–98, 200–201, 205, 221–23, 227, 230, 232–33, 304, 311
alleged, 238
committed, 315
special, 374
criminal code, 196, 200
criminalization, 379, 385
criminal trials, 192, 221, 234–35, 241, 271, 277, 279, 302, 311, 317, 335, 375, 377, 382, 384–85, 387–89. *See also* cases

capoeira-related, 382
crioula(s), 9–11, 15–16, 20, 84, 93, 97, 143, 146–47, 157, 161–62, 199, 202, 217, 219, 222
emancipated, 10, 13, 20
young, 22, 92
crioulo(s), 5, 28–29, 54, 70, 74, 79, 147, 161, 170, 199, 207, 217, 229, 397
little, 11, 15, 196
crisis, 124, 338, 340, 349, 360
crops, 177, 197, 206, 218–19
abandoned, 201
cruelties, 47, 336, 348
cultural artifacts, 48, 358
cultural practices, 385, 417
culture, 5, 33, 37, 51, 56–57, 77, 82, 217, 256, 262–63, 323, 363–64, 375, 387, 393
black, 371, 385
feminized, 286
local, 26
masculinized, 380
popular, 352
currency, 4, 8, 21, 25, 36, 40, 86, 107, 127, 148, 152, 180, 186, 206, 228
curses, 47, 49, 95
custodians, 107, 109, 117–18, 123, 151, 154, 157, 165
customs, 17, 39, 56, 131, 194, 310
agent, 203
good, 355, 358
offices, 222
Dahomey, 208
daily payment, 39, 43–44, 53–54, 183. *See also* earnings
dances, 43, 47–48, 60, 72, 159, 356–59, 371–72, 376
batuque, 47
daughter, 6–8, 13–14, 21, 24–25, 52, 100, 115–17, 131, 133, 182, 185–86, 218–19, 283, 289–91, 395–96
alleged, 25
illegitimate, 127
legitimate, 20, 26, 28, 115, 204, 223, 271
dealers, 181, 328

rich, 186
death, 2, 12–15, 61, 76, 143–44, 181, 183–85, 216–17, 230–32, 270–71, 276–77, 348, 363–64, 395, 397–99
  child's, 276, 281
  owner's, 118
  person's, 141
  violent, 234
debtors, 108, 141, 181
debts, 8, 13, 108, 112–14, 148, 151, 155–56, 179, 181–82, 185–86, 206, 214, 395, 397, 399
  marital, 151
deceased husband, 141, 399
declaration, 22, 156, 181, 200–201, 218, 272, 362
  personal, 15
dedication, 246, 252, 255, 257–58, 343–44, 361
  passive, 259
defects, 86, 99, 327, 337
  intrinsic moral, 265
defendant, 145, 151, 154–56, 164–65, 169–71, 196–97, 199, 201, 237–41, 273–75, 279, 303, 315, 382–84, 387–89
defense, 103, 109, 112, 122, 156–57, 201, 230, 232, 240, 275, 298, 317, 387
degree, 78, 176, 180, 205, 324, 368, 393
  bachelor's, 112, 222
dehydration, 275
delicacies, 135, 137, 256, 335
democracy, 362
  racial, 278
dependence, 30, 177, 186, 255, 267
dependents, 22, 29, 182, 255, 336–37
deponent, 113, 229–30, 272–73, 275–77
deposit, 123, 170, 242
destiny, 101, 351, 361, 363
devil, 46–47, 49, 58, 351
devotion, 15, 81, 88, 356–57
  judge for, 67, 69, 72
  pervasive, 305
diaper, 276, 280

diaspora, 33, 144, 172–73, 219, 306, 393, 400, 418. *See also* African diaspora
  transatlantic, 208
difficulties, 6, 40, 117, 175, 294, 339, 345
  financial, 113
dignitaries, 284
dignity, 157, 234, 292, 365
diploma, 205, 349, 368
directorates, 64, 66, 68, 77, 198, 367
disagreements, 140, 152, 233–34, 289, 294, 310
disappearance, 208, 238–39, 253, 260
discourse, 94, 102, 259, 262, 266, 280, 286, 289, 292, 308, 351
  abolitionist, 287
  dominant, 251
  educated, 274
  hygienist, 270
  literary, 88
  medical, 264, 266, 274
discoveries, 265
  modern, 265
  new, 265, 351
discriminations, 141, 411
diseases, 81, 178, 230, 327, 392
  children's, 251
  suspicious, 249
disorder, 27, 129, 230, 385
disputes, 49, 113, 140, 147, 154, 156, 159–60, 164–65, 199, 220, 294
  complicated, 165
  electoral, 375
  judicial, 26, 399
  marital, 157
diversity, 39, 55, 121
divinations, 46–47
divorce, 23, 31, 145–47, 150, 153, 157–59, 164, 166, 168–70, 173–74, 188, 190
  dealing with their, 147
  ecclesiastical, 148, 151, 154–55, 160, 165
doblas, 397–98
dobras, 395–96, 399

doctors, 83, 249–52, 254, 260, 265, 267, 278, 343, 346, 348, 350–51, 355, 362–63, 415
  hygienist, 249–50
  medical, 248, 252, 259, 262, 280
  requirements, 272
  visiting, 52
domesticity, 264, 266, 290, 297, 299, 341
domestic servants, 189, 290–92, 295, 327–28, 333, 337–38, 340, 347
domestic services, 290–92, 325–26, 328–33, 337–40
  characterized, 339
  performed, 211
  regulating, 340
  rental of, 331
domestic slavery, 277, 323–25, 335
  sentimentalized, 263
domestic slaves, 25, 88–89, 97, 130, 137, 177, 179, 264, 301–2, 311, 324–27, 335
  female, 325
domestic work, 129, 189, 254, 323–25, 327, 331–32, 336–37, 339–40
  performed, 323, 331
domestic workers, 246, 255, 333–34, 339–40, 402, 404, 407–8, 410–12
donations, 61, 65, 72, 75, 78–79, 236, 286
  annual, 78
dowries, 21, 75, 133, 149, 155, 167, 212, 218–19
drama, 85, 87, 102, 311, 378
  short, 176
dreams, 84, 190, 234, 238, 304–5, 309, 314
drinking, 41, 240, 275
  poison, 84
droughts, 142, 216, 392
  major, 121
drumming, 43, 48, 51, 348, 362
drunkenness, 44, 48
duties, 76, 89, 145, 154, 157–58, 222, 269, 274, 324, 333, 339
  domestic, 302, 326

marital, 155, 157
performing, 222
reciprocal, 252
earnings, 40–42, 51, 175, 335
  daily, 51, 199
earrings, 11, 355, 397
Ecclesiastical Court, 146, 151, 153–54, 157–58, 160, 164, 170, 173
economy, 110, 175, 324, 349
  subsistence, 260
education, 57, 99, 251, 290, 297, 299, 320, 344, 351–52, 354, 357, 359, 363–64
  basic, 349, 352
  higher, 354, 408–10
  history of, 320, 364
  improved, 362
  physical, 371
elite, 37, 90, 98, 155, 168, 224, 267, 290–92, 295, 297, 310
  couples, 159, 291, 352
  educated, 395
  local, 239
  socio-economic, 130
  urban, 139
Elmina, 169
emancipated slaves, 14–16, 42, 48, 67, 71, 113, 146, 149, 160–62, 166, 254
emancipation, 5, 12–13, 19, 41–43, 48, 163–65, 202–5, 208–13, 229–30, 235–37, 239–40, 242, 284–85, 288, 294–96
  acquired, 41, 127, 200
  conditional, 198, 254
  letter of, 19, 30, 85, 108–9, 115–16, 118–20, 128, 163, 165, 197, 207–8, 211, 221–22, 286
  unconditional, 117
emancipation ceremony, 293
emancipation fund, 120–21, 283–85, 288, 298
emancipation laws, 312, 348
embargo, 107, 112, 182
embroidery, 3, 332, 346, 363
empire, 33, 82, 123, 200, 229, 327, 332, 338, 340. *See also* Brazilian empire

employers, 249, 253, 257, 332, 336–37, 339–40, 402–3
  category of, 405, 409
empress, 283, 286–87, 293, 296
enemies, 7, 91, 199, 376
enslaved women, 31, 73, 108, 110, 112, 114, 116, 118–22, 124–25, 292–93, 295, 324, 336, 392–94
  poor, 239
enslavement, 5, 122, 208, 302, 304, 306, 311
enslavers, 120, 122
entities
  ancestral, 314
  sacred Yoruba, 11
escape, 6, 36, 48, 83, 89, 158, 196, 199, 202–5, 209, 213, 215–16, 221, 240, 348
  helping enslaved people, 393
  punishment, 164
  route, 36, 198, 203
  unsuccessful, 209
escravas ("enslaved females"), 104, 123–24, 192, 278–79, 308, 416
escravos ("slaves"), 18, 57, 79–80, 123–24, 172, 224, 244, 297–99, 310, 319–22, 370, 416–17
estate, 92, 138, 153, 155, 168, 179, 182, 184–85, 201, 211, 216
  mother-in-law's, 132
  real, 138, 141, 216
Ethiopia, 74
ethnic identities, 81, 172–73, 225, 418
ethnicity, 49, 57–58, 69, 71, 81, 131, 136, 140–41, 162, 172, 175, 209, 320, 372, 376
  diverse, 12, 20, 345, 352
Europe, 5, 91, 249, 260, 265–66, 290, 376
  travelers, 83, 89
evil, 63, 83, 90, 265, 273, 305
evolution, 350, 405
Ewe, 24, 208, 219
exile, 46, 55, 242
exploitation, 53, 227, 234–35, 326, 336, 347

sexual, 53
extramarital affairs, 19, 154
faith, 15, 35, 237, 344, 354, 356, 359, 394
fame, 39, 45, 354
families, 27, 89–91, 131–34, 149–50, 177–78, 187–88, 248–53, 255–58, 269–72, 290–92, 324, 326–28, 332–33, 337–38, 384
  black, 48, 214, 244, 393, 413
  imperial, 283–84, 286–87
  invented, 182, 186
  large, 132, 150, 178
  mothers of, 251–52, 291, 295
  new, 149
  noble, 220, 284
  nuclear, 115
  poor, 52, 260, 324
  slaveholding, 89
  wealthy, 324, 360
  white, 90, 245–46, 252, 256–57, 291
family
  life, 134, 241, 393, 416
  members, 6, 120, 132, 134, 221, 253, 260, 293
  structure, 12, 52, 120, 128, 131, 134, 140, 233, 337, 394
farm, 7–8, 20–21, 24, 37, 97, 130, 176–77, 187, 189, 196, 205–6, 398
  coffee, 185, 187
farmers, 130, 187–88, 196–97, 272, 321
gaúcho, 198
fate, 221, 267–68, 304, 414
  biologic, 264
father, 9, 11, 14, 25, 27, 85, 203, 207, 210, 214, 216, 289, 291, 302, 305–6
fear, 46, 54, 85, 89–90, 251–52, 339
Federal Writers Project, 268, 279–80
female, slaves, 19, 30, 83, 86, 130, 167, 185, 219, 323, 326
females, 130, 133, 135, 243, 326, 371, 375, 391
  white, 77
festival, 63, 65, 72, 75–76, 81, 173, 356–58, 417
  lavish, 356

literary drama, 355
literary music, 359–60
traditional, 356
fever, 178
yellow, 249
fidelity, 30, 170, 222, 246
fights, 44, 107, 110–11, 120, 142, 188, 220, 231, 254, 284–85, 294, 376–77, 379–84
daily, 227
woman's, 108
fireworks, 65, 349, 356–57
flowers, 3, 95, 105, 224, 256
food, 24, 37–39, 43, 47, 65, 135, 145, 156, 159, 250, 252, 256, 268, 270, 335–36
selling, 45, 108, 155, 158–59, 166
foolishness, 93, 102
foreigners, 141, 223, 325, 374
forests, 6, 36, 111, 177, 310, 321
fortune, 2, 13, 33, 35, 41, 127, 135, 145, 152–53, 159, 171, 240
largest, 11, 13
small, 152, 167
freed Africans, 130, 138, 141, 152, 184, 190
freed black woman, 19–20, 22, 24, 28–31, 114–15, 129, 142, 144, 180–81, 185, 228, 230, 283–84, 294–96, 331–32
freedmen, 5, 27, 31, 124, 128–29, 133, 139, 142, 160, 163, 242, 244, 310, 312–13, 349
freed Mina people, 146, 155, 160
freedom, 42, 107–9, 113–16, 119–21, 163–67, 171–72, 178–88, 199–201, 207–8, 211–12, 255, 283–85, 291–96, 299, 348
fights for, 107, 110, 120
letter of, 108–9, 113, 116–18, 120, 123, 180, 184, 191, 199, 207, 211, 283, 286, 293–94, 317–18
obtaining, 203, 311
promises of, 211, 270
purchase, 42, 184
freedwoman, false, 92

free womb, 93, 109, 111, 118, 285, 298, 395
logic of the, 284–85, 288, 297
Freyre, Gilberto, 99, 103, 138, 143–44, 335, 342
friendship, 89, 134, 140, 151–52, 186, 237, 337, 344, 362
sincere, 141, 196, 221–22, 234
fruits, 6, 37–38, 92, 158, 180–81, 197, 258–59, 344, 378
street vendor, 145, 148, 154, 394
fund, 121, 284–85, 288, 295
municipal, 288
funeral rites, 81, 173, 271
funerals, 61, 64, 76, 128, 139–41, 345
dignified, 76, 140
furnishings, 14, 29, 138–39, 143, 248, 257
gallery, 84–85, 95, 364
game, 35–36, 38, 40, 42, 44, 46, 48, 50, 52, 54, 56, 58, 157, 377, 379
child's, 89
complex, 99
political, 220, 374
street gambling, 385
game houses, 155
gangs, 224, 315, 374, 385
Gbe-speakers, 25
gender, 19, 30–31, 42–43, 172–73, 281, 283, 295, 299–300, 352, 369, 371, 388, 390–92, 408–9, 415–18
hierarchy, 28, 405
relations, 103, 227, 241, 323, 363, 387, 394, 400–401
generations, 14, 116, 290, 343, 345, 362, 400
gesture, 133, 184, 253, 344
leaping, 384
gifts, 112, 212, 218, 288, 296, 363
physical, 95
girls, 8, 12, 84, 88, 90–91, 97–101, 251, 254, 258–59, 290–92, 332, 346, 352, 381
beautiful, 99
childlike, 91
creole, 134

dark-skinned black, 21
little black, 3, 258–59, 328, 333
servant, 329, 331, 333, 335
small white, 245
young black, 12, 21, 26, 91, 101, 179
young *mulatta*, 12–13, 91, 95
God, 14–15, 46, 93–94, 238, 306–7, 309, 314, 344, 363, 365
godchildren, 8, 132–34, 185, 344, 395–96
freed, 133
godparents, 26, 115–16, 132–34, 150, 163, 186, 207, 209–10, 222, 362
Goiânia, 73, 78–79, 81
Goiás, 60, 62, 65, 67, 69, 71–75, 78–81
captaincy of, 59–60, 65, 72, 74, 79, 81
city of, 63, 68, 72–73, 77–78
gold, 3, 5, 10–11, 13, 35, 37, 39–41, 49–50, 64–67, 74, 76, 78, 136, 138, 301
age of, 347, 349
amount of, 40, 47, 67
contraband, 39
donations of, 60, 66–68, 72, 75
powdered, 41
Gold Coast, 169
goods, 2, 4, 19–20, 27, 36–37, 40–41, 43, 57, 108, 153, 156, 215, 218, 220, 230
baked, 35, 394
basic, 39, 117
confiscated, 36
gourds, 47, 181
government, 80, 142, 241, 284, 344, 362
head of, 112
governors, 24, 27, 48, 55, 344, 363
grandchildren, 13, 66, 116, 134, 194, 296, 398, 400
grandmother, 251, 258–59
child's, 272, 275, 277
gratitude, 30, 246, 252, 255, 344, 360
graves, 15, 27, 139, 344, 362, 397
groceries, 129, 137, 166, 181, 302–3, 416, 418
groups

ethnic, 49, 70, 145, 147, 152, 208, 310
ruling, 64, 339
social, 9, 42, 132, 149, 155, 157, 302, 310, 387–88
guardianship, 123, 131–32
guilt, 222, 251, 274, 314
habits, 37, 265, 272, 290, 305, 311, 353
happiness, 85, 87, 96, 256, 284, 357
hardships, 100, 113, 234
hardworking, 86, 188, 292, 365, 383
healers, 38, 47, 60
health, 14, 83, 94, 153, 206, 251–52, 267, 272, 307, 351, 382
good, 237, 304–5, 307
poor, 263
heart, 43, 48, 85, 96, 98, 100–101, 164, 258, 286, 338, 411
heavy, 84, 289, 314
heavens, 90, 95, 251, 344, 395
heirs, 20, 24–25, 27–31, 115–16, 128, 134, 141, 153, 179, 182–83, 185–86, 207, 215, 218, 398–400
direct, 132, 396
legitimate, 151, 154, 183
universal, 13, 17, 21–22
hierarchy, 19, 139, 172, 220, 270, 335
social, 30, 283, 315
socio-familial, 212
hinterlands, 6–7, 10
historiography, 9, 16, 86, 92, 321, 392. *See also* Brazilian historiography
traditional, 121
homeland, 63, 309, 344
homicide, 222, 242
horses, 20, 140, 196, 199, 203, 206, 216, 222, 230
tame, 216, 218
house
brothel, 51
candomblé, 373
detention, 289
master's, 232, 236, 315
households, 12, 94, 110, 134, 256–57, 264, 272, 312, 324, 337, 391
slaveholding, 12

430

urban, 325
wealthy, 257
house servants, 253, 325, 327, 334
humiliation, 255–56, 287, 335, 348, 413
hunger, 36, 257, 275, 392
husband, 6–7, 22–24, 131–34, 137–38, 140–41, 145–50, 154–59, 163–64, 166–70, 186–88, 219–20, 302–6, 313–14, 395–97, 399–400
illiterate, 180, 182, 196–97, 213, 271, 296, 302
illness, 146, 230, 233, 263, 395, 399
    cardiac, 223
    mental, 271
imperial Brazil, 110, 112, 114, 162, 169, 172, 323, 325–26, 334, 390
imprisonment, 36, 60, 137, 196, 201, 204, 376
income, 10, 52, 94, 117, 138, 153, 158, 183, 236, 326, 411
independence, 167, 176, 188
Independence Day, 117, 284, 354
Indians, 5–6, 8, 40, 64, 114, 177
indictments, 147, 151, 154, 156, 158, 164, 169–70, 315
inequalities, 364, 391–92, 394, 396, 398, 400, 402, 406, 408, 410, 414, 416–18
    social, 122
infant, 209, 267–68, 270
    sicknesses, 251
infanticide, 393
inferiority, 39, 202, 255
inhabitants, 5, 74, 110, 122, 192, 198, 215, 272, 310, 312, 347, 360
    local, 221
inheritance, 41, 127–28, 132–33, 154, 167, 205, 214, 218, 220, 236, 395–96
    material, 12
    paternal, 216
innocence, 101, 200–201, 207, 210, 273
    absolute, 199
institutions, 72, 90, 105, 108, 146, 170, 187, 290, 300, 345, 373
    ethnic, 163
    religious, 47
    social, 290, 363

intellectuals, 346, 350, 375, 385, 387, 400
intermediary, 178, 204, 237, 328, 350
interrogation, 46, 171, 232–33, 279, 302–3, 315, 392
intimacy, 220, 248, 267–68, 274, 299, 336–37, 341
intimate relationships, 92, 211
invention, 265, 278, 372, 385
iron neck collars, 347
jail, 188, 238, 385
Jeje
    Mina, 24–26, 49, 147, 182, 208
    nation in Bahia, 33, 173
jewelry, 10–11, 13, 41, 133, 138, 148, 152, 165, 248–49, 256, 400
jobs, 2, 130, 259–60, 323, 331, 333, 337, 339, 403, 408
    domestic, 131, 324
journalists, 346, 355, 363
judges, 59–60, 62, 64, 66–70, 72, 74–76, 78, 80, 82, 113, 118, 201, 215–16, 271, 273
    district court, 118
    female, 65, 69, 72, 75
    male, 65, 72
    municipal, 271, 277
    presiding, 69–71, 76
judgment, 49, 52, 187
justice, 11, 107, 111, 252, 373–74
kingdom, 22, 155, 171, 208
kinship, 82, 134, 206, 209, 362
    spiritual, 125, 140, 144
    symbolic, 267
kisses, 100, 231, 287
kitchen, 63, 139, 183, 188–89, 199, 292
knife, 11, 93, 155, 316, 373, 375, 378, 380–81, 383
    large, 383
    short, 189
knowledge, 109, 205, 237, 388
    exclusionary, 264
    medical, 415
    monopolized, 266
knowledge production, 413
Kongo, 82. *See also* Congo

labor, 124, 158, 166–67, 196, 269, 326, 332–33, 336, 373, 409
  cheapest, 332
  domestic, 331, 403, 405, 408
  forced, 373
  unwaged, 405, 409
labor market, 342, 392–93, 400–402, 408, 411, 416
Lady of Mercy, 60, 63, 70, 74–75, 78–79
landowners, 205, 299, 393
landscape, 111, 130, 312
  urban, 347
languages, 49, 51, 57, 77, 122–23, 175, 318, 320, 349, 354, 374, 393
  feminine abolitionist, 295
  figurative, 96
  moral, 51
Laranjeiras, city of, 343–49, 351–55, 357–69
Laranjeiras School, 366
laundresses, 129–30, 328, 383
laws, 35, 37, 39–40, 43–44, 112, 118–20, 131–32, 184, 192, 222, 294–95, 300, 312–13, 315–16, 336–37
  white, 148, 154, 167
  zoning, 336
lawsuits, 112–14, 117, 123, 146–47, 154
lawyers, 85, 92, 108, 112, 151, 157, 169, 205, 239–40, 254–55, 273, 346, 355, 363, 384
legal status, 147, 229, 284–85
letters, 117–19, 176, 178, 197, 211, 221–23, 237–38, 240, 283, 289, 293–94, 296, 303–6, 308–10, 313–19
  complete, 304
  exchanging, 309–11, 353
  false, 92
  official, 215
  personal/intimate, 310
liberation, 33, 74, 109, 124, 144, 191, 224, 244, 293, 298–300, 303, 313, 320, 341–42, 348–49
  limited, 12, 112
Lisbon, 23, 46, 79–81, 103, 122, 190, 320–21

literate, 292, 296, 312, 316–17
  elite, 264, 270
literature, 87, 93, 98, 100, 102–3, 372, 374, 400
  naturalist, 87
livestock, 5, 215
Livro de Ouro fund, 283–84, 286, 288–90, 292–96, 298, 300. *See also* emancipation fund
loan, 13, 50, 85, 153, 156, 163, 240
love, 84–85, 89–90, 100–101, 151–52, 221–22, 245–46, 248, 250, 252, 254, 256, 258–60, 262, 359, 413–14
  holy, 287
  loyal, 278
  maternal, 251, 287, 351
  new, 168
  sublime, 287
loyalty, 25, 134, 186, 252–53, 256, 365, 383
  blind, 88
Luanda, 38, 309, 398
luck, 49, 168, 211, 216, 234, 250, 399
luxury, 22, 138, 248, 257
mãe (mother), 52, 85, 102, 104, 260–61, 278–79
magic, 47, 49, 58, 320
magistrates, 114, 137
maids, 86, 97, 101, 104, 134, 253, 257, 264, 271, 287, 291, 295, 328, 334–36, 338
  favorite, 88, 98, 189, 327
  immoral, 84, 91
  old, 90
malnutrition, 263
malungos, 134, 321
mammy, 263, 269, 281
manioc, producing, 38, 228, 399–400
mansions, 144, 360
manumission, 15, 21, 113, 140, 211, 236, 285, 292, 394, 398–99
markets, 2, 5, 38, 93, 150–51, 159, 163, 167, 180, 334
Maroon women, 416
marriage registries, 25–26, 169

432

INDEX

marriages, 22–23, 26, 131–32, 145–46, 148–55, 160–63, 167–70, 172, 180–81, 187, 212, 215, 292, 351, 395–96
   arranged, 150
   common-law, 8
   condition of, 153
   legalization of, 154, 165
   maintaining, 134
   new, 146
   prior, 395
martial art, 372, 385
masculine, 7, 44, 52, 131
masses, 14, 64, 141, 188, 355–58, 363, 397–98
   celebrate, 64, 398
   chapel, 2
   solemn, 65, 355
masters, 25–28, 47, 88–90, 92, 207–8, 211, 213–14, 216–17, 231–33, 240–42, 252–56, 303–6, 312–16, 333–39, 347–49
   alleged, 118
   assassinated, 348
   dear, 84, 360
   deceased, 214, 344
   new, 254–55
   priest, 306
   unhappy, 86
   unknown, 133, 178
maternity, 260, 270, 283, 287–88, 292, 351, 417
   scientific, 264, 266
mayor, 355, 361, 363
medical care, 81, 249, 343
medicine, 252, 259, 395
melons, 197, 228
melting pot, 5
memoirs, 190, 194, 259, 268
memory, 80–81, 102, 105, 179, 209, 224, 255, 257, 320, 343–45, 362–65, 367, 369, 395
   childhood, 309
   historical, 287
   place of, 364
   wrong side of, 57, 415

mercenary, 278, 280
merchandise, 38, 214, 249, 379
merchants, 129, 180, 187, 302
   entrepreneurial, 149
mercy, 23, 52, 60, 63, 70, 74–75, 78–79
middle classes, 228, 239, 264
military, 210, 374, 402–3, 405, 408
milk, 37, 249–50, 257, 265–67, 270, 275–78, 382
   animal, 251, 260
   contaminated, 265
   donkey, 266
   good, 280
   maternal, 251, 267
   modified powder, 267
   nutritious, 265
   pasteurization of, 265–66
   producing, 263
   purest, 250
mills, 117, 346, 397
   small flour, 399
Minas Gerais, 1–2, 4–7, 9, 12–14, 16, 18, 36–37, 40–42, 49–50, 56–57, 80–81, 176–77, 189–90, 193–94, 415–17
   captaincy of, 47, 50, 190, 194
miners, 49–50
mines, 39, 44, 56–57
   black men of the, 51
   rich, 66
minister, 193, 284, 314, 374
miscegenation, 46, 54
mistresses, 51, 53, 55, 88, 90, 120–21, 197, 199, 205–6, 212–13, 220, 254, 286, 288, 316
   foreign, 294
   little, 90, 135
   old, 11, 91, 101
mixed race, 5, 20, 79, 87, 110–11, 161, 167, 234, 236, 289, 294, 397
   children, 12–13
mobility, 20, 27–28, 30–31, 188, 235, 293–94, 315
   social, 5, 19, 30–31
modernity, 103, 298, 375

money, 131, 133, 148, 151–52, 154–55, 164, 166, 169, 179–84, 235–41, 288–89, 305, 308, 314, 399–400
saving, 184, 285, 305
morality, 13, 54, 103, 174, 337, 352, 355, 358
morbid, 351–52
mortgage, 87, 112, 156
mother, 26, 28–29, 85, 115–17, 178–79, 183–85, 210, 248–52, 263–65, 269–71, 273–75, 283, 285–87, 289, 291–92
black, 259–61, 263
enslaved, 285–86
new, 248–49, 252
sanitary, 249, 252
spiritual, 360
motherhood, 11, 94, 220, 363
mountains, 6, 35, 37, 223
movement, 10, 33, 39, 102, 129, 136, 171, 196, 306, 372, 383, 389
abolitionist, 119, 124, 285–86, 312, 348
feminist, 415
social, 400
Mozambique, 135, 161, 320
mulatas, 16, 27–28, 44, 84–86, 95, 97–99, 101, 104, 108, 115
beautiful, 84, 96–97, 101
vain, 95–96
mulattos, 5, 13, 20, 27, 30, 44, 48, 54, 64, 79, 103, 111, 217, 261, 350
emancipated, 30
little, 12, 27
municipality, 109, 290, 326, 338, 352, 357, 363, 366
rural, 110, 187
murder, 229, 233, 241, 273
music, 48, 65, 348, 357–58, 393
sacred, 359
myth, 33, 57, 365, 416
nagô, 49, 147, 182, 208, 227, 347, 357–58
nannies, 263–64, 271, 274–75, 300, 328

nations (*nações*), 83, 103, 140, 144, 157, 161–63, 166, 168, 171–73, 194, 298–99, 300, 418
ethnic, 3
labyrinth of, 162, 172–73, 194, 299
mestiça, 97
natural breastfeeding, 264–66, 280–81
rejecting, 264
natural children, 20–21, 25, 258
natural sciences, 353, 366
navy, 152, 299, 374
necklaces, 3, 8, 355
negotiations, 85, 104, 116, 120, 125, 127, 185, 204, 214, 254, 268, 288, 337, 387
neighborhood, 21–22, 25, 111, 128–30, 136–37, 140–42, 180, 238, 326, 357, 374
central, 130, 384
networks, 3, 6, 58, 167, 185, 207, 209, 212, 220, 252, 293, 355, 360–61, 385
commercial, 5, 149
social, 16, 112, 127, 140, 209
newspapers, 248, 287–88, 293–94, 343, 346, 351, 360, 385, 388
abolitionist, 294, 348
N'golo, 371–72
nickname, 245, 257–58, 379
norms, 259, 351
religious, 49
social, 202
Nossa Senhora, 7, 15, 18, 22–23, 25, 28–29, 56, 69, 78–79, 81, 357, 399, 414
nostalgia, 253, 364
notaries, 116, 211, 222, 395
nurses, 129, 245–46, 248–51, 253–60, 265, 267–73, 275–78
captive, 278
dry, 246, 253, 256, 334
rented, 270
sick, 253
nursing, 89, 248, 264–65, 268, 277
artificial, 265–66, 279–81
obedience, 104, 120, 134, 170, 221, 246, 251, 257–58, 261, 342, 416

objects, 2, 4, 23, 72, 133, 136, 138, 256, 286, 303, 376
obligations, 53, 76, 118, 164, 178, 185, 188, 254, 301, 314, 340, 397
occupations, 44, 135, 137–38, 152, 155, 180, 229, 331–32, 402, 405
  honest, 155
  lack of, 155
  position of, 404–5, 407, 411–12
  repressive, 44
officials, 35, 65, 68–69, 137
offspring, 25, 27, 150, 167, 199, 209, 211–12, 214–15, 221, 235, 251, 264, 268
oppression, 119, 241, 387, 393, 395, 400, 413, 415
opulence, 56, 347
oral transmission, 59, 394
orixás, 143, 357
ornaments, 77, 139, 356
orphans, 37, 109, 117, 184, 215
ouro (gold), 6, 17, 58, 79, 284, 289, 417
overseers, 39, 97, 347–48
owners, 41–45, 47–48, 53, 112–13, 115, 117–23, 178–79, 184–85, 187–88, 196–98, 203–6, 218–20, 233–37, 326–28, 335–37
  former, 115, 185, 197, 200, 206, 255
pain, 40, 121, 230, 233, 256, 289, 344, 413
  emotional, 338
  sick with stomach, 232
painters, 325, 346–47
Paraíba
  province of, 107–14, 117, 120–25, 144, 222
  slavery in, 114, 124
  valley of, 175–76, 187
Paraíba river, 111
pardas, 16, 20, 22, 64, 84, 108, 161, 167, 234, 292–94, 345
  emancipated, 51
  young, 289
parents, 9, 25, 52, 85, 91, 116, 163, 171, 179, 186, 216, 249, 254, 290–91, 353–54
  married, 272
  mulatto, 5, 20
parishes, 4, 15, 160, 172, 191, 209–10, 329–30, 397–98, 414
  urban, 325
partners, 7, 93, 134, 141, 146, 149–50, 159, 161–62, 165–66, 168, 200–201, 203, 218, 229, 232
passion, 15, 86, 221, 349
  transient, 101
paternalism, 85, 252, 255, 267, 336–37
paternity, 21, 25, 30
patience, 120, 166, 361
patriarchy, 135, 142
patriotism, 354, 358
patronage, 63, 74, 108, 112, 140–41, 185–86, 361
pearls, 3, 86
peddling, 159, 168, 364
penal code, 375, 377, 379, 382, 384–85
penal infractions, 222
Pernambuco, 2, 17, 95, 103, 114, 124, 128, 143, 193, 368
petitions, 56, 107, 147, 154, 168, 239, 283, 289
Philippine Code, 155, 171
piano, 97, 248, 349, 354, 358–59
plaintiff, 112, 145–47, 152, 154–56, 158, 164–66, 169, 171, 195, 235, 240
plantations, 27, 51, 99, 111, 176–77, 204, 212, 217, 220, 224, 310, 349, 393, 400
  corn, 177
  inherited, 27
  sugarcane, 25
pleas, 23, 109, 155
pledge, 60, 62, 70–71, 73–77
poetry, 83, 88, 96–97, 190, 261, 363, 388
  popular, 102, 369
police, 83, 91, 93, 188, 294, 311, 339, 372–74, 384
  chief, 200, 293, 355
  secret, 382
  slaver, 293–94

politics, 40, 141, 202, 221, 298, 336, 342
  internal, 220
  popularizing, 298
population, 5–6, 36–37, 39, 50, 54, 110–11, 117, 125, 130, 142, 144, 308, 310, 347, 403
  black, 94, 401
  largest, 16, 42
  total employed, 405
  working, 331
Porto Alegre, 124, 174, 211, 222–24, 369
Portugal, 18, 20, 28, 46, 103, 171, 190, 418
Portuguese, 5–6, 20, 22, 41, 53, 66–67, 92–93, 102, 104, 135, 198, 238, 374, 384, 393
  colonization, 37, 63, 323
  empire, 1, 202. *See also* empire.
  language, 103, 309, 318. *See also* Brazilian language
  spoken, 318, 333
  written, 309
Portuguese Inquisition, 47
possessions, 28–30, 86, 108, 113, 128–29, 142, 164, 179, 185–86, 237, 239, 316–17, 324, 339, 397–99
post-abolition period, 128, 299, 331, 341, 391, 394, 415, 417
post-partum depression, 263, 271
poverty, 36, 51–52, 58, 64, 342
  extreme, 52
  generalized, 64
  urban, 142
power, 32–33, 107–8, 202, 204–5, 220, 222, 317, 319, 321, 337, 339, 341, 393–94, 413, 415
  economic, 22
  spiritual, 393
power relations, 19, 267, 335–36, 373, 382
  interpersonal, 25
prayers, 61, 64, 76, 141, 346
  ordered mass, 395
prestige, 141, 180, 324, 343, 347
  social, 41, 137
pride, 95, 167, 257, 365
  racial, 364
priests, 15, 64, 66, 74, 210, 346, 395, 416
  wicked, 309, 314
primitivism, 83
prison, 40, 46, 52, 55, 114, 240–41, 254, 277, 373
privileges, 28, 158, 253, 315
  granting of, 335
processions, 65–66, 270, 345, 356–57
  evening, 65
  great, 356
  majestic, 355
proclamation, 23, 44, 109, 120
production, 110, 211–12, 252, 268, 349, 387, 404, 407, 410, 412
  domestic, 324
  literary, 94
profits, 138, 311
  yielded, 326
property, 25, 27, 29, 128–30, 137, 141, 148–49, 153–55, 177–78, 181, 183–84, 186–87, 196–97, 201, 396–97
  endow, 186
  rental, 138, 140
  residential, 29–30
  small rural, 111, 122
prostitutes, 13–14, 41, 50–54, 85, 142, 157–58, 188, 192, 380–84, 387, 415
Protection and obedience, 104, 251, 261, 342, 416
provision, 29, 287, 330, 336, 339
  legal, 285
public spaces, 334, 336, 382
pubs, 379–80
punches, 145, 254
punishments, 40, 54, 90, 166–67, 204, 289, 335, 337, 347, 373–74
  excessive, 101, 373
purgatory, 76, 398
queens, 60, 65, 67–73, 75–76, 78, 305–6, 314
  elected, 75

INDEX

perpetual, 67, 69
quilombos, 39, 43, 45, 48, 56, 66, 204, 373
quitanda, 181, 183, 188, 416
rábula, 112, 205
race, 42, 81, 102, 105, 281, 298, 300, 345, 351–52, 391, 401–2, 410–11, 415–17
   inferior, 350
   relations, 391, 401, 416
   white, 404
racial identity, 357, 364
racial inequalities, 401, 404, 407
racialized concepts, 99, 295
racial paradise, 414
racial prejudice, 50, 92
racism, 388
   scientific, 350–51
rage, 93, 99, 277
ramalhetes, 67, 72
ranch, 195, 197–98, 200, 221, 399
razors, 375, 378, 380, 382, 384
Recife
   city of, 2, 4, 17, 37, 103, 114, 118, 124–25, 127–28, 130–31, 135–39, 141–44, 222, 288, 375
   nineteenth-century, 127
recognition, 311, 352, 362
Recôncavo Baiano, 23–24, 227, 234
regime, 103, 173, 233
   monarchist, 374
   old, 212
registries, 11, 26, 116, 160–61
   historical, 61
   marital, 163
regulation, 222, 249, 288, 338–40
relatives, 115–16, 119–20, 134, 159, 163, 205, 207, 214, 219, 234, 236, 257, 260, 396, 400
   blood, 150
   distant, 311
   spiritual, 209
religion, 82, 170, 320, 347, 354
religious life, 60, 66, 355, 363
religious practices, 14–15, 45, 60, 64, 143, 175, 347

remembrance, 257, 363
rent(ing), 29, 41, 140, 153, 159, 179, 248–50, 254, 264, 287, 326–29, 332
representatives, 338–39, 345, 374
   civil, 361
   municipal, 338
   public, 338
repression, 39, 373, 380, 385
   judicial, 387
reputation, 25, 49, 77, 89, 181, 186, 237, 328, 358
resistance, 18, 57, 92, 98, 204, 222, 244, 321, 340, 348, 368, 393, 414–15, 417–18
   cultural, 415
   potential, 48
respect, 252, 255, 277, 307, 311, 335, 350, 357–59, 376, 387, 391, 393
   garnering, 355
retribution, 222, 299, 341
revenge, 211, 255
revolts, 49, 199, 204, 258, 320, 348. *See also* resistance
rhythms, 9, 308, 310, 372
rice, selling, 378
rights, 76, 94, 107, 111, 119, 141, 154, 160, 165, 252, 256, 258, 294, 319, 339
   civil, 337
   sexual, 294
Rio Grande, 168, 174, 198, 211–12, 216, 221, 223–24, 414
rites, 256, 312, 319, 358
rituals, 33, 46–47, 60, 64–65, 149, 173, 210, 371–72, 375, 389, 395
   initiation, 371
rivers, 6, 37, 111, 177, 193, 195, 198
roads, 36–38, 44, 47, 51–52, 177
   open, 190
robbery, 301, 303, 348
Roman law, 148, 184
roof, 51, 78, 183
   straw, 228
rooms, 52, 129, 145, 156, 183, 199–200, 228, 271, 274, 277, 381
   dining, 139, 183, 277

living, 84, 88, 139, 228
rented, 303, 316
ropes, 3, 11, 397
rosaries, 63, 65, 79, 356
rule, 114, 131–32, 142, 148, 169, 290, 326, 338–39, 351, 355, 358
  legal, 118
  seigniorial, 221
runaway slaves, 93, 111, 293
  captured, 373
Sacramento, principal church of, 22, 29, 160–63, 170, 330
sacraments, 64, 76, 395
sacrifice, 113, 164–65, 252
  maternal, 265
sadness, 101, 270, 344, 361
saints, 14–15, 63–64, 67, 77, 80, 305, 355
salary, 166, 295, 337–38, 402
  daily, 160, 164, 167. See also earnings and daily payment
sale, 43–44, 83, 87, 177, 179, 203–4, 206, 248, 250, 254–55, 287, 302, 304, 327–28, 332
  obliged, 43
  public, 215
sales contract, 43, 254
saleswomen, 38, 180, 182, 378–79. See also street vendors
Salvador, 24–25, 32–33, 179, 181, 183, 190–93, 234–36, 239, 242–44, 368–69, 375–76, 379–83, 386, 388–90, 416–18
samba(s), 86, 95, 356
savings, 42, 53, 57, 91, 121, 163, 165, 183–84, 207, 212, 214, 229, 235–37, 242, 288
  accumulating, 113, 117, 236
  personal, 242
  stolen, 241
scarcity, 60, 64, 268, 345
schemes, 327–28
school, 290–91, 344, 346, 350–55, 358, 361, 363–64
  boarding, 291
  high, 363–64

medical, 267
municipal, 297
primary, 354
public, 349
scientists, 2, 105, 300
scribe, 35, 67, 77, 180, 289, 296, 303–4, 307–8, 313, 316
  anonymous, 306
seal, 35, 150, 258, 348
seamstresses, 229, 334
secretary, state business, 44, 224, 239, 298, 363, 374
secrets, 22, 84–85, 88, 90–91, 141, 380
  tortuous, 87
secularization, 139
security, 4, 149, 157, 168
seigniorial family, 91, 120, 269, 271
  nuclear, 220
seizure, 107, 196
sellers, 43, 135, 181, 183, 186, 188
  female, 149, 383
sensations, 63, 309–10
sentence (legal), 46, 113, 201, 233, 240–41
separation, 146, 149, 153–54, 156, 181, 211, 258, 269–70, 294–95, 304
  avoiding, 158
  ecclesiastical, 153, 180
Sergipe, cities of, 9, 193, 343–46, 348–49, 360, 363–70
servants, 13, 24, 177, 238, 261, 321, 323, 326, 329–30, 333–34, 336–40
  booking, 328
  enslaved, 324
  female, 329
  gifted, 290–91
  good, 120
  poor, 253
  room, 217, 229, 334, 352, 401–2, 404–5, 407, 409–10, 412
sexual acts, 116, 295
sexuality, 19, 95, 102, 173–74, 318, 372, 391
shame, 50–51, 99, 237–38
shelter, 45, 252, 256, 359
shops, 43–45, 51, 129, 328

INDEX

sicknesses, 131, 206, 249, 252, 256, 265, 336, 351, 362
  moral, 99, 252
silence, 33, 35, 88, 258, 298, 369, 391
silk, 3, 11, 13, 253, 316, 327
silver, 3, 8, 11, 13, 112, 138
sin, 52, 95, 174, 414
  of the color of, 96
sisterhoods, 59–61, 63–64, 67–68, 70, 72, 75–77, 79, 395, 397–98
  black, 59–60, 62, 64–65
  religious, 55
  rosary, 60
skirts, 3, 11, 13, 96, 135, 355
slave couple, 200, 215, 398
slave culture, 81, 202, 318, 394
slave emancipation, 42, 182, 268, 278, 283, 285, 290–92, 300, 349
slave escapes, 39, 45, 204, 215, 224, 348. *See also* runaway slaves
slave family, 105, 116, 185, 221, 415
slave labor, 32, 119, 177, 192, 198, 243, 313, 323–25, 347, 370
slave ownership, 6, 15–17, 27, 140, 324, 326, 373
slave partners, 306, 315
slave population, 43, 48, 87, 124, 129–30, 284, 325, 348
slave practices, 325, 332
slave quarters, 105, 341
slave regime, 109, 119, 121
slave relations, 19, 114, 128, 263, 267, 278, 312, 339
slavery, 28–30, 53–54, 88–90, 108–10, 118–20, 123–24, 193–94, 262–64, 270, 284, 295–301, 337–42, 391–92, 400, 417
  urban, 311, 342, 389, 394, 415
slaves
  adult, 4, 26, 187
  urban, 179, 185, 187, 315, 324
slave ships, 219, 393
slave society, 19, 33, 54, 108, 119–21, 128, 202, 227, 241, 263, 285, 311–12, 317, 324, 392

slave trade, 80, 129, 140, 179, 318, 327, 393. *See also* Atlantic slave trade
slave women, 20, 23, 27–29, 41–42, 44–45, 47, 51, 53–54, 86, 88–89, 91–92, 284–85, 329, 331, 414
  emancipated, 28, 42, 290
  naming, 30
  purchase of, 41, 95
sleep, 54, 195, 237, 257, 274
snakes, 45–46, 251
sociability, 48, 52, 315, 359, 392, 417
social dominance, 335, 340
social history, 81, 261, 300, 415, 418
social relations, 33, 268, 274, 327, 336
social roles, 94, 157, 290
social status, 76–77, 135, 138, 142, 147, 159, 165, 324, 347
social stigma, 44, 144, 415
solidarity, 30, 45, 127, 140–41, 150, 153, 223, 234
  narrowed, 48
songs, 95–97, 103–4, 257, 372
soul, 2, 14–15, 53, 61, 64, 76, 101, 141, 368, 372, 395, 397–98
  kindhearted, 85
  noble, 98
spaces, domestic, 157, 220, 324, 333–34
spectacle, 105, 284, 300
speeches, 83, 88, 94, 102, 216, 293, 311, 344–45, 349, 363
sponsorship, 140–41, 185, 203–4, 208, 210, 213
  ties, 203
sport, 375–76, 385
spouses, 132, 140, 146, 148–50, 153–55, 157, 160, 163, 170, 218, 393
  arranged, 162
  divorced, 146
squares, 38, 170, 176, 181, 188, 229, 357
  public, 36, 40, 114, 135, 371
stability, 7, 44, 166
  political, 43
standards, 9, 157–58, 274, 339, 397
  body beauty, 388
  cultural, 41

INDEX

current, 17–18, 55, 102, 123, 241–43, 296–97, 389, 413–14
  hygienic, 274
  patriarchal, 132
statistics, 191, 194, 373, 401
  contemporary, 400
stereotypes, 84, 86, 98–99, 102, 350, 388
  animalizing, 94
  literary, 84
  masculinized, 379
  recurring, 88
  sexualized, 101
sterilization, 265, 278
stigmas, 37, 51, 89, 142, 391
  negative, 350
street vendors, 38, 108, 135, 159, 172, 187, 377, 394, 417
  black female, 54, 57, 135, 299
  excellent, 167
students, 6, 101, 134, 266, 312–13, 343, 346, 349–50, 352–54, 356, 358–63, 387
  beautiful female, 355
  distinguished, 343
  enrolled, 360
  former, 344, 359–62, 364
  served, 352
styles, 10, 138–39, 235, 248, 305, 355
  personal, 84
sugar, 40, 86, 110, 117, 128–30, 177, 189, 346, 349
  brown, 117
  plantations, 117, 130, 345, 347. *See also* plantations
suicide, 84, 93, 393
superiority, 255, 338
  genetic, 87
supplies, 39–40, 44, 152, 251
Suriname, 416
surveillance, 249, 336
survival, 52, 121, 142, 212, 227, 252, 268, 270, 276, 332, 387
  daily, 142
suspicions, 39, 46, 222, 227, 248, 252, 256, 311, 313, 315, 337–38
sustenance, 15, 37, 149, 155, 252
  financial, 157
sweets, 37, 79, 82, 97, 129, 268, 327, 335, 378
  sold, 183, 416
swindlers, 382, 385
symbols, 10, 160, 312, 317, 321, 358, 376, 379, 385
  national, 371
  ostentatious, 360
syncretism, 46, 48
tailors, 229, 345–46
talismans, 60, 63
tamed animals, 216
taverns, 51, 103, 166, 348
taxes, 43–44, 74, 183, 242, 328
teaching, 14, 290, 335, 344, 349, 352, 354, 359, 362–63, 365
  moral, 159
tensions, 140, 267–68, 276, 349
  domestic, 270
  dramatic, 214, 268
  emotional, 269
testaments, 1–2, 6–9, 11–12, 14, 18, 22, 26, 57, 128, 143, 217, 395–97, 413–14
testimonies, 7, 112–13, 153, 159, 196, 199–201, 203, 205–8, 210, 229, 232–33, 235–36, 238, 275–77, 279
  direct, 310
  uniform, 203
theatre, 96, 238, 354–55, 371, 388
  cinema, 355
  religious, 371
theft, 43, 140, 196–97, 199–201, 204–5, 213, 222, 231, 315
theses
  medical, 264, 269–70, 278–79
  old, 252
threats, 54, 90, 227, 276, 384
torment, 13, 57, 100
towels, 3, 8, 383
trade, 10, 25, 40–41, 44, 117, 129, 135–36, 167, 169, 331, 347, 349, 360
  fish, 129
  inter-state, 117
  small, 37, 53, 334

transatlantic, 108, 217.
TAB*See also* slave trade
traders, 2–4, 86, 93, 136, 138, 299, 346, 355
  adventurous, 4
  free, 150
  globalized, 9
traditions, 37, 47, 55, 299, 358, 372, 385
  cultural, 372
  new, 375
  old, 215
  oral, 308
  religious, 60, 66
trafficking, 108, 125, 222
  illegal, 44
trails, 7, 36, 125, 261
trance, 45–46, 372
travelers, 2, 138, 325
  foreign, 271
trays, 35–37, 39–41, 53, 135, 181, 229, 377
  carried, 36
  selling, 394
treatment, 235–36, 332, 335–36, 338
  cruel, 98, 336
  medical, 252, 256, 362
  poor, 249, 337
  preferential, 335
trial, 113–14, 118, 196–97, 199, 201, 203, 228–33, 235, 237–38, 240–41, 271, 273, 302–3, 315, 382–85
  civil, 348
tricks, 216, 239–40
trunks, 138, 228
trustees, 67, 76–78, 117–18
  black, 76
  female, 77
  single, 77
turbans, 135, 248
  colored, 135
typologies, 84, 86–88, 90, 92, 94, 96, 98, 100, 102, 104
  literary, 97
unbelievers, 210
uncertainties, 199, 202
uncle, 6, 163, 178, 190

unions, 37, 146, 148–51, 153, 160–61, 163, 170, 202, 305
  consensual, 160, 187
  illicit, 187
  legal, 148
Uruguay, 196–98, 201, 205–6, 213, 216, 221
  abolitionist laws, 198, 224
  river, 197–98, 205, 216
vagrancy, 112, 146, 155, 291, 339, 385
valley, 345, 354, 359, 363
valorization, 108, 260, 266
  hyper, 119
vegetables, 92, 180–81, 394
vehicles, 139, 264, 345
vicar, 4, 79, 154, 158, 209–10, 223, 355–56
victims, 94, 217, 232–33, 364, 375, 382, 387
  defenseless, 16
  naïve, 315
villages, 2, 5, 8, 10, 16, 37–39, 42–43, 51, 162, 200
  adjacent, 42
  humble, 45
  small, 167
villas, 10–11, 29, 180, 192
  small, 346
violence, 6, 18, 40, 44, 48, 53, 101, 105, 241, 267, 277, 293, 295, 312, 318
  excessive, 155
  moral, 335, 337
virtue, 358–59, 381, 396
visions, 53, 102, 266, 298, 311, 341, 391
  idealized, 292
  modern, 266
  national, 267
  positive, 385
voting, 142, 291
waitresses, 328, 334
walls, 50, 59, 257
  mud, 228
warehouses, 43, 177, 347
wars, 199, 208, 417
  internal civil, 199
  pre-civil, 268

INDEX

washing, 77, 86, 89, 160, 274, 291, 332, 334
   collective, 334
washwomen, 86, 88, 95, 229, 334
wax, 65, 79
   candle, 64–65
wealth, 36, 138, 141, 177, 180, 182–83, 213, 216, 218, 252, 256, 258, 393, 396, 400
   bequeathed, 400
   diverse, 357
   generating, 360
   material, 78
weapons, 35, 373, 375–76, 385, 387
weaving, 349, 361
weddings, 149, 158, 160, 190
West Africa, 24, 60, 149, 161, 169, 181, 188, 394
wet nurses, 229, 246, 249–56, 258–59, 263–65, 267–70, 272, 280, 334
   fulfilled, 261
   good, 327
   hired, 280–81
   prospective, 278
white child, 246, 256, 267–69, 278
   small, 256
   well-nourished, 263, 291
whiteness, 98, 101, 368
white people, 347
   to the power of, 158
white women, 13, 24, 37, 50, 95–96, 167, 228, 263, 402, 408–11
   employed, 402, 409
   poor, 142
   well-bred, 264
whore, 158, 382
widow, 22, 29–30, 87–88, 91, 100, 103, 109, 115, 127, 131, 182, 206–7, 215, 217–18, 396–99
wife, 22, 140, 147, 149, 155, 158–59, 164, 166, 170, 187–88, 197, 203–4, 208, 305, 308–9
   former owner's, 197
   good, 158, 351
   ideal, 157, 170
   respectable, 292
wills, 9, 19–22, 24, 28–30, 47, 67, 128, 134, 137, 140, 167, 206, 395, 397
window, 86, 137, 183, 228, 230, 382
   new, 284
   open, 388
witchcraft, 46–47, 49, 58, 60, 373
witnesses, 112, 136, 153, 156, 165–66, 197, 199–201, 205–7, 213, 230, 232–33, 238–39, 253–54, 272–73, 396–99
   alleged, 231
   black, 205
   partial, 213
   wedding, 137
womb, 211, 235, 258, 284–85, 295, 297
   preservation of the, 25
women
   black, 35, 59, 180, 227, 323
   captive, 53, 113–14, 120, 219, 235
   dark-skinned, 84, 108–9, 376
   divorced, 168
   emancipated, 2, 14, 19, 23, 28–30, 41, 43–45, 48–49, 181, 185, 188, 329, 332, 336, 397–400
   employed, 408
   married, 145, 154, 157
   mixed-race, 20, 23, 37, 40, 48, 50, 54, 84, 293, 331, 395, 411, 417
   old, 28, 85, 87, 273
   poor, 37, 264, 286, 292, 418
   rule of, 145–46, 148, 150, 152, 154, 156, 158, 160, 162, 164, 166, 168, 170, 172, 174
   working, 332, 377
   young, 95, 245, 288
woods, 145, 196, 199, 203, 221, 335
wool, 3, 316
workers, 95, 103, 142, 205, 229, 328–29, 331–32, 338, 380, 387, 400, 402, 411
   autonomous, 405, 409
   enslaved, 332, 336
   free, 328, 332, 337, 373
   public, 402–3
   quarry, 334
work ethic, 290

workforce, 323, 332, 401, 414
    enslaved, 137
wounds, 45, 155, 177, 180, 311
    bullet, 381
Xango, 11, 140, 143, 358
Yoruba, 147, 149–50, 161–62, 169, 172, 181, 193, 208, 219, 227, 368
    entries, 161
    ethnicities, 161, 163, 182
    slave, 152, 156
Yorubaland, 167, 193
zones, rural, 176, 185, 302